C000141074

STREET
Suffolk

Bury St Edmunds, Felixstowe, Ipswich, Lowestoft, Newmarket

First published in 2003 by

Philip's, a division of
Octopus Publishing Group Ltd
2-4 Heron Quays, London E14 4JP

Second edition 2007
Second impression 2010
SUFBA

ISBN   978-1-84907-101-7 (pocket)

© Philip's 2007

Ordnance Survey®

This product includes mapping data licensed from Ordnance Survey® with the permission of the Controller of Her Majesty's Stationery Office. © Crown copyright 2007. All rights reserved. Licence number 100011710.

Printed by Toppan, China

Contents

II   **Key to map pages**

IV   **Route planning**

VIII   **Administrative and Postcode boundaries**

1   **Key to map symbols**

2   **Street maps** at 1⅓ inches to 1 mile

109   **Street maps** at 2⅔ inches to 1 mile

154   **Street maps of centres of Bury St Edmunds and Ipswich** at 5⅓ inches to 1 mile

156   **Index** of towns and villages

159   **Index** of streets, hospitals, industrial estates, railway stations, schools, shopping centres, universities and places of interest

Digital Data

The exceptionally high-quality mapping found in this atlas is available as digital data in TIFF format, which is easily convertible to other bitmapped (raster) image formats.

The index is also available in digital form as a standard database table. It contains all the details found in the printed index together with the National Grid reference for the map square in which each entry is named.

For further information and to discuss your requirements, please contact Philip's on 020 7644 6932 or victoria.dawbarn@philips-maps.co.uk

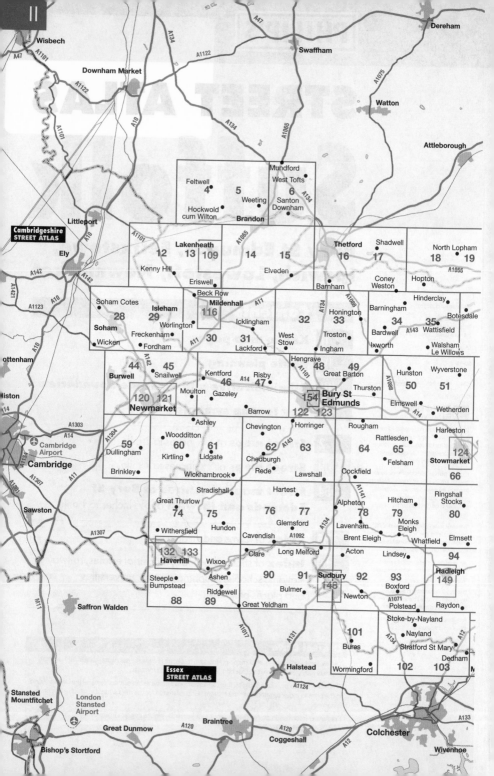

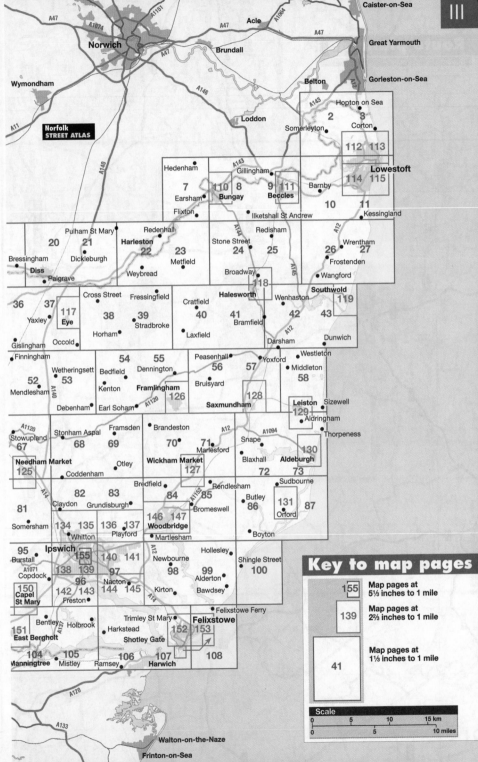

III

Caister-on-Sea
Great Yarmouth
Gorleston-on-Sea

Norwich
Acle
Brundall
Belton
A47
A1074
A1151
A1064
A47
A47
A146

Wymondham

A11
Norfolk
STREET ATLAS

Loddon

A143
Hopton on Sea
2
3
Corton
Somerleyton
112 113
Lowestoft
114 115

A140

Hedenham
7
Earsham
Flixton
110 8
Bungay
9 111
Beccles
Barnby
10
11
Kessingland
Gillingham
A143
Ilketshall St Andrew

Pulham St Mary
20
21
Dickleburgh
Harleston
22
Weybread
23
Metfield
Redenhall
Redisham
Stone Street
24
25
Wrentham
26
27
Frostenden
Wangford
Bressingham
Diss
Palgrave

36
37
Yaxley
117
Eye
38
39
Stradbroke
Horham
Cross Street
Fressingfield
Cratfield
40
Laxfield
41
Bramfield
42
43
Dunwich
Broadway
118
Halesworth
Wenhaston
Southwold
119
Gislingham
Occold
Finningham
Darsham

Wetheringsett
52
53
Mendlesham
Kenton
Debenham
Earl Soham
54
Bedfield
55
Dennington
Framlingham
126
Bruisyard
Saxmundham
128
56
57
Middleton
58
Peasenhall
Yoxford
Westleton
Leiston
129
Sizewell
Aldringham

A1120
Stowupland
67
Needham Market
125
Stonham Aspal
68
Coddenham
69
Framsden
Otley
70
Brandeston
71
Marlesford
Wickham Market
127
Snape
Blaxhall
72
Aldeburgh
73
130
Thorpeness

81
Somersham
82
Claydon
83
Grundisburgh
84
Bredfield
85
Rendlesham
Bromeswell
Butley
86
131
Orford
87
Sudbourne
146 147
Woodbridge
Martlesham
Boyton

95
Burstall
Ipswich
155
140 141
138 139
Copdock
97
96
Nacton
142 143
144 145
Freston
Kirton
98
Newbourne
Hollesley
99
Alderton
Bawdsey
Shingle Street
100

150
Capel
St Mary
151
East Bergholt
Bentley
Holbrook
Harkstead
Trimley St Mary
Shotley Gate
Felixstowe Ferry
Felixstowe
152 153

104
Manningtree
Mistley
105
106
Ramsey
107
Harwich
108

A120
A133

Walton-on-the-Naze
Frinton-on-Sea

A1071
A137
A14
A12
A1152
A1094
A12
A12
A145
A144
A1120
A140
A146

Key to map pages

155
Map pages at
5½ inches to 1 mile

139
Map pages at
2⅔ inches to 1 mile

41
Map pages at
1⅓ inches to 1 mile

Scale
0   5   10   15 km
0   5   10 miles

IV

Route planning

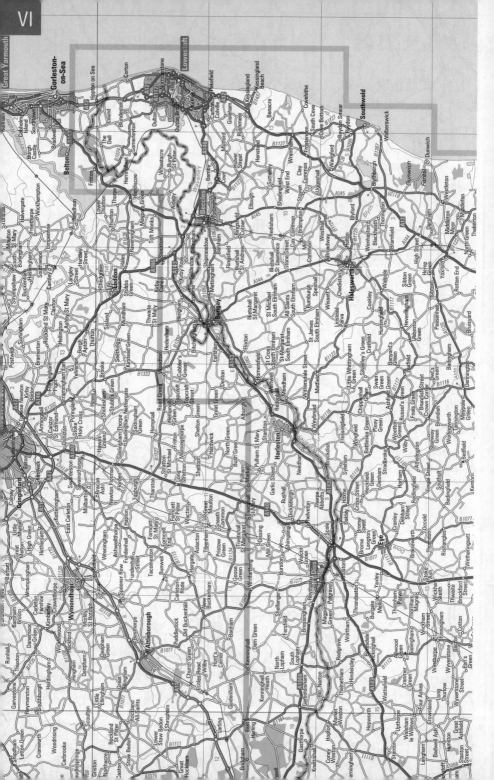

VIII

Administrative and Postcode boundaries

Scale

| County and unitary authority boundaries |
| District boundaries |
| Postcode boundaries |
| Area covered by this atlas |

Key to map symbols 1

(22a)	**Motorway** with junction number
	Primary route – dual/single carriageway
	A road – dual/single carriageway
	B road – dual/single carriageway
	Minor road – dual/single carriageway
	Other minor road – dual/single carriageway
	Road under construction
	Tunnel, covered road
	Rural track, private road or narrow road in urban area
	Gate or obstruction to traffic (restrictions may not apply at all times or to all vehicles)
	Path, bridleway, byway open to all traffic, road used as a public path
	Pedestrianised area
DY7	**Postcode boundaries**
	County and unitary authority boundaries
	Railway, tunnel, railway under construction
	Tramway, tramway under construction
	Miniature railway
Walsall	**Railway station**
	Private railway station
South Shields	**Metro station**
	Tram stop, tram stop under construction
	Bus, coach station

♦	**Ambulance station**
♦	**Coastguard station**
♦	**Fire station**
♦	**Police station**
✚	**Accident and Emergency entrance to hospital**
H	**Hospital**
+	**Place of worship**
i	**Information Centre** (open all year)
	Shopping Centre
P P&R	**Parking, Park and Ride**
PO	**Post Office**
Ⓧ 🚐	**Camping site, caravan site**
✕	**Picnic site**
►	**Golf course**
Prim Sch	**Important buildings, schools, colleges, universities and hospitals**
	Built up area
	Woods
River Ouse	**Tidal water, water name**
	Non-tidal water – lake, river, canal or stream
	Lock, weir, tunnel
Church	**Non-Roman antiquity**
ROMAN FORT	**Roman antiquity**
87	**Adjoining page indicators and overlap bands** The colour of the arrow and the band indicates the scale of the adjoining or overlapping page (see scales below)
237	

Enlarged mapping only

	Railway or bus station building
	Place of interest
	Parkland

Acad	Academy	Inst	Institute
Allot Gdns	Allotments	Ct	Law Court
Cemy	Cemetery	L Ctr	Leisure Centre
C Ctr	Civic Centre	LC	Level Crossing
CH	Club House	Liby	Library
Coll	College	Mkt	Market
Crem	Crematorium	Meml	Memorial
Ent	Enterprise	Mon	Monument
Ex H	Exhibition Hall	Mus	Museum
Ind Est	Industrial Estate	Obsy	Observatory
IRB Sta	Inshore Rescue Boat Station	Pal	Royal Palace
		PH	Public House
Recn Gd	Recreation Ground		
	Resr	Reservoir	
Ret Pk	Retail Park		
Sch	School		
Sh Ctr	Shopping Centre		
TH	Town Hall/House		
Trad Est	Trading Estate		
Univ	University		
W Twr	Water Tower		
Wks	Works		
YH	Youth Hostel		

■ The small numbers around the edges of the maps identify the 1 kilometre National Grid lines ■ The dark grey border on the inside edge of some pages indicates that the mapping does not continue onto the adjacent page

The scale of the maps on the pages numbered in blue is 4.2 cm to 1 km • 2⅔ inches to 1 mile • 1: 23810

0	¼	½	¾	1 mile
0	250 m	500 m	750 m	1 kilometre

The scale of the maps on pages numbered in green is 1.96 cm to 1 km • 1⅓ inches to 1 mile • 1: 50688

0	¼	½	¾	1 mile
0	250m	500m	750m	1 kilometre

The scale of the maps on pages numbered in red is 8.4 cm to 1 km • 5⅓ inches to 1 mile • 1: 11900

0	220 yards	440 yards	660 yards	½ mile
0	125m	250m	375m	½ kilometre

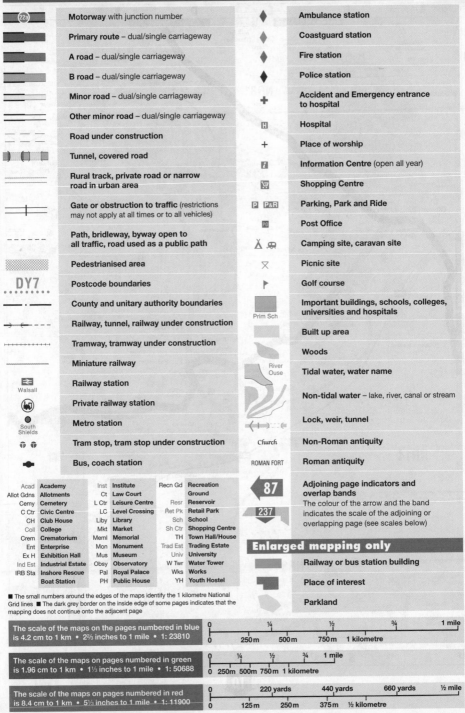

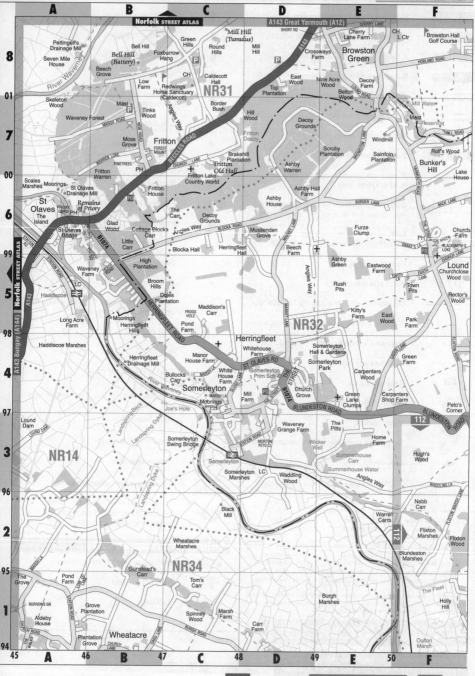

Scale: 1½ inches to 1 mile

B7		7 HALL RD	14 ST VINCENT WK
0 ¼ ½ mile	1 RACKHAM CL	8 THE LAURELS	15 ST CLARE CT
0 250m 500m 750m 1 km	2 RANDALL CL 3 ST MARGARET'S WAY	9 WALTERS CL 10 BISHOPS WK	
	4 FLOWERDAY CL 5 GROOMES CL 6 HOPTON GDNS	11 MARINERS PK CL 12 JULIAN WY 13 ST CLEMENT MEWS	

3

A12 Great Yarmouth

Norfolk STREET ATLAS

B8
1 THE FAIRWAY
2 MARINER'S CL
3 MARINE CL
4 MEADOW CT
5 JOSHUA CT

Gorleston
Golf Course

NR31

Hopton
on Sea

Holiday
Village

A4
1 ST ANDREW CL
2 BARN CL
3 WATSONS CL

B6
1 OLD CHURCH RD
2 CULLEY WY
3 SEAFIELDS DR

C6
1 CADIZ WAY
2 TURIN WAY
3 ZURICH CL
4 GENEVA GDNS
5 NAPLES CL
6 MISBURGH WAY
7 MANOR GD
8 PEBBLE VW WK
9 SANDS CL

St Margaret's
Church (rems)

Holiday &
Leisure Centre

Bloodman's
Corner

Cuckoo
Green

Fourways
Farm

Woburn
Farm

Corton
Cliffs

D4
1 BAKER'S SCORE
2 FOWLER'S CR
3 WIGG'S WY
4 COLMAN RD
5 CORNFIELD CR
6 TIBBENHAM'S SCORE
7 THE CLOSE
8 STATION RD
9 RUBY CL
10 MILLS DR
11 LINDA CL

Church
Farm

A4
1 MEADOWLANDS
2 ORCHARD CL
3 ORCHARD LA
4 MICAWBER MEWS
5 PICKWYK DR
6 DICKENS CT

Blundeston

NR32

Corton CE VC Prim Sch

Corton
Village

Corton
Furze
Plantation

112

113

Pleasurewood
Hills
Leisure Park

Gunton

Lowestoft
North Roads

Pleasurewood
Farm

113

Lowestoft
Danes

North
Beach

St Andrew's
Church
(rems)

The
Ashley
School

Maritime
Mus

LOWESTOFT

Normanston

For full street detail of the
highlighted area see pages
112 and 113

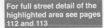

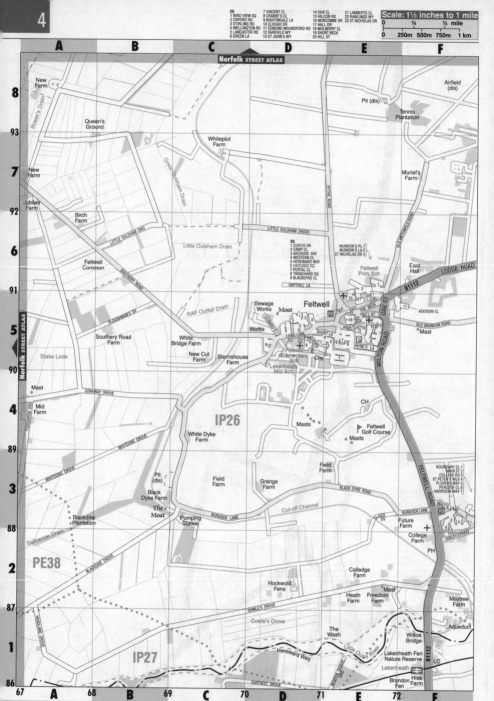

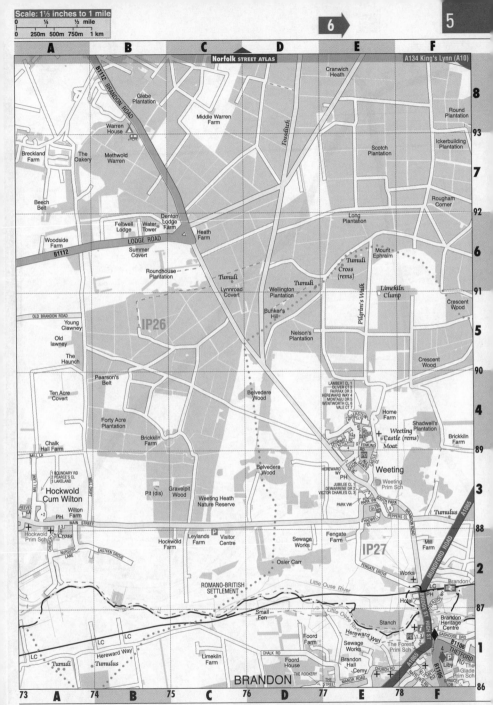

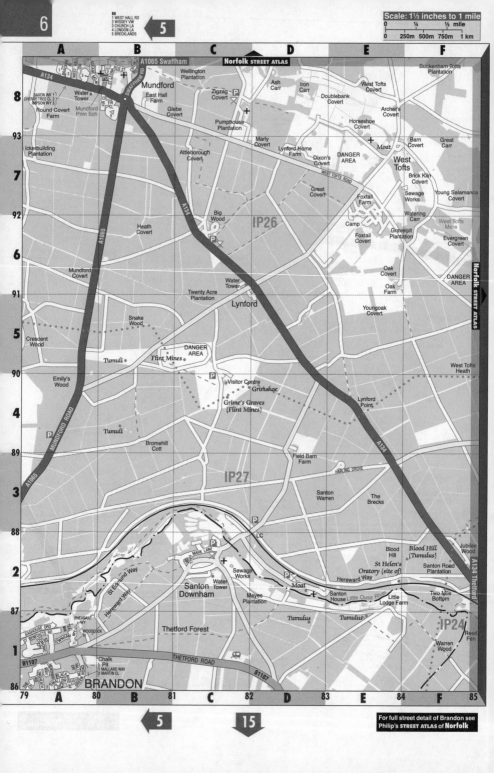

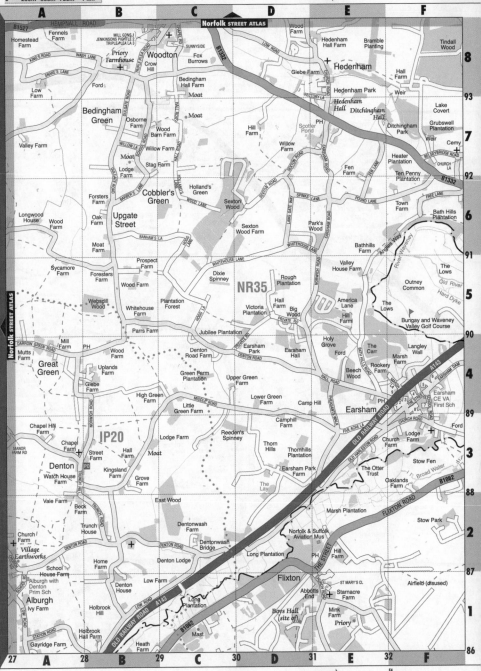

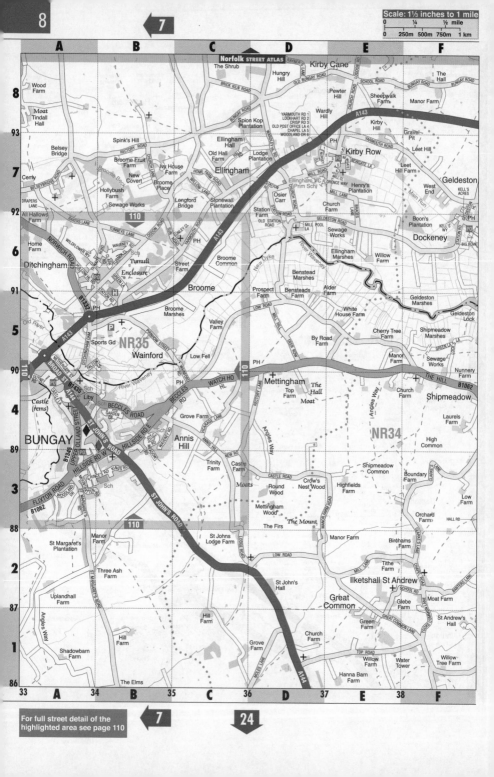

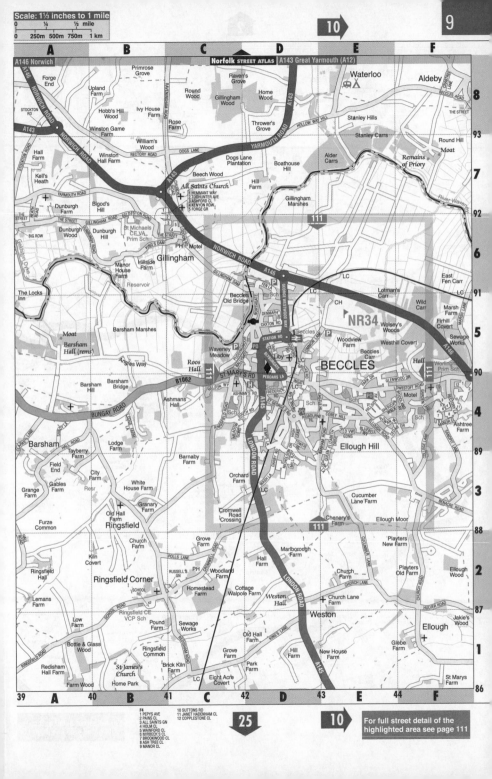

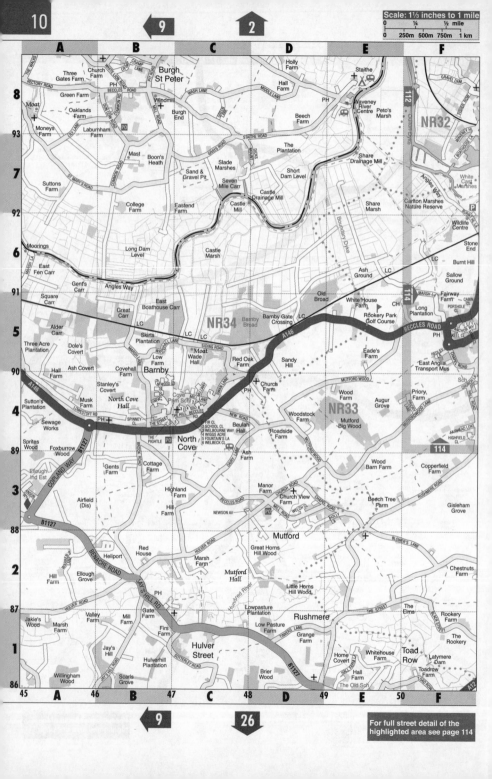

Scale: 1⅓ inches to 1 mile

0   ¼   ½ mile
0   250m 500m 750m 1 km

Norfolk STREET ATLAS

A1101 Littleport

B1382 MILE END ROAD

MILDENHALL RD

A1101

Letter F Farm

Flanders Farm

Cross Bank Farm

Redmere Fen

Decoy Farm

IP27

Decoy Fen

Plantation Farm

Decoy Fen

HEREWARD WAY

Peacock's Farm

ASCOT RD

LC

Lodge Farm

SEDGEFEN ROAD

Burnt Fen

Bulldog Bridge

Shippea Hill

STATION ROAD

Hereward Way

Sedge Fen

Shippea Hill Farm

LC

LC

Sparrow Hall Farm

Willow Farm

FARTHING DROVE

DUCK DROVE

Engine Drain

Engine Farm

Grosvenor House Farm

Elderberry Farm

BURNT FEN TURNPIKE

CB7

Spooner's Farm

River Lark

WHISTLE DROVE

Whistle Farm

Harris Farms

Friesland Farm

Mildenhall Drain

Lark Grange

Townmoor Farm

Great Fen

A1101

Kings Farm

Row Fen

Crossbank Farm

Poplar Farm

Great Fen

IP28

Baldwin's Lode

B1104

County Farm

FISHER'S DRO

SNARE DROVE

MILDENHALL DROVE

Cock Inn Farm

Summers Farm

Kenny Hill

P

FRICKSOLLOW ROAD

Alder Farm

BIRCHINHILL DROVE

Birchinhill Farm

Isleham Fen

ENGINE DROVE

TUNNEL DROVE

Forty Farm

Chestnut Farm

Stargate Farm

Fen Bank Farm

FODDERFEN DROVE

Ranville Farm

Waverley Farm

Cambria Farm

Fen Farm

Mildenhall Fen

Mayfield Farm

PURDLE DROVE

Sedge Bush Drain

B1104

Isleham Fen

Three Tree Farm

West Row Fen

Tree Farm

NEW DROVE

High Post Farm

PARISH BUSH DROVE

Great Fen

DELPH DRO

28   29

61   A   62   B   63   C   64   D   65   E   66   F

8 85 7 84 6 83 5 82 4 81 3 80 2 79 1 78

Cambridgeshire STREET ATLAS

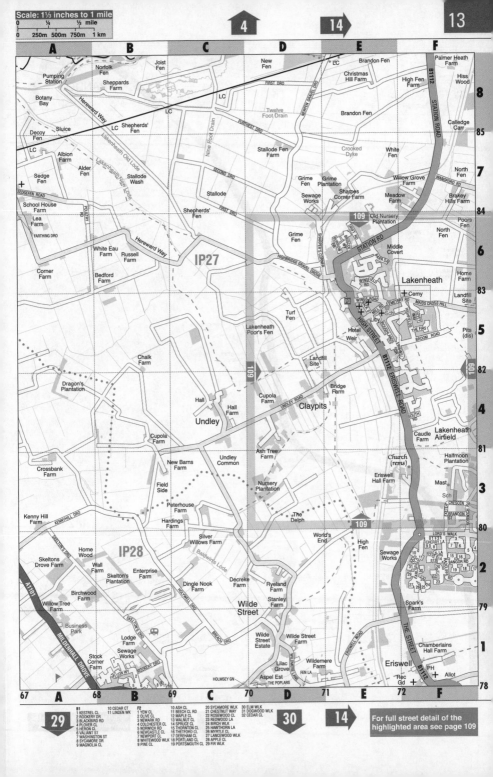

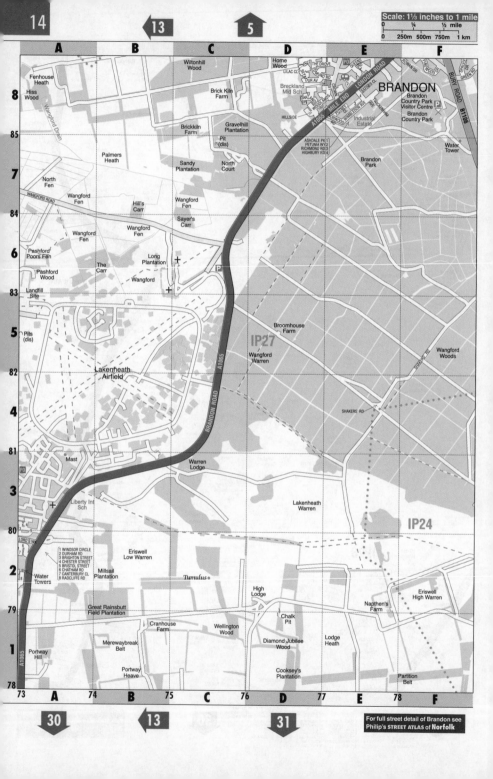

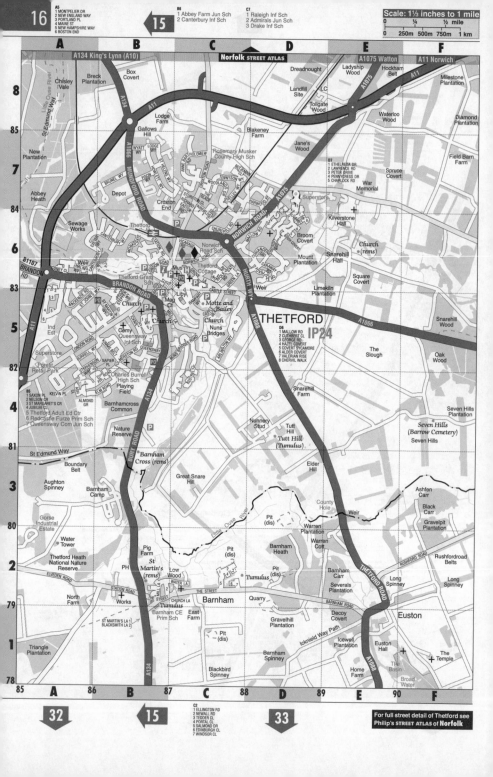

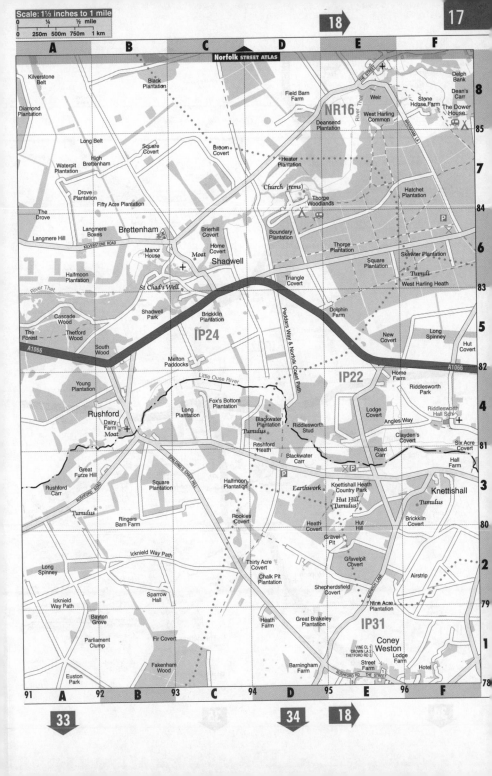

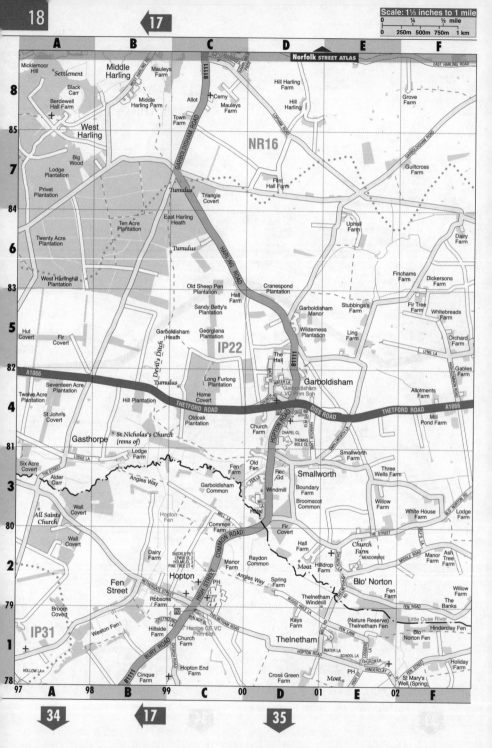

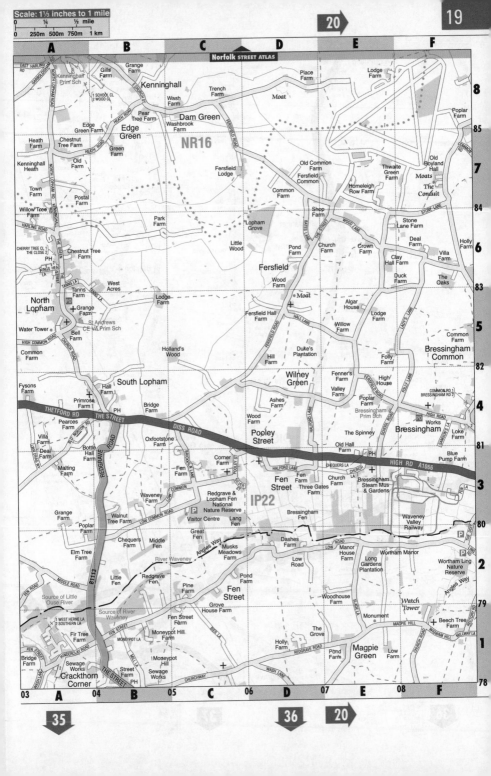

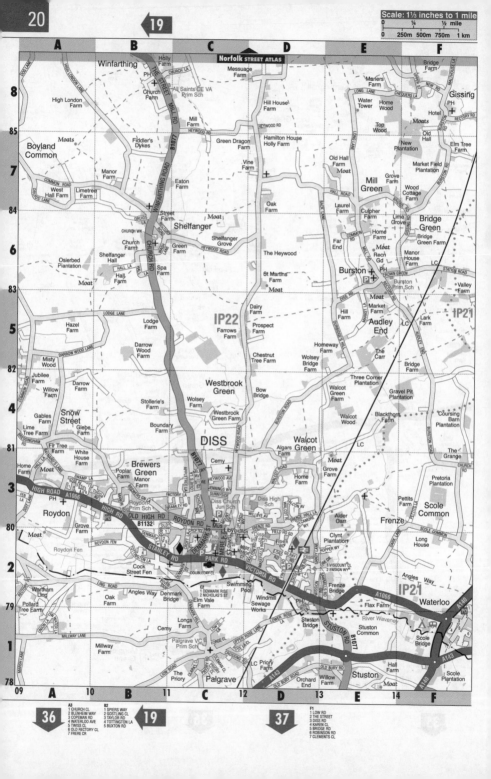

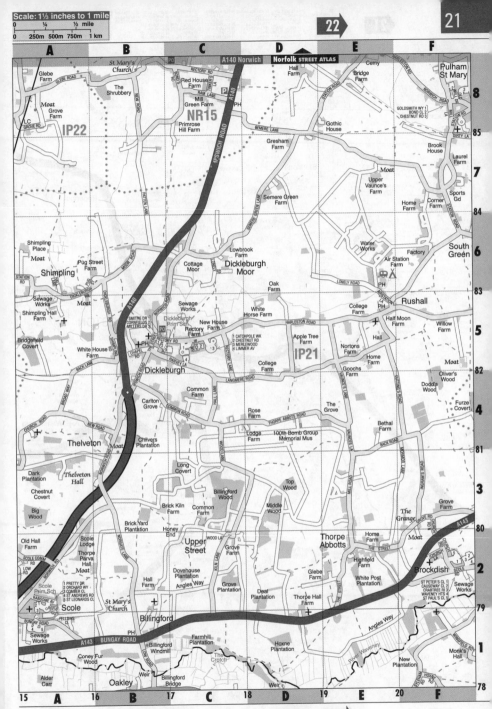

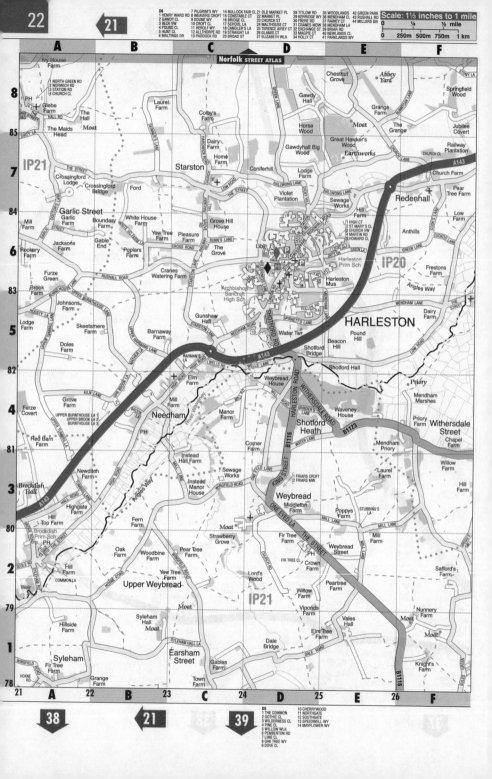

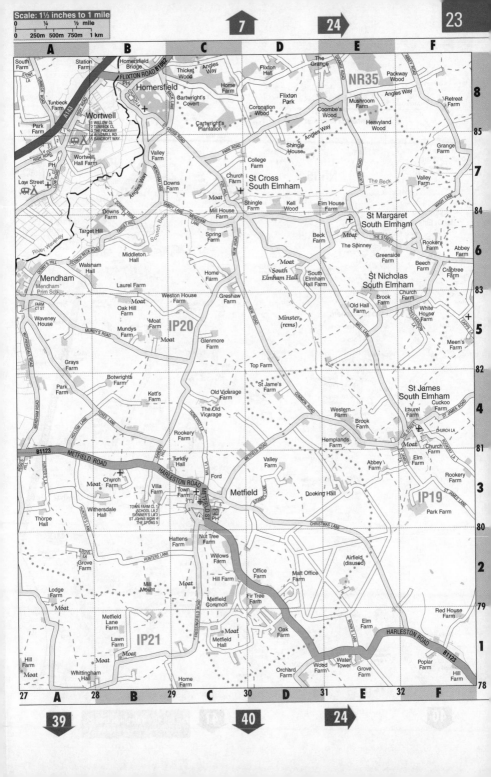

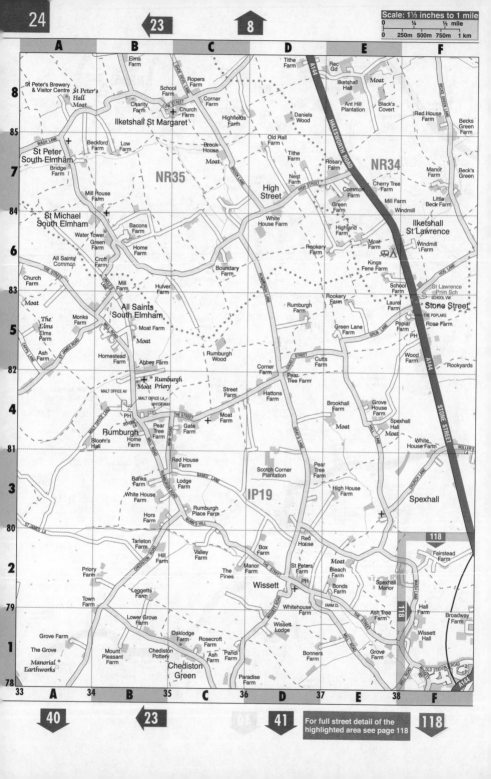

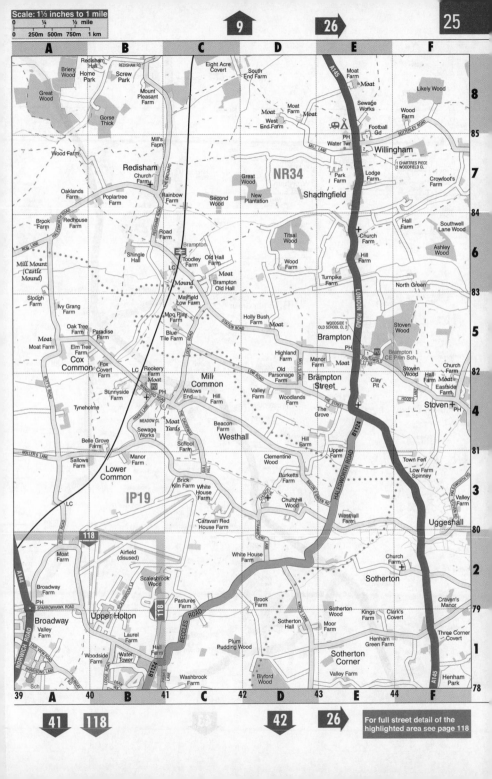

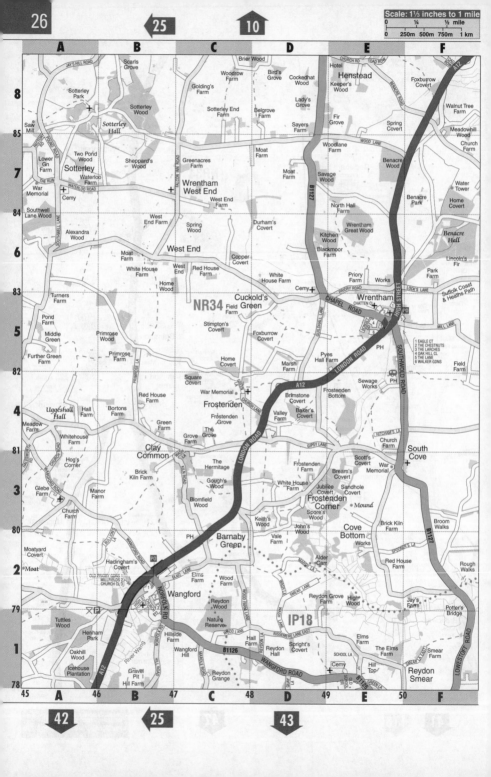

Scale: 1⅓ inches to 1 mile
0   ¼   ½   mile
0   250m 500m 750m   1 km

A   B   C   D   E   F

Kessingland Beach
NR33
Blackcap Wood
PH
CHURCH RD
Sewage Works
MARSH
Churchfarm Marshes
HOLLY GRANGE ROAD
8
Suffolk Coast & Heaths Path
Kessingland Level
85
Benacre
War Memorial
Beachfarm Marshes
Pumping Station
7
Church Covert
THE STREET
Northwalk Plantation
The Denes
Beach Farm
84
Hall Farm
Blackwater Covert
Alder Carr
6
Wood Farm
Coney Hill
Boathouse Covert
Holly Hang
Craft Plantation
Benacre National Nature Reserve
83
NR34
Benacre Broad
Holly Grove
Long Covert
5
North Common Wood
Chancel Covert
Ausgates
St Andrew's Church
82
Church Farm
Covehithe
4
Porter's Farm
Green Heath
Covehithe Cliffs
81
Covehithe Broad
Warren House
The Warren
3
Suffolk Coast & Heaths Path
Easton Wood
80
Benacre National Nature Reserve
Easton Home Covert
2
Easton Broad
Pottersbridge Marshes
Easton Marshes
79
IP18
Easton Bavents
1
EASTON LA.
Easton Cliffs
78

51   A   52   B   53   C   54   D   55   E   56   F

Scale: 1½ inches to 1 mile

0 ¼ ½ mile
0 250m 500m 750m 1 km

D5
1 NORTH DR
2 ST FELIX CL
3 CALFE FEN CL
4 OLD SCHOOL CL
5 HOLMES LA
6 SNOWBERRY WY

7 FOX WOOD N
8 MARTIN CL
9 POPPY FIELDS
10 PRIMROSE LA
11 FOX WOOD S

The Dunstalls
Mow Sides
Lay Clerks Farm
Nornea Farm
St John's Farm
Water Tower
Great Fen
Harlock's Farm
Hitherthree Farm
Hundred Acres
Castles Farm
Turf Fen
Delph Bridge
Eye Hill Farm
Barcham Farm
Westfields Farm
Broadhill Farm
Slack's Hill
Great Hasse Farm
Blockmoor Farm
Orchard Farm
Crow Hall Farm
Broad Hill
Saxon Farm
Longfield Farm
Blockmoor Fen
Orchard Farm Business Park
North Field
North Horse Fen
Granary Farm
Hodson Farm
The Hasse
Barway Fen
Dolver Farm
Willow Farm
Soham Cotes
Shade Common
Northfield Windmill
Bancroft Field
Soham Fen
Mardon Farm
Sedge Fen
Engine Farm
Tiled House Farm
Partile Farm
CB7
Hotel
Soham
Middlemere Farm
Spencer Drove
Qua Fen Common
East Fen Farm
Moor Farm
Angie Common
Horse Bridge
East Fen Common
Soham Mere
North Angle Farm
The Causeway
Soham Lode
Horse Fen
South Angle Farm
The Ross Peers Sports Centre
Libly
Wet Horse Fen
Low Barn
Cherry Tree Farm
Wicken Dolves
Cherrytree Lane
Ash Closes
Small Path Hill
Water Tower
Horse Croft
Windmill
Down Field
Down Field Windmill
Lark Hall Farm
The Bracks
South Horse Fen
Horse Fen
No Ditch Bridge
Block Farm
Lark Hall Bridge
Football Ground
North Corner
Visitor Centre
Wicken
Hall Farm
Cemy
No Ditch Field
Westside Farm
National Trust
Windmill
Chancel Farm
CB5
Little Fen
Moat

CB5

D3
1 LODE CL
2 COLLEGE RD
3 REGENT PL
4 FRANK BRIDGES CL
5 REDHOUSE GDNS
6 THE CRESCENT
7 FORDHAM RD
8 MEADOW CL
9 MILL CFT

D4
1 ROSEBAY GDNS
2 BLUEBELL WK
3 HERBERT HUMAN CL
4 HONEYSUCKLE CL
5 NIGHTALL RD
6 CHESTNUT DR
7 GIMBERT RD
8 QUEENSWAY
9 WEATHERALLS CL

10 TEN BELL LA
11 BERRYCROFT
12 GUNTONS CL
13 BELL GDNS
14 FREDERICK TALBOT CL
15 CHURCHGATE ST
16 MARKET ST
17 ADELAIDE CL
18 EASTERN AV
19 BREWHOUSE LA

20 WHITE HART LA
21 GARDENERS LA
22 BROOK DAM LA

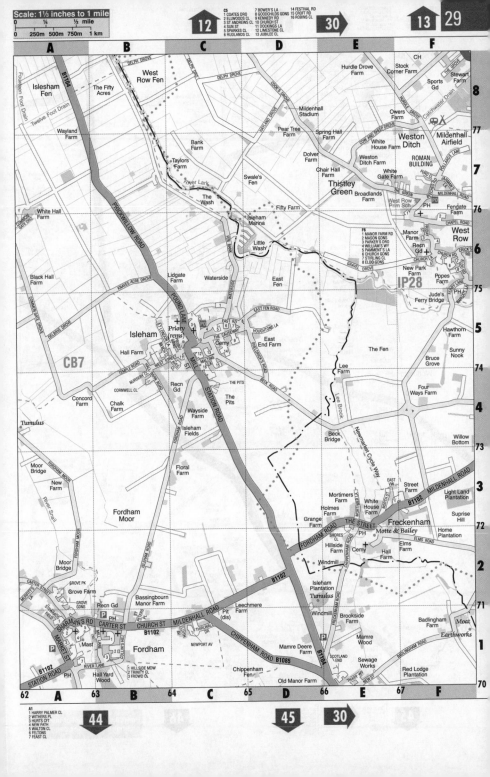

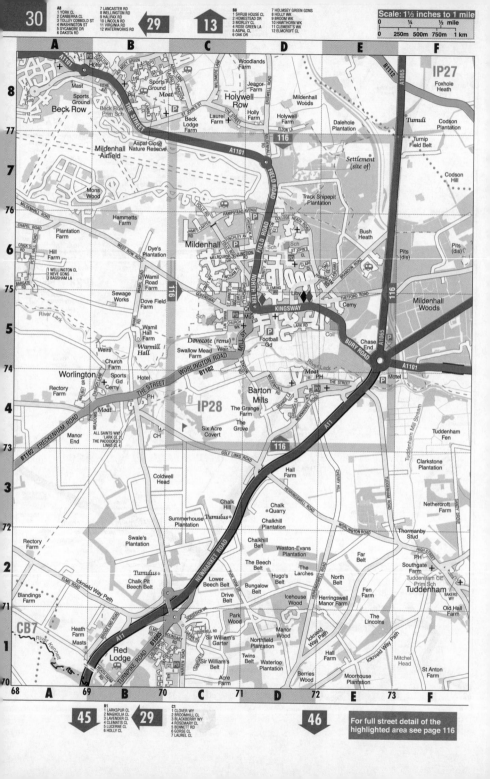

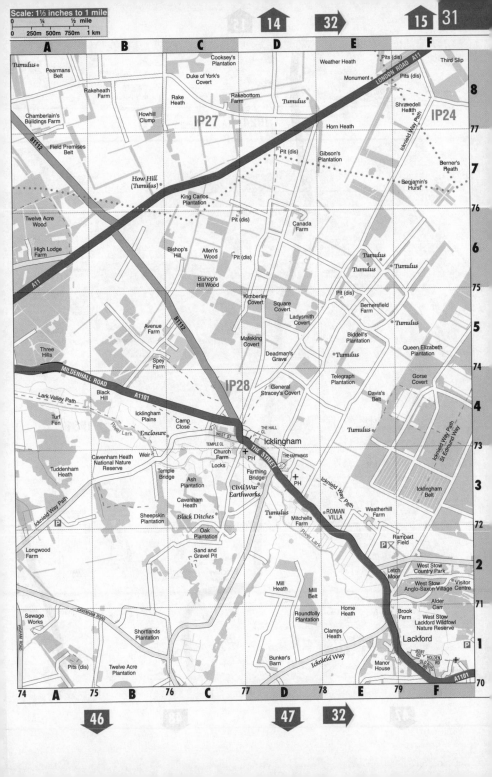

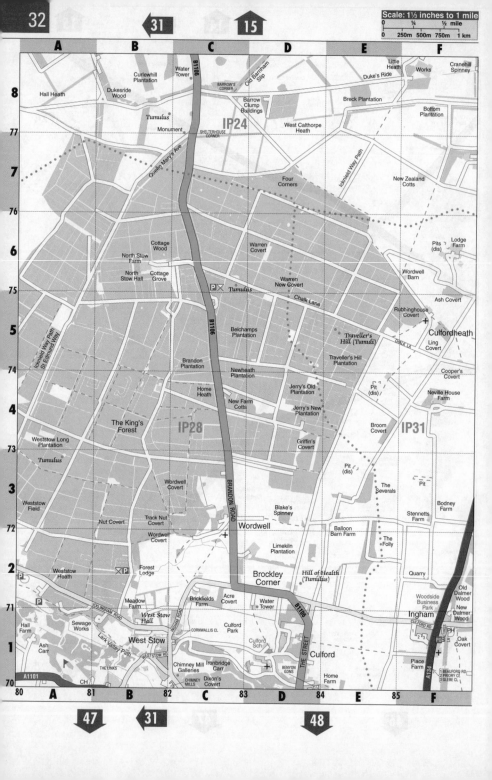

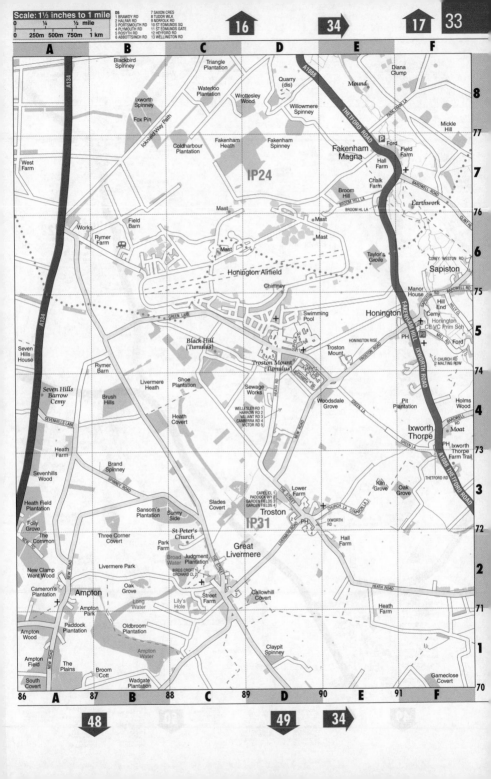

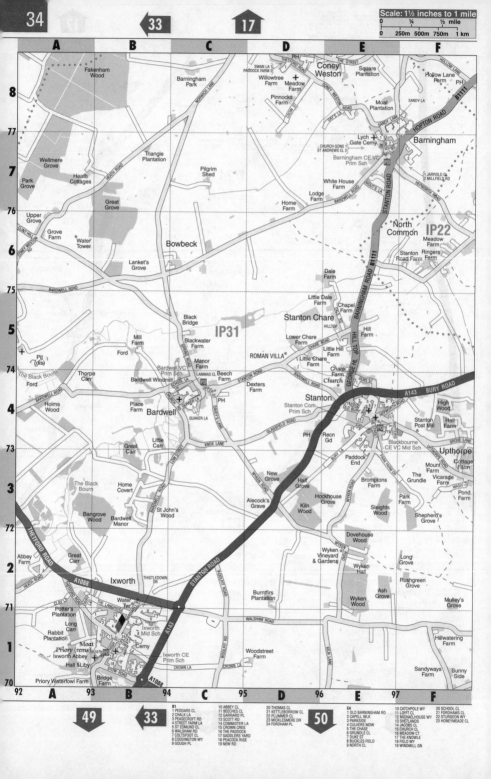

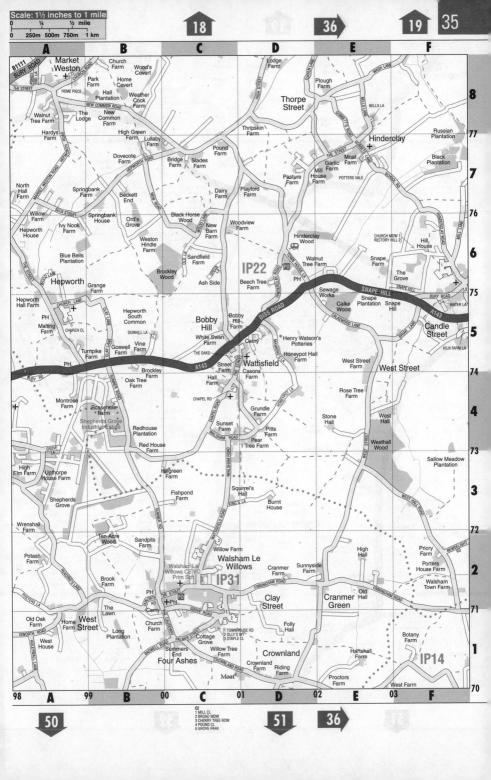

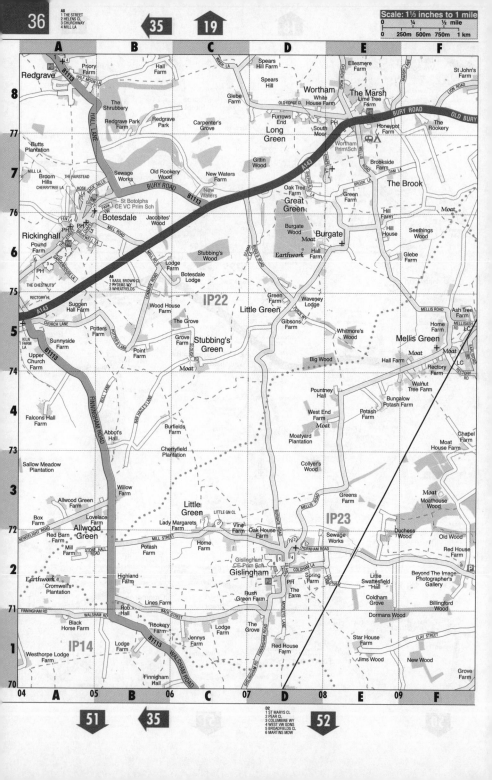

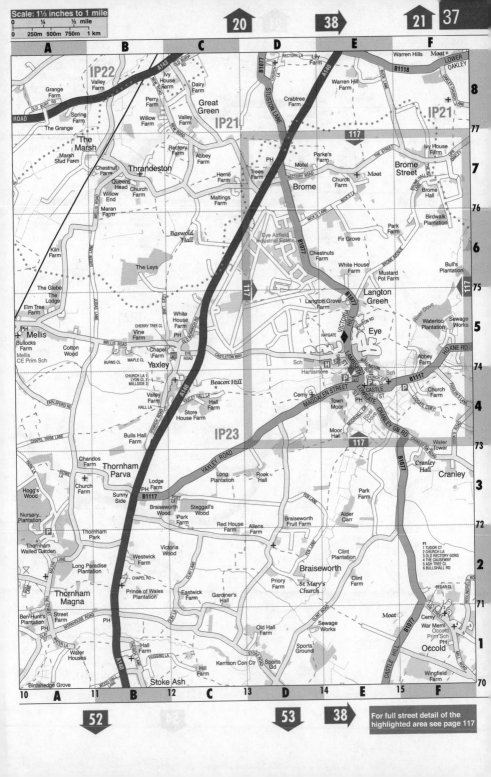

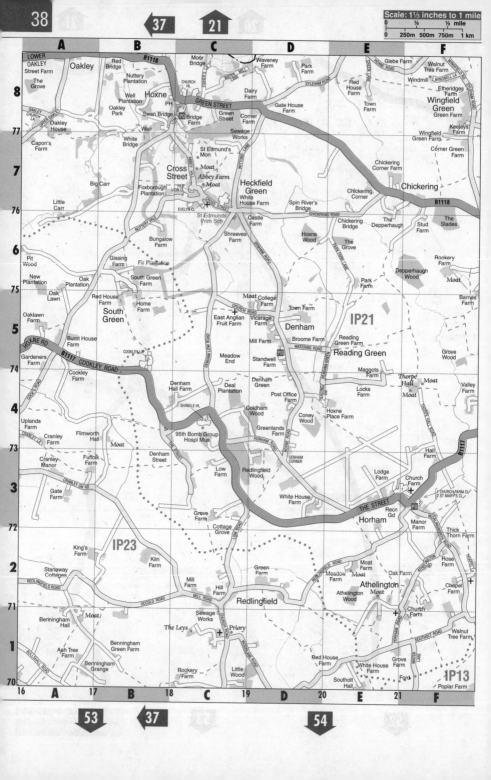

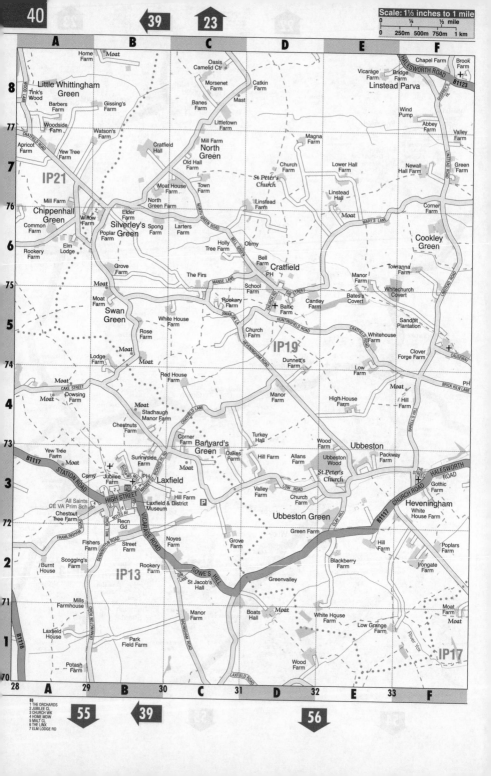

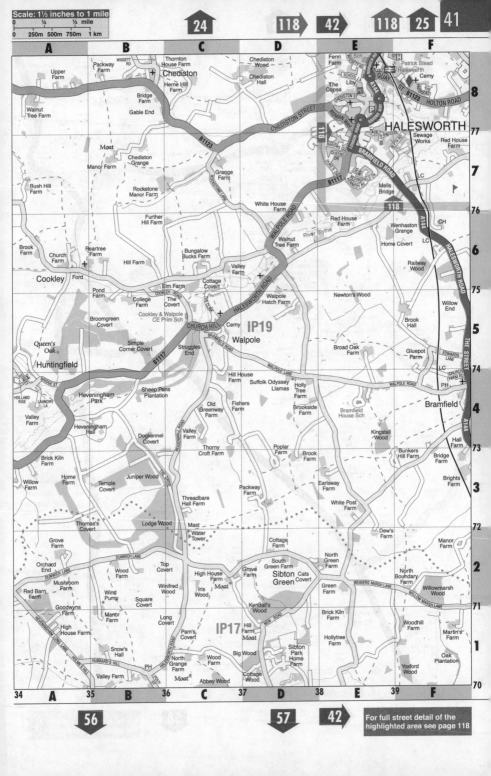

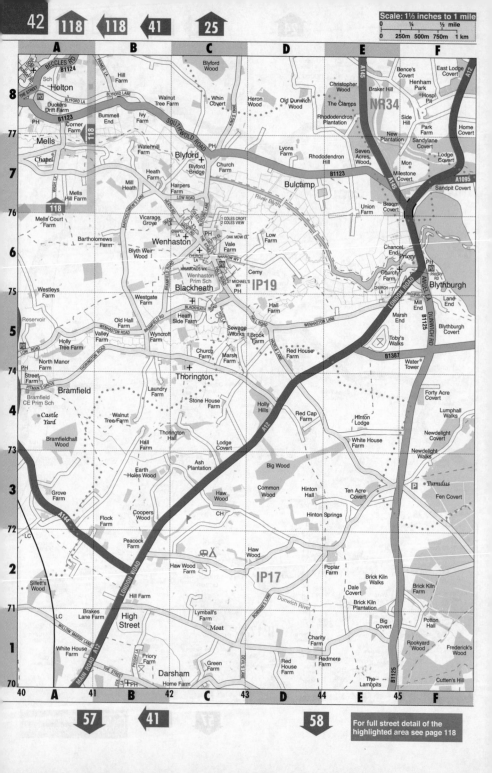

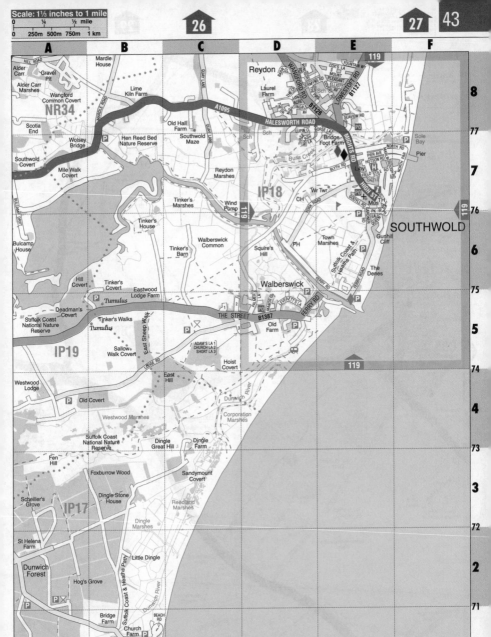

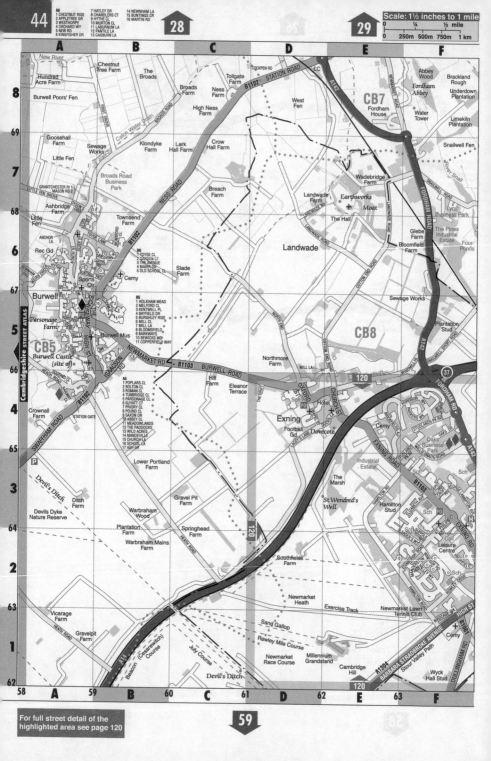

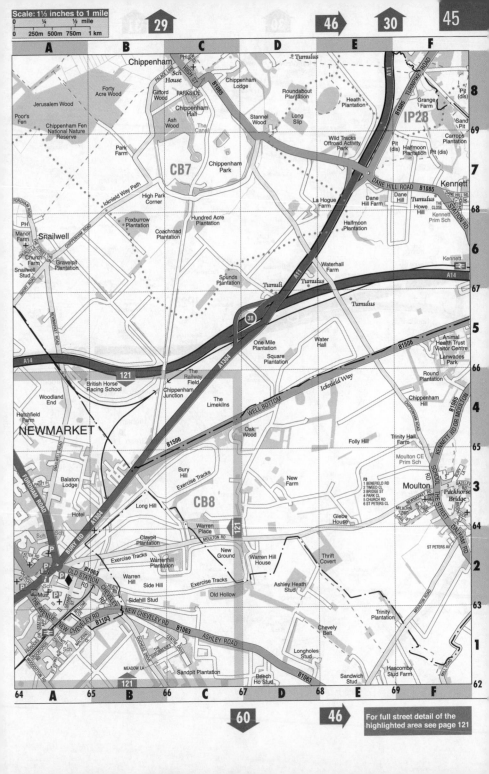

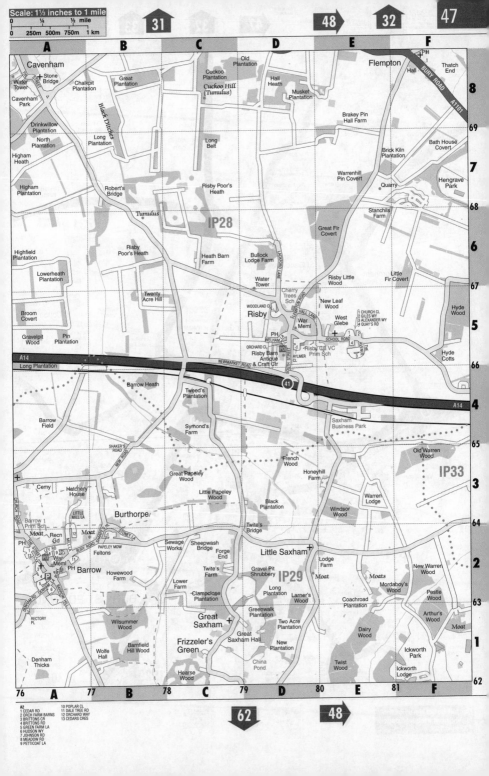

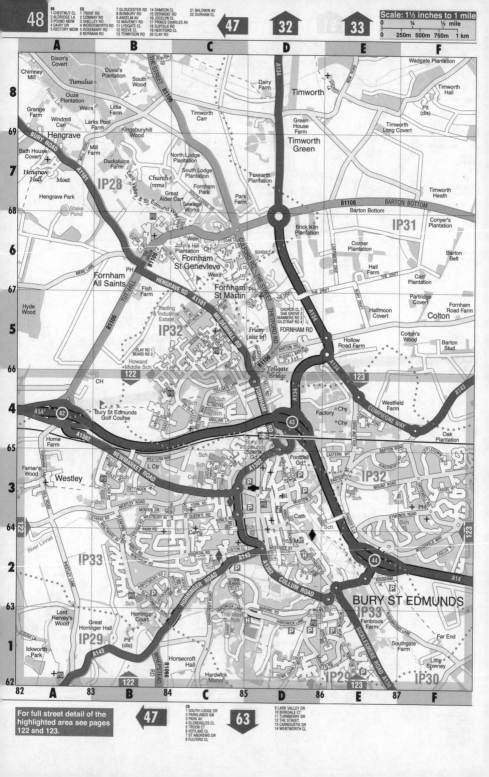

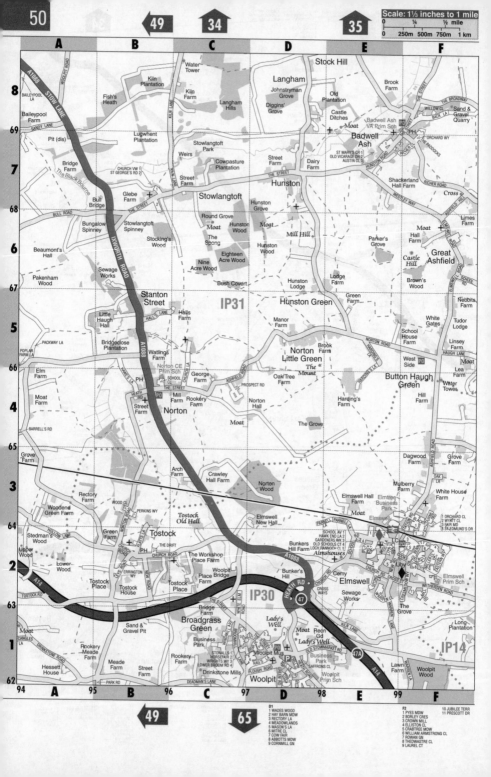

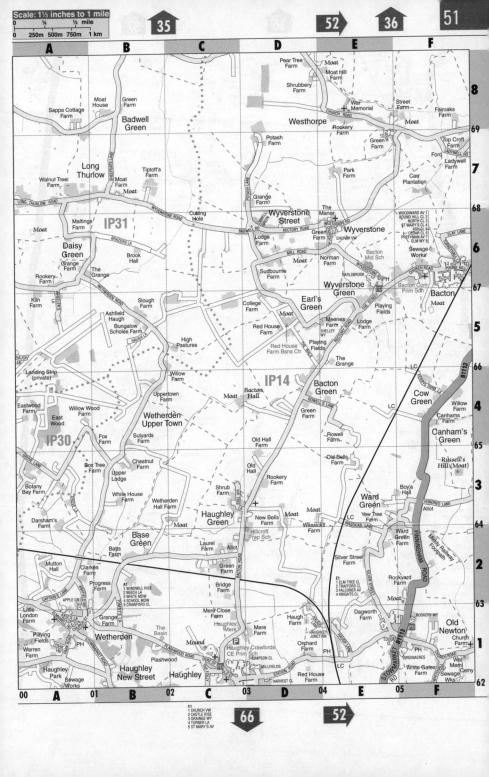

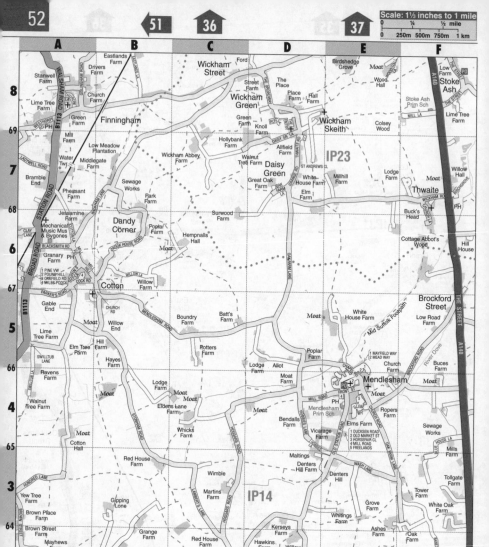

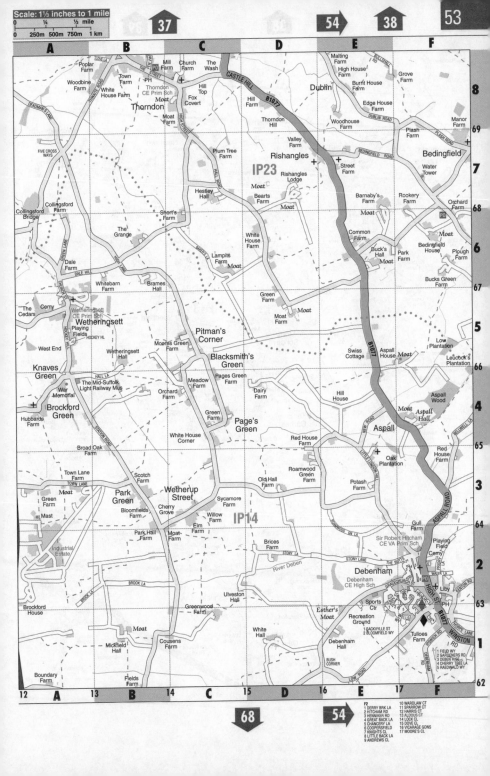

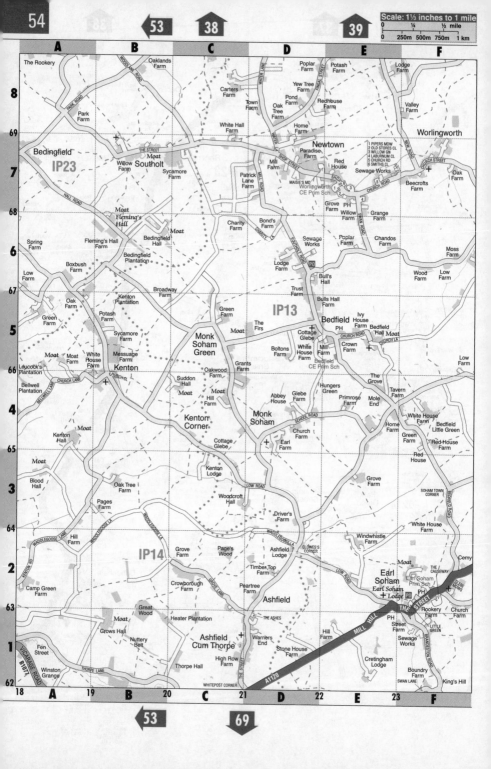

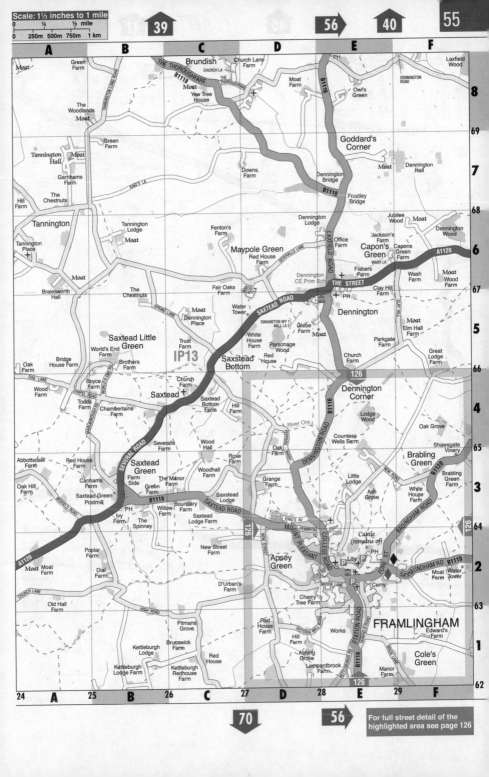

A   B   C   D   E   F

Darsham
THE STREET
Old Hall
GORSE VW 1
STUDIO CL 2
THE STREET 3
Westleton Heath
National Nature
Reserve
WESTLETON ROAD
Greyfriars
Wood
Dunwich
Cliffs

8

The
Wilderness
Darsham
House
DUNWICH ROAD
Mount Pleasant
Farm
Cliff
House
PH

Mill Hill
Farm
Chatburn
Farm
The
Grange
PH
PH
King's
Farm
Grimston's
Covert
Dunwich
Nature
Reserve
Minsmere
Cliffs

69

YOXFORD ROAD
IP17
Walk Barn
Farm
Shepherdswalk
Covert
Stuart
Spinney

Low
Farm
Westleton
Westleton
Common

7

Watermill
Farm
Vale House
Farm
Westleton
Walks
North
Walks
Scottshall
Coverts
The
Warren
Visitor
Centre

Causeway
Farm
Middleton
Middleton
Prim Sch
Whin
Covert
Scott's
Hall
SHEEPWASH LA
Visitor
Centre
Coney
Hill

68

**Middleton
Moor**
PH
THE STREET
MINSMERE RD
New
Wood
Minsmere
Nature Reserve

Rose
Farm
Reckford
Farm
Bank Top
Vault
Hill

6

Hill
Farm
ANNEDNS
CORNER
EAST LA
THE DRIFT
Hangmans
New Wood
Minsmere
Level

Valley View
Farm
Fenn
Farm
Alder
Carr
Stonehill
Covert
Dovehill
Plantation
The
Sluice

67

Trust
Farm
Yew Tree
Farm
RATTLA
CORNER
Redhouse
Farm
PH Cemy
Sandypytle
Plantation

Hawthorn
Farm
Theberton Hall
Farm
Holly
Tree Farm
England
Covert
CHAPEL ROAD
Willow
Farm
Eastbridge

5

Plumtreehills
Covert
Theberton
Church
Farm
Mill
Drift
Farm
Lower Abbey
Farm
The
Grove

Dove House
Farm
Peckover
Wood
Brown's
Plantation
DOUGHTY WYLIE
CR
Game
Plantation
Potter's
Farm
Ash
Wood

66

Jubilee
Wood
Kiln
Grove
MOAT ROAD
Moat
Farm
Hotel
Theberton
House
Birchwood
Farm
Greenhouse
Plantation
Dunwich
Forest
Goose
Hill

4

Theberton
Woods
Moat
House
Fishpond
Grove
Upper
Abbey
IP16
Hilltop
Covert
Nursery
Covert

Hill
Farm
Harrow
Lane
Farm
Spring
Covert
Hill
Farm
Old Abbey
Farm
Kenton
Hills

65

Crossing
Farm
Leiston
Abbey
129
Aldhurst
Farm
LOVER'S LANE
Leiston
Carr
Sizewell Belts
Nature Reserve
Sizewell
Visitor
Centre
Sewage
Works

3

Buckle's
Wood
Fishers
Farm
Leiston
Common
Reckham
Pits Wood
Rookyard
Wood
Sizewell
Power Station
Chimney

64

LC
129
Cemy
Brick Kiln
Farm
Sewage
Works
Beirnfels
Round
Covert
Coronation
Wood
Hill
Wood

2

B1119
SAXMUNDHAM ROAD
WATERLOO
AVENUE
Liby
Works
B1119
VALLEY ROAD
129
Broom
Covert
Timber
Top
Sizewell

Woodfield
Pit
IP17
LEISTON
Sports
Gd
Recreation
Gd
EASTLANDS
RD
KING GEORGE'S AV
Crown
Farm
Halfway
Cottages
Home
Farm

1

B1119
HIGH ST
SEAWARD RD
Recn Gd
GRIMSEY'S LA
PH
SIZEWELL GAP

62

42   A   43   B   44   C   45   D   46   E   47   F   48

57 129 73

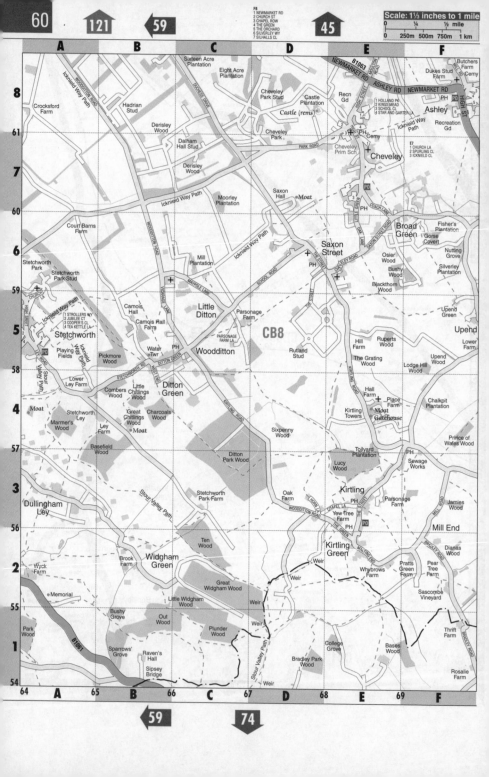

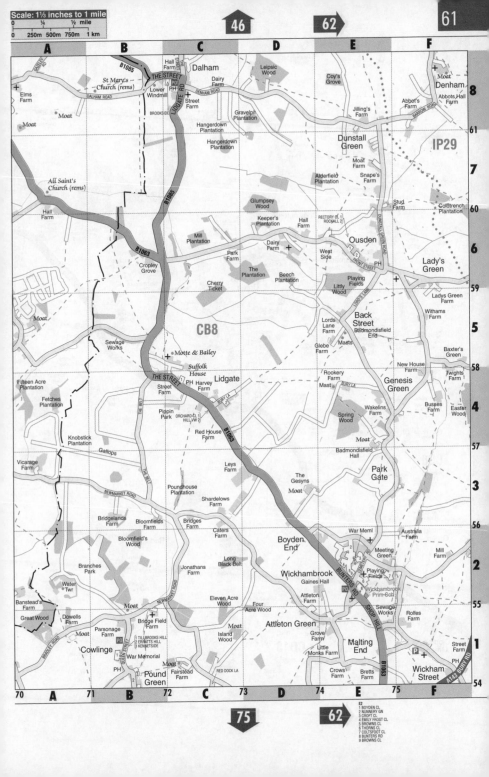

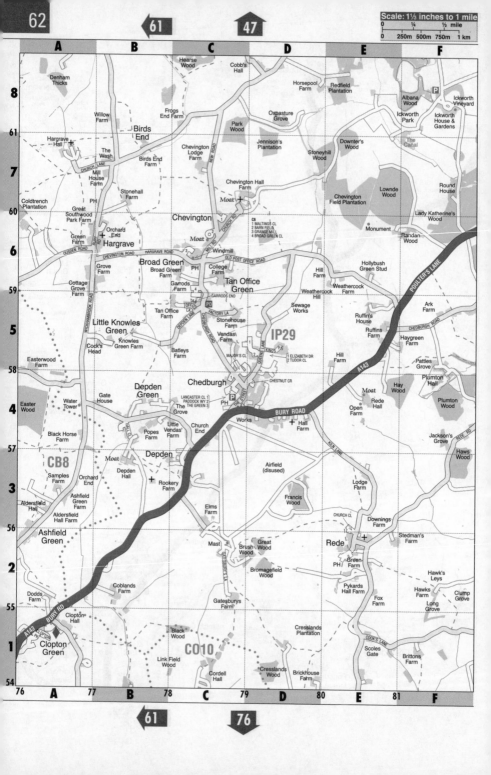

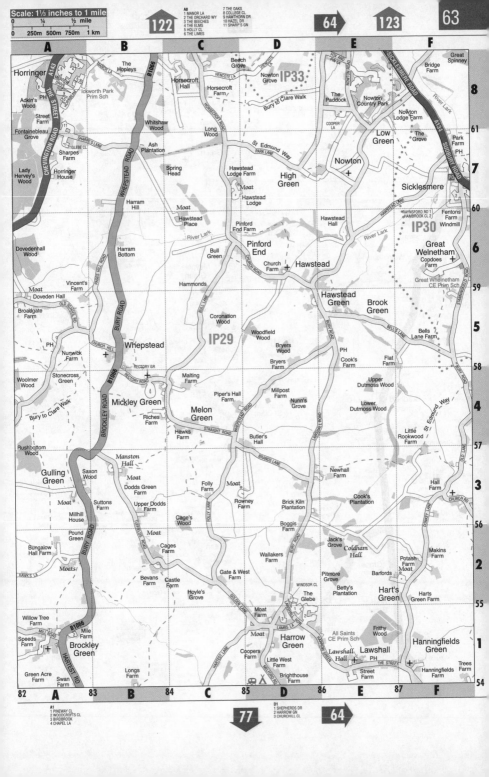

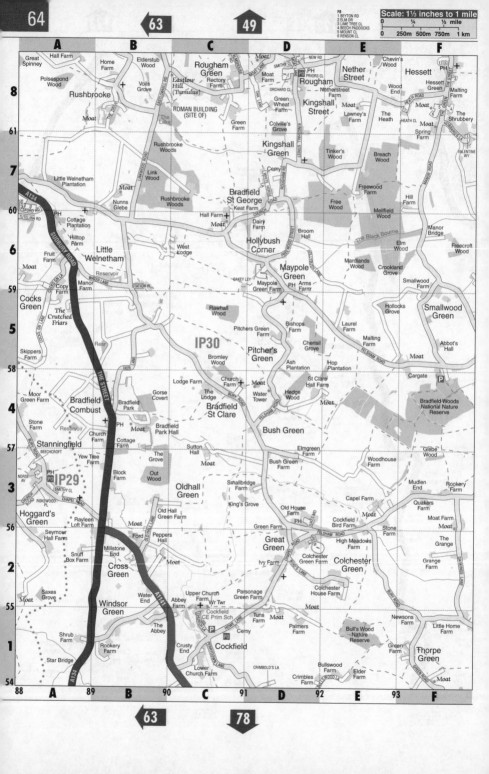

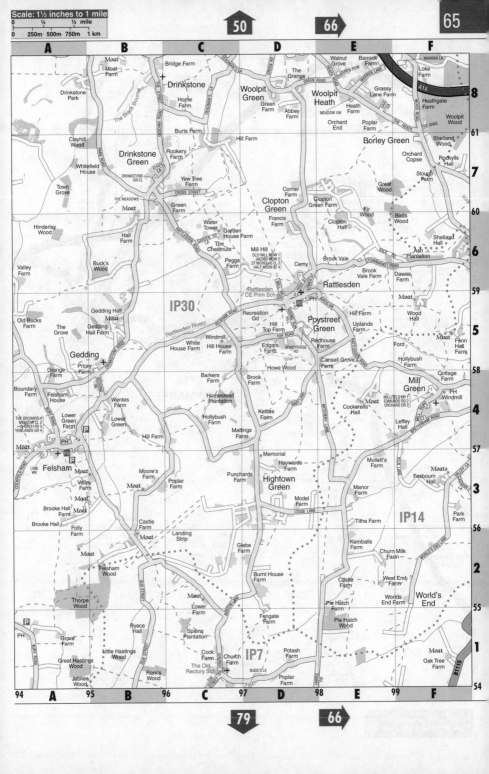

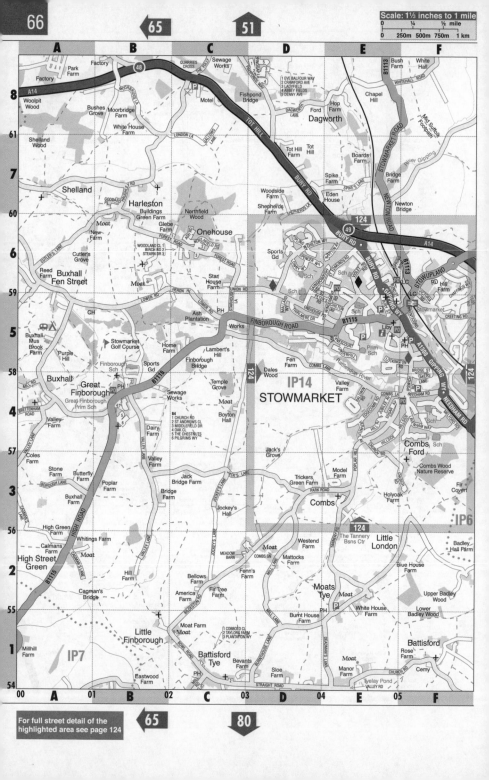

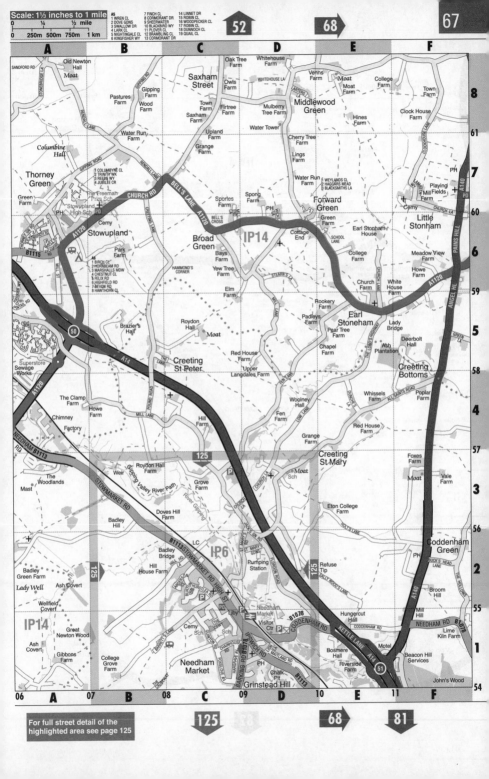

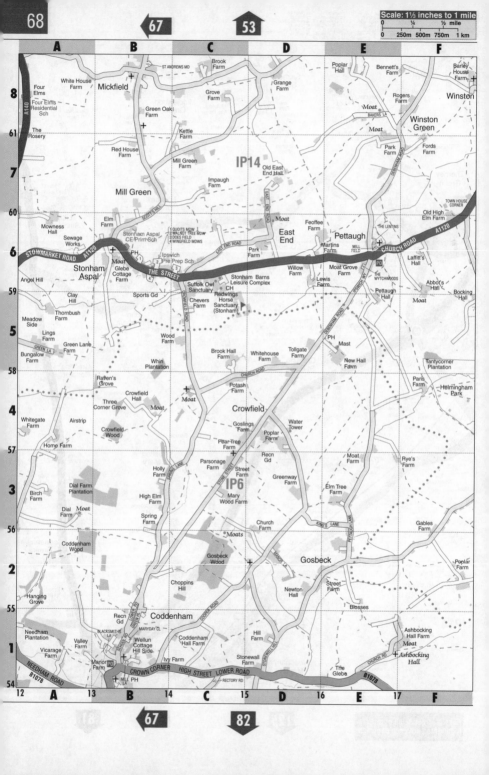

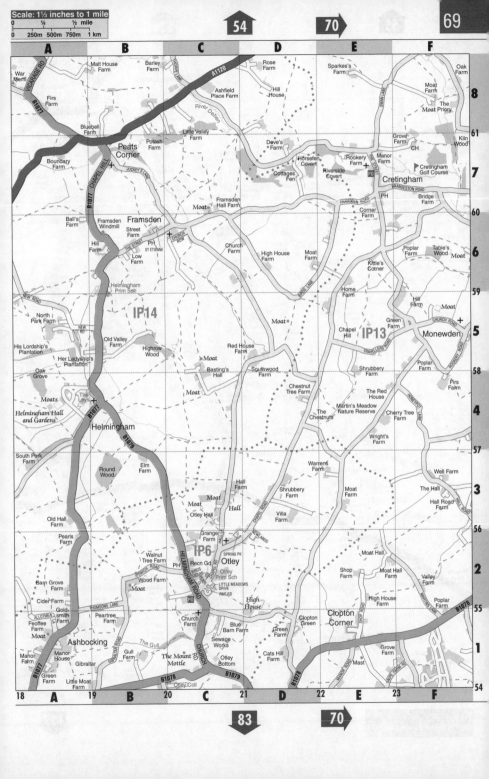

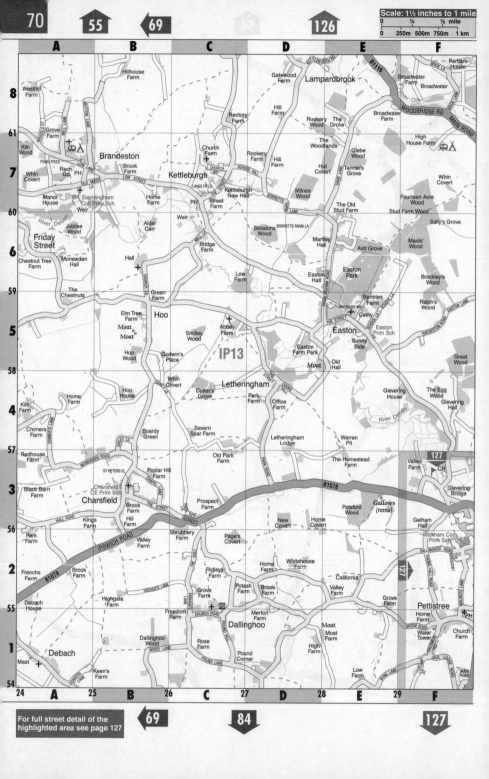

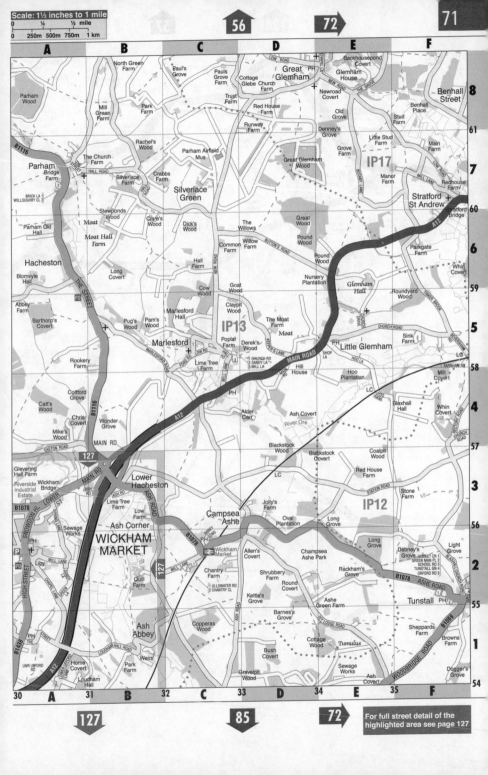

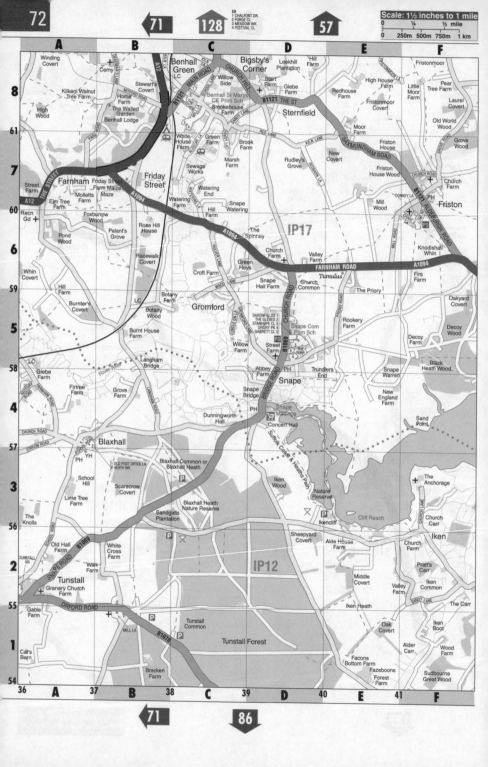

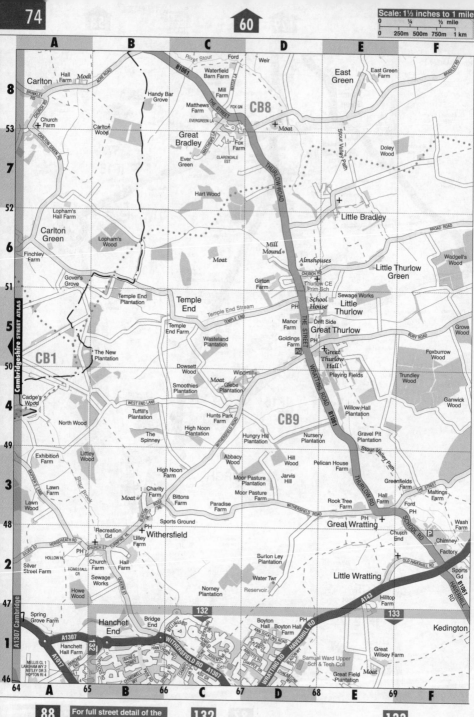

Scale: 1½ inches to 1 mile

0 ¼ ½ mile
0 250m 500m 750m 1 km

A **B** **C** **D** **E** **F**

60

Cambridgeshire STREET ATLAS

Carlton
Hall Farm
Moat
Brinkley Rd
Church Farm
Handy Bar Grove
Carlton Wood
Carlton Green Rd
Church Rd

River Stour
Ford
Waterfield Barn Farm
Mill Farm
Matthews Farm
Weir
Fox Gn
Evergreen La
CB8
East Green
East Green Farm
Bradley Rd
Moat

Great Bradley
Ever Green
Fox Farm
Clarendale Est
Stour Valley Path
Doley Wood

Hart Wood
Thurlow Road
Little Bradley
Broad Road
Wadgell's Wood

Lopham's Hall Farm
Carlton Green
Finchley Farm
Lopham's Wood
Moat
Mill Mound
Almshouses
Church Rd
Thurlow CE Prim Sch
Little Thurlow Green

Gover's Grove
Temple End Plantation
Temple End
Girton Farm
Sewage Works
Little Thurlow

CB1
The New Plantation
Temple End Stream
Temple End
PH
School House
Great Thurlow
Grove Wood
Bury Road

Temple End Farm
Wasteland Plantation
Manor Farm
Goldings Farm
Great Thurlow Hall
Foxburrow Wood

Cadge's Wood
Dowsett Wood
Smoothies Plantation
Moat
Windmill
Glebe Plantation
Playing Fields
Trundley Wood
Ganwick Wood

North Wood
West End Lane
Tuffill's Plantation
Hunts Park Wood
Withersfield Road
CB9
Willow Hall Plantation
Stour Valley Path

The Spinney
High Noon Plantation
Hungry Hill Plantation
Nursery Plantation
Gravel Pit Plantation

Exhibition Farm
Littley Wood
High Noon Farm
Abbacy Wood
Hill Wood
Pelican House Farm
Greenfields Farm
The Street
Maltings Farm

Lawn Farm
Stour Brook
Charity Farm
Moor Pasture Plantation
Jarvis Hill
Hall Farm
Ford
PH
Wash Farm

Lawn Wood
Moat
Bittons Farm
Paradise Farm
Moor Pasture Farm
Withersfield Road
Rook Tree Farm
Great Wratting
Chimney Factory

Recreation Gd
Sports Ground
PH
Lilley Farm
Church End
Old Haverhill Rd

Silver Street Farm
Hollow Hl
Horseheath Rd
Withersfield
Church Farm
Hall Farm
Burton Ley Plantation
Little Wratting
Sports Gd
Haverhill Rd

Howe Wood
Sewage Works
Norney Plantation
Water Twr
Reservoir
Hilltop Farm
B1061

Spring Grove Farm
A1307 Cambridge
132
A143
133
Kedington

Hanchet End
Bridge End
Hanchett Hall Farm
A1307
A1017
Withersfield Rd
Haverhill Rd
Boyton Hall
Boyton Hall Farm
PH
Great Wilsey Farm

MELLIS CL 1
LANGHAM WY 2
NOTLEY DR 3
HOPTON RD 4
Samuel Ward Upper Sch & Tech Coll
Great Field Plantation
Moat

A **B** **C** **D** **E** **F**
64 65 66 67 68 69

88

132

133

For full street detail of the highlighted area see pages 132 and 133

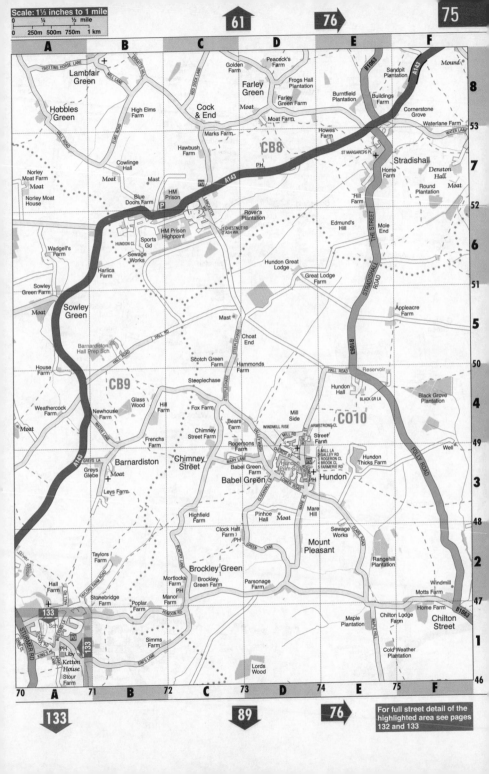

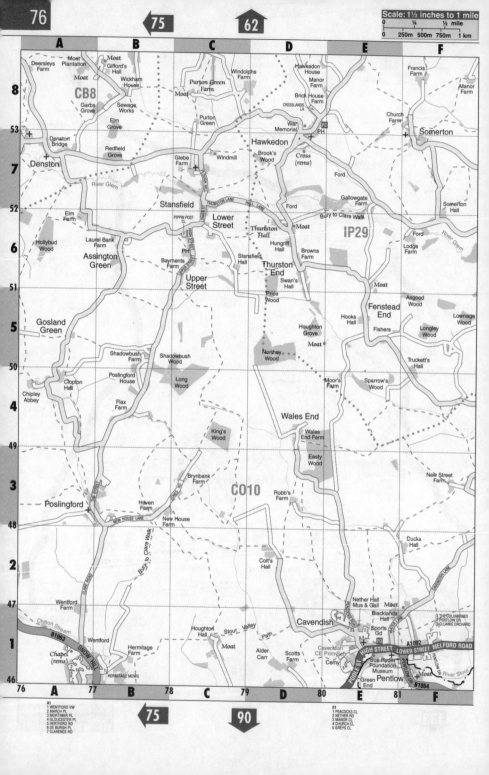

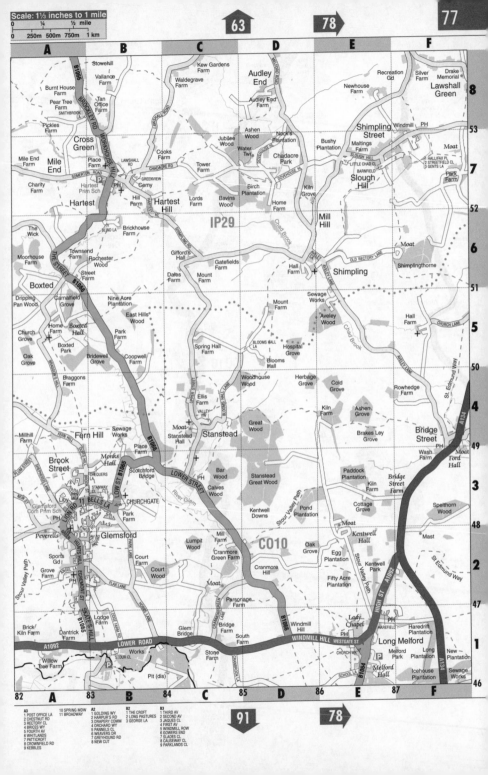

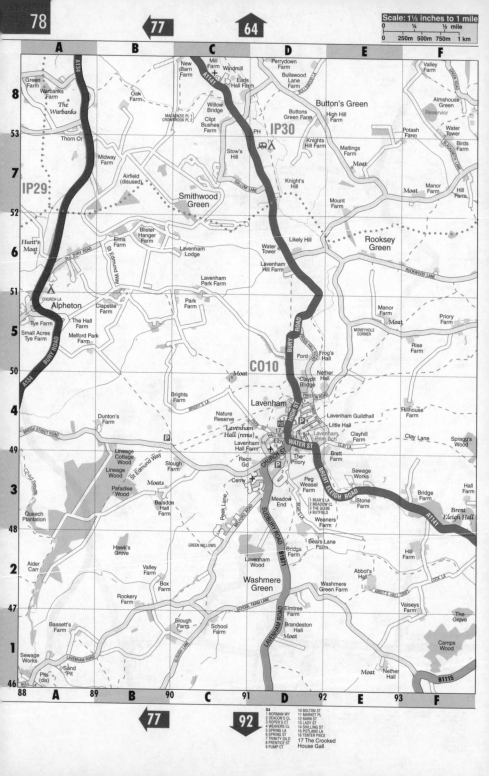

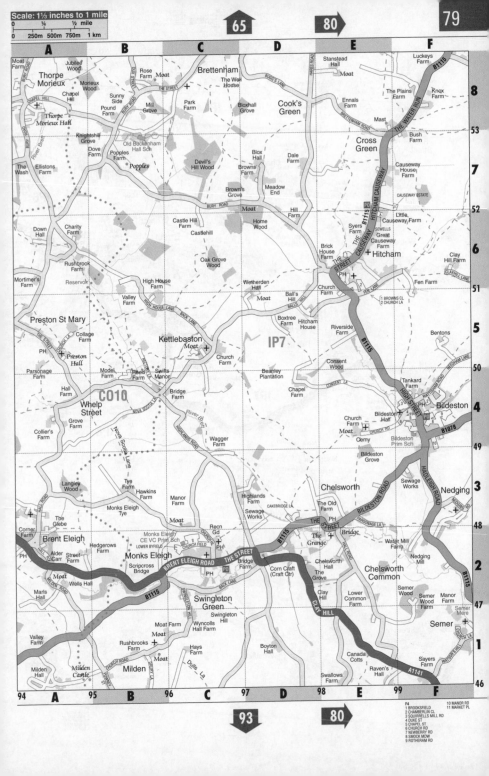

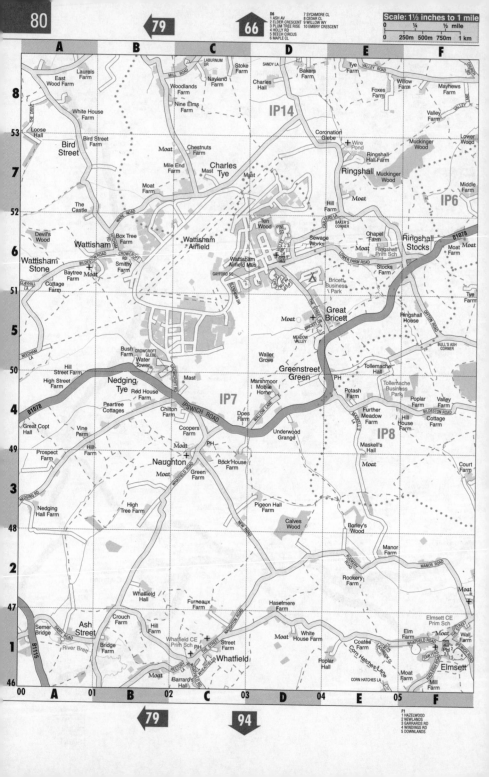

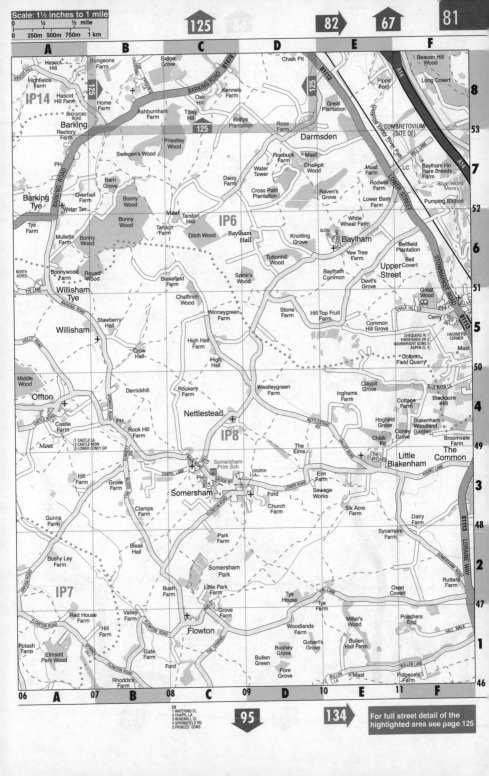

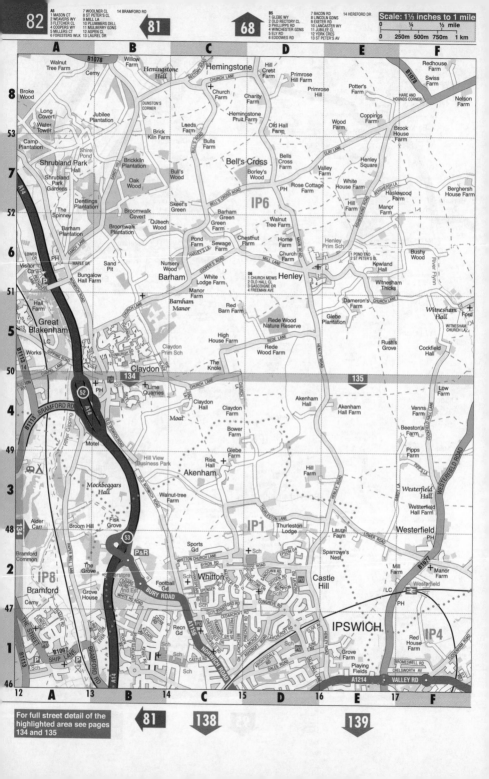

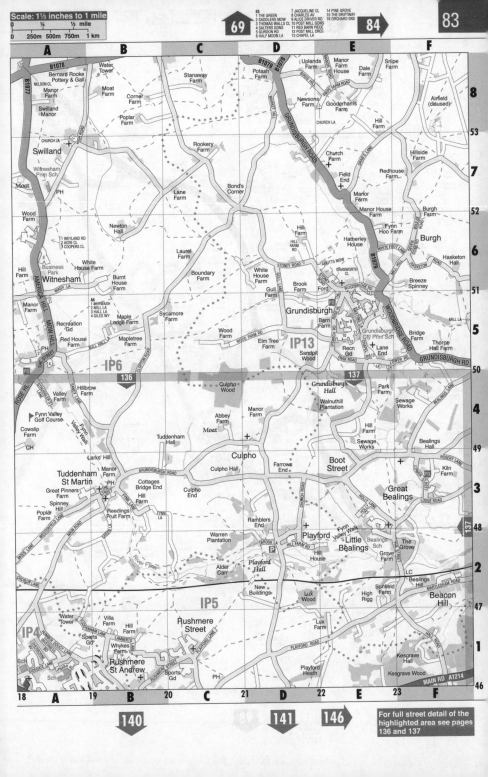

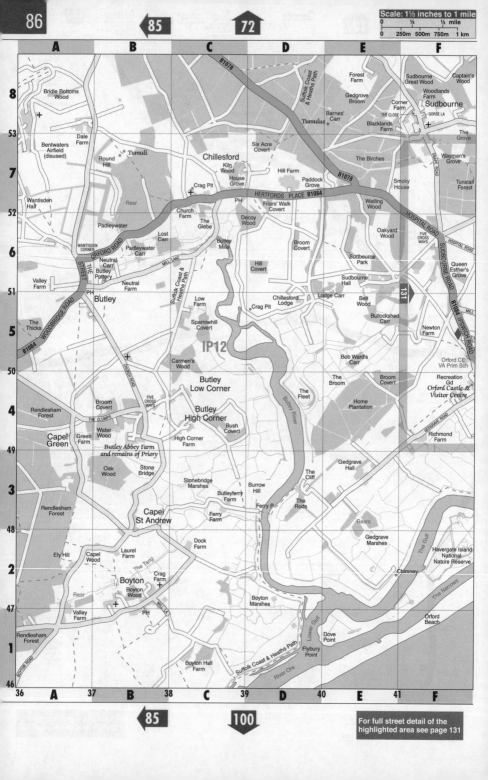

Aldeburgh Bay

IP15

River Alde

Firs Farm

The Firs

Longdrift Carr

Sudbourne Marshes

The White House

SCHOOL ROAD

131

Valley Farm

High House Farm

HIGH HOUSE FARM ROAD

Elm Covert

Crag Farm

Crag Pit

FERRY ROAD

CRAG FARM ROAD

Chaplin's Carr

Sudbourne Beach

Moss' Carr

Church Farm

Ox Carr

Blackstakes Reach

Lantern Marshes

Masts

Prettyman's Whin

IP12

Masts

131

Lodge Farm

Cobbins Farm

Bullockshed Grove

Ash Carr

BROADWAY

BULLOCKSHED

Raydon Hall

Wireless Station

Orford

RECTORY RD

Pig Pail Bridge

Town Marshes

FRONT ST

QUAY ST

BROAD ST

Town Hall

P PH

P P

King's Marshes

Chantry Farm

River Ore

Sewage Works

Orfordness

131

Orford Ness

Chantry Point

Orford Ness National Nature Reserve

Orfordness Lighthouse

Stony Ditch

Stonyditch Point

Cuckold's Point

Orford Beach

53

7

52

6

51

5

50

4

49

3

48

2

47

1

46

42   A   43   B   44   C   45   D   46   E   47   F

For full street detail of the highlighted area see page 131

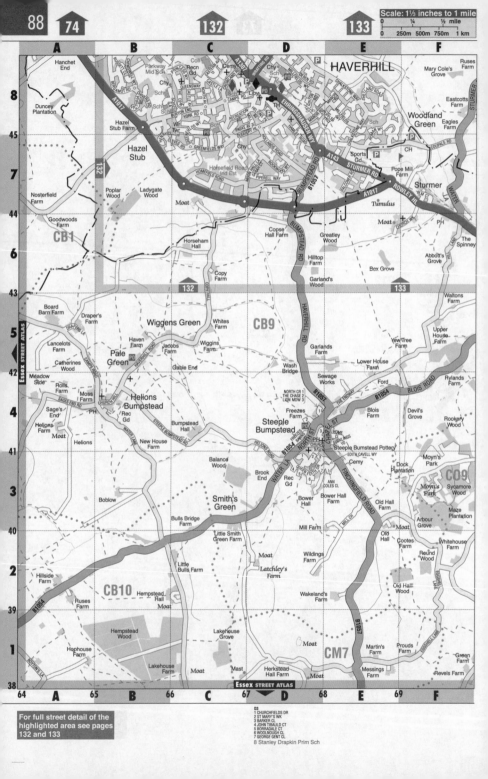

Scale: 1½ inches to 1 mile

¼ ½ mile
250m 500m 750m 1 km

HAVERHILL

Hanchet End
Mary Cole's Grove
Ruses Farm
Eastcotts Farm

Duncey Plantation
Woodland Green
Eagles Farm

Hazel Stub Farm
CH

Hazel Stub
Pope Mill Farm
Sturmer

Nosterfield Farm
Poplar Wood
Ladygate Wood
Moat
Tumulus
Rowley Hl

CB1
Goodwoods Farm
Moat
PH
The Spinney

Horseham Hall
Copse Hall Farm
Greatley Wood
Abbott's Grove

132
Copy Farm
Hilltop Farm
Bex Grove
133

Waltons Farm

Board Barn Farm
Draper's Farm
Wiggens Green
Whites Farm
CB9
Garlands Farm
Yew Tree Farm
Upper House Farm

Lancelots Farm
Haven Farm
Jacobs Farm
Wiggins Farm
Lower House Farm

Catherines Wood
Pale Green
Gable End
Wash Bridge
Garlands Farm
Ford
Rylands Farm

Meadow Side
Moss Farm
Sewage Works
Blois Road
Devil's Grove
Rookery Wood

Rolls Farm
Helions Bumpstead
PH
Rec Gd
NORTH CR 1 / THE CHASE 2 / LION MDW 3
Freezes Farm
Blois Farm

Sage's End
Bumpstead Hall
Steeple Bumpstead
HOME
Steeple Bumpstead Pottery
Moyn's Plantation
CO9
Moyn's Park
Sycamore Wood

Helions Farm
New House Farm
EDITH CAVELL WY
Cemy
Dock Plantation
Maze Plantation

Moat
Helions
Balance Wood
Brook End
Rec Gd
ANN COLES CL
Arbour Grove
Whitehouse Farm

Boblow
Bower Hall
Bower Hall Farm
Old Hall
Round Wood

Bulls Bridge Farm
Smith's Green
Mill Farm
Old Hall
Cootes Farm

Hillside Farm
CB10
Little Smith Green Farm
Little Bulls Farm
Moat
Latchley's Farm
Wildings Farm
Old Hall Wood

Ruses Farm
Hempstead Hall Farm
Moat
Wakeland's Farm

Hophouse Farm
Hempstead Wood
Lakehouse Grove
CM7
Martin's Farm
Prouds Farm
Green Farm

Lakehouse Farm
Moat
Mast
Herkstead Hall Farm
Moat
Messings Farm
Revels Farm

For full street detail of the highlighted area see pages 132 and 133

D3
1 CHURCHFIELDS DR
2 ST MARY'S WK
3 BARKER CL
4 JOHN TIBAULD CT
5 BORRADALE CT
6 WOOLNOUGH CL
7 GEORGE GENT CL

8 Stanley Drapkin Prim Sch

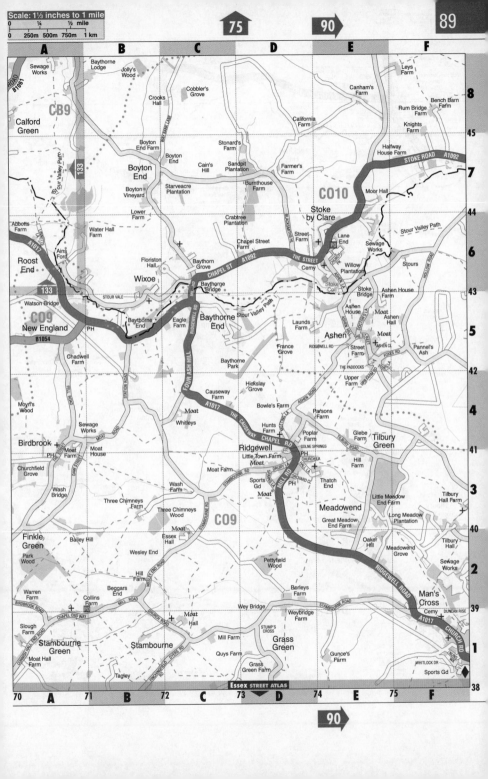

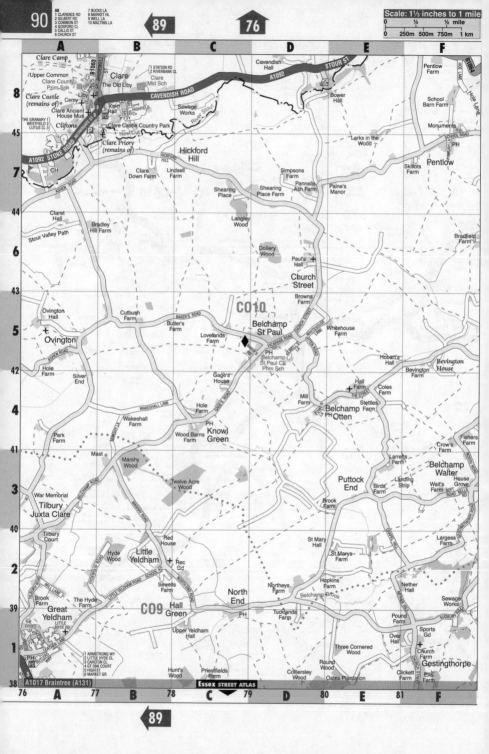

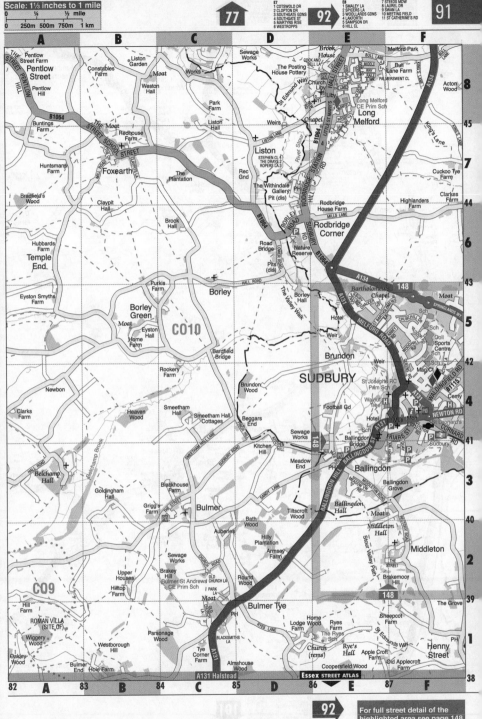

For full street detail of the highlighted area see page 148

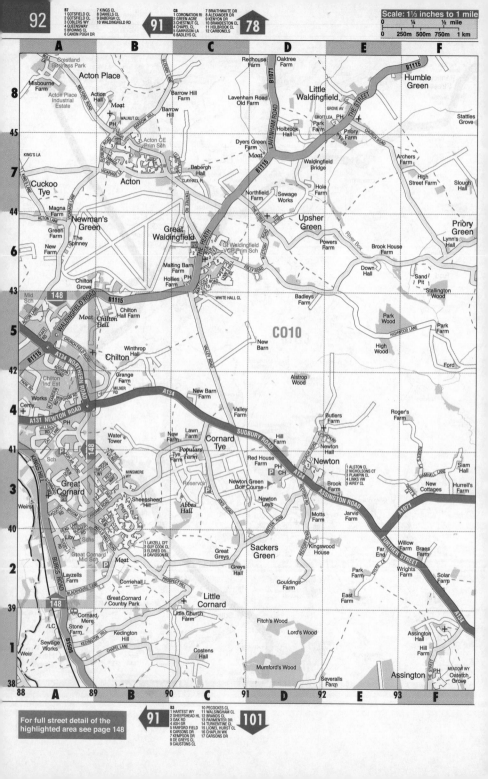

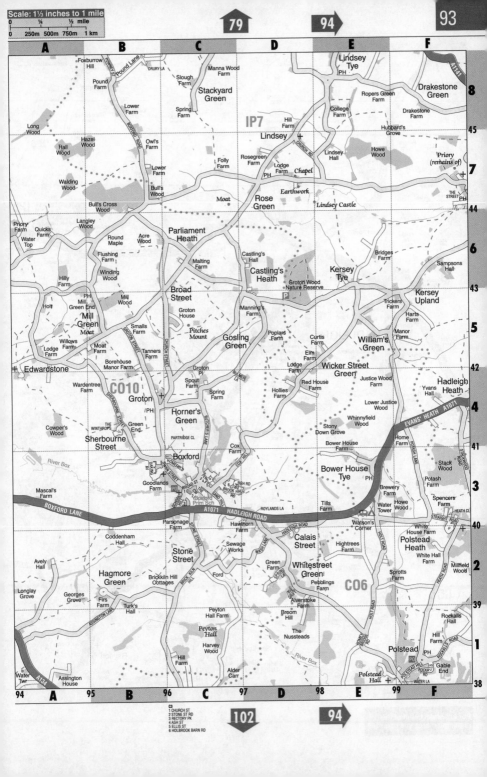

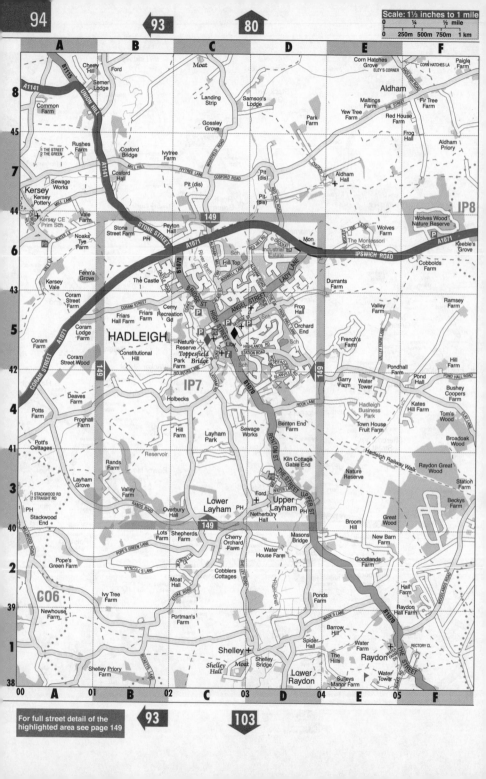

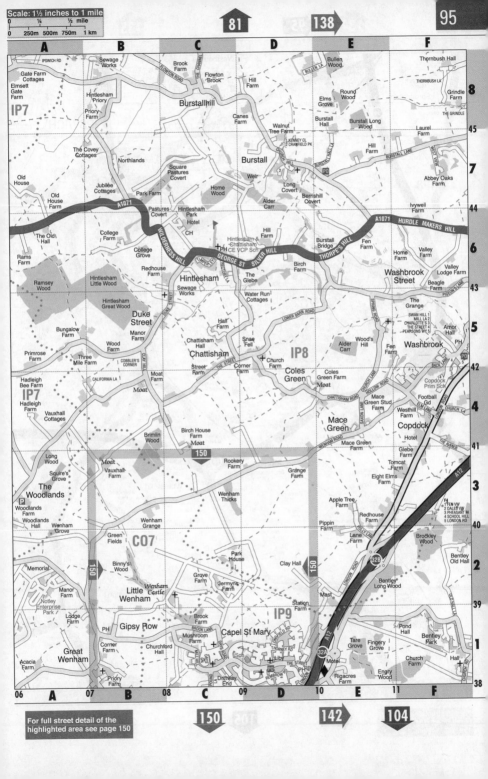

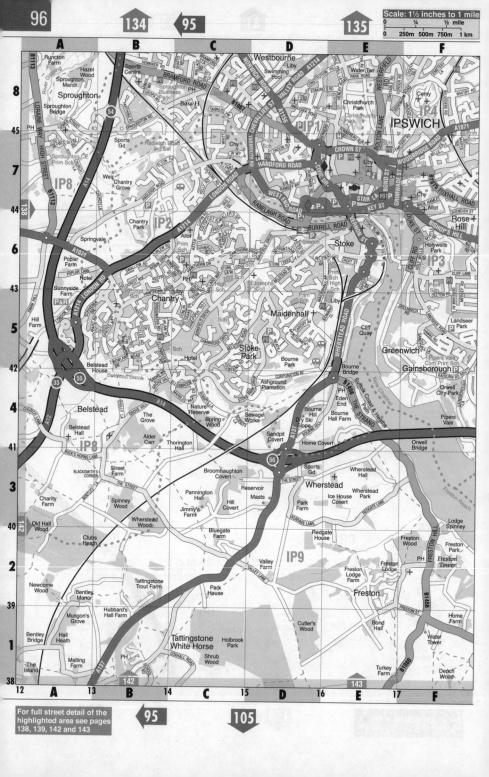

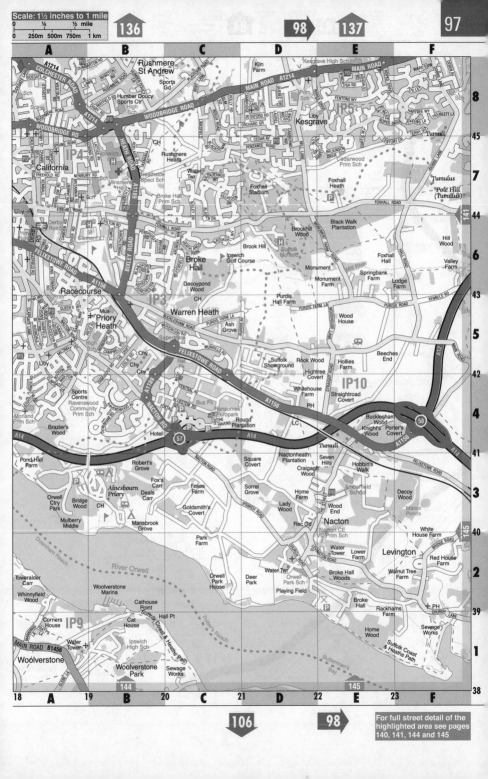

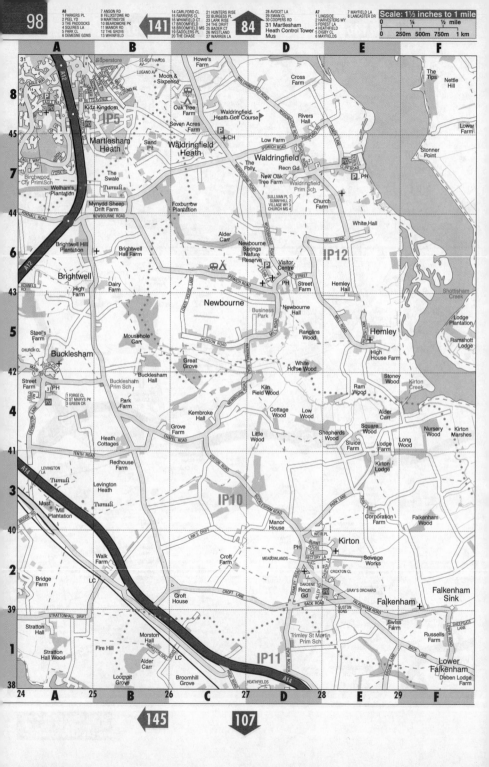

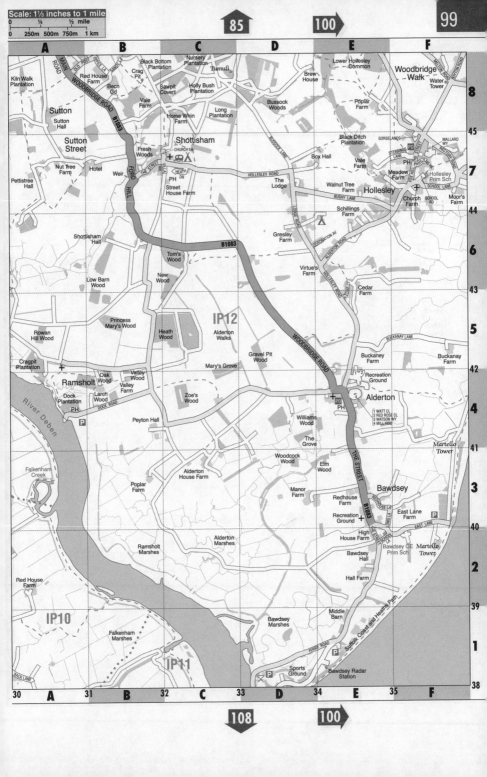

99
86

Scale: 1½ inches to 1 mile

0   ¼   ½ mile

0   250m 500m 750m 1 km

Oak Hill

HM Prison

Sports Ground

Grove House

The Grove

IP12

River Ore

Hollesley Bay Colony
(HM Young Offender
Institution)

Hollesley Bay

Orford Haven

Sewage Works

Oxley Dairy

Oxley Marshes

North Weir Point

P

Shingle Street

Martello Tower

Suffolk Coast & Heaths Path

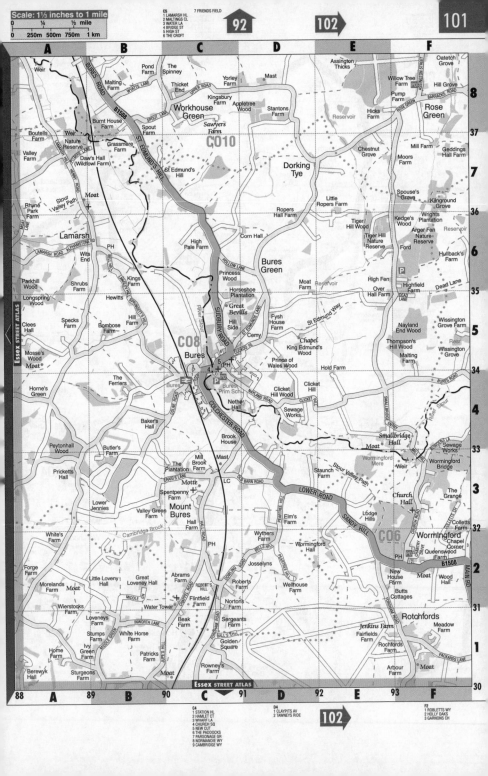

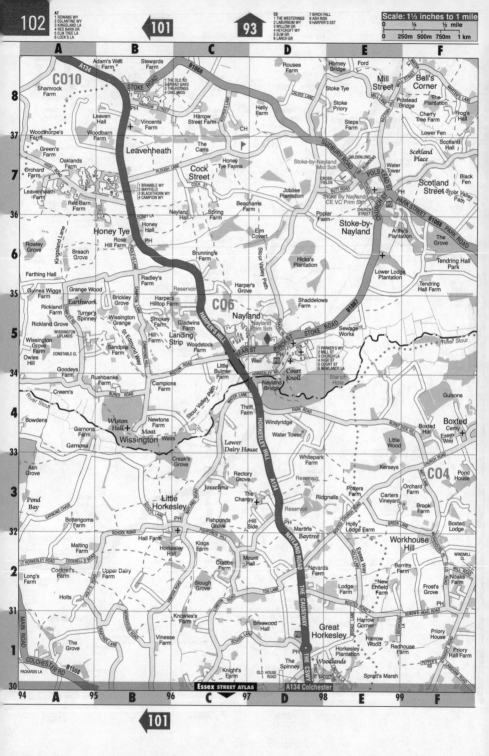

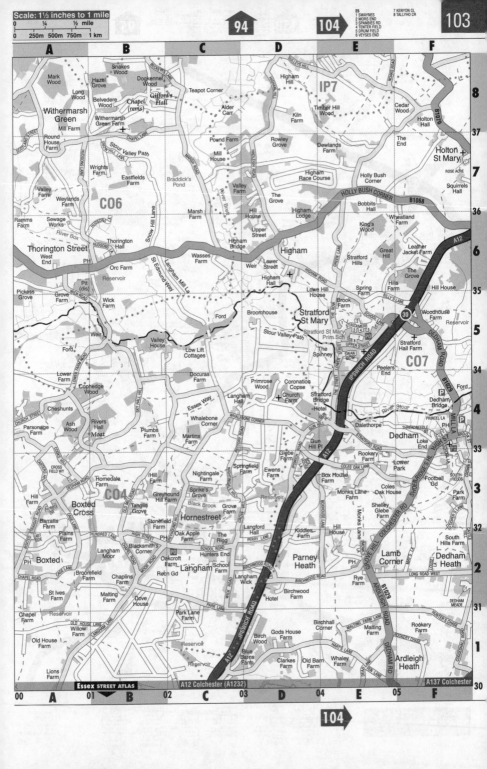

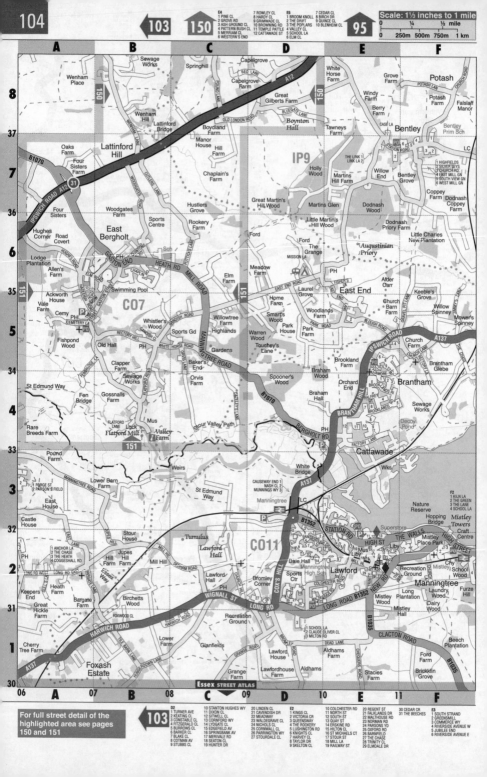

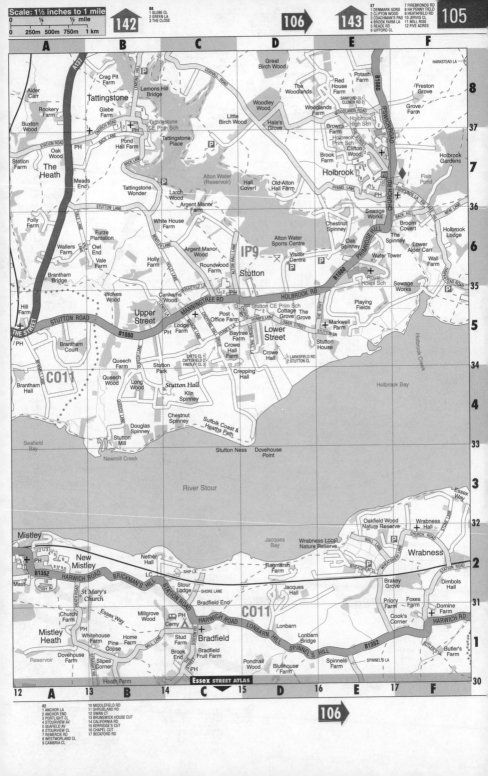

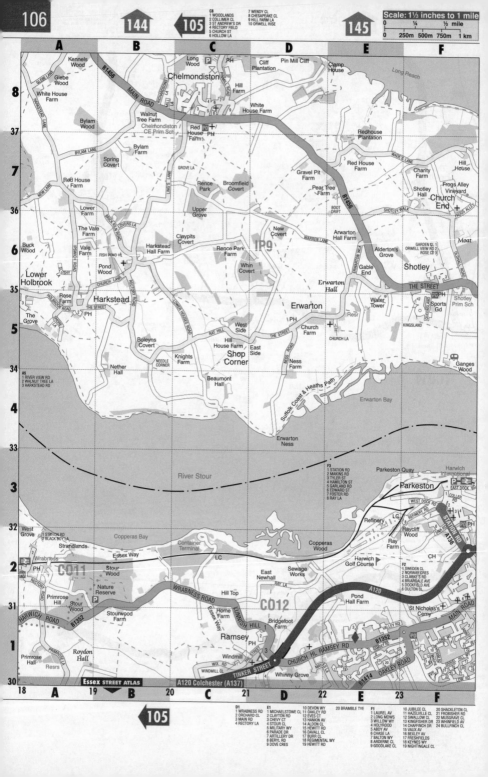

Scale: 1⅓ inches to 1 mile

0   ¼   ½ mile
0   250m 500m 750m 1 km

For full street detail of the highlighted area see page 152

98 108

107

A5
1 CHILDERS CL
2 GATE FARM RD
3 TUDOR CL
4 BLAKE AV
5 KITCHENER WY
6 HERVEY CL

7 LINK RD

D8
1 MILL CL
2 HIGH HALL CL
3 RED HOUSE CL
4 CAPEL CL
5 SANDY CL
6 CROWSELL CT

7 CRAIG CL
8 MEADOW CL
9 JASMINE CL
10 ASH GROUND CL
11 JUBILEE CL
12 HEATH CT
13 BLUE BARN CL

14 ST MARTINS GN
15 BRICK KILN CL

A4
1 GANGES RD
2 BAKER RD
3 LLOYD RD
4 LOWER HARLINGS
5 ESTUARY CRES
6 BROADWATER GDNS
7 ESTUARY RD
8 CALEDONIA RD
9 SCHOOL RD
10 BATTERY LA

B3
1 THE QUAY
2 GEORGE ST
3 CHURCH LA
4 FERNLEA RD
5 ALBEMARLE ST
6 MARIA ST
7 ALEXANDRA ST

C3
1 ST AUSTIN'S LA
2 KING'S HEAD ST
3 MARKET ST
4 ANGELGATE ESPLANADE
5 CHURCH ST
6 WELLINGTON RD
7 HARBOUR CRES
8 MAYFLOWER AV

E3
1 CARR RD
2 ADASTRAL CL
3 DOCK RD

A1
1 DEANE'S CL
2 WILLIAM GROOM AV
3 ALGFIELDS
4 QUEEN'S RD
5 GORDON RD
6 SEAFIELD RD
7 KRESWELL GR
8 RICHMOND CRES
9 REBOW RD
10 HUDSON CL
11 ST DENIS CL
12 ST EDMUNDS CL
13 LOUNAIN RD
14 BRUGES CL
15 BRUSSELS CL
16 WEST END LA

A2
1 HARCOURT AV
2 THE VINEWAY
3 KING GEORGE'S AV
4 SHAFTESBURY AV
5 LARKSFIELD CRES
6 DEEPDALE RD
7 FRYATT AV
8 POUND FARM DR
9 THE CLOSE
10 THE RIDGEWAY
11 DOUGLAS RD
12 PRINCES RD
13 OLD VICARAGE RD
14 MANOR LA
15 ELIZABETH RD
16 GRANGE RD
17 NEWTON RD
18 ICONFIELD PK

B1
1 BEACH RD
2 ST GEORGE'S AV
3 FRONK'S AV
4 ST MICHAEL'S RD

B2
1 INGESTRE ST
2 GRAFTON RD
3 PARK RD
4 GWYNNE RD
5 WADDESSON RD
6 EAST ST
7 VICTORIA ST
8 STATION RD
9 KINGSWAY

D1
1 ORWELL RD
2 GRAFTON RD
11 BAY RD
12 MARINE PARADE
13 STATION LA
14 BROOKLYN RD
15 OAKLAND RD
16 PORTLAND AV
17 ELMHURST RD

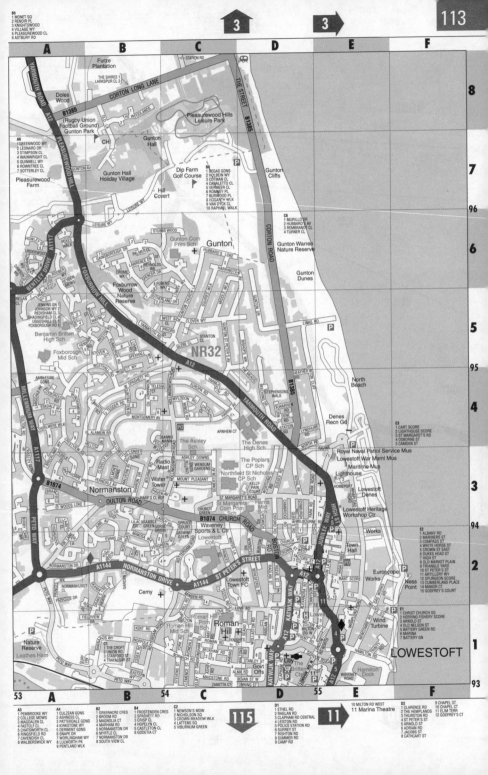

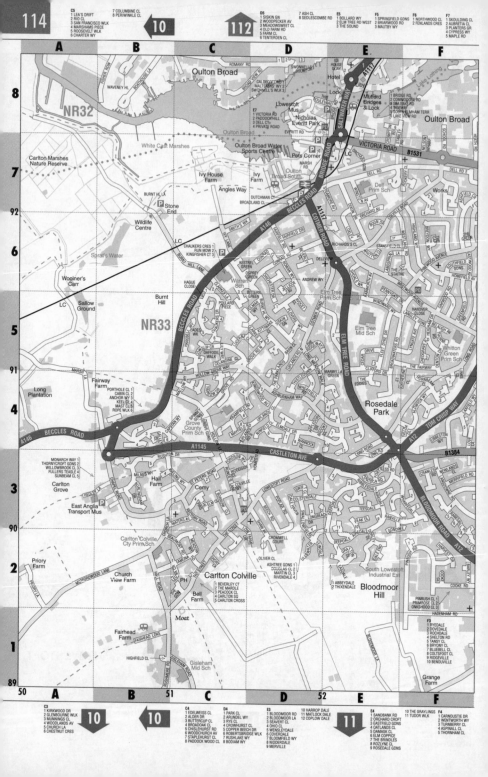

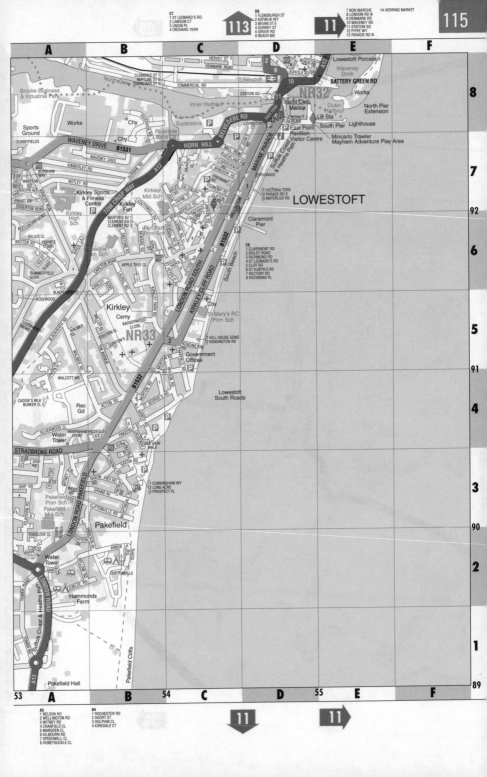

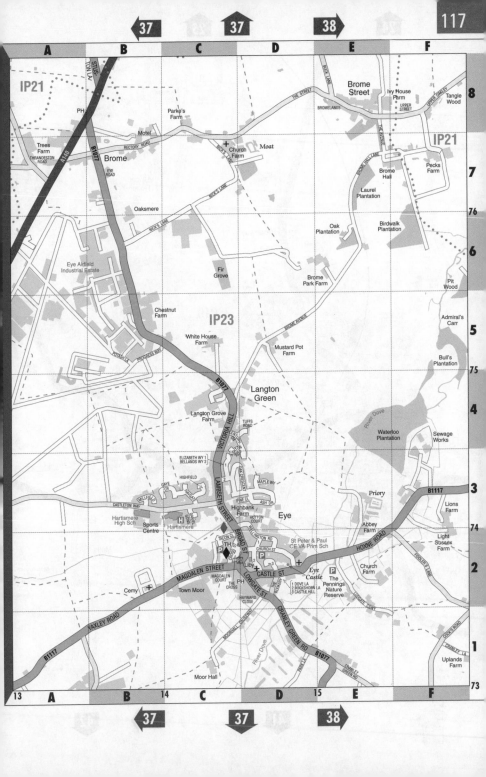

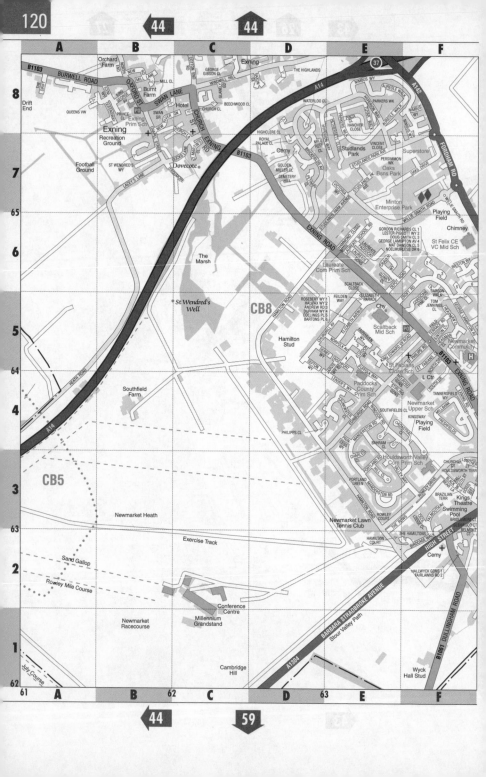

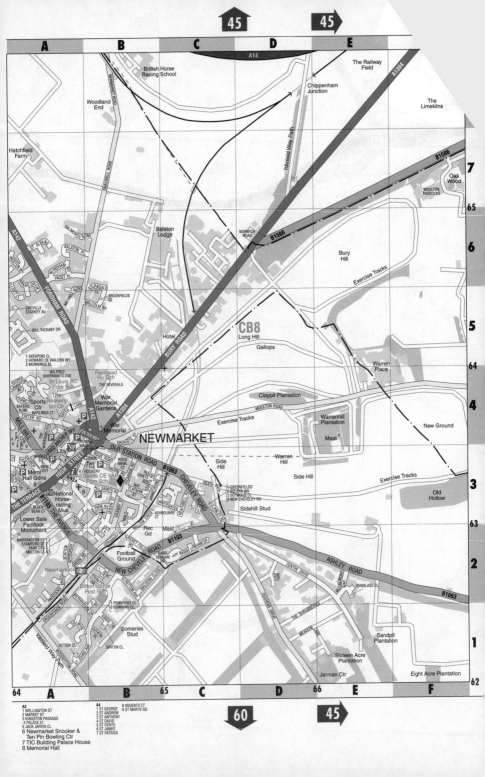

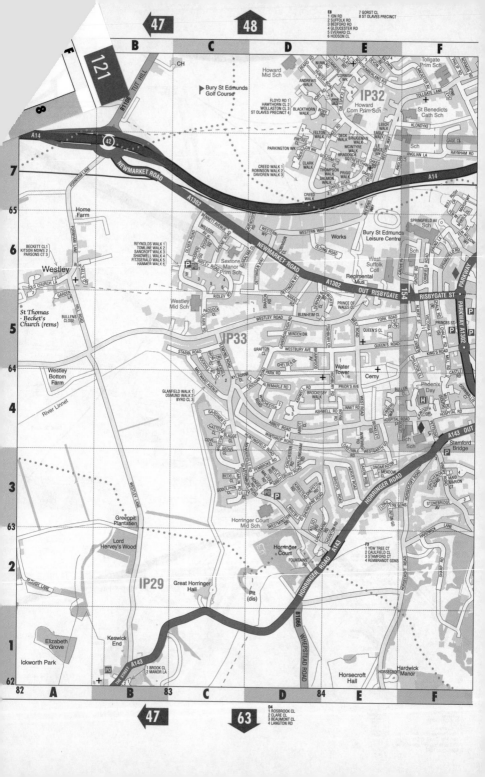

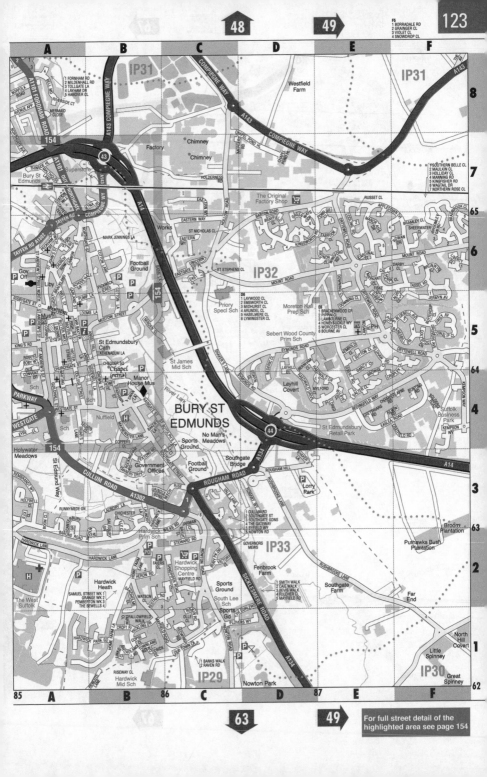

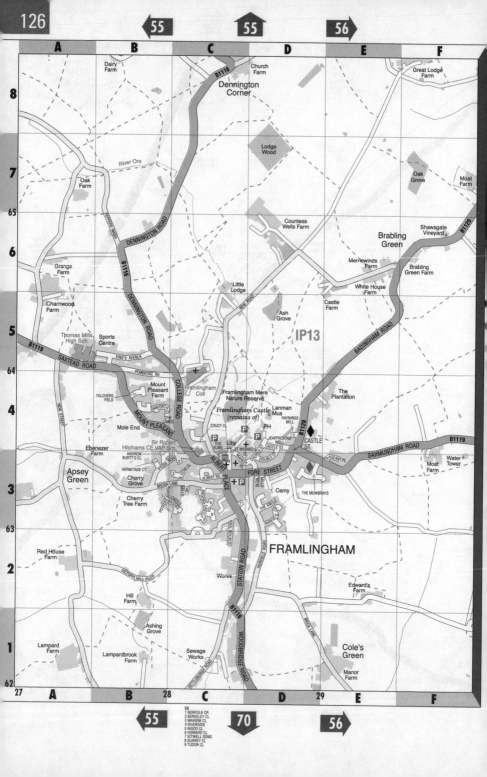

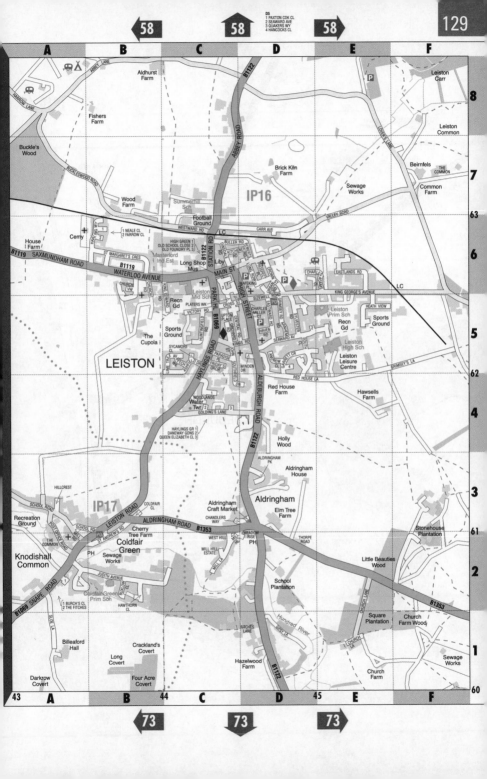

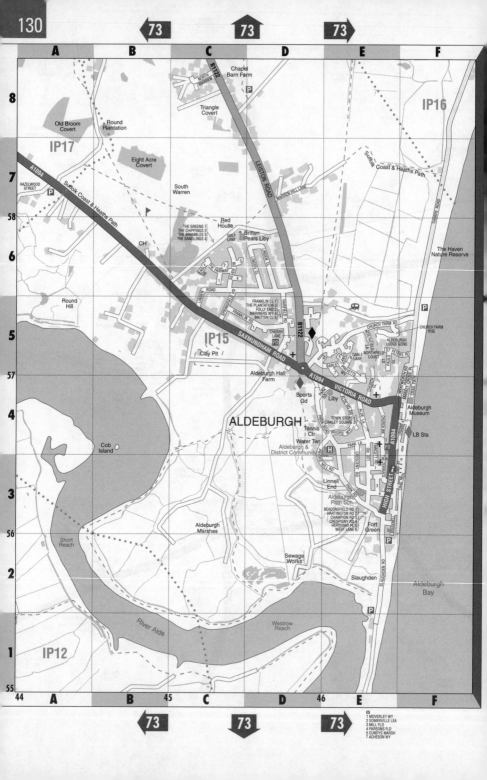

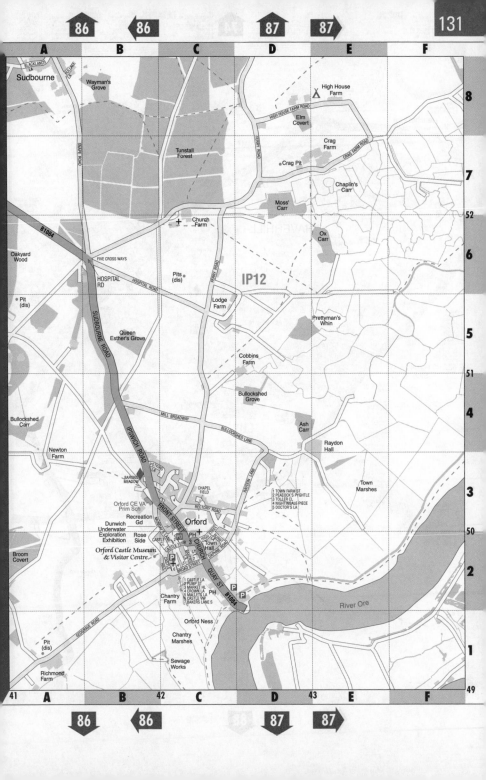

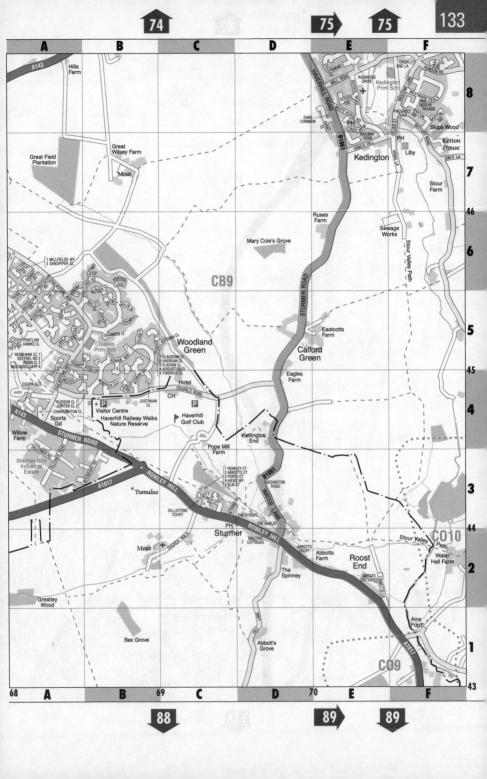

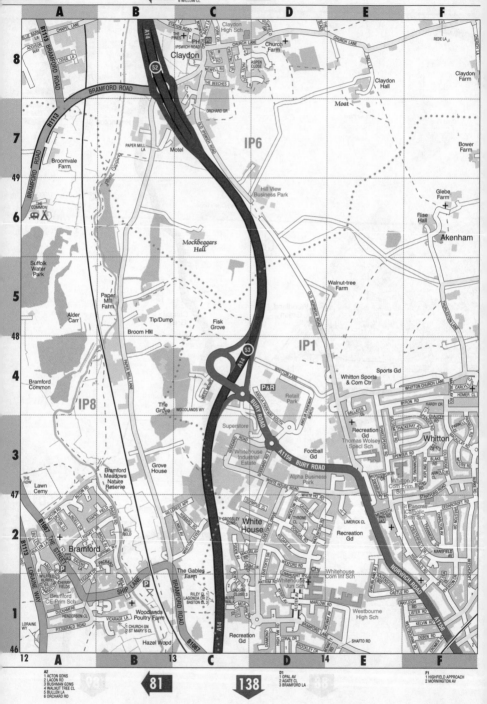

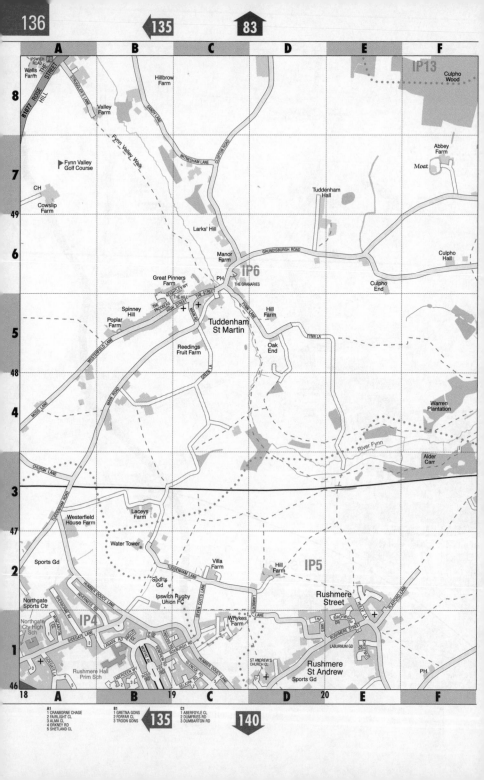

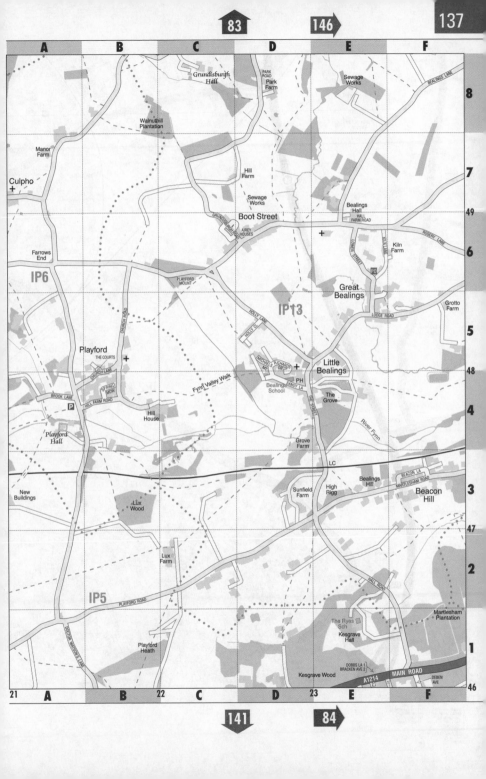

Grundisburgh Hall

PARK ROAD
Park Farm

Sewage Works

Walnuthill Plantation

Manor Farm

Culpho

Hill Farm

Sewage Works

Bealings Hall

HALL FARM ROAD

Farrows End

IP6

Boot Street

GRUNDISBURGH ROAD

AIREY HOUSES

PLAYFORD MOUNT

Kiln Farm

LOWER STREET

BALK LANE

ROSERY LANE

Great Bealings

CHURCH ROAD

HOLLY LANE

HOLLY CL

IP13

LODGE ROAD

Grotto Farm

Playford

THE COURTS

CHURCH LANE

SPRING VIEW

BROOK LANE

HILL FARM ROAD

Hill House

Fynn Valley Walk

MICHAEL S RICHARDS DR

MH

Bealings School

SANDY LA

Little Bealings

PH

The Grove

THE STREET

River Fynn

Playford Hall

Grove Farm

LC

New Buildings

Lux Wood

Sunfield Farm

High Rigg

Bealings Hill

BEACON LA

MARTLESHAM ROAD

Beacon Hill

Lux Farm

IP5

PLAYFORD ROAD

DOCTOR WATSONS LANE

HALL ROAD

Martlesham Plantation

Playford Heath

The Ryes Sch

Kesgrave Hall

DOBBS LA 1
BRACKEN AVE 2

Kesgrave Wood

A1214 MAIN ROAD

DEBEN AVE

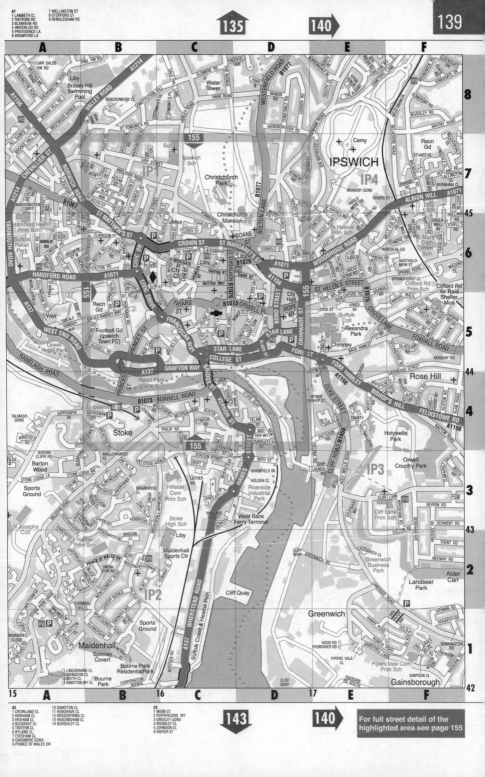

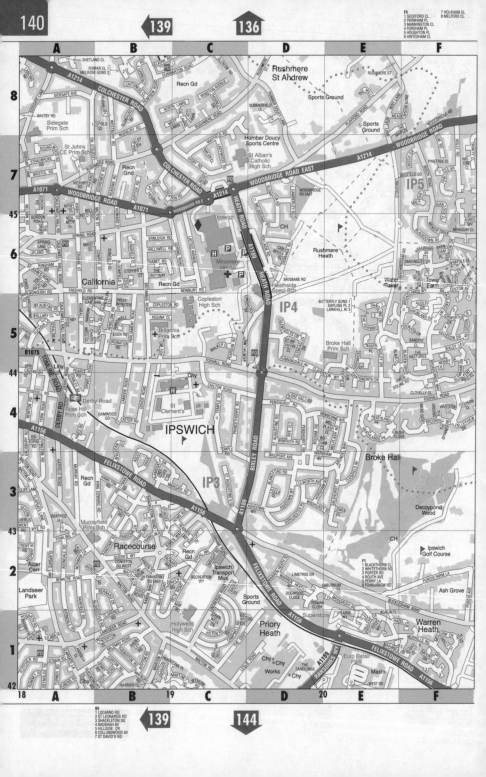

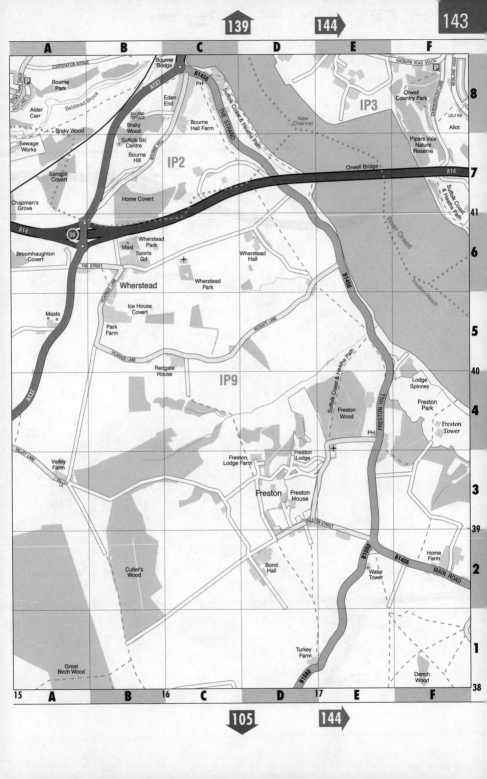

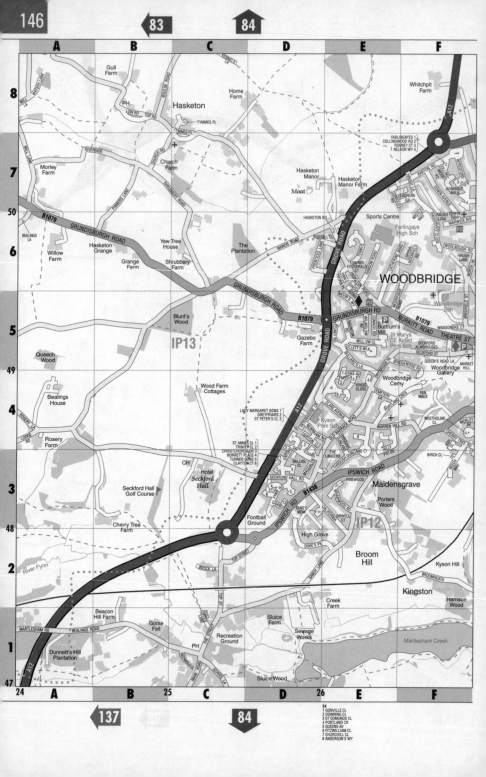

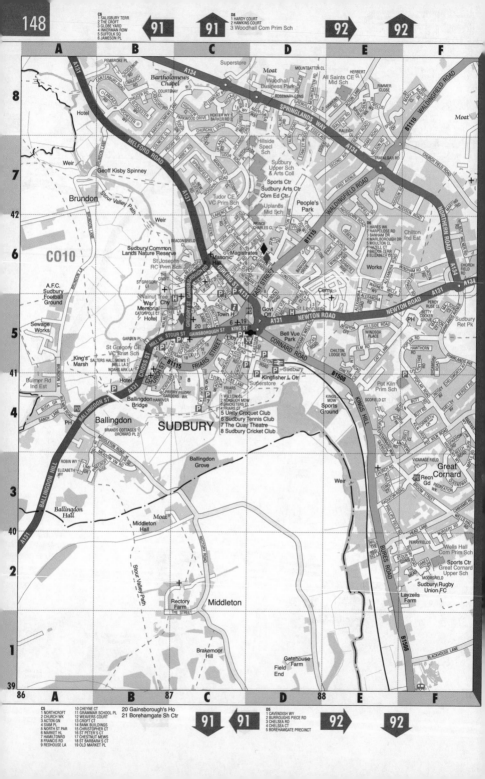

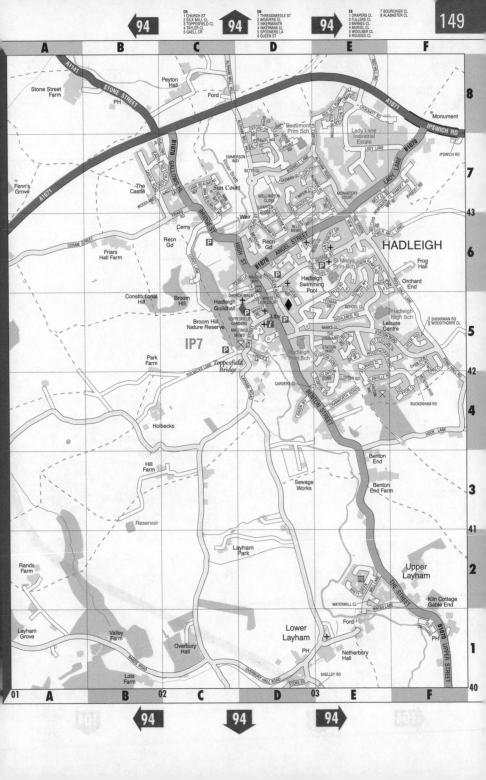

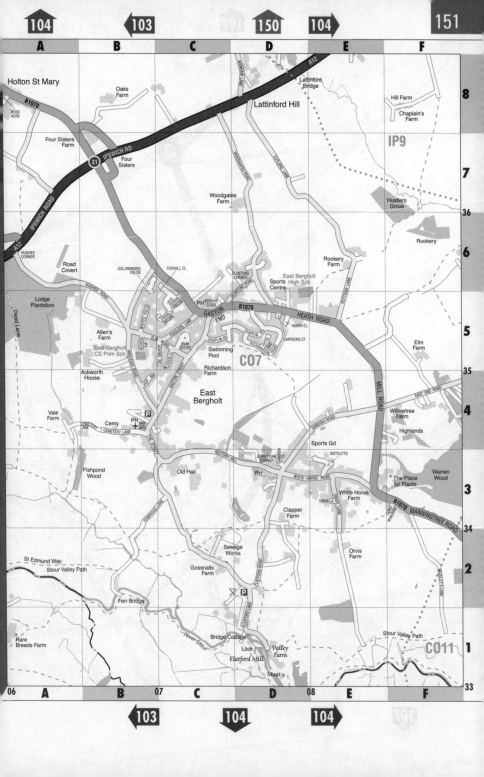

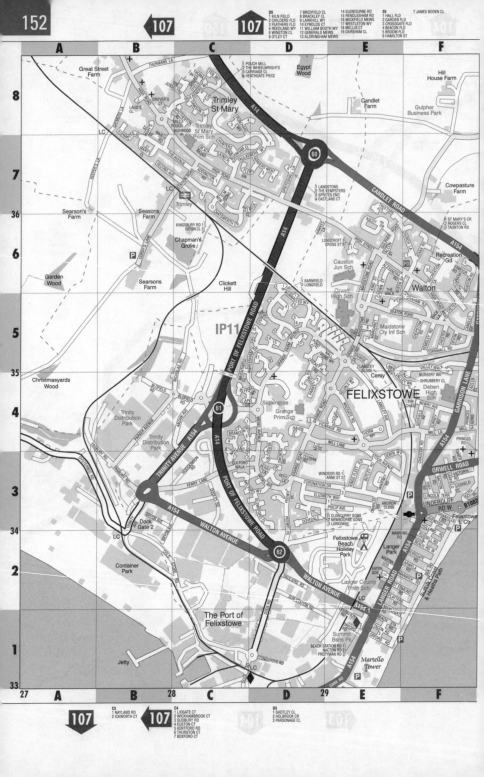

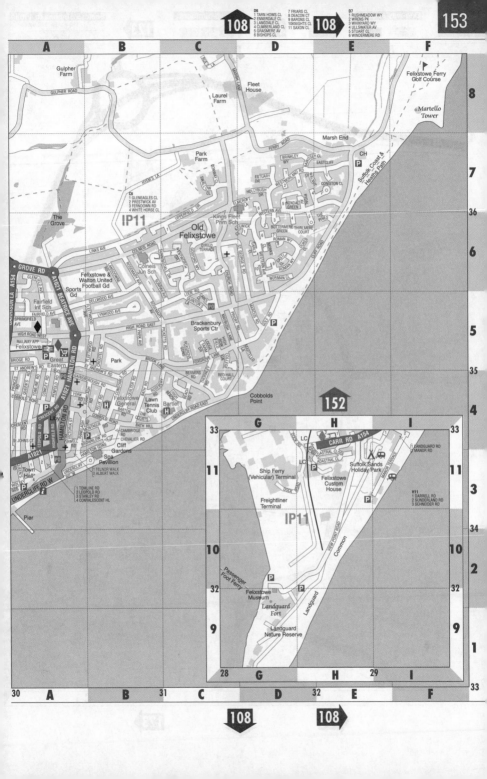

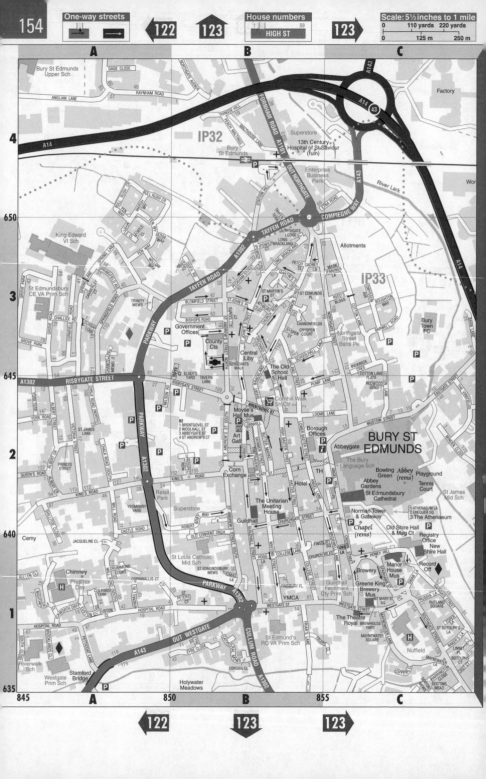

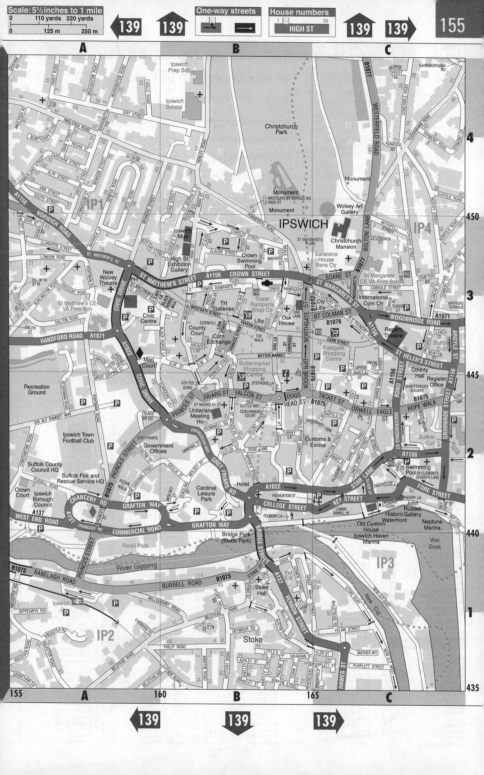

Index

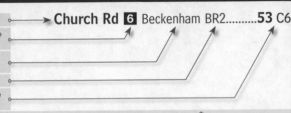

Place name May be abbreviated on the map	Church Rd
Location number Present when a number indicates the place's position in a crowded area of mapping	6
Locality, town or village Shown when more than one place has the same name	Beckenham
Postcode district District for the indexed place	BR2
Page and grid square Page number and grid reference for the standard mapping	53 C6

Church Rd 6 Beckenham BR2..........53 C6

Public and commercial buildings are highlighted in magenta **Places of interest are highlighted in** blue **with a star**★

Abbreviations used in the index

Acad	Academy	Comm	Common	Gd	Ground	L	Leisure	Prom	Promenade
App	Approach	Cott	Cottage	Gdn	Garden	La	Lane	Rd	Road
Arc	Arcade	Cres	Crescent	Gn	Green	Liby	Library	Recn	Recreation
Ave	Avenue	Cswy	Causeway	Gr	Grove	Mdw	Meadow	Ret	Retail
Bglw	Bungalow	Ct	Court	H	Hall	Meml	Memorial	Sh	Shopping
Bldg	Building	Ctr	Centre	Ho	House	Mkt	Market	Sq	Square
Bsns, Bus	Business	Ctry	Country	Hospl	Hospital	Mus	Museum	St	Street
Bvd	Boulevard	Cty	County	HQ	Headquarters	Orch	Orchard	Sta	Station
Cath	Cathedral	Dr	Drive	Hts	Heights	Pal	Palace	Terr	Terrace
Cir	Circus	Dro	Drove	Ind	Industrial	Par	Parade	TH	Town Hall
Cl	Close	Ed	Education	Inst	Institute	Pas	Passage	Univ	University
Cnr	Corner	Emb	Embankment	Int	International	Pk	Park	Wk, Wlk	Walk
Coll	College	Est	Estate	Intc	Interchange	Pl	Place	Wr	Water
Com	Community	Ex	Exhibition	Junc	Junction	Prec	Precinct	Yd	Yard

Index of localities, towns and villages

A

Acton 92 B7
Acton Place 92 B8
Akenham 134 F6
Alburgh 7 A1
Aldeburgh 130 D4
Aldeby 9 F8
Alderton 99 E4
Aldham 94 E8
Aldringham 129 D3
All Saints South Elmham 24 B5
Allwood Green 36 A2
Alpheton 78 A5
Ampton 33 A2
Annis Hill 110 E3
Apsey Green 126 A3
Ardleigh Heath 103 F1
Ash Abbey 127 F3
Ashbocking 69 A1
Ash Corner 127 F7
Ashen 89 E5
Ashfield 54 D2
Ashfield Cum Thorpe 54 C1
Ashfield Green
 Stradbroke 39 D4
 Wickhambrook 62 A2
Ashley 60 F8
Ash Street 80 A1
Aspall 53 E4
Assington 92 F1
Assington Green 76 B6
Athelington 38 E2
Attleton Green 61 D1
Audley End
 Burston and Shimpling 20 E5
 Lawshall 77 D8

B

Babel Green 75 D3
Back Street 61 E5
Bacton 51 F5
Bacton Green 51 E4
Badingham 56 A6
Badwell Ash 50 E7
Badwell Green 51 B8
Ballingdon 148 B4
Banyard's Green 40 C4
Bardwell 34 C4
Barham 82 C6
Barking 125 A1
Barking Tye 81 A7
Barley Green 39 C5
Barnaby Green 26 C2
Barnardiston 75 B3
Barnby 10 B5
Barnham 16 C2
Barningham 34 F7
Barrow 47 A2
Barsham 9 A4
Barton Mills 116 D2
Base Green 51 B2
Bath Side 107 B3
Battisford 66 F1
Battisford Tye 66 C1
Battlesea Green 39 A6
Battlies Green 49 C3
Bawdsey 99 E3
Baylham 81 E6
Baythorne End 89 C5
Beacon Hill 137 F3
Beccles 111 D5
Beck Row 30 A8
Bedfield 54 E5
Bedingfield 53 F7
Bedingham Green 7 B7
Belchamp Otten 90 E4
Belchamp St Paul 90 D5
Belchamp Walter 90 F3
Bell's Corner 102 F8
Bell's Cross 82 D7
Belstead 142 C7
Benacre 27 A7
Benhall Green 72 C8
Benhall Street 71 F8
Bentley 104 F8
Beyton 49 F1
Beyton Green 49 F2
Bigsby's Corner 72 D8
Bildeston 79 F4
Billingford 21 B1
Birdbrook 89 A4
Birds End 62 B7
Bird Street 80 A7
Blackheath 42 C5
Blacksmith's Green 53 C5
Black Street 11 A2
Blackthorpe 49 C2
Blaxhall 72 B4
Bleach Green 39 A8
Blo' Norton 18 E2
Bloodman's Corner 3 A6
Bloodmoor Hill 114 E2
Blundeston 3 A4
Blyford 42 C7
Blythburgh 42 F6
Bobby Hill 35 C5
Boot Street 137 D6
Borley 91 C5
Borley Green
 Borley 91 B5
 Woolpit 65 E7
Botesdale 36 B6
Bowbeck 34 C6
Bower House Tye 93 E3
Boxford 93 C3
Boxted
 Colchester 77 A6
 Glemsford 102 F4
Boxted Cross 103 A3
Boyden End 61 D2
Boyland Common 20 A7
Boyton 86 B2
Boyton End 89 B7
Brabling Green 126 E6
Bradfield 105 C1
Bradfield Combust 64 A4
Bradfield St Clare 64 C4
Bradfield St George 64 D7
Braiseworth 37 D2
Bramfield 41 F4
Bramford 134 A2
Brampton 25 E5
Brampton Street 25 E4
Brandeston 70 B7
Brandon 6 A1
Brantham 104 F4
Bredfield 84 C7
Brent Eleigh 79 A2
Bressingham 19 F4
Bressingham Common 19 F5
Brettenham
 Stowmarket 79 C8
 Thetford 17 B6
Brewers Green 20 B3
Bridge Green 20 F6
Bridge Street 77 F4
Brightwell 98 A6
Brinkley 59 E2
Broadgrass Green 50 C1
Broad Green
 Cheveley 60 F6
 Chevington 62 B6
 Creeting St Peter or West Creeting 67 C6
Broad Street 93 C5
Broadway 118 C6
Brockdish 21 F2
Brockford Green 53 A4
Brockford Street 52 F5
Brockley Corner 32 D2
Brockley Green
 Hartest 63 A1
 Hundon 75 C2
Broke Hall 140 E3
Brome 117 B7
Brome Street 117 E8
Bromeswell 85 A5
Brook Green 63 E5
Brook Street 77 A3
Broome 110 D7
Broome Heath 110 D7
Broom Hill 146 E2
Broom's Barn 46 F4
Brown Street 52 A2
Browston Green 2 E8
Bruisyard 56 C5
Brundish 55 C8
Brundish Street 39 E1
Brundon 148 A7
Bucklesham 98 A5
Bulcamp 42 D7
Bulmer 91 C3
Bulmer Tye 91 D1
Bungay 110 B3
Bures 101 C5
Bures Green 101 D6
Burgate 36 E6
Burgh 83 F6
Burgh St Peter 10 B8
Burrough End 59 E2
Burrough Green 59 F2
Burstall 95 D7
Burstallhill 95 C8
Burston 20 E6
Burthorpe 47 B3
Burwell 44 A5
Bury St Edmunds 154 C2
Bush Green 64 D4
Butley 86 B5
Butley High Corner 86 C4
Butley Low Corner 86 C4
Button Haugh Green 50 F4
Button's Green 78 E8
Buxhall 66 A4
Buxhall Fen Street 66 A6

C

Calais Street 93 D2
Calford Green 133 D5
California 140 B6
Camps Heath 112 D3
Candle Street 35 F5
Canham's Green 51 F4
Capel Green 86 A4
Capel St Andrew 86 B3
Capel St Mary 150 E4
Capon's Green 55 E6
Carlton
 Carlton 74 A8
 Kelsale cum Carlton 128 C6
Carlton Colville 114 C2
Carlton Green 74 A6
Castle Hill 135 A3
Castling's Heath 93 D6
Cattawade 104 E4
Cavendish 76 D1
Cavenham 47 A8
Cay Hill 52 C2
Chantry 138 D2
Charles Tye 80 C7
Charsfield 70 B3
Chattisham 95 C5
Chedburgh 62 C4
Chediston 41 C8
Chediston Green 24 C1
Chelmondiston 106 C8
Chelsworth 79 E3
Chelsworth Common 79 E2
Cheveley 60 E7
Chevington 62 C6
Chickering 38 F7
Chillesford 86 C7
Chilton 92 B5
Chilton Street 75 F1
Chimney Street 75 C3
Chippenhall Green 40 A6
Chippenham 45 C8
Church End 106 F7
Church Street 90 D6
Clare 90 B8
Clay Common 26 B4
Claydon 134 C8
Claypits 109 B4
Clay Street 35 D2
Clopton Corner 69 E1
Clopton Green
 Wickhambrook 62 A1
 Woolpit 65 D7
Cobbler's Green 7 C6
Cock & End 75 C8
Cockfield 64 C1
Cocks Green 64 A5
Cock Street 102 C7
Coddenham 68 C1
Coddenham Green 67 F2
Colchester Green 64 E2
Coldfair Green 129 B2
Coles Green 95 D4
Cole's Green 126 E1
Colton 48 F5
Combs 124 C1
Combs Ford 124 D4
Coney Weston 17 E1
Conyers Green 49 B7
Cookley 41 A6
Cookley Green 40 F6
Cook's Green 79 D8
Copdock 95 F4
Cornard Tye 92 C4

Corton 3 C4
Cotton 52 B6
Cove Bottom 26 E3
Cowehithe 27 B4
Cow Green 51 F4
Cowlinge 61 B1
Cox Common 25 A5
Crackthorn Corner 19 A1
Cranley 37 F3
Cranmer Green 35 E2
Cransford 56 B3
Cratfield 40 D6
Creeting Bottoms 67 E5
Creeting St Mary 125 F8
Creeting St Peter 67 C5
Cretingham 69 F7
Cross Green
  Cockfield 64 B2
  Hartest 77 A7
  Hitcham 79 E7
Cross Street 38 C7
Crowfield 68 C4
Crown Corner 39 D1
Crownland 35 D1
Cuckold's Green 26 C5
Cuckoo Green 3 A6
Cuckoo Tye 92 A5
Culford 32 D1
Culfordheath 32 F5
Culpho 137 A7
Curlew Green 128 C7

D

Dagworth 66 E8
Daisy Green
  Great Ashfield 51 A6
  Wickham Skeith 52 D7
Dalham 61 C8
Dallinghoo 70 D5
Dam Green 19 C8
Dandy Corner 52 B6
Darmsden 125 F1
Darsham 42 C1
Debach 70 A1
Debenham 53 E2
Dedham 103 F4
Dedham Heath 103 F2
Denham
  Denham 61 F8
  Hoxne 38 D5
Denham End 46 F2
Dennington 55 E8
Dennington Corner 126 C8
Denston 76 A7
Denton 7 A3
Depden 62 B3
Depden Green 62 B4
Dickleburgh 21 B5
Dickleburgh Moor 21 D6
Diss 20 C4
Ditchingham 110 C7
Ditton Green 60 B4
Dockeney 8 F6
Dorking Tye 101 D7
Dorley's Corner 128 D8
Dovercourt 107 D2
Down Field 28 F2
Drakestone Green 93 F8
Drinkstone 65 C8
Drinkstone Green 65 D8
Dublin 53 E8
Duke Street 95 B5
Dullingham 59 F5
Dullingham Ley 60 A3
Dunstall Green 61 E7
Dunwich 43 B1

E

Earl's Green 51 D5
Earl Soham 54 E2
Earl Stoneham 67 E5
Earsham 7 E4
Earsham Street 22 C1
East Barton 49 C4
East Bergholt 151 C4
Eastbridge 58 D4
East End
  East Bergholt 104 E6
  Stonham Aspal 68 D6
East Green
  Great Bradley 74 E8
  Kelsale cum Carlton . . . 57 E4
Easton 70 E5
Edge Green 19 B8
Edwardstone 93 A5
Ellingham 8 D7
Ellough 9 F1
Ellough Hill 111 D3
Elmsett 80 F1
Elmswell 50 D8
Elveden 15 D3
Eriswell 13 F1
Erwarton 106 D5
Euston 16 F5
Exning 120 B8
Eye 117 D3
Eyke 85 B6

F

Fakenham Magna 33 E7
Falkenham 98 E2
Falkenham Sink 98 F2

Farley Green 75 D8
Farnham 72 A7
Felixstowe 152 E4
Felixstowe Ferry 108 C8
Felsham 64 E5
Feltwell 4 A3
Fenstead End 76 E5
Fen Street
  Hopton 18 B2
  Redgrave 19 C2
Fern Hill 77 B4
Fersfield 19 C6
Finkle Green 89 A2
Finningham 52 B8
Flempton 47 F8
Flixton 7 D1
Flowton 81 C1
Foals Green 39 D2
Fordham 29 B1
Fornham All Saints 48 B6
Fornham St Genevieve . . 48 C6
Fornham St Martin 48 B6
Forward Green 67 E7
Four Ashes 35 C1
Foxash Estate 104 B1
Foxearth 91 B7
Framlingham 126 E2
Framsden 69 B6
Freckenham 29 F3
Frenze 20 F3
Fressingfield 39 D8
Freston 143 D1
Friday Street
  Benhall 72 B7
  Brandeston 70 A6
  Rendlesham 85 D7
Friston 72 F7
Fritton 2 B7
Frizzeler's Green 47 C1
Frostenden 26 C4
Frostenden Corner 26 D3

G

Gainsborough
  Ipswich 139 F1
  Ipswich 144 B8
Garboldisham 18 D4
Garlic Street 22 A6
Gasthorpe 18 A4
Gazeley 46 B3
Gedding 65 A5
Geldeston 8 F7
Genesis Green 61 F4
Gestingthorpe 90 F1
Gillingham 9 C6
Gipping 52 B2
Gipsy Row 150 A4
Gisleham 11 A3
Gislingham 36 D5
Gissing 20 F8
Glemsford 77 B2
Goddard's Corner 55 E7
Gosbeck 68 D2
Gosland Green 76 A5
Gosling Green 93 C5
Grass Green 89 D1
Great Ashfield 50 F6
Great Barton 49 A6
Great Bealings 137 E6
Great Blakenham 68 A3
Great Bradley 74 C7
Great Bricett 80 E5
Great Common 8 C2
Great Cornard 148 F3
Great Finborough 66 B4
Great Glemham 71 D8
Great Green
  Burgate 36 D7
  Cockfield 64 D4
  Denton 7 A4
  Thrandeston 37 C8
Great Horkesley 102 E1
Great Livermere 33 C2
Great Saxham 47 C1
Great Thurlow 74 E5
Great Waldingfield 92 C6
Great Welnetham 63 F6
Great Wenham 150 A3
Great Wratting 74 E3
Great Yeldham 90 A1
Greenstreet Green 80 D5
Greenwich 139 E1
Grimstone End 49 F8
Grinstead Hill 125 E3
Gromford 72 C5
Groton 93 B4
Grundisburgh 83 D5
Gulling Green 63 A3
Gunton 113 C6

H

Hacheston 71 A6
Hadleigh 149 F6
Hadleigh Heath 93 F4
Hagmore Green 93 B2
Halesworth 118 A4
Hall Green 90 C2
Hanchet End 132 A8
Hanningfields Green 63 F1
Hargrave 62 B6
Harkstead 106 B5
Harleston
  Harleston 66 B7
  Redenhall with Harleston . . . 22 E5

Harrow Green 63 D1
Hartest 77 A7
Hartest Hill 77 C7
Hart's Green 63 E2
Harwich 107 A3
Hasketon 146 C8
Haughley 51 C1
Haughley Green 51 C3
Haughley New Street . . . 51 B1
Haverhill 132 C6
Hawstead 63 C6
Hawstead Green 63 E5
Hazel Stub 132 A5
Heckfield Green 38 D7
Hedenham 7 E8
Helions Bumpstead 88 B4
Helmingham 69 B4
Hemingstone 82 C8
Hemley 98 E5
Hemp Green 57 C8
Hengrave 48 A7
Henley 82 D6
Henny Street 91 F1
Henstead 26 E8
Hepworth 35 A6
Herringfleet 2 D4
Herringswell 46 C8
Hessett 64 F8
Heveningham 40 B6
Hickford Hill 90 C7
Higham
  Bury St Edmunds 47 B3
  Stratford St Mary 103 D6
High Green 63 D7
High Rougham 49 E1
High Street
  Darsham 42 B1
  Iken 73 B2
  St Margaret, Ilketshall . . . 24 D7
High Street Green 66 A2
Hightown Green 65 D3
Hinderclay 35 E7
Hintlesham 95 C6
Hitcham 79 E6
Hobbies Green 75 A8
Hockwold cum Wilton . . . 5 A3
Hoggard's Green 64 A3
Holbrook 105 E7
Hollesley 99 F7
Hollybush Corner 64 D6
Holly Hill 110 B8
Holton 118 E4
Holton St Mary 151 B4
Holywell Row 30 C8
Homersfield 23 B8
Honey Tye 102 B6
Honington 33 E5
Hoo 70 B5
Hopton 18 C2
Hopton on Sea 3 C7
Horham 38 E3
Horner's Green 93 C4
Hornerstreet 103 C3
Horringer 63 A8
Hoxne 38 B8
Hulver Street 10 C1
Humble Green 92 F8
Hundon 75 E3
Hunston 50 D7
Hunston Green 50 D5
Huntingfield 41 A5

I

Icklingham 31 D3
Iken 72 F2
Ilketshall St Andrew 8 E3
Ilketshall St Lawrence . . . 24 F6
Ilketshall St Margaret . . . 24 B8
Ingham 32 F1
Ipswich 155 B3
Isleham 29 B5
Ixworth 34 B2
Ixworth Thorpe 33 F4

K

Kedington 133 E7
Kelsale 128 C2
Kennett 45 F7
Kenninghall 19 B8
Kenny Hill 12 F2
Kentford 46 A5
Kenton 54 B5
Kenton Corner 54 C4
Kersey 94 A7
Kersey Tye 93 E6
Kersey Upland 93 F5
Kesgrave 141 C8
Kessingland 11 C2
Kessingland Beach 27 C8
Kettlebaston 79 C5
Kettleburgh 70 C7
Kingshall Green 64 D7
Kingshall Street 64 D8
Kingston 146 F2
Kirby Cane 8 E8
Kirby Row 8 E7
Kirkley 115 B5
Kirtling 60 E3
Kirtling Green 60 E2
Kirton 98 E2
Knaves Green 53 A5
Knettishall 17 F3
Knodishall 73 A8

Knodishall Common . . . 129 A2
Knowl Green 90 C4

L

Lackford 31 F1
Lady's Green 61 F6
Lakenheath 109 E7
Lamarsh 101 A6
Lamb Corner 103 D3
Lambfair Green 75 A8
Lampardbrook 70 E8
Landwade 44 D6
Langham
  Bury St Edmunds 50 D8
  Stratford St Mary 103 C2
Langton Green 117 C3
Lattinford Hill 151 D8
Lavenham 78 D4
Lawford 104 E2
Lawshall 63 E1
Lawshall Green 77 F8
Laxfield 40 C3
Leavenheath 102 B7
Leiston 129 B5
Letheringham 70 C2
Levington 145 E3
Lidgate 61 C4
Lindsey 93 D7
Lindsey Tye 93 E8
Linstead Parva 40 E8
Liston 91 D7
Little Bealings 137 E5
Little Blakenham 81 F3
Little Bradley 74 E6
Little Cornard 92 C2
Little Ditton 60 C5
Little Finborough 66 B1
Little Glemham 71 E5
Little Green
  Burgate 36 D5
  Gislingham 36 C3
Little Horkesley 102 B3
Little Knowles Green 62 B5
Little London 66 E2
Little Saxham 47 D2
Little Stonham 67 F6
Little Thurlow 74 E5
Little Thurlow Green 74 E6
Little Waldingfield 92 D8
Little Welnetham 64 B6
Little Wenham 150 B5
Little Whittingham
  Green 40 A8
Little Wratting 74 E2
Little Yeldham 90 B2
Long Green 36 D8
Long Melford
  Long Melford 77 F1
  Long Melford 91 E8
Long Thurlow 51 B7
Lound 2 F5
Lower Common 25 B3
Lower Falkenham 98 F1
Lower Green 46 E4
Lower Hacheston 127 F8
Lower Holbrook 106 A6
Lower Layham 149 D1
Lower Raydon 94 D1
Lower Street
  Stansfield 76 C5
  Stutton 105 D5
Lowestoft 113 F1
Low Green 63 E7
Lynford 6 C5

M

Mace Green 95 E4
Magpie Green 19 C1
Maidenhall 139 B1
Maidensgrave 146 E3
Malting End 61 E1
Manningtree 104 F2
Man's Cross 89 F2
Market Weston 35 A8
Marlesford 71 C5
Martlesham 84 A1
Martlesham Heath 98 B7
Marpole Green
  Bradfield St George 64 D6
  Dennington 55 D6
Meadowend 89 E3
Mellis 37 A5
Mellis Green 36 F5
Mells 118 E2
Melon Green 63 C4
Melton 147 C8
Mendham 23 A6
Mendlesham 52 E4
Mendlesham Green 52 D2
Metfield 23 C3
Methersgate 84 E1
Mettingham 8 D4
Mickfield 68 B8
Mickley Green 63 B4
Middle Green 46 E4
Middle Harling 18 B8
Middleton
  Leiston 58 B6
  Sudbury 148 C2
Middleton Moor 58 A6
Middlewood Green 67 D8
Milden 79 B1
Mildenhall 116 D6
Mile End 77 A7

Mill Common 25 C4
Mill End 60 F3
Mill Green
  Burston and Shimpling . . . 20 E7
  Buxhall 65 F4
  Edwardstone 93 B5
  Stonham Aspal 68 B7
Mill Hill 77 E6
Mill Hills 147 A6
Mill Street 102 E8
Mistley 105 A2
Mistley Heath 105 A1
Moats Tye 66 E2
Monewden 69 F5
Monks Eleigh 79 B2
Monk Soham 54 D4
Moulton 45 F3
Mount Bures 101 C3
Mount Pleasant 75 D2
Mundford 6 B8
Mutford 10 D2

N

Nacton 145 C5
Naughton 80 C3
Nayland 102 C5
Nedging 79 F3
Nedging Tye 80 B4
Needham 22 C4
Needham Market 125 E5
Needham Street 46 B4
Nether Street 64 B8
Nettlestead 81 C4
Newbourne 98 C5
New England 89 A5
Newman's Green 92 A6
Newmarket 121 B4
New Mistley 105 A2
Newton 92 D3
Newtown 54 D7
Normanston 113 B3
North Common 34 F6
North Cove 10 C4
North End 90 C2
North Green
  Cratfield 40 C7
  Kelsale cum Carlton . . . 57 D5
  Parham 56 B1
North Lopham 19 A5
Norton 50 B4
Norton Little Green 50 D5
Nowton 63 E7

O

Oak Hill 100 A8
Oakley 38 A8
Occold 37 F1
Offton 81 A4
Old Felixstowe 153 C6
Oldhall Green 64 C3
Old Newton 51 F1
Onehouse 66 C6
Orford 131 C3
Otley 69 C2
Oulton 112 F5
Oulton Broad 114 C8
Ousden 61 E6
Ovington 90 A5

P

Page's Green 53 C4
Pakefield 115 B3
Pakenham 49 E6
Pale Green 88 B5
Palgrave 20 C1
Parham 71 A7
Parkeston 106 F3
Park Gate 61 E3
Park Green 53 B3
Parliament Heath 93 C5
Parney Heath 103 D2
Peasenhall 56 E8
Peats Corner 69 B7
Pentlow
  Pentlow 76 E1
  Pentlow 90 F7
Pentlow Street 91 A8
Pettaugh 68 E6
Pettistree 127 B4
Pinford End 63 D6
Pitcher's Green 64 D5
Pitman's Corner 53 C5
Playford 137 B5
Polstead 93 F1
Polstead Heath 93 F2
Pooley Street 19 D4
Poslingford 76 A3
Potash 104 F8
Pound Green 61 B1
Poystreet Green 65 E5
Preston St Mary 79 A5
Priory Green 92 F6
Priory Heath 140 D1
Pulham St Mary 21 F8
Puttock End 90 E3

R

Racecourse 140 B2
Ramsey 106 C1
Ramsholt 99 A4

Rattlesden.....65 E6
Raydon.....94 E1
Reading Green.....38 E5
Rede.....62 E2
Redenhall.....22 E7
Redgrave.....36 A8
Redisham.....25 B7
Redlingfield.....38 D2
Red Lodge.....30 B1
Rendham.....56 E3
Rendlesham.....85 C8
Reydon.....119 C7
Reydon Smear.....26 F1
Rickinghall.....36 A6
Ridgewell.....89 D4
Ringsfield.....9 B3
Ringsfield Corner.....9 B2
Ringshall.....80 E7
Ringshall Stocks.....80 F6
Risby.....47 D5
Rishangles.....53 D7
Rodbridge Corner.....91 E6
Roman Hill.....113 C1
Rooksey Green.....78 E6
Roost End.....133 E2
Rosedale Park.....114 E4
Rose Green
  Assington.....101 F8
  Lindsey.....93 D7
Rose Hill.....139 F4
Rotchfords.....101 F1
Rougham.....64 D8
Rougham Green.....64 C8
Roydon.....20 A3
Rumburgh.....24 A4
Rushall.....21 F5
Rushbrooke.....64 B8
Rushford.....17 B4
Rushmere.....10 D1
Rushmere St Andrew.....136 E1
Rushmere Street.....136 E2
Russel's Green.....39 C3

S
Sackers Green.....92 D2
St Cross South Elmham.....23 D7
St James South Elmham.....23 F4
St Margaret South Elmham.....23 E6
St Michael South Elmham.....24 A6
St Nicholas South Elmham.....23 E6
St Olaves.....2 A6
St Peter South Elmham.....24 A7
Santon Downham.....6 C2
Sapiston.....33 F6
Saxham Street.....67 C8
Saxmundham.....128 D3
Saxon Street.....60 D6
Saxstead Bottom.....55 C5
Saxtead.....55 C4
Saxtead Green.....55 B3
Saxtead Little Green.....55 B5
Scole.....21 A2
Scole Common.....20 F3
Scotland Street.....102 F7
Semer.....79 F1
Shadingfield.....25 E7
Shadwell.....17 C6
Shelfanger.....20 C6

Shelland.....66 A7
Shelley.....94 C1
Sherbourne Street.....93 B4
Shimpling
  Burston and Shimpling.....21 A6
  Shimpling.....77 E6
Shimpling Street.....77 E8
Shingle Street.....100 A5
Shipmeadow.....8 F4
Shop Corner.....106 C5
Shotford Heath.....22 D4
Shotley.....106 F6
Shotley Gate.....107 A4
Shottisham.....99 C7
Sibton.....57 A8
Sibton Green.....41 D2
Sicklesmere.....63 F7
Silverlace Green.....71 C7
Silverley's Green.....40 B6
Sizewell.....58 F1
Slough Hill.....77 E7
Smallwood Green.....64 F5
Smallworth.....18 D3
Smith's Green.....88 C3
Smithwood Green.....78 C7
Snailwell.....45 A6
Snape.....72 D4
Snow Street.....20 A4
Soham.....28 D4
Soham Cotes.....28 B6
Somersham.....81 C3
Somerton.....76 F8
Sotherton.....25 E2
Sotherton Corner.....25 E1
Sotterley.....26 A7
South Cove.....26 F4
South Green
  Hoxne.....38 B5
  Pulham St Mary.....21 F6
South Lopham.....19 B4
Southolt.....54 B7
Southwold.....119 C5
Sowley Green.....75 A5
Spexhall.....24 F3
Spratt's Street.....85 D5
Sproughton.....138 A7
Stackyard Green.....93 C8
Stambourne.....89 B1
Stambourne Green.....89 A1
Stanningfield.....64 A4
Stansfield.....76 C7
Stanstead.....77 C4
Stanton.....34 D4
Stanton Chare.....34 D5
Stanton Street.....50 B5
Stanway Green.....39 C1
Starston.....22 C7
Steeple Bumpstead.....88 D4
Sternfield.....72 D8
Stetchworth.....60 A5
Stock Hill.....50 E8
Stoke.....155 B1
Stoke Ash.....37 B1
Stoke by Clare.....89 E6
Stoke-by-Nayland.....102 E6
Stoke Park.....138 F1
Stone Street
  Boxford.....93 C2
  Spexhall.....24 F5
Stoven.....25 F4
Stonham Aspal.....68 A6
Stowlangtoft.....50 C7
Stowmarket.....124 E6

Stowupland.....67 B6
Stradbroke.....39 A5
Stradishall.....75 F7
Stratford St Andrew.....71 F7
Stratford St Mary.....103 D5
Stubbing's Green.....36 C5
Sturmer.....133 C2
Stuston.....20 E1
Stutton.....105 D6
Sudbourne.....86 F8
Sudbury.....148 C4
Sutton.....85 A1
Sutton Street.....99 A7
Swan Green.....40 B5
Swefling.....56 E2
Swilland.....83 A7
Swingleton Green.....79 C2
Syleham.....22 A1

T
Tannington.....55 A6
Tan Office.....52 F2
Tan Office Green.....62 C6
Tattingstone.....105 B8
Tattingstone White
  Horse.....142 D1
Temple End
  Foxearth.....91 A6
  Little Thurlow.....74 C5
Theberton.....58 B4
The Brook.....36 E7
The Common.....81 F3
The Heath.....105 A7
Thelnetham.....18 D1
Thelveton.....21 A4
The Marsh.....36 E8
The Port of Felixstowe.....152 C1
Thetford.....16 D5
The Woodlands.....95 A3
Thistley Green.....29 E7
Thorington.....42 C4
Thorington Street.....103 A6
Thorndon.....53 B8
Thorney Green.....67 A7
Thornham Magna.....37 A2
Thornham Parva.....37 B3
Thorpe Abbotts.....21 E2
Thorpe Common.....107 C8
Thorpe Green.....64 F1
Thorpe Morieux.....79 A8
Thorpeness.....73 E6
Thorpe Street.....35 D8
Thrandeston.....37 B7
Thurston.....49 E3
Thurston End.....76 D6
Thwaite.....52 F7
Tilbury Green.....89 E4
Tilbury Juxta Clare.....90 A3
Timworth.....48 D8
Timworth Green.....48 D7
Toad Row.....10 F1
Tostock.....50 B2
Tower Hill.....107 C3
Trimley Lower Street.....107 C7
Trimley St Martin.....107 D8
Trimley St Mary.....152 C8
Troston.....33 D3
Tuddenham.....30 F2
Tuddenham St Martin.....136 C5
Tunstall.....71 F2

U
Ubbeston.....40 E4
Ubbeston Green.....40 D3
Ufford.....84 F7
Uggeshall.....25 F3
Undley.....13 C4
Upend.....60 F5
Upgate Street.....7 B6
Upper Green.....46 E3
Upper Holton.....118 E7
Upper Layham.....149 F2
Upper Street
  Baylham.....81 E6
  Dickleburgh and Rushall.....21 C2
  Stansfield.....76 C6
  Stutton.....105 B5
Upper Town.....49 E7
Upper Weybread.....22 B2
Upsher Green.....92 D6
Upthorpe.....34 F3

W
Wainford.....110 D5
Walberswick.....119 A2
Walcot Green.....20 D4
Waldingfield.....98 D7
Waldringfield Heath.....98 C7
Wales End.....76 D4
Walpole.....41 C5
Walsham Le Willows.....35 C2
Walton.....152 F6
Wangford.....26 B2
Ward Green.....51 E3
Warren Heath.....140 F1
Washbrook.....95 F5
Washbrook Street.....95 F6
Washmere Green.....78 D2
Waterloo
  Aldeby.....9 E8
  Dickleburgh and Rushall.....20 F2
Wattisfield.....35 D5
Wattisham.....80 B6
Wattisham Stone.....80 A6
Weeting.....5 E3
Wenhaston.....42 C6
Westbourne.....138 F7
Westbrook Green.....20 C4
West End.....26 B6
Westerfield.....135 E4
Westhall.....25 C4
West Harling.....18 A8
Westhorpe.....51 D8
Westleton.....58 B7
Westley.....122 A6
Westley Waterless.....59 E3
Weston.....9 D1
Weston Ditch.....29 F7
West Row.....29 F6
West Stow.....32 B1
West Street
  Rickinghall Inferior.....35 E5
  Walsham-le-willows.....35 A1
West Tofts.....6 F7
Wetherden.....51 B1
Wetherden Upper Town.....51 B4
Wetheringsett.....53 A5
Wetherup Street.....53 C3
Weybread.....22 D3
Whatfield.....80 C1

Wheatacre.....2 B1
Whelp Street.....79 B4
Whepstead.....63 B5
Wherstead.....143 B6
Whitestreet Green.....93 D2
Whitton.....134 F3
Wicken.....28 B1
Wicker Street Green.....93 E5
Wickhambrook.....61 E2
Wickham Green.....52 C8
Wickham Market.....127 B6
Wickham Skeith.....52 E8
Wickham Street
  Wickhambrook.....61 F1
  Wickham Skeith.....52 C8
Widgham Green.....60 B2
Wiggens Green.....88 C5
Wilby.....39 C2
Wilde Street.....13 D2
William's Green.....93 E5
Willingham.....25 E7
Willisham.....81 A5
Willisham Tye.....81 A6
Wilney Green.....19 D4
Windsor Green.....64 B2
Winfarthing.....20 B8
Wingfield.....39 B8
Wingfield Green.....38 F8
Winston.....68 F8
Wissett.....24 D2
Withermarsh Green.....103 A8
Withersdale Street.....22 F4
Withersfield.....74 B2
Witnesham.....83 A6
Wixoe.....89 B6
Woodbridge.....146 E6
Woodbridge Walk.....99 F8
Wooddition.....60 C5
Woodland Green.....133 C5
Wootton.....7 C8
Woolpit.....50 D1
Woolpit Green.....65 D8
Woolpit Heath.....65 E8
Woolverstone.....144 B1
Wootten Green.....39 B3
Wordwell.....32 D3
Workhouse Green.....101 C8
Workhouse Hill.....102 F2
World's End.....65 F2
Worlingham.....111 F3
Worlington.....30 A4
Worlingworth.....54 F8
Wormingford.....101 F2
Wortham.....36 D8
Wortwell.....23 B8
Wrabness.....105 F2
Wrentham.....26 E5
Wrentham West End.....26 C7
Wyverstone.....51 E6
Wyverstone Green.....51 E6
Wyverstone Street.....51 D6

Y
Yaxley.....37 B5
Yoxford.....57 D7

1

13th Century Hospl of St Saviour* IP32 ... 154 B4
100th Bomb Group Meml Mus* IP21 ... 21 D4

9

95th Bomb Group Hospl Musuem* IP21 ... 38 C4

A

Abbey Cl 10 Burwell CB5 ... 44 A5
10 Ixworth IP31 ... 34 B1
Rendlesham IP12 ... 85 D7
Abbey Farm Jun Sch 1 IP24 ... 16 B6
Abbey Fields IP14 ... 66 D8
Abbey Gdns IP13 ... 71 C2
Abbey Hill IP21 ... 38 C7
Abbey La IP16 ... 129 B8
Abbey Rd Flixton NR35 ... 23 F8
Leiston IP16 ... 129 C7
Sudbury CO10 ... 148 C7
Abbey Sch The IP12 ... 147 A4
Abbeydale NR32 ... 114 E2
Abbeygate St 3 IP33 ... 154 B2
Abbot Cl IP33 ... 122 D4
Abbot Rd IP33 ... 122 D4
Abbot's Hall Drift CO10 ... 78 E2
Abbot's Hall Rd IP14 ... 124 D5
Abbots Cotts CB9 ... 133 E2
Abbots Hall* IP14 ... 124 D5
Abbots Hall Prim Sch IP14 ... 124 C5
Abbotsbury Cl IP2 ... 139 A1
Abbotsbury Rd IP33 ... 122 D3
Abbott Rd CO12 ... 106 F1
Abbotts Croft CB9 ... 133 D2
Abbotts Ct CB9 ... 133 C3
Abbotts Gn Com Prim Sch IP32 ... 49 A3
Abbotts Meadow 8 IP30 ... 50 D1
Abbotts Rd CB9 ... 132 E7
Abbottsinch Rd 6 IP31 ... 33 D5
Abdy Ave 5 CO12 ... 106 F1
Abercorn Ct 2 CB9 ... 132 D4
Aberdeen Way IP4 ... 136 B1
Aberfoyle Cl 1 IP4 ... 136 C1
Abingdon Cl IP2 ... 139 A1
Abington Pl CB9 ... 132 E7
Ablitts Meadow IP13 ... 83 E6
Acacia Ave IP32 ... 48 C5
Acacia Cl IP3 ... 140 E1
Acer Gr IP8 ... 138 C1
Acer Rd IP12 ... 85 D8
Acheson Way 7 IP15 ... 130 E5
Acorn Cl 9 IP8 ... 138 C2
Acorn Way IP5 ... 98 B8
Acorns The IP30 ... 49 E3
Acre Cl IP6 ... 83 A6
Acre Rd CB8 ... 74 B8
Action France CB8 ... 59 E5
Acton CE Prim Sch CO10 ... 92 B7
Acton Cl Bramford IP8 ... 134 A2
Sudbury CO10 ... 148 D6
Acton Gdns 1 IP8 ... 134 A2
Acton Gn 3 CO10 ... 148 C5
Acton La Acton CO10 ... 92 A6
Sudbury CO10 ... 148 D6
Acton Pl Ind Est CO10 ... 92 A8
Acton Rd Bramford IP8 ... 134 A2
Lowestoft NR33 ... 115 B4
Adair Rd IP1 ... 138 D8
Adam's La IP18 ... 43 C5
Adams Pl IP5 ... 141 C7
Adamson Rd IP18 ... 119 B8
Adastral Cl
Felixstowe IP11 ... 153 H11
Newmarket CB8 ... 120 E4
Addington Rd IP11 ... 152 C7
Addison Cl IP26 ... 4 F5
Addison Rd CO10 ... 148 E7
Addison Way IP8 ... 134 A8
Adeane Meadow IP26 ... 6 A8
Adelaide Cl 17 CB7 ... 28 D4
Adelaide Rd IP4 ... 140 D6
Admiral Rd IP8 ... 142 E8
Admirals Jun Sch 2 IP24 ... 16 C7
Admirals Wlk IP12 ... 146 F7
Adrian Rd 6 NR32 ... 113 D2
Africa Alive* NR33 ... 11 A1
Agate Cl 2 IP1 ... 134 D1
Ailwin Rd IP32 ... 123 E4
Ainslie Rd IP1 ... 139 A6
Airedale NR33 ... 114 E2
Airey Cl Lowestoft NR32 ... 112 F5
Newton CO10 ... 92 E3
Airey Houses IP13 ... 137 D6
Airfield Rd IP32 ... 49 A3
Airstation La IP21 ... 21 E6
Aisthorpe IP9 ... 150 D3
Akethorpe Way NR32 ... 113 A3
Alabaster Cl 8 IP7 ... 149 E6
Alan Rd IP3 ... 139 F4
Alandale Dr 25 NR33 ... 11 C1
Alasdair Pl 9 IP6 ... 134 C8
Alban Sq 2 IP12 ... 84 A1
Albany Rd 1 NR32 ... 113 E2
Albany The IP4 ... 139 E8
Albemarle Rd IP33 ... 122 D4
Albemarle St 6 CO12 ... 107 B3
Albert Cres IP33 ... 154 A2
Albert Pl IP13 ... 126 C3
Albert Pye Prim Sch NR34 ... 111 B4
Albert Rd IP13 ... 126 C3
Albert Rolph Dr IP27 ... 109 E4
Albert St IP33 ... 154 A2
Albert Wlk IP11 ... 153 B3
Alberta Cl IP5 ... 141 A8
Albion Hill IP4 ... 139 F7
Albion Rd NR35 ... 110 D3
Albion St IP17 ... 128 C3
Alburgh with Denton Prim Sch IP20 ... 7 A1
Alde House Dr IP15 ... 130 E4
Alde La IP15 ... 130 E4
Alde Rd CB9 ... 132 E7
Aldeburgh & District Com Hospl IP15 ... 130 D4
Aldeburgh Cl CB9 ... 132 C5
Aldeburgh Lodge Gdns IP15 ... 130 E5
Aldeburgh Mus* IP15 ... 130 F4
Aldeburgh Prim Sch IP15 ... 130 E3
Aldeburgh Rd
Friston IP17 ... 72 F7
Leiston IP16 ... 129 D4
Aldecar La IP17 ... 72 C7
Alder Carr Farm & Ctyd Craft Ctr* IP6 ... 125 E5
Alder Covert 6 IP24 ... 16 D6
Alder Dr 2 NR33 ... 114 C4
Alder Way CO10 ... 148 D6
Aldercroft Cl IP1 ... 135 B3
Aldercroft Rd IP1 ... 135 B3
Aldergrove Cl IP19 ... 118 A3
Alderlee IP2 ... 142 F8
Alderman Rd IP1 ... 155 A2
Alderton Cl CB9 ... 132 C8
Alderton Rd IP12 ... 99 E6
Aldham Ct 1 CB9 ... 132 C5
Aldham Gdns IP14 ... 124 E4
Aldham Mill Hill IP7 ... 149 C8
Aldham Rd IP7 ... 149 E7
Aldis Ave IP14 ... 124 D4
Aldon Cl 14 CO12 ... 106 E1
Aldous Cl CO7 ... 151 C5
Aldous Ct 13 IP14 ... 53 F2
Aldridge La 2 IP28 ... 48 B6
Aldringham Craft Mkt* IP16 ... 129 C3
Aldringham Mews 13 IP11 ... 152 D5
Aldringham Pk IP16 ... 129 D3
Aldringham Rd IP17 ... 129 B3
Aldwyck Way NR33 ... 114 F4
Alexander Cl NR34 ... 111 C2
Alexander Dr
8 Great Waldingfield CO10 ... 92 C6
Needham Market IP6 ... 125 C5
Alexander Way IP28 ... 47 E5
Alexanders Int Sch IP12 ... 108 D8
Alexandra Rd
Beccles NR34 ... 111 B5
Felixstowe IP11 ... 152 E6
Ipswich IP4 ... 139 E6
Lowestoft NR32 ... 113 D1
Sudbury CO10 ... 148 E5
Alexandra St 8 CO12 ... 107 B3
Alfred Corry Mus* IP18 ... 119 C2
Algar Dr CB8 ... 59 F4
Alice Driver Rd 9 IP13 ... 83 E5
Alicia Ct IP33 ... 123 C3
All Hallows' Hospl NR35 ... 110 C7
All Saints IP27 ... 5 E3
All Saints CE Mid Sch CO10 ... 148 E8
All Saints CE Prim Sch IP29 ... 63 E1
All Saints CE VA Prim Sch
Laxfield IP13 ... 40 A3
Newmarket CB8 ... 121 B3
Winfarthing IP22 ... 20 C8
All Saints Cl CB8 ... 46 C3
All Saints Ct IP33 ... 154 B3
All Saints Dr NR34 ... 111 C3
All Saints Gn 6 NR34 ... 111 F4
All Saints Rd IP6 ... 125 F8
All Saints' Rd
Ipswich IP1 ... 139 A7
Lowestoft NR33 ... 115 B4
All Saints Rd CB8 ... 121 B3
All Saints Wlk IP28 ... 30 B4
Allen Rd Hadleigh IP7 ... 149 D7
Lowestoft NR32 ... 112 D1
Allenby Rd IP2 ... 138 F6
Alley Rd IP10 ... 98 D2
Allfields 3 CO12 ... 107 A1
Allington Cl IP4 ... 139 F7
Allington Rd 7 IP19 ... 118 A3
Allington Wlk CB9 ... 132 C6
Allotment La IP6 ... 69 A1
Allthorpe Rd 12 IP20 ... 22 D6
Alma Cl 3 IP4 ... 136 A1
Alma Pl IP17 ... 128 D3
Alma Rd NR32 ... 113 C1
Almond Gr IP24 ... 16 A4
Almondhayes IP2 ... 139 B3
Almshouse Rd IP30 ... 49 C1
Alnesbourn Cres
1 Gainsborough IP2 ... 144 D8
Ipswich IP3 ... 144 D7
Alnesbourne Priory IP10 ... 144 C6
Alpe St IP1 ... 155 A4
Alpha Bsns Pk IP1 ... 134 D3
Alphamstone Rd CO8 ... 101 A6
Alston Cl CO10 ... 92 D3
Alston Rd IP3 ... 139 F4
Alton Hall La IP9 ... 105 C6
Alton Wr Sports Ctr IP9 ... 105 D6
Alvis Cl IP32 ... 123 F5
Alvis Wlk IP1 ... 134 C1
Amber Mus The* IP18 ... 119 D5
Amberfield Sch IP10 ... 145 C6
Amberley Ct 3 NR32 ... 112 F4
Ambleside Gdns NR32 ... 113 A4
America Hill IP6 ... 83 A6
Amis Ct IP27 ... 109 D4
Amy Johnson Ct 6 IP28 ... 116 B5
Ancaster Rd IP2 ... 155 A1
Anchor End 2 CO11 ... 105 A2
Anchor La Burwell CB5 ... 44 A6
Dedham CO7 ... 104 A2
Lakenheath IP27 ... 109 C6
1 Mistley CO11 ... 105 A2
Anchor St NR33 ... 115 C6
Anchor Way NR33 ... 114 B4
Anderson Cl IP6 ... 125 C5
Anderson Wlk IP32 ... 122 D7
Anderson's Way 8 IP12 ... 146 E4
Andrew Burtt's Cl IP13 ... 126 B3
Andrew Cl
Felixstowe IP11 ... 152 E3
Leiston IP16 ... 129 D5
Andrew Johnston Way IP19 ... 118 B3
Andrew Rd CB8 ... 120 E5
Andrew Way NR33 ... 114 D6
Andrews Cl 9 IP14 ... 53 F2
Andrews Wlk IP32 ... 122 D8
Andros Cl IP3 ... 144 A7
Angel Hill
Bury St Edmunds IP33 ... 154 C2
Stonham Earl IP14 ... 67 F5
Angel La Blythburgh IP19 ... 42 F6
Bury St Edmunds IP33 ... 154 B2
Glemsford CO10 ... 77 A2
Ipswich IP4 ... 155 C2
2 Woodbridge IP12 ... 147 A5
Angel Link IP19 ... 118 B3
Angel Rd IP8 ... 134 A2
Angel St IP7 ... 149 D6
Angela Cl IP12 ... 84 A1
Angelgate Espl 4 CO12 ... 107 C3
Angerstein Cl IP27 ... 5 E4
Anglesea Rd IP1 ... 155 A4
Anglesey Pl 6 IP31 ... 49 A5
Anglia Parkway N IP1 ... 134 D4
Anglia Parkway S IP1 ... 134 D3
Anglian La IP32 ... 154 A4
Anglian Way NR31 ... 3 B7
Angus Cl IP4 ... 136 B1
Animal Health Trust Visitor Ctr* CB8 ... 45 F5
Anita Cl E IP2 ... 138 E5
Anita Cl W IP2 ... 138 E5
Ann Beaumont Way IP7 ... 149 C7
Ann Coles Cl CB9 ... 88 E3
Ann St IP1 ... 155 A4
Ann Suckling Rd CB9 ... 132 E8
Annandale Dr NR34 ... 111 D4
Annbrook Rd IP2 ... 138 E1
Anne Bartholomew Rd IP24 ... 16 C7
Anne St IP11 ... 152 E3
Annesons Cnr IP17 ... 58 B6
Annis Hill NR35 ... 110 E3
Annis Hill La 2 NR35 ... 110 D3
Annis Hill Rd NR35 ... 110 D3
Annison Cl NR33 ... 115 B5
Ansell Cl IP7 ... 149 D6
Anselm Ave 9 IP32 ... 48 C5
Anson Rd 7 IP5 ... 98 A8
Anson Way NR34 ... 10 A3
Antonia Cl CB9 ... 133 C5
Antrim Rd IP1 ... 134 D1
Anzani Ave IP11 ... 152 C4
Apple Acre Rd CB9 ... 132 A7
Apple Cl 28 IP27 ... 13 F2
Apple Gr IP14 ... 51 A2
Apple Tree Cl NR33 ... 115 B6
Appleby Cl IP8 ... 138 C1
Appledore Dr NR33 ... 114 D4
Appledown Dr IP30 ... 123 E7
Appletree Gr 2 CB5 ... 44 A6
Appletree La IP22 ... 20 C3
Approach Cotts CB9 ... 132 B8
Aragon Rd CB9 ... 132 B4
Arbor La NR33 ... 115 A2
Arcade St IP1 ... 155 B3
Archangel Gdns IP2 ... 138 E4
Archbishop Sancroft High Sch IP20 ... 22 C6
Archers' Ave 3 IP26 ... 4 D5
Arderne Cl 8 CO12 ... 106 F1
Ardleigh Rd CO7 ... 103 E2
Arger Fen Nature Reserve* CO10 ... 101 F6
Argyle St IP4 ... 155 C3
Argyll Ct 7 CB9 ... 132 D5
Ark Cl 7 NR33 ... 11 B1
Arkle Ct IP5 ... 141 D7
Arkwright Rd IP2 ... 138 E6
Arlington Way IP24 ... 16 C5
Arms La CB9 ... 133 F7
Armstrong Cl
Hundon CO10 ... 75 D4
Newmarket CB8 ... 121 B3
Armstrong Way CO9 ... 90 A1
Arnhem Ct NR32 ... 113 C4
Arnhem Rd IP16 ... 129 D5
Arnold Cl IP1 ... 134 F3
Arnold St 3 NR32 ... 113 E1
Arras Rd IP33 ... 122 D5
Arrendene Rd CB9 ... 132 D7
Arrowhead Dr IP27 ... 109 C7
Arthurs Terr IP4 ... 155 C3
Artillery Dr 7 CO12 ... 106 E1
Artillery Way 11 NR32 ... 113 E2
Arundel Cl 4 IP32 ... 123 D6
Arundel Way
Ipswich IP3 ... 140 E3
2 Lowestoft NR33 ... 114 D4
Arundel Wlk 11 CB9 ... 132 C6
Arwela Rd IP11 ... 152 F2
Ascot Dr
Felixstowe IP11 ... 152 E6
Ipswich IP3 ... 140 B3
Ash Ave 1 IP7 ... 80 D6
Ash Cl Bacton IP14 ... 51 F6
10 Lakenheath IP27 ... 13 F2
7 Lowestoft NR33 ... 114 D5
Thetford IP24 ... 16 A4
Warren Heath IP3 ... 140 F1
Woodbridge IP12 ... 146 F4
Ash Dr IP23 ... 117 D3
Ash Gd Cl
3 Brantham CO11 ... 104 E4
10 Felixstowe IP11 ... 107 D8
Ash Gr 17 Burwell CB5 ... 44 A5
Capel St Mary IP9 ... 150 E3
Haverhill CB9 ... 132 C7
4 Sudbury CO10 ... 92 B3
Ash Rd
Campsey Ash IP12 ... 71 C1
Hacheston IP13 ... 127 F7
Onehouse IP14 ... 66 C6
Rendlesham IP12 ... 85 C7
Ash Rise 8 CO6 ... 102 C5
Ash St 4 CO10 ... 93 C3
Ash Tree Cl
8 Beccles NR34 ... 9 F4
7 Fessingfield IP21 ... 39 D8
5 Occold IP23 ... 37 F1
Ash Wlk CB8 ... 75 C6
Ashbocking Rd IP6 ... 82 E6
Ashbourne Ct CB8 ... 121 B3
Ashburnham Rd IP6 ... 125 C4
Ashburnham Way NR33 ... 114 D4
Ashby Rd NR32 ... 113 C1
Ashcroft Rd IP1 ... 135 A1
Ashdale Dr NR34 ... 111 E4
Ashdale Pk IP27 ... 14 E8
Ashdale Rd IP5 ... 141 D8
Ashdown Way IP3 ... 140 D3
Ashe Rd IP12 ... 71 F2
Ashen Cl CO10 ... 89 E5
Ashen Hill CO10 ... 89 E5
Ashen La CO10 ... 89 E6
Ashen Rd Ashen CO10 ... 90 A7
Ridgewell CO9 ... 89 D4
Ashes The IP14 ... 54 D1
Ashfield Cres NR33 ... 114 F7
Ashfield Dr IP16 ... 129 C5
Ashfield Hill IP31 ... 50 F6
Ashfield Rd
Elmswell IP30 ... 50 F3
Norton IP31 ... 50 C4
Wetherden IP14 ... 51 A2
Ashford Cl NR34 ... 9 B6
Ashfords Cl IP17 ... 128 B4
Ashlea Cl CB9 ... 132 F4
Ashlea Rd CB9 ... 132 F4
Ashley Downs NR32 ... 113 C3
Ashley Rd Cheveley CB8 ... 60 E8
Harwich CO12 ... 107 A2
Newmarket CB8 ... 121 E2
Ashley Sch The NR32 ... 113 C4
Ashley St IP2 ... 155 B1
Ashman's Rd NR34 ... 111 A4
Ashmere Gr IP4 ... 139 F6
Ashmere Rise CO10 ... 148 E6
Ashness Cl 2 NR32 ... 113 A4
Ashton Cl IP2 ... 138 C2
Ashton Rd IP23 ... 117 C3
Ashtree Gdns NR33 ... 114 D3
Ashwell Rd IP33 ... 122 D4
Askins Rd CO7 ... 151 C5
Aspal Cl 5 IP28 ... 30 B8
Aspal Close Nature Reserve* IP28 ... 30 B7
Aspal Hall Rd IP28 ... 30 B8
Aspal La IP28 ... 30 C8
Aspal Pk IP28 ... 30 B8
Aspall Rd IP14 ... 53 F3
Aspel Est IP28 ... 13 D1
Aspen Cl Claydon IP6 ... 134 D8
Great Barton IP31 ... 49 B6
Haverhill CB9 ... 132 C7
3 Woodbridge IP12 ... 147 B6
Aspen Coppice 6 NR32 ... 112 F5
Aspinall Cl 4 NR33 ... 114 F4
Assington La CO6 ... 93 A1
Assington Rd CO10 ... 92 D3
Assington St CO10 ... 101 F8
Astbury Rd 6 NR32 ... 113 B5
Aster Rd IP2 ... 138 E4
Aston Cl IP1 ... 134 C1
Ataka Rd IP11 ... 152 F6
Athelington Rd IP21 ... 38 F2
Athenaeum La IP33 ... 154 C2
Athenaeum The* IP33 ... 154 C2
Atherton Rd IP2 ... 138 D2
Atterton Rd CB9 ... 132 B7
Aubretia Cl 2 NR33 ... 114 F7
Audley End IP21 ... 20 F5
Audley Gr IP4 ... 140 F5
Augusta Cl IP10 ... 144 E7
Augustus Cl CB9 ... 133 B5
Aureole Wlk CB8 ... 120 E8
Austin Cl IP31 ... 50 E7
Austin St IP2 ... 155 B1
Aveley La IP29 ... 77 D6
Aveling Way NR33 ... 114 B3
Avenue App IP32 ... 123 A8
Avenue Rd IP27 ... 109 E4
Avenue The
Brome & Oakley IP23 ... 117 E8
3 Burwell CB5 ... 44 B6
Copdock & Washbrook IP8 ... 95 F4
Felixstowe IP11 ... 152 B7
Great Barton IP31 ... 123 F8
Halesworth IP19 ... 118 B5
Ipswich IP1 ... 135 C1
4 Kessingland NR33 ... 11 B1
Lowestoft NR33 ... 115 B5
Newmarket CB8 ... 121 A3
Risby IP28 ... 47 E5
Ufford IP13 ... 84 F7
Woodbridge IP12 ... 147 A4
Aves Cl CB7 ... 29 C5
Avocet Cl NR33 ... 114 D5
Avocet Gr 12 CB7 ... 28 D5
Avocet La 20 IP5 ... 98 A8
Avondale Rd
Ipswich IP3 ... 140 A2
Lowestoft NR32 ... 113 C1
Aylmer Cl IP28 ... 47 D5
Aylward Cl IP7 ... 149 E4
Ayr Rd IP4 ... 136 B1

B

Babb's La IP14 ... 52 F2
Babergh Cl 9 CO10 ... 92 B7
Babington Dr IP19 ... 118 B2
Baby La IP30 ... 65 D4
Back Hamlet IP3 ... 139 E5
Back Hill IP9 ... 105 F6
Back Hills IP22 ... 36 A7
Back La
Badwell Ash IP31 ... 50 F8
Burrough Green CB8 ... 59 F2
Claydon IP6 ... 134 C8
Copdock & Washbrook IP8 ... 95 F5
Diss IP22 ... 20 D7
Falkenham IP10 ... 98 F1
Felixstowe IP11 ... 152 F5
Kettlebaston IP7 ... 79 C5
Lound NR32 ... 2 F6
Monks Eleigh IP7 ... 79 C2
St Mary, South Elmham otherwise Homersfield IP20 ... 23 C8
Scole IP21 ... 21 A5
Tattingstone IP9 ... 105 B7
Wicken CB7 ... 28 A1
Back Rd Brockdish IP21 ... 21 E4
Middleton IP17 ... 58 B6
Rattlesden IP30 ... 65 E6
Trimley St Martin IP10 ... 98 D2
Wenhaston with Mells Hamlet IP19 ... 42 C6
Back St
Garboldisham IP22 ... 18 D5
Gislingham IP23 ... 36 B1
Lakenheath IP27 ... 109 D6
Bacon Rd 7 IP6 ... 82 B5
Bacon's Gn Rd IP19 ... 25 D3
Bacton Com Prim Sch IP14 ... 51 F6
Bacton Mid Sch IP14 ... 51 E6
Bacton Rd
Felixstowe IP11 ... 152 F3
Haughley IP14 ... 51 C2
Baden Powell Wlk IP5 ... 141 E7
Bader Cl IP3 ... 140 C2
Bader Ct 25 IP5 ... 98 A8
Badger's Holt 10 NR33 ... 11 B1
Badgers Bank IP2 ... 138 E1
Badgers Gr CO6 ... 102 D1
Badgerwood Cl NR33 ... 115 B5
Badingham Rd
Badingham IP13 ... 56 A4
Framlingham IP13 ... 126 E5
Laxfield IP13 ... 40 C1
Peasenhall IP17 ... 56 D7
Badley Hill IP6 ... 125 B7
Badley Wlk IP6 ... 125 A7
Badleys Cl 6 CO10 ... 92 C6
Badlingham Rd CB7 ... 29 E1
Badshah Ave 4 IP3 ... 140 B3
Badwell Ash VA Prim Sch IP31 ... 50 E8
Badwell Rd
Walsham le Willows IP31 ... 35 B1
Wyverstone IP14 ... 51 C6
Bagsham La IP28 ... 30 A6
Bahram Cl CB8 ... 120 E4
Bailey Ave IP5 ... 141 E7
Bailey Cl Haverhill CB9 ... 133 B5

Bailey Cl *continued*
 Ipswich IP2 ....138 E6
Bailey La CO10 ....90 B8
Baileypool La IP31 ....49 F8
Baines Coney CB9 ....132 A7
Baird Cl IP7 ....138 F7
Baird Gr IP5 ....141 B6
Bakehouse Hill CB8 ....59 F4
Baker Dr **6** CB5 ....44 B6
Baker Rd **2** IP29 ....107 A4
Baker's Cnr IP14 ....80 E6
Baker's Hill IP16 ....58 C4
Baker's La
 Bury St Edmunds IP33 ....154 C1
 Thorndon IP23 ....53 C6
 Westleton IP17 ....58 C8
Baker's Rd CO10 ....90 D5
Baker's Score **1** NR32 ....3 D4
Bakers La
 Ditchingham NR35 ....110 B8
 Orford IP12 ....131 C2
 Winston IP14 ....68 E8
 1 Woodbridge IP12 ....147 A4
Bakers La S IP12 ....131 C2
Bakers Row CB8 ....121 A4
Bakers Way IP28 ....30 F2
Balaton Pl CB8 ....121 A6
Baldry Cl IP8 ....138 C1
Baldrys Wlk NR35 ....110 B7
Baldwin Ave IP12 ....122 E8
Baldwin Rd IP14 ....124 C4
Ball's Chace CO6 ....101 C1
Ballater Cl IP1 ....134 E4
Ballingdon Hill CO10 ....148 A3
Ballingdon St CO10 ....148 A4
Balliol Cl IP12 ....146 D3
Balls Hill IP7 ....79 D5
Ballygate NR34 ....111 A5
Balmoral Cl IP2 ....138 F1
Balmoral Dr **9** CB9 ....132 C6
Balton Way IP7 CO12 ....106 F1
Bancroft La CB7 ....28 D5
Bangor Rd IP2 ....13 F2
Banham Dr **8** CO10 ....148 D6
Banham Rd NR34 ....111 C2
Banham's La NR35 ....7 B6
Bank Alley **8** IP18 ....119 D5
Bank Bldgs **14** CO10 ....148 C5
Bank Rd IP4 ....139 E6
Banks Cl IP7 ....143 C5
Banks' La IP19 ....24 C3
Banks Wlk IP33 ....129 C5
Bannocks La IP13 ....56 B4
Banters La NR34 ....8 F2
Bantocks Rd CO10 ....92 C5
Bantoft Terr IP3 ....140 C2
Banyard Cl **4** IP3 ....141 D7
Barbara Stradbroke Ave
 CB8 ....120 D1
Barber Cl **3** NR33 ....11 B1
Barber's La NR35 ....7 B6
Barcham Rd CB7 ....28 C7
Bardolph Rd NR35 ....110 B3
Bardwell Rd IP31 ....33 F5
Bardwell VC Prim Sch
 IP31 ....34 C5
Bardwell Windmill*
 IP31 ....34 B4
Barell's Hill IP19 ....40 F4
Bargate La
 Beck Row, Holywell Row
  & Kenny Hill IP28 ....29 F5
 Dedham CO7 ....104 A2
Bargate Rd IP28 ....30 A6
Barham Picnic Site Visitor
 Ctr* IP6 ....82 A6
Barhams Way IP13 ....127 C7
Barker Cl Ipswich IP2 ....138 D5
 6 Manningtree CO11 ....104 D2
 3 Steeple Bumpstead CB9 ...88 D3
Barker Rd CO10 ....148 C8
Barking Rd
 Barking IP6 ....125 A1
 Willisham IP8 ....81 A5
Barkis Meadow NR32 ....3 A4
Barkways **9** CB5 ....44 B5
Barley Lands IP15 ....130 E3
Barley Meadow **5** IP19 ....118 A3
Barley Way NR33 ....114 F2
Barlings Ct CB8 ....121 A4
Barn Cl
 2 Hopton on Sea NR31 ....3 C7
 Lowestoft NR33 ....114 D5
 Southwold IP18 ....119 B8
Barn Field **2** IP29 ....62 C6
Barn La IP33 ....154 C3
Barn St **12** CO10 ....78 D4
Barnaby Gn IP18 ....119 C5
Barnardiston Hall Prep Sch
 CB9 ....75 A5
Barnards Way NR32 ....113 B1
Barnby & N Cove Prim Sch
 NR34 ....10 C4
Barnes Cl Brandon IP27 ....14 E8
 3 Hadleigh IP7 ....149 E6
Barnfield
 Capel St Mary IP9 ....150 F3
 Felixstowe IP11 ....152 D6
 20 Manningtree CO11 ....104 E2
Barnham CE Prim Sch
 IP24 ....16 B1
Barnham Pl IP25 ....140 F6
Barnham Rd IP24 ....16 E2
Barningham CE VC Prim Sch
 IP31 ....34 E7

Barningham Rd IP31 ....34 E5
Barons Cl
 9 Felixstowe IP11 ....153 D6
 Halesworth IP19 ....118 A2
Barons Ct **17** CB9 ....132 C5
Barons Meadow IP12 ....131 B3
Barons Rd IP7 ....123 A2
Baronsdale Cl IP1 ....135 B1
Barr Dr IP27 ....109 D7
Barrack La
 Harwich CO12 ....107 C2
 Ipswich IP1 ....155 A3
 Ufford IP13 ....84 F7
Barrack Sq IP5 ....98 A8
Barracks Rd CO10 ....101 F8
Barrell's Rd IP31 ....49 F3
Barrett's La IP6 ....125 C4
Barrow Hill Acton CO10 ....92 B8
 Barrow IP29 ....47 A2
Barrow Prim Sch IP29 ....47 A3
Barrow Rd IP29 ....47 A3
Barrow's Cnr IP28 ....32 C8
Barry Lynham Dr CB8 ....121 B2
Barsey Cl IP31 ....132 A7
Bartholomew Gn
 IP18 ....119 D5
Bartholomew St IP4 ....139 F6
Bartholomew's La IP19 ....42 B6
Bartlet Hospl IP11 ....153 C4
Bartlow Pl IP28 ....137 F7
Barton Bottom IP31 ....48 E7
Barton Rd CB9 ....133 F8
Barton Hamlet IP31 ....49 C6
Barton Hill IP31 ....48 D5
Barton Rd
 Bury St Edmunds IP32 ....123 D6
 Felixstowe IP11 ....153 B4
 Thurston IP31 ....49 C4
 Woodbridge IP12 ....146 F7
Bartons Pl CB8 ....120 E5
Bartrum La J IP5 ....141 C7
Barvens The IP8 ....138 A1
Barway Rd CB7 ....28 A6
Barwell Rd IP31 ....33 C3
Basil Brown Cl **B** IP22 ....36 A6
Bates La IP22 ....19 D6
Bath Ct CB9 ....132 D4
Bath Hill IP11 ....153 B4
Bath Hills Rd NR35 ....7 A4
Bath Rd IP11 ....153 D3
Bath St IP2 ....139 D3
Battery Gn **7** NR32 ....113 E1
Battery Gn Rd **5** NR32 ....113 E1
Battery La **10** IP9 ....107 A4
Battisford Rd IP6 ....125 A1
Battles La IP5 ....141 D7
Battlesea Hill IP21 ....39 A6
Bawdsey CE Prim Sch
 IP12 ....99 E2
Bawdsey Cl IP11 ....153 D7
Bawdsey Manor Workshops*
 IP12 ....108 D8
Bawdsey Radar Sta*
 IP12 ....99 E1
Bay Rd **11** CO12 ....107 B2
Bayfield Dr **4** CB5 ....44 B5
Baylham House Rare Breeds
 Farm* IP6 ....81 F7
Baynard's La IP22 ....20 A3
Bays The **4** IP16 ....73 F6
Beach Mews **8** NR32 ....115 D8
Beach Rd
 1 Harwich CO12 ....107 B1
 Hopton on Sea NR31 ....3 C6
 Kessingland NR33 ....27 C8
 Lowestoft NR32 ....115 D8
Beach Rd E **6** NR32 ....115 C4
Beach Rd W IP11 ....152 F2
Beach Sta Rd IP11 ....152 E1
Beacon Field **4** IP11 ....152 E5
Beacon Hill Ave CO12 ....107 C2
Beacon Hill La IP16 ....73 F7
Beacon Hill Specl Sch
 IP2 ....138 F2
Beacon La IP12 ....137 F3
Beaconsfield Cl CO10 ....148 C6
Beaconsfield Ct **9** CB9 ....132 D5
Beaconsfield Rd
 Aldeburgh IP15 ....130 E3
 Ipswich IP1 ....135 E1
 21 Kessingland NR33 ....11 C1
 Lowestoft NR33 ....115 C4
 Sudbury CO10 ....148 C6
 3 Woodbridge IP12 ....147 A5
Bealings La IP13 ....137 F8
Bealings Rd IP12 ....146 A6
Bealings Sch IP13 ....137 D4
Bear Meadow **5** IP30 ....49 F2
Bear St CO6 ....102 C5
Beard Rd IP32 ....122 D8
Beardmore Pk **10** IP5 ....98 A8
Bear's La IP7 ....78 D3
Beatrice Ave IP11 ....153 B5
Beatrice Cl IP3 ....140 A3
Beatty Rd Ipswich IP3 ....140 B2
 Sudbury CO10 ....148 E7
Beauford Rd IP31 ....32 F8
Beaufort Ct **10** CB9 ....132 D5
Beaufort St IP1 ....139 A7
Beaumont Cl **3** IP33 ....122 D4
Beaumont Cotts IP17 ....128 C6
Beaumont Ct CB9 ....132 F4
Beaumont Prim Sch
 IP7 ....149 D8
Beaumont Rd NR33 ....114 B2
Beaumont Vale CB9 ....132 F4
Beaumont Way IP24 ....124 B5

Beccles & District Mus*
 NR34 ....111 A5
Beccles & District War Meml
 Hospl NR34 ....111 B4
Beccles Gall* q0 NR34 111 B5
Beccles Mid Sch
 NR34 ....111 C4
Beccles Rd Aldeby NR34 ....9 F8
 Aldeby/Wheatacre/Burgh
  St Peter NR34 ....19 C1
 Blyford IP19 ....25 C1
 Bungay NR35 ....110 C8
 Carlton Colville NR33 ....114 A4
 Fritton & St Olaves NR31 ....2 C7
 Holton IP19 ....118 F4
 Lowestoft NR33 ....114 D7
 Mutford NR34 ....10 C3
Beccles Sports Ctr
 NR34 ....111 A4
Beccles Sta NR34 ....111 C5
Beccles Way **1** NR34 ....111 B6
Beck Cl **5** IP17 ....85 D8
Beck Rd CB7 ....29 D4
Beck Row Prim Sch
 IP28 ....30 B8
Beck St IP22 ....35 A7
Beck View **3** IP20 ....22 D6
Becketts La **3** NR34 ....22 A6
Becketts The IP14 ....124 B8
Beckford Rd **17** CO11 ....105 A2
Beckham Rd NR32 ....113 C1
Becks Gn La NR34 ....24 F8
Bedell Cl IP33 ....122 C3
Bederic Cl IP32 ....123 D4
Bedfield CE Prim Sch
 IP13 ....54 D5
Bedfield Rd IP13 ....54 D5
Bedford Rd **3** IP22 ....122 E8
Bedford St IP1 ....155 A3
Bedingfeld Way IP21 ....123 E4
Bedingfield Rd IP23 ....53 E7
Beech Circus **5** IP7 ....155 B6
Beech Cl
 Halesworth IP19 ....118 A4
 Isleham CB7 ....29 B5
 11 Lakenheath IP27 ....13 F2
 Sproughton IP8 ....138 A6
Beech Croft CB8 ....59 E1
Beech Gr Haverhill CB9 ....132 C7
 Stutton IP9 ....51 A1
Beech La **8** IP7 ....94 B1
Beech Paddocks **4** IP30 ....64 F8
Beech Pk IP31 ....49 B6
Beech Rd Ipswich IP5 ....140 F7
 Lowestoft NR33 ....114 D3
 Sudbury CO10 ....148 D3
Beech Rise IP30 ....123 C3
Beech Row CB8 ....46 C1
Beech Terr IP14 ....124 D7
Beech Tree Cl NR34 ....111 B4
Beech Tree Way **9** NR35 ....7 F4
Beech Way
 Dickleburgh IP21 ....21 C5
 Woodbridge IP12 ....146 F3
Beech Wlk IP16 ....129 C5
Beechcroft IP29 ....64 A3
Beechcroft Rd IP1 ....134 F2
Beeches **6** CO11 ....81 E3
Beeches Rd IP28 ....29 F7
Beeches The
 Benhall Green IP17 ....72 C8
 Claydon IP6 ....74 C8
 Horringer IP29 ....63 A8
 Ipswich IP3 ....139 F4
 10 Lawford CO11 ....104 E2
 Little Blakenham IP8 ....81 E3
Beeching Dr NR32 ....113 D4
Beechwood Cl CB8 ....120 E8
Beechwood Gdns
 NR33 ....115 A6
Beehive Cl CO7 ....151 C5
Beetons Way IP32 ....122 E7
Beevors Gdn NR33 ....110 B7
Belaugh Ave NR33 ....114 F5
Belcham Hall* CO10 ....91 A3
Belcham Rd CO10 ....90 A3
Belcham St Paul CE Prim
 Sch CO10 ....90 D5
Belcher Gn IP18 ....119 C8
Belfry Rd IP7 ....144 F7
Belgrave Cl IP4 ....135 E1
Bell Cl IP2 ....155 B1
Bell Gdns **13** CB7 ....28 C4
Bell Gn IP19 ....40 C6
Bell Hill CO8 ....101 B6
Bell La
 Barton Mills IP28 ....116 D2
 Ipswich IP2 ....155 B1
 Marlesford IP13 ....71 C4
Bell Meadow IP32 ....123 A8
Bell Mews IP7 ....4 E5
Bell Pk IP26 ....4 E5
Bellands Way IP33 ....117 C3
Bell's Cross IP14 ....67 C6
Bell's Cross Rd IP14 ....67 B6
Bell's La Hawstead IP29 ....62 C7
 Stowupland IP14 ....67 A7
Belle Vue Rd
 Ipswich IP4 ....139 F6
 Sudbury CO10 ....148 D5
Bellings Rd CB9 ....132 C8
Bells Hill CO8 ....101 D2
Bells La Glemsford CO10 ....77 A3
 Hinderclay IP22 ....36 E8
Bells Rd CO10 ....90 F3

Bellwell La
 Debenham IP14 ....53 F4
 Kenton IP14 ....54 A4
Belmont Ct
 14 Haverhill CB9 ....132 C5
 Newmarket CB8 ....120 F3
Belmont Gdns NR32 ....113 B3
Belmont Rd IP8 ....138 C1
Belsay Ct CB9 ....132 B6
Belseybridge Rd NR35 ....7 F7
Belstead Ave IP2 ....155 A1
Belstead Rd IP2 ....155 A1
Belstead Sch IP8 ....138 C2
Belt The CB8 ....61 B4
Belvedere Dr **28** NR33 ....11 C1
Belvedere Rd
 Ipswich IP4 ....139 F8
 Lowestoft NR33 ....115 C7
Belvoir Ct **7** CB9 ....132 C6
Benacre National Nature
 Reserve* NR34 ....27 B6
Benacre Rd
 Ellough NR34 ....111 F1
 Henstead with Hulver Street
  NR34 ....26 E8
 Ipswich IP3 ....140 A2
Benefield Rd **1** CB8 ....48 F3
Benezet St IP1 ....155 A2
Benhall St Marys CE Prim
 Sch IP17 ....72 C8
Benjamin Britten High Sch
 NR32 ....113 A5
Bennett Ave
 Bury St Edmunds IP33 ....122 C6
 Elmswell IP30 ....50 F2
Bennett Rd
 Ipswich IP1 ....134 E1
 5 Red Lodge IP28 ....30 C1
Benouville **10** NR33 ....114 F3
Bensly's Drift IP19 ....118 C4
Bent La IP4 ....140 E8
Bentley Dr NR32 ....113 A6
Bentley La
 Belstead IP9 ....105 B6
 11 Stutton IP9 ....50 F8
Bentley Prim Sch IP9 ....104 F8
Bentley Rd IP1 ....134 C2
Benton Cl **7** IP4 ....65 C1
Benton St IP7 ....149 D4
Benton Way IP19 ....118 B4
Benyon Gdns IP28 ....32 D1
Beresford Dr IP4 ....140 F5
Beresford Rd NR32 ....113 D2
Bergamot Rd IP9 ....132 A6
Berghersh La IP6 ....82 E7
Bergholt Rd CO11 ....104 D4
Berkeley Cl
 2 Framlingham IP13 ....126 C3
 Ipswich IP4 ....135 E1
Berkeley Gdns
 5 Framlingham IP13 ....122 C8
 Lowestoft NR32 ....113 A4
Bermuda Rd IP10 ....144 D7
Bernard Cres IP3 ....140 B2
Bernard Pottery &
 Gall* IP6 ....83 A8
Berners Rd IP3 ....153 C4
Berners St IP1 ....155 A3
Bernham Cl IP32 ....123 D5
Berry Cl Ipswich IP3 ....140 F1
 Lowestoft NR32 ....112 E1
Berrycroft **11** CB7 ....28 C4
Beryl Rd **8** CO12 ....106 E1
Bethel Dr **24** NR33 ....11 C1
Betjeman Cl IP24 ....16 C7
Betony Wlk CB9 ....132 B6
Betts Cl IP7 ....149 D7
Betty Cocker Gr CO10 ....148 F5
Bevan St E **3** NR33 ....115 D8
Bevan St W NR32 ....113 C1
Beverley Cl NR33 ....114 D6
Beverley Ct NR33 ....114 C2
Beverley Rd IP4 ....139 F8
Bevilla Dr IP11 ....71 F5
Bevis Wlk IP33 ....123 D3
Bewicks Mead **10** CB5 ....44 B5
Bexley Ave **16** CO12 ....106 F1
Beyond the Image
 Photographers Gall*
 IP23 ....36 F2
Beyton Mid Sch IP30 ....49 F2
Beyton Rd IP30 ....49 F3
Bibb Way IP1 ....139 A5
Bickers Hill Rd IP13 ....49 A6
Bier La IP23 ....19 C1
Big Row NR34 ....8 F6
Bigod Cl
 5 Framlingham IP13 ....126 C3
 Halesworth IP19 ....118 B2
Bigod Rd NR35 ....110 D3
Bilberry Rd IP3 ....144 C7
Bildeston Gdns **2** IP1 ....135 D1
Bildeston Prim Sch IP7 ....79 E4
Bildeston Rd
 Chelsworth IP7 ....79 E3
 Combs IP14 ....124 A1
 Offton IP7 ....80 F4
 5 Wattisham IP7 ....94 C4
Bill Rickaby Dr CB8 ....121 A5
Billy's La CO7 ....151 D6
Bilney Rd IP12 ....146 E5
Birch Ave CO12 ....107 A2
Birch Cl
 Lowestoft NR32 ....112 D2
 1 Thetford IP24 ....67 A6
 Wickham Market IP13 ....127 C6
 Woodbridge IP12 ....146 F3
Birch Covert IP24 ....16 D6

Birch Cres IP27 ....109 D7
Birch Dr **8** CO11 ....104 E5
Birch Fall **7** CO6 ....102 C5
Birch Gr IP5 ....98 A7
Birch Rd Onehouse IP14 ....66 C6
 10 Thurstow IP31 ....49 E4
Birch St CO6 ....102 D5
Birch Wlk **24** IP27 ....13 F2
Birchcroft Rd IP1 ....135 B2
Birches The
 Kennett IP28 ....46 A8
 Soham CB7 ....28 C5
Birchgrove IP23 ....52 F7
Birchinhill Dro IP28 ....30 E3
Birchwood Cty Prim Sch
 IP5 ....98 A8
Birchwood Dr IP5 ....136 E1
Birchwood Rd CO7 ....103 D2
Bird View Sq **1** IP26 ....4 E5
Bird's La IP30 ....64 D2
Birds Rd IP13 ....49 F3
Birdbrook **3** IP29 ....63 A1
Birdcage Wlk CB8 ....120 F2
Birds Croft IP31 ....33 C2
Birds Gn IP30 ....65 E5
Birds Hill IP13 ....83 D8
Birds La Framsden IP14 ....69 D5
 Rickinghall NR34 ....115 B6
Birds Meare IP6 ....57 C2
Birkdale Ave IP28 ....116 B5
Birkdale Cl **10** IP28 ....48 C6
Birkfield Cl IP2 ....139 A4
Birkfield Dr IP2 ....138 E1
Biscay Cl CB9 ....133 A5
Bishop Mews IP8 ....138 B2
Bishop's Hill IP3 ....139 E4
Bishops Cl
 6 Felixstowe IP11 ....153 D6
 Haverhill CB9 ....132 C6
Bishops Ct **1** CB9 ....132 C6
Bishops Rd IP33 ....154 B3
Bishops Way IP21 ....39 A4
Bittern Cl IP2 ....138 E3
Bittern Gn NR33 ....114 C6
Bittern Rd IP17 ....128 B3
Bixley Dr IP4 ....140 E5
Bixley La IP4 ....140 F5
Bixley Rd Ipswich IP3 ....140 D3
 2 Lowestoft NR33 ....114 C6
Black Barns IP11 ....152 C7
Black Bear Cl CB8 ....121 A3
Black Bear La CB8 ....120 F3
Black Boy La CO11 ....106 A2
Black Boy Meadow
 NR34 ....111 B4
Black Dyke Rd IP26 ....4 E3
Black Gr La CO10 ....75 C4
Black Hill (Tumulus)*
 IP31 ....33 C5
Black Horse La
 Ditchingham NR35 ....110 C7
 Ipswich IP1 ....155 A3
Black Horse Wlk IP1 ....155 B3
Black Mill Rd IP18 ....119 C5
Black Slough IP17 ....58 B7
Black St IP33 ....10 F1
Blackberry Way
 Lowestoft NR32 ....112 E2
 3 Red Lodge IP28 ....30 C1
Blackbird Ave IP27 ....6 A1
Blackbird Cl **16** IP19 ....49 D4
Blackbird Dr IP32 ....49 A3
Blackbird Rd IP32 ....13 B1
Blackbird Way **2** IP14 ....67 A7
Blackbourne CE VC Mid Sch
 IP31 ....34 F4
Blackbourne Rd IP30 ....50 F3
Blackdike Dro IP26 ....4 A2
Blackdown Ave IP5 ....140 F6
Blackdyke Cl **9** IP13 ....4 D5
Blackfriars CO10 ....148 B4
Blackheath Rd
 Wenhaston with Mells Hamlet
  IP19 ....42 C5
Blackhouse La CO12 ....148 F1
Blacklands La IP12 ....131 A8
Blackmore Cl CB8 ....132 D7
Blacksmith La
 Barnham IP24 ....16 B2
 Thorpe Morieux IP30 ....78 F7
Blacksmith Rd IP14 ....52 A6
Blacksmith's Cnr IP28 ....142 C6
Blacksmiths Hill CO10 ....89 D6
Blacksmiths La
 Bulmer CO10 ....91 C1
 Coddenham IP6 ....68 B1
 Stonham Earl IP14 ....67 D6
Blackthorn Ct IP31 ....140 F1
Blackthorn Ct CB7 ....28 C5
Blackthorn Way CO6 ....102 B7
Blackthorn Wlk IP32 ....122 D8
Blacktiles La IP12 ....84 A1
Bladen Dr IP4 ....141 A7
Bladon Way IP28 ....137 F7
Blagge Cl IP33 ....122 C4
Blair Cl IP3 ....140 E5
Blair Par **8** CB9 ....132 C6
Blake Ave **4** IP9 ....107 A5
Blake Cl **7** CO11 ....104 D2
Blake Rd Ipswich IP1 ....134 F3
 Stowmarket IP14 ....124 B7
Blakenham Cl **4** NR32 ....112 F4

Blakenham Woodland Gdn* IP6 81 F4
Blakes Cl IP12 147 C7
Blanche St IP4 155 C3
Blandford Rd IP3 140 D3
Blaxhall Church Rd IP12 71 F2
Blaxhall Ct 2 CB9 132 C5
Blaxhall Heath Nature Reserve* IP12 72 C3
Blenheim Cl
10 Brantham CO11 104 E5
Bury St Edmunds IP33 122 D5
Haverhill CB9 132 F7
Blenheim Dr IP7 80 C6
Blenheim Rd 3 IP1 139 A7
Blenheim Way 2 IP22 20 A3
Blickling Cl IP2 139 B2
Blinco Rd NR32 112 C1
Blind La IP29 77 B6
Blo' Norton Rd
Blo' Norton IP22 18 F3
South Lopham IP22 19 A4
Block Rd CB7 28 E1
Blocka Rd NR32 2 C6
Blockmoor Rd CB7 28 A6
Blofield Rd IP11 152 B4
Blois Rd CB9 88 F4
Blomfield St IP33 154 B3
Blood Hill IP8 81 B3
Bloodmoor La 2 NR33 114 E3
Bloodmoor Rd 1 NR33 114 E3
Bloomfield St IP4 140 B6
Bloomfield Way
Debenham IP14 53 E1
7 Lowestoft NR33 114 E3
Blooms Ct IP28 116 D5
Blooms Hall La CO10 77 D5
Bloomsbury Cl NR32 112 E4
Bloomsfield 8 CB5 44 B5
Blower's La NR33 10 E2
Blue Barn Cl 13 IP11 107 D8
Blue Barn La IP8 134 A8
Blue House La IP14 52 F3
Bluebell Ave IP32 123 F5
Bluebell Cl Ipswich IP2 138 E4
7 Lowestoft NR33 114 F3
Bluebell Gr IP6 125 D3
Bluebell Way NR34 111 E3
Bluebell Wlk 2 CB7 28 D4
Bluegate La IP9 150 F1
Bluestem Rd IP3 144 D8
Blundens The CO6 102 E7
Blundeston Rd
Corton NR32 112 F8
Somerleyton, Ashby & Herringfleet NR32 112 B8
Blyburgate 2 NR34 111 C4
Blyford La Blyford IP19 42 B8
Holton IP19 118 E3
Wenhaston with Mells Hamlet IP19 42 C6
Blyford Rd NR32 113 A5
Blyford Way IP11 152 C4
Blyth Cl Ipswich IP2 139 A1
Wenhaston IP19 42 C6
Blyth Rd
Halesworth IP19 118 C2
Southwold IP18 119 B5
Blythburgh Rd IP17 58 C8
Boathouse La
Carlton Colville NR32 114 B8
Lowestoft NR32 112 B1
Boatman Cl 16 IP8 142 E8
Bobbits La
Pinewood IP9 142 E8
Wherstead IP9 143 A7
Boby Rd IP32 122 D8
Bockhill Rd IP33 122 C5
Bodiam Cl IP3 140 D4
Bodiam Rd IP3 140 D4
Bodiam Way 8 NR33 114 D4
Bodian Wlk 8 CB9 132 C6
Bodmin Cl IP5 141 A6
Boeing Way IP28 116 B5
Boldero Rd IP32 123 F4
Boleyn Way CB9 132 B5
Boleyn Wlk CB8 121 C3
Bollard Way NR33 114 E5
Bolton Cl 2 CB5 44 A5
Bolton La IP1 155 C3
Bolton St 10 CO10 78 D4
Bon Marche 7 NR32 115 D8
Bond Cl IP21 21 F8
Bond St Ipswich IP4 155 C2
Stowmarket IP14 124 D7
Bond's Rd NR15 21 C8
Bonds Meadow NR32 112 E2
Bonnington Rd IP3 139 F1
Bonny Cres IP3 144 C8
Bonsey Gdns NR34 26 E5
Boon Cl IP33 123 A3
Boon Dr NR33 114 E6
Boot Drift IP9 106 E7
Booth La IP5 141 E8
Border Cot La IP13 127 B7
Border La NR32 2 E6
Borehamgate Prec 5 CO10 148 D5
Borehamgate Sh Ctr 21 CO10 148 C5
Borley Cres 2 IP30 50 F2
Borley Rd CO10 91 D6
Borough End 8 NR34 111 C3
Borough La IP14 66 A3
Borradale Ct 5 CB9 88 D3
Borradale Rd IP32 123 F5
Borrett Pl IP12 146 D3
Borretts Farm La IP13 70 D6
Borrow Cl NR33 114 C3
Borrow Rd NR32 112 C1
Borrowdale Ave 1 IP4 135 D1
Bosmere Prim Sch IP6 125 D4
Bosquet Cl 1 NR32 112 F5
Boss Hall Ind Est IP1 138 E7
Boss Hall Rd IP1 138 E7
Bostock Rd IP2 139 C1
Boston End 6 IP24 16 A5
Boston Rd Ipswich IP4 139 F7
Lowestoft NR32 113 D2
Boswell La IP7 149 D7
Botany La IP17 71 E7
Botolphs Ct IP33 154 C1
Bouchain Ct 1 IP19 118 A3
Boughton Way IP33 154 C3
Boulevard The NR32 114 D8
Boulge Rd Burgh IP13 83 F6
Hasketon IP13 146 B8
Boulters Cl IP14 124 B6
Boulters Way IP14 124 B6
Boundary Cl IP26 4 F3
Boundary Rd
Haverhill CB9 133 B3
1 Hockwold cum Wilton IP26 5 A3
Red Lodge IP28 30 C1
Bourchier Cl 7 IP7 149 E6
Bourne Ave 6 IP32 123 E6
Bourne Hill IP2 143 B7
Bourne Pk Residential Park IP2 139 B1
Bourne Rd
Haverhill CB9 132 F6
Lowestoft NR32 113 B3
Bourne Terr IP2 143 B8
Bowdens La CO6 101 F3
Bower's La 7 CB7 29 C5
Bowl Rd IP14 66 C1
Bowland Dr IP8 138 C1
Bowman's La IP17 42 D1
Bowthorpe Cl IP1 155 A4
Box Bush La IP13 55 D5
Boxford Cl 2 IP14 124 E3
Boxford Ct
7 Felixstowe IP11 152 C4
3 Haverhill CB9 132 C5
Boxford La CO10 93 A3
Boxford Prim Sch CO10 93 C3
Boxford Rd IP7 93 B8
Boxhouse La CO7 103 D3
Boxted Church Rd CO6 102 E2
Boxted Rd CO6 102 E2
Boxted Straight Rd CO4 103 A2
Boyden Cl 1 CB8 61 E2
Boydlands IP9 150 E3
Boyne Rd IP33 122 E4
Boyscott La 1 NR35 110 B3
Boyton Cl CB9 132 E8
Boyton Rd
Hollesley IP12 86 A1
Ipswich IP3 140 B1
Boyton Vineyard* CO9 89 B7
Boyton's La CB10 88 A1
Braces La NR35 8 E7
Bracken Ave IP5 137 E1
Bracken Rise IP26 6 A8
Bracken Row 6 IP31 49 D4
Brackenbury Cl IP1 139 B8
Brackenbury Sports Ctr IP11 153 C5
Brackenhayes Cl IP2 139 B3
Brackenwood Cres 1 IP32 123 E6
Brackley Cl 8 IP11 152 D5
Bradbrook Cl IP32 123 F6
Braddock Sq IP32 122 E7
Bradfield Ave IP7 149 D7
Bradfield Cres IP7 149 D7
Bradfield Woods National Nature Reserve* IP30 64 F4
Bradley Rd Cowlinge CB8 60 F1
Great Bradley CB8 74 F8
Kirtling CB8 60 F2
Bradley St IP2 155 B1
Braggon's Hill IP29 77 A5
Braithwaite Dr 7 CO10 92 C6
Bramble Cl CB9 132 B7
Bramble Dr IP3 140 E1
Bramble Gn NR32 113 B3
Bramble Tye 20 CO12 106 E1
Bramble Way CO6 102 B7
Brambles The IP15 130 C6
Bramblewood 1 IP8 138 C2
Bramblewood Way IP19 118 C4
Brambling Cl 12 IP14 67 A5
Brames La IP20 23 D3
Bramfield CE Prim Sch IP19 42 A4
Bramfield House Sch IP19 41 E4
Bramfield Rd
Halesworth IP19 118 B2
Lowestoft NR32 113 A3
Walpole IP19 41 C5
Wenhaston with Mells Hamlet IP19 42 B5
Bramford CE Prim Sch IP8 134 A1
Bramford Ct IP14 124 E4
Bramford La 6 IP1 139 A7
Bramford Meadows Nature Reserve* IP1 134 B3
Bramford Rd
Bramford IP8 134 B1
Claydon IP8 134 A8
Great Blakenham IP6 134 A8
Ipswich IP1 138 E8
Bramhall Cl IP2 138 D1
Bramley Chase IP4 140 B7
Bramley Cl IP32 123 F6
Bramley Rd Diss IP22 20 B3
Haverhill CB9 132 A5
Bramley Rise NR34 111 C3
Brampton CE Prim Sch NR34 25 E5
Brampton Gr 9 NR32 112 F4
Brampton Sta NR34 25 C6
Brand Rd IP31 49 C7
Brandeston Cl 10 CO10 92 C6
Brandeston Rd
Cretingham IP13 69 E7
Earl Soham IP13 54 F1
Brandon Ctry Pk Visitor Ctr* IP27 14 F8
Brandon Her Ctr* IP27 5 F1
Brandon Rd
Felixstowe IP11 152 C4
Lakenheath IP27 14 C4
Methwold IP26 5 B8
Mildenhall IP28 116 E5
Thetford IP24 15 F6
Weeting IP27 5 F3
Wordwell IP28 32 C3
Brandon St IP27 109 F1
Brandon Sta IP27 5 F2
Brands Cl 12 CO10 92 B3
Brands La IP29 63 D3
Bransby Gdns IP4 139 E7
Brantham Hill CO11 104 E4
Brawdy Rd 1 IP31 33 D5
Brayfield Cl IP32 123 D6
Braziers La IP31 51 B6
Brazier's Wood Rd IP3 144 B8
Brazilian Terr CB8 120 F3
Breach Dro IP28 13 C1
Breckland Ave IP27 109 D7
Breckland Mid Sch IP27 14 D8
Breckland Way
Lowestoft NR32 113 A3
Mildenhall IP28 116 C5
Brecklands 5 IP26 6 B8
Brecon Cl IP2 139 B2
Bredfield Cl 7 IP11 152 D5
Bredfield Rd IP12 147 A7
Bredfield St IP12 146 F5
Brendon Cl NR32 112 E2
Brendon Dr IP5 140 F6
Brent Cl IP28 116 D4
Brent Eleigh Rd
Lavenham CO10 78 D3
Monks Eleigh IP7 79 B2
Brentgovel St 1 IP33 154 B2
Bressingham Prim Sch IP22 19 E4
Bressingham Rd IP22 19 F4
Bressingham Steam Mus & Gdns* IP22 19 E3
Brett Ave IP7 149 E7
Brett Cl IP1 138 E8
Brett Gn IP7 149 E2
Brettenham Cres 4 IP1 135 D1
Brettenham Rd
Buxhall IP14 65 F4
Hitcham IP7 79 E8
Bretts The IP5 141 E8
Brewers Cl IP27 109 C6
Brewers Gn La IP22 20 B3
Brewhouse La 19 CB7 28 D4
Breydon Way
Gainsborough IP3 144 C7
Lowestoft NR33 114 F6
Briar Cl
Halesworth IP19 118 C4
Lowestoft NR32 113 B5
Briar Hill IP30 50 D1
Briar La IP22 35 F5
Briar Rd 39 IP20 22 D6
Briardale Ave 4 CO12 106 F2
Briarhayes Cl IP2 139 B3
Briarwood Ave IP33 122 D5
Briarwood Rd
Lowestoft NR33 114 F5
Woodbridge IP12 146 E3
Brices Way 4 CO10 77 A3
Bricett Bsns Pk IP7 80 E6
Bricett Gn IP7 80 D5
Brick Kiln Ave NR34 111 C4
Brick Kiln Cl 15 IP11 107 D8
Brick Kiln Hill CO6 93 C2
Brick Kiln La
Huntingfield IP19 40 F4
Melton IP12 147 E7
Brick Kiln Rd
Ellingham NR35 8 C8
Harkstead IP9 106 B6
Mildenhall IP28 116 D5
Brick La
Framlingham IP13 126 D1
Parham IP13 71 A7
Brickfield Cl IP2 155 C1
Brickfields Ave CB8 120 D7
Brickfields The IP14 124 C6
Brickkiln La IP22 19 C3
Brickman's Hill CO11 105 B2
Bridewell Cl IP28 116 B4
Bridewell La
Botesdale IP22 36 A6
Bury St Edmunds IP33 154 C2
Bridewell St CO10 90 B8
Bridge Cl 16 IP20 22 D6
Bridge Cottage* CO7 151 D1
Bridge End Rd IP28 30 B1
Bridge Foot Cnr IP18 119 C7
Bridge Pk (Skate Park)* IP1 155 B1
Bridge Rd
Bromeswell IP12 85 A6
Burston & Shimpling IP22 20 E7
Felixstowe IP11 153 A5
Levington IP10 145 E4
Lowestoft NR32 112 E1
Reydon IP18 119 C7
6 Scole IP21 20 F1
Snape IP17 72 D4
Bridge St Beccles NR34 111 A7
Brandon IP27 5 F2
Bungay NR35 110 B4
4 Bures Hamlet CO8 101 C5
Carlton IP17 128 D6
Framlingham IP13 126 C3
Hadleigh IP7 149 C7
Halesworth IP19 118 B4
Huntingfield IP19 41 A4
Ipswich IP1 155 B2
Moulton CB8 45 F3
Needham Market IP6 125 D5
Stowmarket IP14 124 F5
Thetford IP24 16 B5
Bridge St Rd CO10 78 A4
Bridge Terr 7 CO10 148 D6
Bridge Wood Nature Reserve* IP3 144 B6
Bridgeman Wlk IP32 122 E7
Bridgewood Rd IP12 146 E5
Bridgham La NR16 17 F8
Bridgwater Rd IP2 138 D2
Bridlemere Ct CB8 120 F3
Bridles The 4 NR34 111 F4
Bridport Ave IP3 140 D3
Bright Cl
Bury St Edmunds IP33 123 C3
Saxmundham IP17 128 B4
Bright's La CO10 78 C4
Brighton St 3 IP27 14 A3
Brights Wlk IP5 141 E7
Brightwell Cl IP11 152 C4
Brimstone Rd IP8 142 E8
Brindles The 7 NR33 114 E4
Brinkley Rd Brinkley CB8 59 E1
Carlton CB8 74 A8
Dullingham CB8 59 F4
Brinkley Way IP11 153 D7
Brisbane Rd IP4 140 D6
Briscoe Way IP27 109 C8
Bristol Hill IP9 107 A4
Bristol Rd
Bury St Edmunds IP33 122 E3
Ipswich IP4 140 A7
Bristol St 5 IP27 14 A2
Britannia Prim Sch IP4 140 B5
Britannia Rd IP4 140 B6
Britten Ave IP14 124 C7
Britten Cl IP15 130 D5
Britten Ctr The NR32 113 D1
Britten Rd NR33 115 A6
Brittons Cres 3 IP29 47 A2
Brittons Rd 4 IP29 47 A2
Broad Fleet Cl 2 NR32 112 E4
Broad Gn Cl 4 IP29 62 C6
Broad La CO6 102 E1
Broad Meadow
2 Ipswich IP8 138 C2
2 Walsham le Willows IP31 35 C2
Broad Oaks CO6 102 B8
Broad Piece CB7 28 C5
Broad Rd Cotton IP14 52 A6
Little Thurlow CB9 74 F6
Lowestoft NR32 112 D1
Wickham Market IP13 127 B7
Broad St Boxford CO10 93 C3
Bungay NR35 110 A5
Eye IP23 117 C2
20 Harleston IP20 22 D6
Haverhill CB9 132 D6
Orford IP12 131 C2
Broad View Rd NR32 114 C8
Broad Way IP21 21 A4
Broadcroft Cres CB9 132 C6
Broadfields Rd 5 IP23 36 D2
Broadland Cl
Beccles NR34 111 E4
Lowestoft NR33 114 C7
Broadland Rd IP33 123 B1
Broadlands Way IP4 140 F5
Broadmere Rd IP1 138 E8
Broadoak Cl 4 NR33 114 C4
Broads Rd CB5 44 B8
Broads Rd Bsns Pk CB5 44 B7
Broadwater Gdns 6 IP9 107 A4
Broadwaters Rd NR33 114 E5
Broadway
6 Fressingfield IP21 39 E8
11 Glemsford CO10 77 A3
Pakenham IP31 49 F8
Wickham Market IP13 127 B7
Broadway Dr IP19 118 C6
Broadway The
Badwell Ash IP31 50 F8
Wickham Skeith IP23 52 D8
Brock La IP13 146 C2
Brockdish Prim Sch IP21 22 A2
Brockesby Wlk IP33 122 D4
Brockford Rd IP14 52 F4
Brockley Cres IP1 134 D1
Brockley La IP29 46 F2
Brockley Rd
Hartest IP29 77 A8
Whepstead IP29 63 B4
Brocks Bsns Ctr CB9 132 C3
Broke Ave IP8 134 B2
Broke Hall Gdns IP3 140 D4
Broke Hall Prim Sch IP4 140 E5
Brome Ave IP23 117 D5
Brome Hall La IP23 117 E7
Bromelands IP23 117 E8
Bromeswell Gn Nature Reserve* IP12 147 F7
Bromeswell Rd IP4 135 E1
Bromley Cl 4 IP2 139 C3
Bromley Rd CO11 104 D1
Bronyon Cl IP33 122 C5
Brook Cl
Horringer IP29 122 B1
Hundon CO10 75 D3
Lowestoft NR33 114 D4
Stowmarket IP14 124 B7
Brook Dam La 22 CB7 28 D4
Brook Dr 3 IP17 56 F8
Brook Farm La 4 IP9 105 E7
Brook Farm Rd IP17 128 B4
Brook Hall Rd CO10 93 C3
Brook House Rd IP14 52 B6
Brook La Burgate IP22 36 E7
Capel St Mary IP9 150 C4
Felixstowe IP11 153 B5
Framlingham IP13 126 B3
Mickfield IP14 53 A2
Needham IP20 22 B4
Playford IP6 137 A4
St Margaret, Ilketshall NR35 24 C7
Trimley St Martin IP10 98 E1
Brook Rd NR34 10 B4
Brook Service Rd 1 CB9 132 E5
Brook St Dedham CO7 103 F4
Glemsford CO10 77 A3
Soham CB7 28 D3
Woodbridge IP12 147 A5
Yoxford IP17 57 D7
Brook Way IP8 81 C3
Brooke Bsns & Ind Pk NR33 115 A8
Brookfield Rd IP1 138 F8
Brookfields Cl CB8 121 B5
Brookhill Way IP4 140 F4
Brookhouse Bsns Pk IP2 138 F6
Brooklands Cl IP33 154 A1
Brooklands Rd CO11 104 E4
Brooklands Rise CO11 104 E4
Brooklyn Rd 14 CO12 107 B2
Brooks Castle IP13 126 C3
Brooks Hall Rd IP1 139 A7
Brooksfield 1 IP7 79 F4
Brookside Dalham CB8 61 C8
Moulton CB8 45 F3
Brookview Ipswich IP2 142 E8
Pinewood IP2 138 E1
Brookwood Cl 7 NR34 9 F4
Broom Cres IP3 139 F1
Broom Field 5 IP11 152 E5
Broom Hill La IP24 33 E7
Broom Hill Nature Reserve* IP7 149 C5
Broom Hill Rd IP1 139 A8
Broom Hill Swimming Pool IP1 139 A8
Broom Knoll 1 CO11 104 E5
Broom Rd
Lakenheath IP27 109 E5
2 Lowestoft NR32 113 B2
Broom Rd Cl IP27 109 E5
Broom St CO10 148 F3
Broom Way IP9 150 E4
Broom Wlk 9 IP28 30 B8
Broomfield
Martlesham IP5 141 F7
17 Martlesham Heath IP5 98 A8
Broomfield Comm IP8 138 B6
Broomfield Mews 18 IP5 98 A8
Broomhayes IP2 139 A2
Broomheath IP12 146 F2
Broomhill Cl 2 IP28 30 C1
Broomhill La IP30 50 C1
Broomley Gn Rd IP32 123 F6
Broomspath Rd IP14 67 A6
Brotherton Ave IP11 152 B8
Broughton Rd IP1 155 A4
Brown St IP14 52 A3
Browning Rd
10 Brantham CO11 104 E4
Ipswich IP1 134 F3
Brownlow Rd IP11 153 A4
Browns Cl 2 Acton CO10 92 B7
Hitcham IP7 79 E6
5 Wickhambrook CB8 61 E2
Browns Gr IP5 141 D7
Browse Cl IP32 123 E4
Browston La NR32 2 E7
Broxtead Cl IP12 85 C2
Bruce St NR33 115 C7

Brudenell Cl IP15 ....130 E3
Bruges Cl 14 CO12 ....107 A1
Bruisyard Rd IP13 ....56 C3
Bruisyard Vineyard*
  IP17 ....56 C5
Brundon La CO10 ....148 A5
Brunel Rd IP2 ....138 E6
Brunel Way IP24 ....16 B7
Brunswick House Cut 13
  CO11 ....105 A2
Brunswick Rd IP4 ....135 F1
Brunwyn Cl IP32 ....123 F6
Brussels Cl 15 CO12 ....107 A1
Brybank Rd CB9 ....132 A7
Bryon Ave IP11 ....152 B2
Bryony Cl Haverhill CB9 ..132 C7
  6 Lowestoft NR33 ......114 F3
Buck La IP23 ....117 E8
Buckanay La IP12 ....99 E5
Buckenham Ct 17 IP18 ..119 D5
Buckenham Rd IP7 ......149 F4
Buckfast Cl 4 IP2 ....28 C5
Buckingham Cl 4 IP12 ...84 A1
Buckingham Rd CB9 .....132 C4
Buckingham's Hill IP12 ..39 E8
Buckles Field IP11 ....35 F2
Bucklesham Prim Sch
  IP10 ....98 B4
Bucklesham Rd
  Ipswich IP3 ....140 E2
  Kirton IP10 ....98 D3
Buckleswood Rd IP16 ...129 A7
Bucknam Cl 16 NR33 ....11 C1
Buck's Head La IP6 ......67 F2
Buck's Horns La IP8 ....142 B6
Bucks La 7 CO10 ....90 A8
Buckshorn La IP23 ......117 D2
Buddleia Cl IP2 ....138 E4
Bude Cl IP5 ....141 A6
Bugg's La
  Brettenham IP7 ....65 D1
  Hitcham IP7 ....79 D8
Bugg's Rd IP22 ....36 D6
Buggs Hole La IP22 ......18 D2
Bugsby Way IP5 ....141 E7
Bulcamp Drift IP19 ......43 A7
Bull Dr IP5 ....141 C6
Bull Hall La IP6 ....83 A5
Bull La Acton CO10 ......63 C5
  Hawstead IP29 ....63 C5
  Long Melford CO10 ......91 E8
  Rickinghall Superior IP22 .36 B4
Bull Rd IP31 ....49 F6
Bull Rush Cres IP33 ....154 A4
Bullace La IP12 ....131 A8
Bullen La 5 IP8 ....134 A2
Bull's Ash Cnr IP7 ......26 F5
Bull's Rd IP6 ....82 C7
Bullen Cl Bramford IP8 ..134 A2
  Bury St Edmunds IP33 ..154 A1
Bullen La 5 IP8 ....134 A2
Bullens Cl IP33 ....122 A5
Buller Rd IP16 ....129 C6
Bullfinch Cl 12 CO10 ....106 F1
Bullion's La 4 NR34 .....26 B2
Bullock Fair Cl 14 IP20 ..22 D6
Bullocks Cl CO10 ....148 C5
Bullockshead La 7 CO10 .43 D2
Bull's Wood Nature Reserve*
  IP30 ....64 E1
Bullshall Rd 6 IP23 ......37 F1
Bullswood La IP30 ......64 D1
Bulmer La CO10 ....93 C4
Bulmer Rd CO10 ....148 A4
Bulmer Rd Ind Est
  CO10 ....148 A4
Bulmer St Andrews CE Prim
  Sch CO10 ....91 C4
Bulstrode Rd IP2 ....155 C1
Bulwer Rd IP1 ....139 A6
Bumpstead Rd CB9 .....132 F3
Bunbury Ave
  1 Great Barton IP31 ....49 A5
  Mildenhall IP28 ....116 C5
Bunbury Rd 8 IP32 ......48 C5
Bungay Ave
  1 Great Barton IP31 ....49 A5
  Mildenhall IP28 ....116 C5
Bungay Castle (rems)*
  NR35 ....110 A4
Bungay High Sch
  NR35 ....110 C2
Bungay Mid Sch NR35 ..110 D3
Bungay Mus* NR35 ....110 B4
Bungay Prim Sch
  NR35 ....110 C2
Bungay Rd Barsham NR34 .9 B4
  Beccles NR34 ....111 A4
  Dickleburgh & Rushall
  IP21 ....21 B1
  Ellingham NR35 ....8 C8
  Halesworth IP19 ....118 B4
  Scole IP21 ....21 A1
  Stockton NR34 ....8 F8
Bunker Cl NR33 ....115 A5
Bunn's La IP22 ....22 C6
Bunters Rd 8 CB8 ......61 E2
Bunting Rd
  Bury St Edmunds IP32 ..123 F4
  Ipswich IP2 ....138 D3
Buntings Cres 15 CB5 ....44 A6
Buntings Path CB5 ......44 A6
Buntry La CO10 ....75 C2
Bunyan Cl IP1 ....135 A3
Burch's Cl IP17 ....129 A2
Burdock La IP26 ....4 C3
Buregate Rd 4 IP12 ....152 F2

Bures Cl IP14 ....124 E4
Bures Ct 6 CB9 ....132 C5
Bures Prim Sch CO8 ....101 C4
Bures Rd
  Little Cornard CO10 ....101 A8
  Nayland-with-Wissington
  CO6 ....101 A4
  Sudbury CO10 ....148 E2
Bures Sta CO8 ....101 C4
Burgate Rd
  Gislingham IP23 ....36 D3
  Mellis IP23 ....46 E3
Burgess Cl 8 NR32 .....115 D7
Burgess Pl 2 IP5 ....98 A8
Burgh Rd NR34 ....2 C1
Burghley Cl 14 IP2 .....139 A2
Burghley Rise 5 CB5 ....44 B5
Burke Cl IP1 ....135 A3
Burke Rd 7 IP1 ....135 A3
Burkitt Rd IP12 ....146 E4
Burkitts La CO10 ....148 C5
Burlingham Dr NR33 ....114 B3
Burlington Rd IP1 ......155 A3
Burnet Cl IP8 ....142 D8
Burnham Cl
  Felixstowe IP11 ....152 C7
  Ipswich IP4 ....139 F7
Burnham Way NR33 ....115 A1
Burns Cl IP23 ....37 B5
Burns Rd IP1 ....134 E3
Burnt Cl CO10 ....102 E4
Burnthouse La
  Battisford IP14 ....66 D1
  Needham IP20 ....22 B4
Burnt Hill La NR33 .....114 B7
Burnt Hill Way NR33 ...114 C5
Burnt House Cl 3 CB9 ..132 A2
Burnt House La IP19 ....98 D2
Burnt La IP12 ....131 C2
Burnt Oak Cnr IP7 .....151 D3
Burrell Rd IP2 ....155 B1
Burrell Way IP27 ....16 A5
Burrell's Orch IP33 ....122 A6
Burroughs Gn CE Prim Sch
  CB8 ....59 F2
Burroughs Piece Rd 2
  CO10 ....148 D5
Burrow Dr CO10 ....109 C8
Burrows Cl 5 CO11 ....104 D2
Burrows Gn NR34 ......2 A1
Burrows Rd 7 IP12 .....84 E6
Burstall Hall La IP8 ....95 E7
Burstall La IP8 ....95 C7
Burston Com Prim Sch
  IP22 ....20 E6
Burston Rd
  Dickleburgh & Rushall
  IP21 ....20 F4
  Diss IP22 ....20 D4
  Gissing IP22 ....20 F7
Burton Cl CB9 ....132 C5
Burton Dr IP6 ....125 C5
Burton End CB9 ....132 C5
Burton End Com Prim Sch
  CB9 ....132 B5
Burton Hill CB9 ....74 B3
Burton St NR32 ....113 D2
Burwash 1 IP6 ....83 A5
Burwell Mus* CB5 .....44 B5
Burwell Rd CB8 ....120 A8
Burwood Pl
  7 Lowestoft NR32 .....113 B6
  Trimley St Mary IP11 ...152 C8
Bury Bottom IP27 ......15 A5
Bury Hill IP12 ....147 A7
Bury Hill Cl IP12 ......147 A7
Bury La Lidgate CB8 ....61 C4
  Moulton CB8 ....45 F3
  Stanton IP31 ....34 E3
  Wickhambrook CB8 ....61 E4
Bury Language Sch The
  IP33 ....154 C2
Bury Pk Dr IP33 ....123 C2
Bury Rd Alpheton CO10 .78 A5
  Barrow IP29 ....47 A2
  Beyton IP30 ....49 A2
  Botesdale IP22 ....36 B7
  Bradfield St Clare IP30 ..64 C4
  Brandon IP27 ....14 F8
  Brettenham IP7 ....79 C7
  Brockley IP29 ....63 A2
  Chedburgh IP29 ....62 D4
  Felsham IP30 ....65 A4
  Flempton IP28 ....47 F8
  Great Barton IP31 .....49 A5
  Great Thurlow CB9 ....74 F5
  Great Whelnetham IP30 .63 F4
  Haughley IP14 ....66 D7
  Hengrave IP28 ....48 A7
  Hepworth IP22 ....34 D4
  Ipswich IP1 ....134 D4
  Kentford CB8 ....46 B5
  Lavenham CO10 ....78 D5
  Lawshall IP29 ....63 D2
  Market Weston IP22 ....18 B1
  Mildenhall IP28 ....116 E4
  Newmarket CB8 ....121 C5
  Rickinghall Inferior IP22 .35 F5
  Stanton IP31 ....34 F4
  Stowmarket IP14 ......124 C8
  Thetford IP24 ....16 B3
  Thorpe Morieux IP30 ...64 E2

Bury Rd continued
  Wickhambrook CB8 .....61 F1
  Wortham IP22 ....36 E8
Bury St 3 IP14 ....124 D6
Bury St Edmunds Abbey*
  IP33 ....154 C2
Bury St Edmunds Abbey
  Gdns* IP33 ....154 C2
Bury St Edmunds Art Gall*
  IP33 ....154 B2
Bury St Edmunds Leisure Ctr
  IP33 ....154 B4
Bury St Edmunds Sta
  IP32 ....154 B4
Bury St Edmunds Upper Sch
  IP32 ....154 A4
Bush Cnr IP14 ....53 E1
Bush Gr CO10 ....148 A6
Bushel La CB7 ....28 D4
Bushey Cl IP9 ....150 E3
Bushman Gdns 3 IP8 ...134 A2
Bushy La IP17 ....99 E7
Bussock La IP12 ....99 D7
Buston Rd 5 IP22 ......20 B2
Butcher's La CO10 .....93 C4
Butcher's Rd IP17 .....150 F3
Butchers La IP9 ....150 F3
Bute Ct CB9 ....132 D4
Butfield CO10 ....78 D3
Butler Smith Gdns 6
  IP5 ....141 C7
Butler's La CO11 ......105 F1
Butlers Way CO9 ....90 A1
Butley Cl IP2 ....142 F8
Butley Ct 3 CB9 ....132 C3
Butley Dr 8 NR32 .....112 F3
Butley Mill* IP12 ......86 B6
Butley Rd IP11 ....152 E3
Butt Rd
  Stoke-by-Nayland CO6 ..102 E7
  Sudbury CO10 ....148 F4
Butt's Rd Holton IP19 ..118 D8
  Spexhall IP19 ....25 A4
Butter Mkt
  Bury St Edmunds IP33 ..154 B2
  Ipswich IP1 ....155 B3
Buttercup Cl
  Bury St Edmunds IP32 ..123 F5
  Ipswich IP8 ....138 C1
  3 Lowestoft NR33 .....114 C4
Butterfly Gdns IP4 ....140 E5
Buttermarket Sh Ctr
  IP1 ....155 B3
Buttermere Gn IP11 ...153 D6
Button's Rd IP13 ......71 D6
Buttrum's Mill* IP12 ..146 E5
Butts The
  Debenham IP14 ....53 E2
  Soham CB7 ....28 D3
Buxhall Musuem*
  IP14 ....66 A5
Buxlow CI IP17 ....129 B2
Byfield Way IP33 ......123 C3
Byford Rd CO10 ....148 A3
Bylam La IP9 ....106 A7
Byland Cl 6 IP2 ....139 A2
Byng Hall Rd
  Pettistree IP13 ....84 E8
  Ufford IP13 ....127 A1
Byng La IP33 ....122 C4
Byrd Cl IP33 ....122 C4
Byron Rd IP1 ....134 E4

C

Cabin Cl NR33 ....114 B4
Cable La IP15 ....130 E5
Caddie's Wlk NR33 ....115 A5
Cadiz Way 1 NR31 .....3 C6
Cadmus Rd IP1 ....138 D7
Cadney La IP33 ....154 B3
Cadogan Rd IP33 .....122 D4
Caernarvon Wlk 4 CB9 .132 C6
Cage La Boxted CO4 ...103 A3
  Felixstowe IP11 ....152 E5
Cages Way 1 IP8 ......44 E6
Cagman's La IP14 .....65 F3
Caie Wlk IP4 ....123 D2
Caithness Cl IP4 ......140 B8
Cake St IP13 ....39 F4
Cakebridge La IP7 ....79 D3
Calais St IP7 ....44 C4
Caldecott Rd IP12 ....112 D1
Calder Rd 6 IP22 .....48 C6
Caledonia Rd 6 IP9 ...107 A4
Calfe Fen Cl 3 CB7 ...28 D5
Calfe Fen Dro CB7 ....28 D5
Calford Dr CB9 ....132 A6
California IP21 ....146 D3
California La IP8 ......95 B4
California Rd 14 CO11 .105 A2
Calkewood La IP22 ...35 E5
Callis St 5 CO10 ......90 A8
Calthorpe Cl IP32 ....123 E6
Calves La CO6 ....102 D8
Camberley Cl IP33 ....153 A3
Camberley Rd IP4 ....140 D7
Camborne Rd IP5 .....141 B7
Cambria 9 CO11 ......105 A2
Cambrian Cres 2 NR32 .112 D2
Cambridge Cl CB9 ....132 C7
Cambridge Dr IP2 ....138 E1
Cambridge Rd
  Felixstowe IP11 ....153 B4
  Ipswich IP5 ....141 A7
  Lowestoft NR32 ....113 D3

Cambridge Way
  6 Bures CO8 ....101 C4
  Haverhill CB9 ....132 C7
Camden Rd IP3 ....140 B4
Camden St 5 NR32 ...113 D3
Camp Cl 6 IP26 ....4 D5
Camp Rd NR32 ....113 D1
Campbell Cl 1 IP28 ...116 B5
Campbell Rd IP3 ......140 C1
Campion Cl CB7 ......28 C5
Campion Cres IP14 ...124 C4
Campion La CO6 ......102 B6
Campion Rd CO10 ....148 A6
Campion Way CO6 ....102 B7
Campions Hill CO6 ...102 B5
Camps Rd
  Haverhill CB9 ....132 D5
  Helions Bumpstead CB9 .88 A5
Camwood Gdns IP3 ...140 B4
Canaletto Cl 4 NR32 ..113 B6
Canberra Cl
  Ipswich IP4 ....140 D6
  2 Mildenhall IP28 ....30 A8
Canberra Rd IP3 .....140 C1
Candler's La IP19 ....22 C6
Candlet Gr IP11 ......152 F5
Candlet Rd IP11 ......152 E7
Cangle Junc 18 CB9 ..132 B6
Cangles La IP10 ......49 F1
Canham St IP1 ....155 A3
Canhams Rd CO10 ...148 F3
Cannon St IP33 ......154 B3
Cannonfields IP33 ...154 B3
Canon Cl CB9 ....132 D7
Canon Pugh Dr 6 CO10 .92 B7
Canonbury
  Ipswich IP2 ....142 F8
  7 Lakenheath IP27 ...14 A2
Canterbury Gdns IP7 .149 E6
Canterbury Rd IP24 ..16 B6
Canterbury Way IP24 .16 B6
Capel Cl
  4 Felixstowe IP11 ....107 C5
  Troston IP31 ....33 D3
Capel Dr IP11 ....152 C4
Capel Hall La IP11 ...107 E8
Capel St Mary CE Prim Sch
  IP9 ....150 E3
Capel's Cl IP9 ....95 F4
Copdock IP7 ....95 F4
Capell Wlk 2 IP31 ....34 E4
Capps La IP19 ....23 F5
Capstan Way NR33 ...114 B4
Captain's La IP12 ....51 A2
Caraway Rd IP24 .....16 B4
Carbonells 12 CO10 ..92 C6
Carders Cl IP7 ....149 D4
Cardew Dr IP5 ....141 D8
Cardiff Ave IP12 .....139 B1
Cardigan St
  Ipswich IP1 ....155 A4
  Newmarket CB8 ......121 A3
Cardinal Cl IP32 .....123 E6
Cardinal Pk 2 IP1 ....155 B2
Cardinal St IP1 ....155 B2
Cardinal Way CB9 ...132 D7
Cardinalls Rd IP14 ...124 D7
Carford Cl 14 IP5 ....95 A8
Carlow Mews 13 IP12 .147 A5
Carlton Cl
  Great Yeldham CO9 ...90 A1
  Haverhill CB9 ....132 C5
Carlton Colville Cty Prim Sch
  NR33 ....114 B2
Carlton Cross NR33 ..114 C2
Carlton Gn Rd CB8 ...74 A7
Carlton Marshes Nature
  Reserve* NR33 ....114 A7
Carlton Pk Ind Est
  IP17 ....128 C5
Carlton Rd Brinkley CB8 .59 F1
  Carlton IP17 ....128 C5
  Ipswich IP5 ....141 A7
  Lowestoft NR33 ......115 B6
Carlton Sq NR33 .....114 C2
Carlton Way IP4 .....139 E8
Carlton Wlk IP17 ....149 E4
Carlyle Cl IP1 ....134 F4
Carmarthen Cl IP2 ..139 A2
Carmelite Pl 18 IP12 .147 A5
Carnation Way 2 IP28 .46 A8
Carnoustie Dr
  18 Fornham St Martin IP28 .48 C6
  Lowestoft NR33 ......114 F4
Carol Ave 9 IP12 ....84 A1
Carol Cl IP11 ....153 C5
Carolbrook Rd IP2 ...138 E1
Carr Ave IP16 ....129 D6
Carr Rd IP11 ....152 E1
Carr St IP4 ....155 C3
Carriage Cl IP11 .....152 E5
Carriers Ct CO7 .....151 D5
Carrops The CB8 .....46 A7
Carrs Hill IP13 ......56 B6
Carson Wlk CB8 .....120 F6
Carsons Dr IP28 .....92 B3
Cart Score NR33 .....113 E3
Carter Rd CB5 ....44 A6
Carter St IP7 ....29 B1
Carters Hill CO4 .....103 A3
Carters La IP14 ......80 E6
Carters Teapot Pottery*
  IP17 ....53 F1
Carters Vineyard*
  CO4 ....102 F3
Casburn La 13 CB5 ...44 A6

Case La IP9 ....104 E8
Castle Ave CB9 ....132 C6
Castle Brooks IP6 ....126 B3
Castle Cl
  Felixstowe IP11 ......153 D6
  Orford IP12 ....131 B2
  Weeting-with-Broomhill
  IP27 ....5 E3
Castle Hill
  Beccles NR34 ....111 C4
  Dedham CO7 ....103 F2
  Eye IP23 ....117 D2
  Eyke IP12 ....90 B6
  Halesworth IP19 .....118 C3
  Orford IP12 ....131 C2
  Thornden IP23 ....37 E1
Castle Hill Inf Sch
  IP1 ....135 A3
Castle Hill Jun Sch
  IP1 ....135 A3
Castle Hill Mid Sch
  CB9 ....132 B6
Castle La Bungay NR35 .110 A4
  Hadleigh IP7 ....149 C7
  Haverhill CB9 ....132 C6
  Offton IP8 ....81 A4
  Orford IP12 ....131 C2
Castle Manor Bsns &
  Enterprise Coll CB9 ...132 C6
Castle Meadow IP7 ...81 A4
Castle Orch NR35 ....110 B4
Castle Rd
  Bury St Edmunds IP33 .154 A1
  Hadleigh IP7 ....149 B7
  Ipswich IP1 ....134 E1
  Mettingham NR35 ....110 F2
  Offton IP8 ....81 A4
Castle Rise
  Hadleigh IP7 ....149 B7
  2 Haughley IP14 .....51 C1
Castle St Eye IP23 ...117 D2
  Framlingham IP13 ...126 D4
  Thetford IP24 ....16 C5
  Woodbridge IP12 ....147 A5
Castle Terr IP12 .....131 C2
Castle View IP12 ....131 C2
Castleton Ave NR33 ..114 B4
Castleton Cl 5 NR32 ..113 B4
Castleton Way
  Eye IP23 ....117 B3
  Yaxley IP23 ....37 E5
Catchpole Cl 10 NR33 .11 B1
Catchpole Ct CO10 ..148 B5
Catchpole Way 10 NR33 .34 E4
Catchpole Wlk IP21 ..21 C5
Caters Rd IP33 ....84 C8
Catesbray IP9 ....150 D3
Cathcart St 8 NR32 ..113 D2
Cathedral Meadows
  IP33 ....154 B1
Catherine Rd IP4 ....146 E4
Catkin Cl CB9 ....132 B7
Cat's La CO10 ....148 C5
Cattawade St 12 CO11 .104 E4
Catts Cl IP9 ....105 C5
Cattsfield IP7 ....105 C5
Cauldwell Ave IP4 ...139 F6
Cauldwell Hall Rd IP4 .140 A5
Caulfield Cl IP33 ....122 F3
Causeway
  Haverhill CB9 ....132 C5
  Huntingfield IP19 ....40 F5
  Lowestoft NR33 .....115 B4
Causeway Cl
  Brockdish IP21 ......21 F2
  8 Glemsford CO10 ...77 B3
Causeway End CO11 ..104 D3
Causeway Est IP27 ...79 F7
Causeway The
  Barking IP6 ....125 B2
  Boxford CO10 ....93 C3
  Burwell CB5 ....44 A5
  Great Horkesley CO6 .102 D1
  Hitcham IP7 ....79 E6
  Isleham CB7 ....29 C5
  Middleton IP17 .....58 A9
  Needham Market IP6 .125 D4
  4 Occold IP23 ......37 F1
  Ridgewell CO9 ......89 B7
  Soham CB7 ....28 D3
  Walsham le Willows IP31 .35 B2
  Westhall IP19 ....25 C4
Causton Jun Sch IP11 .152 E6
Caustons Cl 9 CO10 ..92 B3
Cautley Rd IP18 .....119 D6
Cavan Rd IP1 ....134 D2
Cavendish CE Prim Sch
  CO10 ....76 C1
Cavendish Cl
  7 Lowestoft NR32 ...113 A3
  12 Thurstow IP31 ...49 E4
Cavendish Ct 2 CB9 ..132 C4
Cavendish Dr 21 CO11 .104 D2
Cavendish La CO10 ..76 F2
Cavendish Rd
  Bury St Edmunds IP33 .122 C6
  Clare CO10 ....90 B8
  Felixstowe IP11 .....152 F3
  Stowmarket IP14 ...124 B6
Cavendish St 3 IP3 ..139 F4
Cavendish Way 1 CO10 .148 D5
Cavenham Heath National
  Nature Reserve*
  IP28 ....31 C3
Cavenham Rd IP28 ...31 A1

Caville White CB9 ....132 A6
Cawley Rd CO6 ....102 A5
Caxton Mews 4 NR34 ....111 B6
Caxton Rd NR34 ....111 B6
Cecil Lodge CI CB8 ....120 F3
Cecil Rd IP1 ....155 B2
Cecilia St IP1 ....155 B2
Cedar Ave IP1 ....141 A6
Cedar CI Bacton IP14 ....51 F6
  7 Brantham CO11 ....104 E5
  8 Great Bricett IP7 ....80 D6
  32 Lakenheath IP27 ....13 F2
  Occold IP23 ....37 F2
  Stradbroke IP21 ....39 B4
Cedar Cres
  15 Barrow IP29 ....47 A2
  30 Manningtree CO11 ....104 D2
Cedar Ct Alderton IP12 ....99 E5
  16 Beck Row, Holywell
  Row & Kenny Hill IP28 ....13 B1
Cedar Dr
  Lowestoft NR33 ....114 E5
  Worlingham NR34 ....111 F3
Cedar Rd 1 Barrow IP29 ....47 A2
  2 Bentwaters Airfield IP12 ....85 E8
Cedarcroft Rd IP1 ....134 F2
Cedars La IP9 ....150 D3
Cedars The IP27 ....129 C5
Cedarwood Prim Sch
  IP5 ....141 C6
Celandine CI NR33 ....114 C5
Cemetery Hill CB8 ....120 D7
Cemetery La
  East Bergholt CO7 ....151 A4
  Ipswich IP4 ....135 F1
  Woodbridge IP12 ....146 E4
Cemetery Rd
  Ipswich IP4 ....155 C3
  Lakenheath IP27 ....109 D6
  Wickhambrook CB8 ....61 E2
Central Ave IP3 ....144 D8
Central Rd IP16 ....129 C5
Centre CI NR34 ....111 C3
Centre Cliff IP18 ....119 D5
Centre Dr CB8 ....121 D2
Centre CI IP7 ....28 E2
Century Dr IP5 ....141 E7
Century Rd IP3 ....117 C4
Chadacre Rd IP29 ....77 B7
Chaffinch Dr 14 CO12 ....106 F1
Chaffinch Rd IP32 ....49 A3
Chaffinch Way IP14 ....124 F7
Chailey Pieces CB9 ....132 D5
Chainhouse Rd IP6 ....125 D3
Chalfont Dr 3 IP1 ....72 C8
Chalk Hill La IP6 ....81 E5
  2 Ixworth IP31 ....34 B1
Chalk Rd (North)
  IP33 ....154 A2
Chalk Rd (South)
  IP33 ....154 A2
Chalk Rd IP27 ....5 D1
Chalkeith Rd IP6 ....125 E3
Chalkners CI IP32 ....150 E3
Chalkstone Mid Sch
  CB9 ....132 E6
Chalkstone Way CB9 ....133 A6
Chalice Rd IP33 ....154 A3
Chalon St IP1 ....155 A2
Chamberlain Way IP8 ....138 C2
Chamberlayne Rd
  IP32 ....123 E4
Chamberlin CI 2 IP27 ....79 F4
Champion Rd IP15 ....130 E3
Chancellery Mews
  IP32 ....154 A3
Chancery La 5 IP14 ....53 F2
Chancery Rd IP11 ....155 A2
Chandlers Ct 8 CB5 ....44 A6
Chandlers Way IP16 ....129 C3
Chandlers Wlk IP14 ....124 D4
Chandos Ct 3 IP12 ....84 A1
Chandos Dr 5 IP12 ....84 A1
Channel The IP8 ....81 C1
Chantry CI IP11 ....71 C2
Chantry Gn IP21 ....138 D3
Chantry High Sch IP8 ....138 F3
Chantry Rd IP27 ....128 C3
Chapel CI
  Capel St Mary IP9 ....150 E3
  4 Fressingfield IP21 ....39 E8
  Rushbrooke IP28 ....18 D4
  8 Great Waldingfield CO10 ....92 C6
Chapel CI 10 NR32 ....113 D2
Chapel Cut CB11 ....105 A2
Chapel End Way CO9 ....89 A1
Chapel Farm La IP23 ....37 A4
Chapel Field IP14 ....134 A2
Chapel Hill
  Belchamp Walter CO10 ....90 E3
  Framsden IP14 ....69 B7
  Thorpe Morieux IP30 ....79 A8
Chapel La Belstead IP8 ....142 C6
  Botesdale IP22 ....36 A6
  4 Brockley IP29 ....63 A1
  Claydon IP6 ....134 A4
  Copdock & Washbrook
  IP8 ....138 A1
  Drinkstone IP30 ....65 F7
  Great Glemham IP17 ....56 D1
  13 Grundisburgh IP13 ....83 E5
  Horham IP21 ....38 A8
  Kirby Row NR35 ....8 E7
  Kirtling CB8 ....60 E3
  Little Cornard CO10 ....92 B1
  2 Somersham IP8 ....81 C3

Chapel La continued
  Stoke-by-Nayland CO6 ....103 B7
  Wenhaston with Mells Hamlet
  IP19 ....42 C6
  Wicken CB7 ....28 A1
  Wickham Market IP13 ....127 C5
  Wortham IP22 ....36 D7
Chapel Pond Hill IP32 ....123 C8
Chapel Rd
  Beck Row, Holywell Row
  & Kenny Hill IP28 ....29 F6
  Bedingham NR35 ....7 C8
  Boxted CO4 ....103 A2
  Bradfield Combust with
  Stanningfield IP29 ....64 A3
  Bucklesham IP10 ....98 A6
  Cockfield IP30 ....64 D2
  Grundisburgh IP13 ....83 E5
  Langham CO4 ....103 B2
  Lowestoft NR33 ....114 B3
  Mendlesham IP14 ....52 E5
  Mutford NR34 ....10 D3
  Old Newton with Dagworth
  IP14 ....52 A1
  Otley IP6 ....69 D3
  Rendham IP17 ....56 E3
  Ridgewell CO9 ....89 D4
  St Andrew, Ilketshall
  NR34 ....8 F2
  Saxmundham IP17 ....128 C3
  Saxtead IP13 ....55 A4
  Scole IP21 ....21 B5
  Stoke Ash IP23 ....37 B2
  Theberton IP16 ....58 C5
  Wattisfield IP22 ....35 C4
  Wrentham NR34 ....26 D5
Chapel Row 3 CB8 ....60 F8
Chapel St 5 Bildeston IP7 ....79 F4
  Diss IP22 ....20 C2
  Exning CB8 ....120 B8
  9 Lowestoft NR32 ....113 D2
  Peasenhall IP17 ....56 F8
  Steeple Bumpstead CB9 ....88 E4
  Stoke-by-Clare CO9 ....89 C6
  Woodbridge IP12 ....147 A5
Chapelfield IP22 ....131 C3
Chaplains CI IP12 ....132 D7
Chaplin Rd CO7 ....151 C5
Chaplin Wlk 16 CO10 ....92 B3
Chappel Rd IP4 ....101 C2
Chapple Dr CB9 ....132 E7
Chare Rd IP31 ....34 D5
Charity La IP13 ....54 D6
Charles Adams CI
  IP16 ....129 D6
Charles Ave 8 IP13 ....83 E5
Charles Burrell High Sch
  IP24 ....16 B4
Charles CI CB8 ....120 E3
Charles Ind Est IP14 ....124 C7
Charles Melrose CI 1
  IP28 ....116 B4
Charles Miller Ct
  IP16 ....129 D5
Charles Rd IP11 ....152 E3
Charles St IP1 ....155 B3
Charlock Rd 5 IP24 ....16 D7
Charlotte's IP4 ....134 F2
Charlton Ave IP1 ....134 F2
Charrington CI IP4 ....133 A4
Charsfield CE Prim Sch
  IP13 ....70 B3
Charter CI IP7 ....149 D7
Charter Way 6 NR33 ....114 F3
Chartres Piece NR34 ....25 E7
Chartwell Cl IP4 ....140 A5
Chase CI CB9 ....132 E7
Chase La 8 CO12 ....106 F1
Chase Rd IP28 ....48 C5
Chase The
  Beccles NR34 ....111 E5
  Brandon IP27 ....6 A1
  Brantham CO11 ....104 F5
  Dedham CO7 ....103 A4
  Felixstowe IP11 ....152 F4
  Foxearth CO10 ....91 B7
  20 Manningtree CO11 ....104 E2
  20 Martlesham Heath IP5 ....98 A8
  3 Stanton IP31 ....34 E4
  Steeple Bumpstead CB9 ....88 D4
Chaser CI 3 IP3 ....144 C8
Chase's La IP17 ....72 F6
Chatham Rd 3 IP27 ....14 A2
Chatsworth Cl 8 NR32 ....113 A1
Chatsworth Cres
  Felixstowe IP11 ....152 C7
  Ipswich IP4 ....139 A2
Chatsworth Dr IP4 ....140 E4
Chatten Cl NR34 ....26 E5
Chattisham CI IP10 ....124 E3
Chattisham Rd IP8 ....95 F4
Chaucer Rd
  Felixstowe IP11 ....152 F3
  Ipswich IP1 ....134 F3
  Sudbury CO10 ....148 B8
Chaucer St NR35 ....110 A4
Chaukers Cres CO10 ....114 C5
Chauntry Rd CB9 ....132 D5
Chedburgh Pl 8 CB9 ....132 F6
Chedburgh Rd
  Chevington IP29 ....62 C5
  Whepstead IP29 ....62 F5
Chedgrave Rd NR33 ....114 F5
Chediston Pottery*
  IP19 ....41 D8
Chediston Rd IP19 ....24 B2
Chediston St
  Chediston IP19 ....41 D8

Chediston St continued
  Halesworth IP19 ....118 A3
Chelmer Rd CB9 ....132 F6
Chelmondiston CE Prim Sch
  IP9 ....106 B8
Chelsea CI
  Bury St Edmunds IP33 ....122 D5
  Ipswich IP1 ....134 F1
Chelsea CI 4 CO10 ....148 D5
Chelsea Rd 3 CO10 ....148 D5
Chelsworth Ave IP1 ....135 E1
Chelsworth Rd IP11 ....152 D3
Chelsworth Way IP14 ....124 E3
Cheltenham Ave IP1 ....135 B1
Chepstow Rd
  Bury St Edmunds IP33 ....122 D3
  Felixstowe IP11 ....152 F5
  Ipswich IP1 ....135 B1
Chequer Field IP2 ....85 C2
Chequer Sq IP33 ....154 C2
Chequers CI
  Bressingham IP22 ....19 E3
  Burston & Shimpling IP22 ....20 E8
  Glemsford CO10 ....77 B3
Chequers CI CO11 ....104 E1
Chequers Rise IP6 ....81 F5
Cherry Blossom CI
  IP8 ....138 B2
Cherry Hill IP18 ....30 E3
Cherry Hill CI 1 NR34 ....111 F4
Cherry La
  Aldeburgh IP15 ....130 D5
  Belton with Browston NR31 ....2 E8
  Lakenheath IP27 ....13 F2
Cherry La Gdns IP14 ....140 B7
Cherry Tree CI
  Mundford IP26 ....6 A8
  North Lopham IP22 ....19 A6
  Yaxley IP23 ....37 B5
Cherry Tree La IP14 ....53 F1
Cherry Tree Rd
  Stowmarket IP14 ....124 C8
  Woodbridge IP12 ....146 F4
Cherry Tree Row 3 IP14 ....35 C2
Cherry Tress Sch IP14 ....47 D5
Cherryfields IP8 ....134 A1
Cherrytree La
  Rickinghall Inferior IP22 ....36 A7
  Soham CB7 ....28 D3
Cherrywood 10 IP20 ....22 D5
Chervil Wlk 8 IP14 ....16 D6
Chesapeake CI 8 IP9 ....106 C8
Chesapeake Rd 3 IP3 ....144 A8
Chesham Rd IP2 ....155 A1
Chessington Gdns IP1 ....138 F8
Chester Ct 8 CB9 ....132 C4
Chester PI 5 IP31 ....49 A5
Chester Rd
  Felixstowe IP11 ....152 F5
  6 Southwold IP18 ....119 D5
Chester St 4 IP27 ....14 A1
Chesterfield Dr IP1 ....134 F2
Chesterton CI IP2 ....138 F1
Chestnut Ave
  Great Bricett IP7 ....80 D6
  Lowestoft NR32 ....112 E2
Chestnut CI
  4 Beccles NR34 ....111 E3
  8 Bentwaters Airfield IP12 ....85 E8
  1 Fornham All Saints IP28 ....48 B6
  Great Barton IP31 ....49 B4
  8 Great Waldingfield CO10 ....92 C6
  Haverhill CB9 ....132 D6
  8 Mildenhall IP28 ....116 D4
  Rushmere St Andrew
  IP5 ....136 E1
  4 Stowupland IP14 ....67 A6
Chestnut Cres
  Chedburgh IP29 ....62 D4
  Lowestoft NR33 ....114 C3
Chestnut Dr
  Claydon IP6 ....134 C8
  6 Soham CB7 ....28 D4
Chestnut Gr 2 IP14 ....124 E5
Chestnut Mews 17
  CO10 ....148 C5
Chestnut Rd
  Dickleburgh IP21 ....21 C5
  Glemsford CO10 ....77 A3
  Pulham St Mary IP21 ....21 F8
  Stradishall CB8 ....75 C6
Chestnut Rise CB5 ....44 A6
Chestnut Way 21 IP7 ....13 F2
Chestnuts The
  5 Great Finborough IP14 ....66 B4
  7 Ipswich IP3 ....138 C2
  Rickinghall Superior IP22 ....36 A6
  Wrentham NR34 ....26 E5
Chevalier Rd IP11 ....153 B4
Chevallier St IP1 ....139 A7
Cheveley Prim Sch CB8 ....60 E7
Cheveley Rd
  Newmarket CB8 ....121 C3
  Woodditton CB8 ....60 E6
Chevington Rd
  Hargrave IP29 ....62 B6
  Horringer IP29 ....63 A7
Cheviot Rd 3 NR32 ....112 D2
Chevy CI 10 CO10 ....106 E1
Cheyne St IP33 ....123 B3
Chichester Dr NR33 ....114 D6
Chichester Rd IP19 ....118 A5
Chickering Rd IP21 ....38 D2
Childer Rd IP14 ....124 D6

Childers CI 1 IP9 ....107 A5
Childers Field 2 IP11 ....152 D5
Chiltern Cres IP11 ....152 E2
Chilton Ave IP14 ....124 C6
Chilton Corn Prim Sch
  IP14 ....124 C7
Chilton Ct CO10 ....148 E5
Chilton Ind Est CO10 ....148 F6
Chilton Lodge Rd
  CO10 ....148 E5
Chilton Rd IP3 ....140 C4
Chilton Way IP14 ....124 B7
Chilton Way Sports Club
  IP14 ....124 A7
Chimer's La IP13 ....70 A4
Chimney Mill Galleries*
  IP19 ....32 C1
Chimney Mills IP28 ....32 C1
Chimswell Way CB9 ....132 A6
Chippenham Fen National
  Nature Reserve* CB7 ....45 A8
Chippenham Rd
  Chippenham IP29 ....29 E2
  Fordham CB7 ....29 C1
  Moulton CB8 ....45 F3
Chipperfield Rd 20 NR33 ....11 C1
Chippings The IP15 ....130 C6
Chiselhurst Rd 5 NR33 ....114 C4
Chisnall CI IP7 ....149 D8
Chiswick Rd IP28 ....116 C6
Chivers Rd CB9 ....132 B5
Christ Church Sq
  NR32 ....113 C1
Christchurch Dr IP12 ....146 D3
Christchurch Mansion*
  IP1 ....155 C3
Christchurch St IP4 ....155 C3
Christmas La
  Lowestoft NR32 ....112 C1
  Metfield IP20 ....23 C3
Christopher Ct 15 CO10 ....148 C5
Christopher La CO10 ....148 C5
Church Ave NR32 ....112 C2
Church CI
  Aldeburgh IP15 ....130 E4
  Bucklesham IP10 ....98 A5
  Carlton IP17 ....128 D7
  4 Cavendish CO10 ....76 E1
  Creeting St Mary IP6 ....125 F8
  Dullingham CB8 ....59 F4
  Exning CB8 ....120 B8
  Fornham St Martin IP28 ....48 D5
  Hepworth IP22 ....35 A5
  Ipswich IP5 ....141 B8
  Kenton IP14 ....54 B4
  Pulham St Mary IP21 ....22 A8
  Rede IP29 ....62 E3
  Risby IP28 ....47 E5
  1 Roydon IP22 ....20 A4
  18 Stanton IP31 ....34 E4
  Wangford NR34 ....26 B2
  Wilby IP21 ....39 C3
  Wortwell IP20 ....22 E7
Church Cres IP8 ....138 A6
Church Dr IP13 ....71 E5
Church Farm CI IP28 ....38 F3
Church Farm La 3
  IP19 ....118 A3
Church Farm Rd
  Aldeburgh IP15 ....130 E5
  Bramfield IP19 ....41 F4
Church Field
  Monks Eleigh IP7 ....79 C2
  Walberswick IP18 ....119 A2
Church Field Rd CO10 ....148 F7
Church Fm Rise IP15 ....130 F5
Church Gdns
  1 Barningham IP31 ....34 E7
  8 Beck Row, Holywell
  Row & Kenny Hill IP28 ....29 F6
Church Gn
  Bramford IP8 ....134 B1
  Normanston NR32 ....113 C3
Church Hill Benhall IP17 ....72 C8
  Burstall IP8 ....95 D7
  Cookley IP19 ....41 C5
  Helions Bumpstead CB9 ....88 B4
  Hoxne IP21 ....38 C8
  Kersey IP7 ....94 A6
  Lawford CO11 ....104 C2
  Monks Eleigh IP7 ....79 C2
  Pakenham IP31 ....49 E6
  Ramsey & Parkeston
  CO12 ....106 D1
  Saxmundham IP17 ....128 D2
  Starston IP20 ....22 C7
  Westhall IP19 ....25 D3
  Whepstead IP29 ....63 B5
  Wyverstone IP14 ....51 E6
Church La
  Aldeby/Wheatacre/Burgh
  St Peter NR34 ....2 B1
  Aldham IP7 ....94 D7
  Aldringham cum Thorpe
  IP16 ....129 C1
  Alpheton CO10 ....77 F5
  Arwarton IP9 ....106 E5
  Barham IP6 ....16 C2
  Barton Mills IP28 ....116 D1
  Baylham IP6 ....81 E6
  Beck Row, Holywell Row
  & Kenny Hill IP28 ....29 F6
  Bedfield IP13 ....54 E5
  Birds End IP29 ....62 A7
  Blo' Norton IP22 ....18 E2
  Blythburgh IP19 ....42 E6
  Brantham CO11 ....104 F5
  Bressingham IP22 ....19 E3

Church La continued
  Brockdish IP21 ....21 F2
  Bromeswell IP12 ....85 A5
  Broome NR35 ....8 B7
  Brundish IP13 ....55 C8
  Buckleham IP10 ....98 A5
  Burrough Green CB8 ....59 F2
  18 Burwell CB5 ....44 A5
  Carlton IP17 ....128 D7
  1 Cheveley CB8 ....60 E7
  Claydon IP6 ....134 E8
  Clopton IP13 ....83 E8
  Cockfield IP30 ....64 C1
  Copdock & Washbrook
  IP8 ....142 A7
  Corton NR32 ....3 C4
  Creeting St Mary IP6 ....125 D7
  Dalham CB8 ....46 C1
  Ditchingham NR35 ....7 F7
  Dullingham CB8 ....59 F4
  Earl Soham IP13 ....55 A2
  Exning CB8 ....120 B8
  Felixstowe IP11 ....152 E6
  Finningham IP14 ....52 A8
  Fritton & St Olaves NR31 ....2 C7
  Frostenden NR34 ....26 C4
  Harkstead IP9 ....106 B6
  3 Harwich CO12 ....107 B3
  Hemingstone IP6 ....82 C8
  Hemley IP12 ....98 E5
  Henley IP6 ....82 E5
  Hepworth IP22 ....35 A5
  Hitcham IP7 ....79 E6
  Hockwold cum Wilton IP26 ....5 A2
  Hoo IP13 ....70 B6
  Iken IP12 ....72 F3
  Kennett CB8 ....45 F6
  Kenton IP14 ....54 A4
  Kirton IP10 ....98 E2
  Levington IP10 ....145 E3
  Lowestoft NR33 ....114 B2
  Martlesham IP12 ....84 B1
  Mistley CO11 ....104 F2
  3 Mundford IP26 ....6 B8
  Nayland CO6 ....102 D5
  Newmarket CB8 ....121 A3
  Norton IP31 ....50 C4
  2 Occold IP23 ....37 F1
  Playford IP6 ....137 B4
  Preston St Mary CO10 ....79 A5
  Redenhall with Harleston
  IP20 ....22 E7
  Rendlesham IP12 ....85 C7
  Rickinghall Superior IP22 ....36 A5
  Ridgewell CO9 ....89 D3
  St James, South Elmham
  IP19 ....23 F4
  St Mary, South Elmham
  otherwise Homersfield
  IP20 ....23 B8
  Semer IP7 ....79 F1
  Shottisham IP12 ....99 C7
  Somersham IP8 ....81 D3
  Spexhall IP19 ....24 F3
  Sproughton IP8 ....138 B6
  Stetchworth CB8 ....60 A5
  Stoke Ash IP23 ....37 B1
  Stonham Earl IP14 ....67 E6
  Stuston IP21 ....37 D8
  Swilland IP6 ....83 A7
  Thelnetham IP22 ....18 E1
  Thwaite IP23 ....52 F7
  Timworth IP31 ....48 E8
  Troston IP31 ....33 E3
  9 Ufford IP13 ....84 F7
  Walberswick IP18 ....43 C5
  Wenhaston with Mells Hamlet
  IP19 ....42 C6
  Westerfield IP6 ....135 F4
  Westley Waterless CB8 ....59 D3
  Weston NR34 ....9 E2
  Winfarthing IP22 ....20 B8
  Worlington IP28 ....30 B4
  Yaxley IP23 ....37 C4
Church La CI IP28 ....116 D2
Church Meadow
  Barton Mills IP28 ....116 D2
  Rickinghall Inferior IP22 ....35 F6
Church Meadows
  1 Henley IP6 ....82 D6
  Waldingfield IP12 ....98 D7
Church Pk CO10 ....89 E6
Church Rd Alburgh IP20 ....7 A2
  Ashbocking IP6 ....68 E1
  Bacton IP14 ....51 F6
  Bardwell IP31 ....34 B4
  Barningham IP31 ....34 E7
  Barrow IP29 ....47 A3
  Battisford IP14 ....66 E1
  Bedfield IP13 ....54 E5
  Bentley IP9 ....142 A1
  Beyton IP30 ....49 F1
  6 Bildeston IP7 ....79 F4
  Blaxhall IP12 ....71 F4
  Blundeston NR32 ....3 A4
  Boxted CO4 ....102 F3
  Bradfield Combust with
  Stanningfield IP29 ....63 F3
  Bradfield St George IP30 ....64 D6
  Brandon IP27 ....6 E1
  Brettenham IP7 ....65 C1
  Brockdish IP21 ....21 F2
  Bruisyard IP17 ....56 C5
  Bulmer CO10 ....91 C2
  Butley IP12 ....86 B5

Church Rd continued
Carlton CB8 . . . . .74 A8
Chevington IP29 . . . . .62 C6
Combs IP14 . . . . .124 E2
Cotton IP14 . . . . .52 B5
Cratfield IP19 . . . . .40 D5
Crowfield IP6 . . . . .68 C4
Dallinghoo IP13 . . . . .70 C1
Denham IP21 . . . . .38 C5
Dickleburgh & Rushall
IP21 .20 F3
Earsham NR35 . . . . .7 F3
Ellingham NR35 . . . . .8 D7
Ellough NR34 . . . . .111 F1
Elmswell IP30 . . . . .50 E2
Felixstowe IP11 . . . . .153 C6
Felsham IP30 . . . . .65 A4
Flixton NR35 . . . . .7 E2
Friston IP17 . . . . .72 F7
Garboldisham IP22 . . . . .18 D4
Gillingham NR34 . . . . .9 C7
Gisleham NR33 . . . . .11 A3
Great Barton IP31 . . . . .49 A5
1 Great Finborough IP14 . .66 B4
Great Yeldham CO9 . . . . .89 F1
Hasketon IP13 . . . . .146 B7
Hedenham NR35 . . . . .7 C1
Henstead with Hulver Street
NR34 . . . . .26 E8
Heveningham IP19 . . . . .40 E3
Holbrook IP9 . . . . .105 F6
Honington IP31 . . . . .33 F5
Kessingland NR33 . . . . .11 B1
Kettleburgh IP13 . . . . .70 C7
Kirby Cane NR35 . . . . .8 E8
Knodishall IP17 . . . . .58 A1
Leiston IP16 . . . . .129 B6
Lindsey IP7 . . . . .93 D7
Little Glemham IP13 . . . . . . .71 E5
Little Thurlow CB9 . . . . .74 D6
Little Waldingfield CO10 . . . .92 E8
Lowestoft NR32 . . . . .113 C3
Market Weston IP22 . . . . . . .18 C1
Marlesford IP13 . . . . .71 C5
Mendlesham IP14 . . . . .52 E4
Milden IP7 . . . . .79 B1
Monewden IP13 . . . . .69 F5
5 Moulton CB8 . . . . .45 F3
Mutford NR34 . . . . .10 D3
Nacton IP10 . . . . .145 B4
Newton CO10 . . . . .92 D3
North Lopham IP22 . . . . .19 A5
Old Newton with Dagworth
IP14 .51 F1
Otley IP6 . . . . .69 C1
Pettaugh IP14 . . . . .68 E6
Playford IP6 . . . . .137 B5
Redlingfield IP23 . . . . .38 C1
Rushbrooke with Rougham
IP30 .49 C1
Shelfanger IP22 . . . . .20 B6
Snape IP17 . . . . .72 D5
Stowmarket IP14 . . . . .124 D3
Stowupland IP14 . . . . .67 B7
Stutton IP9 . . . . .105 D5
Sudbury CO10 . . . . .148 E3
Sutton IP12 . . . . .85 A1
Tattingstone IP9 . . . . .105 B7
Theberton IP16 . . . . .58 B4
Thistley Green IP28 . . . . .29 F6
6 Thorpeness IP16 . . . . . . .73 F6
Thurston IP31 . . . . .49 E4
Tostock IP30 . . . . .50 B2
Uggeshall NR34 . . . . .26 A3
Weybread IP21 . . . . .22 D2
Wicken CB7 . . . . .28 B1
Wilby IP21 . . . . .39 C3
Wingfield IP21 . . . . .39 A7
Worlingworth IP13 . . . . .54 E7
Wormingford CO6 . . . . .101 F2
Wortham IP22 . . . . .19 F1
Wrabness CO11 . . . . .105 F2
Church Rd N IP21 . . . . .21 F3
Church Row
Bury St Edmunds IP33 . . . . .154 B3
Framsden IP14 . . . . .69 C6
Church St **4** CO8 . . . . . .101 C4
Church St **2** Ashley CB8 . . .60 B5
Belcamp Otten CO10 . . . . . . .90 B8
1 Boxford CO10 . . . . .93 C3
Boxted CO4 . . . . .103 A4
5 Chelmondiston IP9 . . .106 C8
6 Clare CO10 . . . . .90 A8
Diss IP22 . . . . .20 C2
Exning CB8 . . . . .120 C8
Eye IP23 . . . . .117 D2
Fordham CB7 . . . . .29 B1
Framlingham IP13 . . . . .126 D3
2 Fressingfield IP21 . . . . .39 E8
Gestingthorpe CO9 . . . . .90 F1
Groton CO10 . . . . .93 C5
1 Hadleigh IP7 . . . . .149 D5
2 Harleston IP20 . . . . . . .22 D6
2 Harwich CO12 . . . . . . .107 C3
Hundon CO10 . . . . .75 D3
10 Isleham CB7 . . . . .29 C5
Lavenham CO10 . . . . .78 D3
Orford IP12 . . . . .131 C2
Peasenhall IP17 . . . . .56 F8
Saxmundham IP17 . . . . .128 D3
12 Southwold IP18 . . . . .119 D5
Steeple Bumpstead CB9 . . . . .88 D4
Stoke-by-Nayland CO6 . . . . .102 E6

Church St continued
Stradbroke IP21 . . . . .39 B4
Sudbury CO10 . . . . .148 B4
Wangford NR34 . . . . .26 B2
Wetherden IP14 . . . . .51 A1
Wetheringsett-cum-Brockford
IP14 .53 A6
Withersfield CB9 . . . . .74 A2
Woodbridge IP12 . . . . .147 A5
Worlingworth IP13 . . . . .54 F7
Church Terr IP13 . . . . .127 C6
Church View
Halesworth IP19 . . . . .118 E4
Harleston IP20 . . . . .22 E6
1 Haughley IP14 . . . . .51 C1
Leiston IP16 . . . . .129 B6
Stowlangtoft IP31 . . . . .50 B7
Wyverstone IP14 . . . . .51 E6
Church View CI IP12 . . . . .147 C7
Church Walks IP13 . . . . . .154 C1
Church Wlk
Aldeburgh IP15 . . . . .130 E4
Hadleigh IP7 . . . . .149 C5
1 Laxfield IP13 . . . . .40 B3
Long Melford CO10 . . . . .77 C1
Mildenhall IP28 . . . . .116 B4
Shelfanger IP22 . . . . .20 B6
Stowmarket IP14 . . . . .124 D6
Sturmer CB9 . . . . .133 C3
2 Sudbury CO10 . . . . . . .148 C5
Church Wood IP19 . . . . . .118 E4
Churchfields Dr **1** CB9 . . .88 D3
Churchgate CO10 . . . . .77 B3
Churchgate St
Bury St Edmunds IP33 . . . . .154 B2
10 Soham CB7 . . . . .28 D4
Churchill Ave
Hadleigh IP7 . . . . .149 D7
Haverhill CB9 . . . . .132 F7
Ipswich IP4 . . . . .140 B5
Newmarket CB8 . . . . .120 D5
Churchill CI
3 Lawshall IP29 . . . . .63 D1
Lowestoft NR32 . . . . .113 C4
7 Woodbridge IP12 . . . . .146 E4
Churchill Cres IP13 . . . . . .127 C7
Churchill Ct CB8 . . . . .120 F3
Churchill Dr
Mildenhall IP28 . . . . .116 B5
Sudbury CO10 . . . . .148 C8
Churchill Rd
Halesworth IP19 . . . . .118 B5
8 Southwold IP18 . . . . . .119 C8
Thetford IP24 . . . . .16 C6
Churchman CI IP12 . . . . . .147 B8
Churchway **3** IP22 . . . . . . .36 A8
Churchyard IP13 . . . . .154 C2
Churchyard The IP14 . . . . .116 B4
Cinnabar CI **11** IP8 . . . . . .142 E8
Civic Dr IP1 . . . . .155 A2
Clacton Rd CO11 . . . . .104 E1
Clapgate La IP3 . . . . .140 A1
Clapham Rd Central **5**
NR32 . . . . .113 D1
Clapham Rd S NR32 . . . . .113 D1
Clare Ancient House Mus*
CO10 .90 A8
Clare Ave IP12 . . . . .146 E4
Clare Castle (remains of)*
CO10 .90 A8
Clare Castle Ctry Pk* *
CO10 .90 B8
Clare CI
2 Bury St Edmunds IP33 . .122 D4
Mildenhall IP28 . . . . .116 D5
Stowmarket IP14 . . . . .124 E3
Clare Ctry Prim Sch
CO10 .90 A8
Clare Mid Sch CO10 . . . . . .90 B8
Clare PI CB8 . . . . .121 B2
Clare Rd Hundon CO10 . . . .75 E2
Ipswich IP4 . . . . .139 F8
2 Kessingland NR33 . . . . .11 C1
Poslingford CO10 . . . . .76 A2
Claremont Rd **1** NR33 . . .115 C6
Clarence Rd
7 Clare CO10 . . . . .76 A1
Ipswich IP3 . . . . .140 B1
1 Lowestoft NR32 . . . . . .113 D2
Sudbury CO10 . . . . .148 C6
Clarendale Est CB9 . . . . . . .74 C7
Clarendon Rd CB9 . . . . . . .132 D5
Clark Rd NR35 . . . . .110 C7
Clark Wlk IP32 . . . . .122 D7
Clark's Dro CB7 . . . . .28 B4
Clarke Ct IP22 . . . . .20 C1
Clarke's La NR34 . . . . .8 F3
Clarke's Rd **3** CO12 . . . . .106 F2
Clarkes La NR33 . . . . .114 C6
Clarkson Rd NR32 . . . . . . .112 D1
Clarkson St IP1 . . . . .155 A3
Claude Oliver Ct CO11 . . .104 D1
Claude St IP1 . . . . .155 B3
Claudian CI CB9 . . . . .133 B5
Claverton Way IP4 . . . . . . .140 D5
Clay Hill Dennington IP13 . .55 F5
Hintlesham IP8 . . . . .95 B5
Monks Eleigh IP7 . . . . .79 D2
Ubbeston IP19 . . . . .40 E3
Clay La Bacton IP14 . . . . . . .51 A1
Hadleigh IP7 . . . . .94 F4
Henley IP6 . . . . .82 E7
Hepworth IP22 . . . . .35 B5
Ixworth IP31 . . . . .34 A2
Lavenham CO10 . . . . .78 E4
Stoke Ash IP23 . . . . .37 B1
Clay Rd
20 Bury St Edmunds IP32 . .48 C5

Clay Rd continued
Bury St Edmunds IP32 . . . . .122 E8
Fornham All Saints IP32 . . . . .48 B5
Clay St Soham CB7 . . . . .28 D4
Thornham Magna IP23 . . . . . .36 F1
Claydon Dr NR32 . . . . .112 F3
Claydon High Sch IP6 . . . .134 C8
Claydon Prim Sch IP6 . . . .82 B5
Clayhall La CO10 . . . . .92 C7
Clayhall PI CO10 . . . . .92 C7
Clayhill La Hitcham IP7 . . . .79 F6
Wattisham IP7 . . . . .80 A6
Clayhill Rd IP17 . . . . .128 E5
Clayhills IP19 . . . . .118 A3
Clayhive Dr CB8 . . . . .132 D5
Claypits Ave **1** CO8 . . . . .101 C4
Claypits La CO10 . . . . .91 B7
Clayton Ct IP12 . . . . .146 D3
Clayton Rd **2** CO12 . . . . .106 E1
Clearwing CI **10** IP8 . . . . .142 E8
Clematis CI IP4 . . . . .28 B1
Clemence St NR32 . . . . . . .113 C1
Clement Prim Sch
CB9 .132 D5
Clement Rd NR33 . . . . .115 B6
Clement Sq NR33 . . . . .115 B6
Clement's Way **11** IP28 . . .30 B8
Clementine Gdns IP4 . . . . .140 A5
Clements CI
1 Haverhill CB9 . . . . .132 D5
8 Scole IP21 . . . . .20 F1
Clements Dr **2** CB9 . . . . .132 D5
Clements La CB9 . . . . .132 D5
Clements Rd **4** IP12 . . . . .84 E6
Clench CI IP4 . . . . .155 C3
Clench Rd IP9 . . . . .105 E8
Clerk's Piece NR34 . . . . . . .111 D3
Clermont Ave CO10 . . . . . .148 C8
Cleveland Rd NR33 . . . . . . .115 C7
Cleves Rd CB9 . . . . .132 B4
Cley Ct **1** CB9 . . . . .132 A7
Clicket Hill CO8 . . . . .101 D4
Cliff Farm La NR33 . . . . . . .11 B2
Cliff La
Great Yarmouth NR31 . . . . . . .3 B8
Ipswich IP3 . . . . .139 E3
Cliff La Prim Sch IP3 . . . . .139 E3
Cliff Quay IP3 . . . . .139 D2
Cliff Rd
Felixstowe IP11 . . . . .153 D6
Harwich CO12 . . . . .107 B2
Ipswich IP3 . . . . .139 E3
Lowestoft NR33 . . . . .115 C7
Waldringfield IP12 . . . . .98 E7
Clifford Dr NR33 . . . . .114 E5
Clifford Rd IP4 . . . . .139 F5
Clifford Rd Air Raid Shelter
Mus* * 139 F5
Clifford Rd Prim Sch
IP4 . . . . .139 F5
Cliffs The NR33 . . . . .115 B2
Clifton Rd NR33 . . . . .115 C7
Clifton Way IP2 . . . . .138 D2
Clifton Wood **2** IP9 . . . . .105 E7
Cliftonville NR33 . . . . .115 B3
Cliftonville Rd NR33 . . . . . .115 B3
Clink The IP19 . . . . .41 C5
Clint Hill IP23 . . . . .33 F6
Clint Rd IP23 . . . . .37 D1
Clive Ave IP1 . . . . .135 B2
Clockhall La CO10 . . . . .75 D3
Clockhouse La IP14 . . . . . . .67 F7
Cloncurry Gdns IP11 . . . . . .152 D3
Clopton Dr **2** CO10 . . . . . .91 E4
Clopton Gdns IP7 . . . . .149 E4
Clopton Pk CB8 . . . . .62 A1
Clopton Rd IP6 . . . . .136 C2
Close The Corton NR32 . . . . .3 D4
1 Harwich CO12 . . . . .107 A2
Kennett CB8 . . . . .45 F7
North Lopham IP22 . . . . .19 A5
Sudbury CO10 . . . . .148 D6
3 Tattingstone IP9 . . . . . .105 B8
Clough Dr **10** IP26 . . . . .4 E5
Clopton St IP7 . . . . .128 C6
Clovelly CI IP4 . . . . .140 F4
Clovelly Rise IP4 . . . . .113 B3
Clover CI Ipswich IP2 . . . . .138 F4
Needham Market IP6 . . . . . . .125 D3
Clover Field CB9 . . . . .132 B6
Clover Way
Lowestoft NR32 . . . . .113 C5
1 Red Lodge NR28 . . . . . .30 C1
Cloverfield Dr CB7 . . . . .28 C5
Cloverfields **2** IP21 . . . . . .49 E4
Clovers Ct IP14 . . . . .124 C6
Clowes Ct NR34 . . . . .111 B5
Clowes's Cnr IP14 . . . . .54 D2
Cluanie Orch CO10 . . . . . . .76 F1
Clumps The IP12 . . . . .86 A4
Coach La CO8 . . . . .101 A6
Coachman's Paddock **3**
IP9 . . . . .105 E7
Coachmans Ct IP1 . . . . . . .155 B2
Coakers La CO10 . . . . .70 A1
Coalpit La IP29 . . . . .62 A4
Coast Guards The **8**
IP16 . . . . .73 F6
Coast Rd NR32 . . . . .3 C5
Coastguard La IP14 . . . . . . .11 C1
Coates Dro CB7 . . . . .29 C5
Cobbler's Cnr IP6 . . . . .95 B5
Cobbold CI IP14 . . . . .66 C1
Cobbold Mews IP4 . . . . . . .155 C3
Cobbold Rd
Felixstowe IP11 . . . . .153 A4
Woodbridge IP12 . . . . .146 E7
Cobbold St Diss IP22 . . . . . .20 B2

Cobbold St continued
Ipswich IP4 . . . . .155 C3
Cobden PI IP4 . . . . .155 C3
Cobham Rd IP3 . . . . .140 C2
Coblers Way **1** NR33 . . . . .92 B7
Cock & Bel La CO10 . . . . . .91 E8
Cock La CO10 . . . . .78 E2
Cock Rd IP14 . . . . .52 A6
Cock's Rd IP23 . . . . .117 F1
Cockfield CE Prim Sch
IP30 .64 C1
Cockfield Hall La IP6 . . . . .135 E7
Cockfield Rd IP30 . . . . .65 A3
Cockpen Rd CB7 . . . . .27 F3
Cockrell's Rd CO6 . . . . .102 A2
Cocks Gn La IP30 . . . . .64 A5
Coddenham Rd IP6 . . . . . . .67 E1
Coddington Way **8** IP31 . . .34 B1
Codling Rd IP32 . . . . .123 E6
Cody Rd IP3 . . . . .140 C1
Coggeshall Rd
Dedham CO7 . . . . .104 A2
Foxash Estate CO7 . . . . .103 F1
Colbeck Rd CB9 . . . . .132 C8
Colchester Rd
Bures CO8 . . . . .101 C4
Dedham CO7 . . . . .103 E2
Ipswich IP4 . . . . .135 C1
Cold Store Rd IP11 . . . . . .152 B2
Coldfair CI IP17 . . . . .129 B3
Coldfair Gn Prim Sch
IP17 .129 B2
Coldham La IP23 . . . . .36 D2
Cole Ness Rd IP3 . . . . .144 A8
Cole La IP21 . . . . .39 B2
Coleman CI IP22 . . . . .20 C1
Coleridge Rd IP1 . . . . .134 F3
Coles Croft IP19 . . . . .42 C6
Coles Hill IP19 . . . . .42 C7
Coles La CB8 . . . . .59 E1
Coles Oak La CO7 . . . . .103 E3
Coles View IP19 . . . . .42 C6
Colethorpe La IP29 . . . . . . .46 F3
College CI **3** IP23 . . . . . . .117 B3
College Gn IP11 . . . . .153 C5
College Heath Mid Sch
IP28 .116 C6
College Heath Rd
IP28 .116 D6
College La
Bury St Edmunds IP33 . . . . .154 B1
Worlingham NR34 . . . . .111 F2
College Meadows **2**
NR32 . . . . .113 A3
College Rd
Framlingham IP13 . . . . .126 C4
Hockwold cum Wilton IP26 . . .4 F3
Lowestoft NR33 . . . . .115 C6
Soham CB7 . . . . .28 D3
College St
Bury St Edmunds IP33 . . . . .154 B1
Ipswich IP4 . . . . .155 B2
Collett's Wlk IP12 . . . . .146 E5
Colletts Chase CO6 . . . . . . .101 F2
Collier CI **1** IP29 . . . . . . .106 C8
Collin's Hill CB7 . . . . .29 B1
Collings PI CB8 . . . . .120 E5
Collingwood Ave **6** IP13 . .140 B7
Collingwood Fields
CO7 .151 B6
Collingwood Rd IP12 . . . . .146 F7
Collins CI IP17 . . . . .128 B3
Collinson's IP2 . . . . .138 D5
Colman Rd **4** NR32 . . . . . . .3 D4
Colne Springs CO9 . . . . .89 D4
Colne Valley Rd CB8 . . . . . .132 E5
Colneis Jun Sch IP11 . . . . .153 B6
Colneis Rd IP11 . . . . .153 B6
Colneys CI CO10 . . . . .148 B7
Colsterdale NR33 . . . . .114 D3
Coltsfoot CI
7 Ixworth IP31 . . . . .34 B1
Lowestoft NR33 . . . . .114 F3
9 Wickhambrook CB8 . . . .61 E2
Coltsfoot Cnr IP22 . . . . . . .123 F5
Coltsfoot Rd IP2 . . . . .138 E4
Columbia CI IP5 . . . . .141 A7
Columbine CI **7** NR33 . . . .114 C5
Columbine Gdns IP2 . . . . .138 E5
Columbine Way **3** IP23 . . .36 D2
Columbines The CO10 . . . . .76 F1
Columbyne CI IP14 . . . . . . .67 A7
Colville Rd NR33 . . . . .114 C3
Colville Way IP14 . . . . .114 C3
Comber CI IP21 . . . . .21 A2
Combers The IP5 . . . . .141 E7
Combs Ford Prim Sch
IP14 .124 E4
Combs Gn IP14 . . . . .66 D2
Combs La IP14 . . . . .124 E3
Combs Mid Sch IP14 . . . . .124 F3
Combs Wood Dr IP14 . . . . .124 D3
Combs Wood Nature
Reserve* * IP14 . . . . .124 E2
Comet Way IP28 . . . . .116 B5
Comfrey Way IP24 . . . . . . .116 D6
Commerce Way **3**
CO11 . . . . .104 E3
Commercial Rd
Ipswich IP1 . . . . .155 A1
Lowestoft NR33 . . . . .115 C8
Commister La **14** IP31 . . . . .34 B1
Commodore Rd NR32 . . . . .112 E1
Common Gate Dro 29 A5

Common La
Beccles NR34 . . . . .111 C5
Bromeswell IP12 . . . . .147 F7
Syleham IP21 . . . . .22 A2
Troston IP31 . . . . .33 F4
Common La Ind Est
NR34 . . . . .111 C6
Common La N NR34 . . . . . .111 B6
Common Rd
Aldeby NR34 . . . . .10 B7
Botesdale IP22 . . . . .36 B5
Bressingham IP22 . . . . .19 F4
Hopton IP22 . . . . .18 C2
St James, South Elmham
IP19 .23 D4
Scole IP21 . . . . .21 B4
Shelfanger IP22 . . . . .19 F7
Common St CO10 . . . . .90 A8
Common The
Beccles NR34 . . . . .111 C5
Claydon IP8 . . . . .134 A6
1 Harleston IP20 . . . . .22 D5
Knodishall Common
IP17 .129 A1
Leiston IP16 . . . . .129 F7
Southwold IP18 . . . . .119 C5
Compass CI IP27 . . . . .109 C4
Compass St NR34 . . . . .103 D2
Compiegne Way IP33 . . . . .154 B3
Conach Rd IP12 . . . . .146 E5
Coney CI IP24 . . . . .16 A6
Coney Hill NR34 . . . . .111 D3
Coney Weston Rd IP31 . . . . .34 D8
Fakenham Magna IP31 . . . . . .33 F6
Sapiston IP31 . . . . .34 A6
Congreve Rd IP1 . . . . .135 A3
Coniston CI IP1 . . . . .153 E7
Coniston Rd IP3 . . . . .140 B2
Coniston Sq E IP3 . . . . . . .140 B2
Coniston Sq W IP3 . . . . . .140 B2
Connaught Rd
Haverhill CB9 . . . . .132 C5
Ipswich IP1 . . . . .134 D2
Conrad CI NR33 . . . . .114 D6
Conrad Rd NR33 . . . . .114 D6
Consent La IP17 . . . . .79 E4
Constable CI
Halesworth IP19 . . . . .118 A2
Lowestoft NR32 . . . . .112 F1
3 Manningtree CO11 . . . .104 D2
Nayland-with-Wissington
CO6 .102 A5
Constable Ct **15** IP20 . . . . .22 D5
Constable Rd
Bury St Edmunds IP33 . . . . .122 E4
Felixstowe IP11 . . . . .153 B4
Haverhill CB9 . . . . .132 B7
Ipswich IP4 . . . . .155 C4
Sudbury CO10 . . . . .148 C6
Constable Way IP14 . . . . . .124 B7
Constantine Rd IP1 . . . . . . .155 A2
Constitution Hill
Ipswich IP1 . . . . .139 B8
2 Needham Market IP20 . .125 D5
Southwold IP18 . . . . .119 C4
Sudbury CO10 . . . . .148 D6
Convalescent Hill
IP11 .153 A3
Conway CI
Felixstowe IP11 . . . . .153 C7
4 Haverhill CB9 . . . . .132 C6
Ipswich IP2 . . . . .139 B2
Conway Rd **3** IP22 . . . . . . .48 C5
Conyers Way IP31 . . . . .49 A6
Cook's Dro IP28 . . . . .12 D2
Cook's
Hawkedon IP29 . . . . .62 E1
Wortwell IP20 . . . . .22 C6
Cooke CI NR33 . . . . .114 F2
Cooke Rd NR33 . . . . .114 F2
Cookley & Walpole CE Prim
Sch IP19 . . . . .41 B5
Cookley La IP13 . . . . .38 B5
Cookley Rd Cookley IP19 . . .41 B5
Eye IP23 . . . . .38 A5
Cooks Hill Boxted CO4 . . . .103 A8
Letheringham IP13 . . . . .70 D4
Cooks Rd IP30 . . . . .50 E2
Coombers IP29 . . . . .150 D3
Cooper CI **2** IP17 . . . . . . .128 C4
Cooper La IP29 . . . . .63 E8
Cooper Rd IP6 . . . . .68 C1
Cooper's La CB8 . . . . .60 A5
Cooper's La CO7 . . . . .103 B6
Cooper's Rd IP6 . . . . .82 C6
Coopers CI IP5 . . . . .83 A6
Coopers Dr **27** NR33 . . . . . .11 C1
Coopers La IP6 . . . . .11 B1
Coopers Rd **30** IP6 . . . . . . .98 A8
Coopers Rd **1** IP5 . . . . .82 A5
Copperfield **2** IP14 . . . . . . .53 F2
Copdock Intc IP8 . . . . .138 B2
Copdock Prim Sch IP8 . . . . .95 F3
Copellis CI **3** CB8 . . . . . . .132 E8
Copeman Rd **3** IP22 . . . . . .20 A3
Copland Way NR34 . . . . . . .10 A3
Copleston High Sch
IP4 . . . . .140 C5
Copleston Rd IP4 . . . . .140 B5
Coplow Dale **12** NR33 . . . .114 C3
Copper Beech Dr **5**
NR33 . . . . .114 D4
Copper La IP8 . . . . .142 E8
Copperfield Rd IP2 . . . . . . .138 E5
Copperfield Way **11** CB5 . . .44 B5
Coppers CI IP33 . . . . .154 C1

Copperwheat Ave
IP18 ....119 B8
Coppice Cl IP12 ....147 A6
Coppice Ct NR33 ....115 A6
Coppice The IP31 ....49 E4
Copplestone Cl 12 NR34 ....9 F4
Coprolite St IP3 ....139 E5
Copse Cl IP23 ....123 B1
Copswood Cl IP5 ....141 F7
Copy Hill CB9 ....132 C1
Coral Dr IP1 ....134 D1
Coram St 7 IP7 ....149 A6
Cordell Pl CO10 ....91 B8
Cordell Rd CO10 ....91 E8
Corder Rd IP4 ....139 D8
Cordwinders CO7 ....151 F3
Cordy's La IP11 ....152 B6
Coriander Dr IP24 ....16 D6
Corks La IP7 ....149 C6
Corkway Dro IP26 ....4 A4
Cormorant Dr IP14 ....124 F5
Corn Craft (Craft Centre)*
IP7 ....79 D2
Corn Hatches La IP7 ....80 E2
Cornard Rd CO10 ....148 D5
Cornerth Cres CO10 ....148 F4
Cornfield Ave IP27 ....109 D7
Cornfield Cres 5 NR32 ......3 A4
Cornfield Rd IP32 ....154 A3
Cornfields IP21 ....21 B5
Cornflower Cl IP2 ....138 E4
Conford Way 18 CO11 .....104 D2
Cornhill
Bury St Edmunds IP33 ....154 B2
Ipswich IP1 ....155 B3
Cornhill Wlk Sh Ctr
IP33 ....154 B2
Cornish Hall End Rd
CO9 ....89 A1
Cornish Wlk IP22 ....122 E8
Cornmills Gn 9 IP30 ....50 D1
Cornmills Rd CB7 ....28 E2
Cornwall Rd IP11 ....152 F5
Cornwall Rd IP11 ....152 F5
Cornwallis Cl IP28 ....32 C1
Cornwallis Ct IP33 ....154 A1
Cornwallis Rd CB9 ....132 D4
Cornwell Cl CB7 ....29 B4
Coronation Ave IP12 ....99 D6
Coronation Dr IP11 ....152 D3
Coronation Rd IP44 ....144 A2
Coronation Rise 1 CO10 ...92 C6
Corporation Ave IP2 ....139 B1
Corsbie Cl IP33 ....154 B1
Corsican Pine Cl CB8 ......120 F5
Corton CE VC Prim Sch
NR32 ....3 D4
Corton Long La NR32 ......113 B8
Corton Rd Ipswich IP3 ....140 B1
Lowestoft NR32 ....113 D6
Cosford Rd IP7 ....94 C7
Cotes The 28 B6
Cotman Ave IP28 CO11 ....104 D2
Cotman Cl 1 NR32 ....113 B6
Cotman Rd IP3 ....140 A1
Cotmer Rd NR33 ....114 C7
Cotswold Ave IP1 ....135 B1
Cotswold Dr 1 CO10 ....91 E7
Cotswold Way NR32 ....112 E2
Cottesford Cl IP7 ....149 E5
Cottingham Rd IP8 ....138 B2
Cotton End Rd CO10 ....120 C8
Cotton La
Bury St Edmunds IP33 ....154 C3
Cotton IP14 ....52 A6
Cotton La Flats IP33 ......154 C3
Coucy Cl IP13 ....126 C4
Coulson La 1 IP27 ....4 F5
Coupals Prim Sch
CB9 ....133 B5
Coupals Rd CB9 ....133 C4
Courier Cl IP28 ....116 B5
Court Knoll (Earthworks)*
CO6 ....102 D4
Court St CO6 ....102 D5
Courtenay Cl CO10 ....148 B8
Courts The
Felixstowe IP11 ....153 B4
Playford IP6 ....137 B5
Covehite Ct 4 CB9 ....132 C4
Covell Cl IP33 ....122 C4
Coverdale 6 NR33 ....114 E3
Covert Cl CB9 ....132 E7
Covert Rd IP18 ....119 C8
Covert Sycamore 3
IP24 ....16 D6
Covey Dr IP27 ....109 E6
Covey Way IP27 ....109 E6
Cow and Sheep Dro
IP28 ....29 E7
Cow Fair 7 IP30 ....50 D1
Cowell St IP22 ....137 C3
Cowle's Dro IP26 ....4 D1
Cowley Rd IP1 ....153 A4
Cowper St IP4 ....140 B6
Cowslip Cl
Bury St Edmunds IP32 ...123 F5
Ipswich IP2 ....138 E4
Cowslip Cres St IP22 ......114 C5
Cowslip Way IP6 ....125 D3
Cox Cl IP5 ....141 B6
Cox Hill CO10 ....93 C6
Cox La Great Barton IP31 ..49 B4
Ipswich IP4 ....155 C2
Cox's Cl NR34 ....111 C5
Cox's Hill CO11 ....104 D2
Cox's La IP18 ....119 C8

Coxhall Rd IP9 ....142 E1
Coxs Cl CB9 ....132 A5
Coytes Gdns IP1 ....155 B2
Crabbe St
Aldeburgh IP15 ....144 E4
Ipswich IP4 ....140 A6
Crabbe's Cl 8 IP26 ....4 E5
Crabtree Cl IP19 ....118 B2
Crabtree La Aldeby NR34 ...9 F8
Little Horkesley CO6 ....102 B1
Crabtree Meadow 6
IP30 ....50 F2
Crabtree Rise IP21 ....21 F2
Cracks La IP12 ....85 C6
Crag Farm Rd IP12 ....131 E7
Crag Path IP15 ....130 F3
Craig Cl 7 IP11 ....107 D8
Craig's La CO8 ....101 B3
Cramswell Cl NR34 ....132 B4
Cranberry Sq 2 IP3 ....144 C7
Cranborne Chase 1
IP4 ....136 A1
Cranbrook La CO10 ....77 C1
Crane Cl IP12 ....146 D3
Crane Hill London Rd
IP2 ....138 E4
Cranes Meadow 31 IP20 ..22 D6
Cranesbill Rd NR32 ....113 F3
Cranfield Cl 2 NR33 ....115 A3
Cranfield Pk IP8 ....105 D7
Cranleigh Rd NR33 ....114 F3
Cranley Gn Rd IP23 ....117 D2
Cranley La IP23 ....117 F1
Cranmoregreen La
CO10 ....77 C1
Cranwell Cres IP3 ....140 C1
Cranwell Gr 1 IP5 ....141 C7
Cranworth Gdns 1
NR32 ....112 F4
Cranworth Rd IP7 ....149 E4
Cratfield La IP19 ....40 C4
Cratfield Rd
Bury St Edmunds IP32 ....123 C4
Fressingfield IP21 ....39 F8
Huntingfield IP19 ....40 E5
Craven Way CO8 ....28 D3
Crawford Ave IP14 ....66 D8
Crawford Cl 5 IP14 ....51 A1
Crawford La 2 IP5 ....141 C7
Crayford Rd CO10 ....148 B8
Creed Wlk IP32 ....122 D7
Creeting Hills IP6 ....125 F6
Creeting La IP14 ....67 B7
Creeting St Mary Prim Sch
IP6 ....125 F8
Crepping Hall Dr IP9 ....105 C5
Crescent The
Aldeburgh IP15 ....130 E4
Felixstowe IP11 ....153 A3
Ipswich IP1 ....155 A3
Crescent The
Dullingham CB8 ....59 D5
East Harling NR16 ....18 C8
Great Horkesley CO6 ....102 D1
6 Soham CB7 ....28 D3
Stowmarket IP14 ....124 D4
7 Thurstow IP31 ....49 D4
Wicken CB7 ....28 A1
Wickham Market IP13 ......127 B6
Crescents The IP18 ....119 B8
Cresmedow Way IP14 ....50 F2
Crespigny Rd IP15 ....130 E3
Cresslands La IP29 ....76 B3
Crestland Bsns Pk
CO10 ....92 A8
Crestview Dr NR32 ....113 A4
Crick's Rd
Beck Row, Holywell Row
& Kenny Hill IP28 ....30 A6
Thistley Green IP28 ....29 F6
Cricket Field Rd CB8 ....121 B2
Cricket Hill Rd IP11 ....152 D5
Cricketers Cl CO10 ....148 C4
Crimbold's La IP30 ....64 D1
Crimp Cramp La NR34 ......10 B8
Crisp Cl 3 NR32 ....113 B4
Crisp Rd NR35 ....8 E7
Crispin Cl CB9 ....132 B5
Crockatt Rd IP7 ....149 E8
Crockfords Rd CB8 ....121 A1
Croft Cl Beccles NR34 .....111 E4
Diss IP22 ....20 C2
3 Harleston IP20 ....22 D6
3 Wickhambrook CB8 ....61 E2
Croft Rise 6 Bures CO8 ....101 C5
1 Glemsford CO10 ....77 A2
Great Waldham CO9 ....90 A1
5 Lowestoft NR32 ....113 C1
2 Sudbury CO10 ....148 C6
Crofton Rd IP4 ....140 B7
Cromarty Rd IP4 ....140 B8
Crome Wlk NR32 ....113 B6
Cromer Rd IP1 ....134 F1

Crompton Rd
Ipswich IP2 ....138 F7
Lowestoft NR33 ....114 E7
Cromwell Ave NR34 ....111 B3
Cromwell Cl NR34 ....111 B3
Cromwell Ct NR33 ....114 D2
Cromwell Rd
Ringsfield NR34 ....9 C2
Weeting IP27 ....5 E4
Weston NR34 ....111 B3
Cromwell Sq 1 IP1 ....155 B2
Crooked House Gall The*
CO10 ....78 D4
Cropley Cl IP32 ....123 E4
Cross Cl CB9 ....132 E7
Cross Field Way CO4 ....103 A3
Cross La CO7 ....109 D6
Cross Rd IP20 ....22 C6
Cross St 1 Bungay NR35 ..110 B4
Drinkstone IP30 ....65 C7
Elmswell IP30 ....50 E2
Eye IP23 ....117 C2
Felixstowe IP11 ....152 E6
Hoxne IP21 ....38 C7
Leiston IP16 ....129 C5
Sudbury CO10 ....148 B4
Cross The IP23 ....117 C2
Cross Ways IP30 ....50 F2
Crossfields CO6 ....102 C1
Crossgate Field 8 IP11 ...152 E5
Crossing Rd IP22 ....20 C1
Crossley Gdns IP1 ....134 C2
Crotchets Cl 2 IP9 ....150 E3
Croutel Rd IP11 ....153 B5
Crow La IP14 ....124 D5
Crow St IP31 ....124 D8
Crowbrook Pl IP30 ....78 C8
Crowcroft Glebe IP7 ....80 B5
Crowcroft Rd IP7 ....80 B5
Crowe Hall La IP9 ....105 D5
Crowe St IP14 ....124 D6
Crowfield Rd IP14 ....68 C6
Crowfoot Com Prim Sch
NR34 ....111 D4
Crowfoot Gdns 7 NR34 ...111 B5
Crowhurst Cl 4 NR33 ....114 D4
Crowland Cl 1 IP2 ....139 A2
Crowland Rd CB9 ....132 D6
Crowley Rd IP6 ....125 D4
Crown Cl 10 IP22 ....84 A1
Crown Ct IP6 ....68 B1
Crown Cres 15 NR32 ....34 B1
Crown Gn IP22 ....20 C6
Crown La
Coney Weston IP31 ....17 E1
Ixworth IP31 ....34 B1
Orford IP12 ....131 C2
Wickham Market IP13 ......127 C6
Crown Meadow Wlk 3
NR32 ....113 C2
Crown Mill 3 IP30 ....50 F2
Crown Pl IP12 ....147 A4
Crown Rd NR32 ....34 B8
Crown St Brandon IP27 ...14 E8
Bury St Edmunds IP33 ....154 C1
Dedham CO7 ....103 F3
Felixstowe IP11 ....152 E5
Ipswich IP1 ....155 B3
Leiston IP16 ....129 D6
Needham Market IP6 ....125 D5
Stowmarket IP14 ....124 C6
Crown St E 5 NR32 ....113 E2
Crown St W NR32 ....113 D2
Crown Swimming Pool
IP1 ....155 B3
Crown Wlk IP1 ....121 A4
Crownfield Rd 8 CO10 ......77 A3
Crownfields IP13 ....84 F7
Crownland Rd IP31 ....35 C1
Crownswell Ct 6 IP11 ......107 D8
Croxton Cl IP30 ....98 E2
Croxton Rd IP24 ....16 C7
Crunch Croft CB9 ....133 C3
Cryspen Ct IP33 ....154 B3
Cuckfield Ave IP3 ....140 E3
Cuckoo Hill (Tumulus)*
IP28 ....30 A1
Cuckoo Hill CO8 ....101 C5
Cuckoo La IP20 ....22 F6
Cucumber La NR34 ....111 D1
Culford Rd
Bury St Edmunds IP28 .....48 C6
Ingham IP31 ....32 F1
Culford Sch IP28 ....32 F2
Culford Terr IP23 ....154 A1
Culford Wlk IP11 ....152 C3
Culley Way 2 NR31 ....3 B6
Cullingham Rd IP1 ....139 A6
Cullum Rd IP33 ....154 B1
Culvers Meadow 4 IP31 ...34 C4
Culzean Gdns NR32 ....113 A4
Cumberland Cl
4 Felixstowe IP11 ....153 D6
5 Southwold IP18 ....119 D5
Cumberland Mews
IP12 ....147 A4
Cumberland Pl 18 NR32 ...113 E2
Cumberland Rd IP18 ....119 D5
Cumberland St
Ipswich IP1 ....155 A4
Woodbridge IP12 ....147 A4
Cundle Gn La IP17 ....72 C5
Cundys Marsh IP15 ....130 E5
Cunningham Way
NR33 ....115 B3
Curlew Cl IP27 ....109 C5
Curlew Gn NR32 ....112 C1
Curlew Rd IP2 ....138 D4

Curlews The IP33 ....123 C1
Curriers' La IP1 ....155 A2
Curtis Cl IP8 ....138 C1
Curtis Dr 1 IP26 ....4 D5
Curtis Way IP5 ....141 D7
Curzon Rd CO10 ....148 F6
Curzon St IP2 ....139 A6
Cutbert Cl 2 IP24 ....16 D6
Cutler Rd 5 NR32 ....112 D2
Cutler St IP1 ....155 B2
Cutler's La IP14 ....66 A6
Cutlers La CO7 ....151 D7
Cutler's La IP31 ....49 E8
Cutting's Rd IP21 ....21 E4
Cypress Way 4 NR32 ......114 F7

D

Daffodil Cl IP2 ....138 E3
Daffodil Wlk NR33 ....114 C5
Dagworth La IP14 ....66 D8
Daimler Rd IP1 ....134 C2
Dains Pl IP11 ....152 C7
Daires La IP12 ....147 C7
Dairy Dr 4 IP28 ....48 B6
Dairy Hill IP19 ....118 B4
Dairy La Ixworth IP31 ....34 A1
Mutford NR34 ....10 C3
Dairy Rd IP7 ....80 A1
Daisy Ave IP32 ....123 F5
Daisy Gn La IP23 ....52 D7
Daisy Hill IP21 ....39 F8
Daking Ave CO10 ....93 B3
Daking's Drift 8 IP19 ......118 B4
Dakota Rd 6 IP28 ....30 A8
Dale End NR33 ....114 E2
Dale Hall La IP1 ....135 B1
Dale Hall Prim Sch
IP1 ....135 A2
Dale Haven CO10 ....133 D3
Dale Hill IP14 ....53 A6
Dale Rd
Fressingfield IP21 ....22 D1
Stanton IP31 ....34 E5
Dale Tree Rd 10 IP29 ....47 A2
Dales Rd IP1 ....135 A1
Dales View Rd IP1 ....135 A1
Dalham Pl IP32 ....132 C8
Dalham Rd Ashley CB8 .....61 B8
Moulton CB8 ....45 F2
Dallinghoo Rd IP13 ....127 A6
Dalton Rd IP1 ....155 A3
Damask Cl 5 NR33 ....114 E4
Damselfly Rd 5 IP3 ....144 C8
Dandalan Cl IP1 ....138 C8
Dane Cl CB9 ....133 E8
Dane Comm CB9 ....133 D8
Dane Hill Rd CB8 ....45 E7
Danes Cl IP14 ....124 C5
Danes Ct CO10 ....148 F2
Danescourt Ave IP14 ......124 C4
Daneway Rd IP16 ....129 C6
Danforth Cl IP13 ....126 B4
Daniel Gdns IP23 ....117 C3
Daniels Cl 8 CO10 ....92 B7
Daphne Rd IP12 ....131 C2
Darby Pl IP32 ....123 F6
Darby Rd NR34 ....111 B3
Darcy Cl IP32 ....123 E4
Dark La
Dickleburgh & Rushall
IP21 ....20 E2
Easton IP13 ....70 E7
Darkings La IP30 ....22 E4
Darrell Rd 2 IP11 ....153 H11
Darrow Gn IP20 ....7 A4
Darrow Wood La IP22 ....20 A5
Darsham IP17 ....58 E8
Darsham Rd IP17 ....57 E8
Darsham Vale 6 NR32 ...112 F4
Darter Cl 4 IP3 ....144 C8
Darwin Cl IP28 ....116 C6
Darwin Pl CB8 ....121 B1
Darwin Rd IP4 ....139 F5
Dash End Cl CB9 ....133 F8
Dash End La CB9 ....133 C8
Dashwood Cl IP8 ....138 C1
Daundy Cl IP2 ....138 D5
Davall Cl 18 CO10 ....106 E1
Davey Cl Bungay NR35 ...110 B4
Ipswich IP3 ....139 F1
Davey La IP31 ....70 B4
Davey's Cl IP31 ....34 C4
Davidson Cl CO10 ....92 B2
Davoren Wlk IP32 ....122 D7
Daw St CO9 ....89 A3
Dawes Cl IP9 ....150 D4
Dawson Dr IP1 ....152 C8
Dawson Drift 3 IP5 ....141 C7
Dawson Rd IP3 ....143 A6
Day's La IP31 ....34 E8
Days Gn IP9 ....150 D3
Days Rd IP9 ....150 D3
Dazeley's La CO7 ....151 F2
De Burgh Pl 8 CO10 ....76 A1
De Greys Cl CO10 ....92 B3
De Havilland Ct 7 IP28 ....116 B5
De Vere Cl IP3 ....126 C3
Deacon Ct 8 IP11 ....153 D6
Deacon's Cl 2 CO10 ....78 D4
Dead La Ardleigh CO7 .....103 E1

Dead La continued
Bures St Mary CO8 ....101 F5
Lawford CO11 ....104 E1
Deadman's La
Benhall IP17 ....128 A2
Combs IP14 ....66 E1
Rendham IP17 ....57 A3
Stoke Ash IP23 ....53 A8
Woolpit IP30 ....50 C1
Deane's Cl 1 CO12 ....107 A1
Deans Cl CB9 ....132 E7
Deben Ave Ipswich IP5 ....141 F8
Martlesham IP5 ....137 F1
Deben Dr CO10 ....148 E6
Deben High Sch IP12 ....152 F4
Deben La
Waldringfield IP12 ....98 E7
6 Woodbridge Airfield
IP12 ....85 B3
Deben Mill Bsns Ctr
IP12 ....147 B6
Deben Pool IP12 ....147 A4
Deben Rd Haverhill CB9 ..132 F6
Ipswich IP1 ....134 F1
Saxmundham IP17 ....128 C4
Woodbridge IP12 ....147 B5
Deben Rise IP14 ....53 F1
Deben Valley Dr IP5 .....141 C7
Deben Way IP11 ....152 E3
Debenham CE High Sch
IP14 ....53 E2
Debenham Rd
Crowfield IP6 ....68 E5
Winston IP14 ....53 F1
Debenham Sports Ctr
IP14 ....53 E2
Debenside The IP12 ....147 C7
Deck Wlk IP32 ....122 E7
Decoy Rd IP27 ....12 F8
Dedham Dr 4 NR32 ....112 F3
Dedham Meade CO7 .....103 F2
Dedham Rd
Ardleigh CO7 ....103 E1
Boxted CO4 ....103 A3
Lawford CO11 ....104 C2
Deepdale NR33 ....114 E2
Deepdale Rd 6 CO12 ......107 A2
Deer Row NR35 ....8 D5
Defoe Rd IP1 ....135 A4
Degas Gdns 1 NR32 ....113 B6
Delahay Dro CB7 ....29 A5
Delf Cl IP7 ....149 E7
Delius Cl
Lowestoft NR33 ....115 A6
1 Stowmarket IP14 ....124 C7
Dell Cl NR33 ....114 E7
Dell Prim Sch NR33 ....114 E7
Dell Rd E NR33 ....114 F7
Dellview NR33 ....114 D6
Dellwood Ave IP11 ....153 B5
Delph Dro IP28 ....12 D1
Delph Rd IP27 ....109 D7
Demesne Gdns 6 IP5 ......98 A8
Dene Rd NR32 ....113 D4
Denes High Sch The
NR32 ....113 D4
Denham Cl IP33 ....122 D5
Denham Cnr IP21 ....38 D3
Denham La IP29 ....47 A2
Denham Low Rd IP21 ....38 D3
Denham Rd Dalham CB8 ...61 C8
Denham IP29 ....47 A1
Hoxne IP21 ....38 D6
Denmark Gdns 1 IP9 ......105 E7
Denmark Hill IP22 ....20 C2
Denmark La IP22 ....20 B2
Denmark Rd
Beccles NR34 ....111 B6
9 Lowestoft NR32 ....115 D8
Denmark Rise IP22 ....20 C8
Denmark St IP22 ....20 C2
Denney's La IP17 ....128 D7
Dennington CE Prim Sch
IP13 ....55 D6
Dennington Rd
Dennington IP13 ....55 F8
Framlingham IP13 ....126 B5
Laxfield IP13 ....40 B1
Denny Ave IP14 ....66 D8
Denny's Hill IP20 ....23 A6
Denton Cl IP2 ....138 D2
Denton Dr IP14 ....114 F5
Denton Rd IP20 ....7 C2
Depden La IP29 ....62 C5
Depot Rd CB8 ....120 E6
Derby Cl IP4 ....140 A5
Derby Pl 8 IP31 ....49 A5
Derby Rd IP3 ....140 A4
Derby Way CB8 ....120 D5
Dereham Ave IP3 ....139 F3
Dereham Cl 17 IP27 ....13 F2
Derry Brooks La 1 IP14 ...53 F2
Derwent Gdns 8 IP31 .....113 A4
Derwent Rd
1 Bury St Edmunds IP32 ...48 C5
Ipswich IP3 ....139 F3
Desmond Cl 8 NR32 ....112 D2
Dettingen Way IP33 ....122 D5
Devereaux Ct IP4 ....155 C3
Devil's La IP17 ....42 C1
Devils Dyke Nature Reserve*
CB5 ....44 A3
Devlin Rd IP8 ....138 B1
Devon Cl IP32 ....122 E8

Devon Rd
Felixstowe IP11 . . . .**152** F5
☑ Stowupland IP14 . . . .**67** A6
Devon Way ☑ CO12 . . . . . .**106** E1
Devonshire Rd IP3 . . . .**139** F5
Dewar La IP5 . . . .**141** C7
Dewarrene Dr IP27 . . . .**5** E3
Dhobi Pl IP1 . . . .**138** F7
Dial La IP1 . . . .**155** B3
Diamond Cl IP1 . . . .**134** D1
Dickens Ct ☑ NR32 . . . .**3** A4
Dickens Rd IP2 . . . .**138** E6
Dickinson Terr ☑ IP5 . . . . . .**141** D7
Dickleburgh Prim Sch
IP21 . . . .**21** B5
Dickleburgh Rd IP21 . . . .**21** A5
Dicks Mount NR34 . . . .**10** D7
Dicky Hill IP20 . . . .**22** D7
Didsbury Cl IP2 . . . .**138** D2
Digby Cl ⑤ IP5 . . . .**98** A7
Digby Rd IP4 . . . .**140** C7
Dillistone Ct CO8 . . . .**133** C3
Dillwyn St W IP1 . . . .**155** A3
Dinsdale Rd IP16 . . . .**129** C6
Diomed Dr IP31 . . . .**49** A5
Dip The CO8 . . . .**121** D2
Diprose Dr NR34 . . . .**113** A6
Dirty La IP21 . . . .**21** F7
Diss Church Jun Sch
IP22 . . . .**20** C3
Diss High Sch IP22 . . . .**20** D3
Diss Inf Sch IP22 . . . .**20** D2
Diss Mus* IP22 . . . .**20** C3
Diss Rd
Burston & Shimpling IP22 . .**20** E5
Garboldisham IP22 . . . .**18** D4
☑ Scole IP21 . . . .**20** E2
South Lopham IP22 . . . .**19** C4
Wattisfield IP22 . . . .**35** D5
Diss Sta IP22 . . . .**20** D2
Ditchingham Dam
NR35 . . . .**110** B5
Ditchingham Gr IP4 . . . .**140** F6
Ditton Cl CB8 . . . .**121** A1
Ditton Gn CB8 . . . .**60** B5
CB8 . . . .**121** B2
Dixon Cl ⑪ CO11 . . . .**104** D2
Dixon Dr IP3 . . . .**114** E7
Dobbs Drift IP5 . . . .**141** F7
Dobbs La IP5 . . . .**137** E1
Dobson Way NR34 . . . .**111** C5
Dock La IP12 . . . .**147** C7
Dock Rd
Felixstowe IP11 . . . .**152** C1
Ramsholt IP12 . . . .**99** B4
Dock St IP2 . . . .**155** B1
Dockfield Ave ⑤ CO12 . . . .**106** F2
Dockings La IP7 . . . .**29** C5
Doctor Watson's La
IP5 . . . .**137** A1
Doctor's La Ashen CO10 . . . . .**89** E5
Orford IP12 . . . .**131** C3
Pulham St Mary IP21 . . . . . .**22** A6
Doctors La IP21 . . . .**39** B4
Dodmans IP9 . . . .**150** E3
Dodson Vale IP5 . . . .**141** C7
Does Field IP14 . . . .**68** C6
Dog La Shelfanger IP22 . . . . . .**20** A8
Tannington IP13 . . . .**55** A4
Dogs Head St IP4 . . . .**155** B2
Dogs La NR34 . . . .**9** C7
Dogwood Cl IP3 . . . .**140** D2
Dogwood Wlk ☑ IP7 . . . .**13** F2
Doit La IP22 . . . .**20** A3
Doit The IP22 . . . .**19** F2
Dolphin Cl ⑧ NR33 . . . .**115** B4
Dombey Rd IP2 . . . .**138** E5
Dome Leisure Ctr
IP28 . . . .**116** E4
Donegal Rd IP1 . . . .**134** D2
Donkey La
Bradfield Combust with
Stanningfield IP29 . . . .**63** F2
Friston IP17 . . . .**72** F7
Dooley Rd IP11 . . . .**152** C3
Dorchester Rd
Bury St Edmunds IP33 . . . .**122** D3
Ipswich IP3 . . . .**140** D3
Doric Pl IP7 . . . .**147** A4
Doris St CB8 . . . .**120** F3
Dorking Rd IP3 . . . .**3** A6
Dorley Dale NR33 . . . .**114** E3
Dorothy Hodgkin Ct
NR34 . . . .**111** B2
Dorset Cl IP4 . . . .**135** F1
Double St IP13 . . . .**126** D3
Doubleday Cl IP2 . . . .**20** C2
Doug Smith Cl CB8 . . . .**120** F6
Doughty Wylie Cres
IP16 . . . .**58** B4
Douglas Cl
Halesworth IP19 . . . .**118** C5
Lowestoft NR33 . . . .**114** D3
Douglas Rd ⑪ CO12 . . . . . .**107** A2
Doune Way IP20 . . . .**22** D6
Dove Cl ⑥ Debenham IP14 . . .**53** F2
⑦ Harleston IP20 . . . .**22** D6
Saxmundham IP17 . . . .**128** C4
Dove Cres ⑨ CO12 . . . .**106** E1
Dove Gdns IP14 . . . .**67** A5
Dove House Rd CB9 . . . .**132** E7
Dove La IP23 . . . .**117** D2
Dove Rd IP18 . . . .**119** B7
Dove St Ipswich IP4 . . . .**139** E5

Dove St continued
Lowestoft NR32 . . . .**113** D2
Dovedale
Felixstowe IP11 . . . .**152** D3
☑ Lowestoft NR33 . . . .**114** F3
Dovehouse Hill IP29 . . . .**77** D7
Dover Rd IP3 . . . .**140** B4
Dovercourt Sta CO12 . . . . . .**107** B2
Dovercourt Swimming Pool
CO12 . . . .**107** B1
Dowes Hill NR34 . . . .**111** B2
Dowling Rd CO8 . . . .**101** C2
Downham Bvd IP3 . . . .**144** C7
Downham Rd IP27 . . . .**6** A1
Downing Cl
Bury St Edmunds IP32 . . . .**123** E5
Ipswich IP2 . . . .**138** F2
Mildenhall IP28 . . . .**116** D5
Newmarket CB8 . . . .**121** B2
☑ Woodbridge IP12 . . . . . .**146** E4
Downing Dr ④ IP31 . . . .**49** A6
Downing Prim Sch
IP2 . . . .**138** F2
Downlands IP27 . . . .**80** F1
Downs Cres CB9 . . . .**132** D6
Downs Farm La IP20 . . . .**23** B7
Downs Pl CB9 . . . .**132** D6
Downs The
Felixstowe IP11 . . . .**152** D5
Rushbrooke with Rougham
IP30 . . . .**49** C2
Downside IP14 . . . .**124** B6
Downside Cl IP3 . . . .**142** F8
Downton Dr CB9 . . . .**132** C6
Dowson Dr ☑ NR33 . . . .**11** B1
Drab's La IP13 . . . .**83** E7
Drake Cl IP4 . . . .**124** A6
Drake Inf Sch ☑ IP24 . . . . . .**16** C7
Drake Rd CO10 . . . .**148** B4
Drake Sq S IP3 . . . .**140** B2
Drake's Heath NR32 . . . .**113** B2
Drapers Cl ⑪ IP7 . . . .**149** E6
Drapers Hill IP21 . . . .**39** B5
Drapers La
Ditchingham NR35 . . . .**8** A7
Helions Bumpstead CB9 . . . .**88** A5
Drapery Comm ⑧ CO10 . . . . .**77** A2
Draymans Way IP3 . . . .**144** A5
Drays The CO10 . . . .**91** D7
Drift Ct IP6 . . . .**125** D4
Drift Rd IP27 . . . .**109** C8
Drift The Botesdale IP22 . . . . .**36** A7
☑ East Bergholt CO11 . . . .**104** E5
Exning CB8 . . . .**120** A8
Fornham St Martin IP31 . . . .**48** F5
Holbrook IP9 . . . .**105** E5
Ipswich IP5 . . . .**140** C1
Ipswich IP4 . . . .**140** A6
Levington IP10 . . . .**145** E3
☑ Martlesham Heath IP5 . . . .**98** A8
Middleton IP17 . . . .**58** B6
Polstead CO6 . . . .**93** D2
Sudbury CO10 . . . .**92** B3
Tostock IP30 . . . .**50** B2
Wickham Market IP13 . . . . .**127** D8
Driftway The
☑ Grundisburgh IP13 . . . . . .**83** E5
Ipswich IP4 . . . .**140** B6
Drinkstone Gn IP30 . . . .**65** B7
Drinkstone Rd
Beyton IP30 . . . .**49** F2
Gedding IP30 . . . .**65** B5
Drinkwater Cl CB8 . . . .**120** E4
Drive The
Harwich CO12 . . . .**107** A1
Heveningham IP19 . . . .**41** B3
Hitcham IP7 . . . .**80** A8
Lowestoft NR32 . . . .**112** F2
☑ Martlesham Heath IP5 . . . .**98** B8
Rushbrooke with Rougham
IP30 . . . .**64** B8
Southwold IP18 . . . .**119** B7
Drout's La IP31 . . . .**34** E7
Drove La IP14 . . . .**51** A3
Drove The IP27 . . . .**14** D8
Drover's Ct IP11 . . . .**152** B8
Drovers Ave IP22 . . . .**123** F5
Druids La IP22 . . . .**20** B6
Druids' La IP22 . . . .**20** A7
Drum Field ⑤ CO7 . . . .**103** E5
Drummond Cl IP3 . . . .**154** A1
Drury Cl ⑪ NR33 . . . .**11** C1
Drury Dr CO10 . . . .**148** D8
Drury La Milden IP7 . . . .**79** B1
Ridgewell CO9 . . . .**89** D3
Wicken CB7 . . . .**28** B1
Drury Pk IP17 . . . .**72** D5
Drury Rd IP6 . . . .**134** C8
Drybridge Hill IP12 . . . .**146** E4
Dryden Rd IP1 . . . .**135** A3
Dublin Rd IP23 . . . .**53** E8
Duchess Dr
Newmarket CB8 . . . .**121** D2
Woodditton CB8 . . . .**60** C8
Duck Dro CB7 . . . .**12** A6
Duckamere IP8 . . . .**134** A1
Ducks La CB8 . . . .**120** C7
Ducksen Rd IP14 . . . .**52** E4
Duddery Hill CB9 . . . .**132** E5
Duddery Rd ☑ CB9 . . . .**132** E5
Dudley St IP7 . . . .**109** F1
Duffs Hill CO10 . . . .**77** A4
Duke St Beccles NR34 . . . . . .**111** D3
④ Bildeston IP7 . . . .**79** F4
Hadleigh IP7 . . . .**149** D5
Haughley IP14 . . . .**51** C1

Duke St continued
Hintlesham IP8 . . . .**95** C5
Ipswich IP3 . . . .**139** E4
☑ Stanton IP31 . . . .**34** E4
Duke's Dr IP19 . . . .**118** A2
Duke's Meadow IP12 . . . . . .**146** D3
Duke's Pk IP12 . . . .**146** D2
Duke's Rd NR35 . . . .**110** C2
Dukes Cl IP11 . . . .**153** D6
Dukes Head St ⑥ NR32 . . . .**113** E2
Dukes Meadow
⑪ Beccles NR34 . . . .**111** C4
Cockfield IP30 . . . .**64** D3
Dukesway ⑪ NR35 . . . .**7** F4
Dulgate Rd CB8 . . . .**7** B7
Dullingham Rd
Newmarket CB8 . . . .**120** F1
Woodditton CB8 . . . .**59** F7
Dullingham Sta CB8 . . . .**59** D5
Dumbarton Rd ⑧ IP4 . . . . . .**136** C1
Dumfries Rd ☑ IP4 . . . .**136** C1
Dumplingbridge La
IP27 . . . .**109** C6
Dunbar Rd NR34 . . . .**10** B8
Dunburgh Rd NR34 . . . .**9** A6
Duncan Rise CO9 . . . .**89** F1
Dunche's La IP6 . . . .**67** E4
Dunhill La IP2 . . . .**35** B5
Dunlin Rd IP2 . . . .**138** E2
Dunlop Rd IP2 . . . .**138** F6
Dunn Cl IP7 . . . .**149** E4
Dunnock Cl ⑪ IP14 . . . .**67** A5
Dunsey Wood Cl CB9 . . . . . .**132** C7
Dunstall Gn Rd CB8 . . . .**61** E6
Dunster Dr ⑫ CB9 . . . .**132** C6
Dunston Dr NR32 . . . .**112** E4
Dunston's Cnr IP6 . . . .**82** B8
Dunton Gr IP7 . . . .**149** E4
Dunwich Cl ⑤ CB9 . . . .**132** C6
Dunwich Heath Nature
Reserve* IP17 . . . .**58** F7
Dunwich La IP17 . . . .**41** A2
Dunwich Mus* IP17 . . . .**43** B1
Dunwich Pl ☑ IP31 . . . .**49** A5
Dunwich Rd
Blythburgh IP19 . . . .**42** F5
☑ Southwold IP18 . . . .**119** D5
Westleton IP17 . . . .**58** D8
Dunwich Underwater
Exploration Ex*
IP12 . . . .**131** B3
Dunwich Way ⑪ NR32 . . . . .**112** F4
Durban Cl IP19 . . . .**118** B2
Durban Rd NR33 . . . .**115** B7
Durbar Terr IP33 . . . .**154** A3
Durbidge's Hill IP22 . . . .**20** E5
Durham Cl ⑧ IP22 . . . .**48** C5
Durham Rd ☑ IP27 . . . .**14** A3
Durham Way CB8 . . . .**120** E5
Durrant Rd IP7 . . . .**149** E6
Durrant View IP15 . . . .**141** E7
Durrant's Cl ⑧ NR33 . . . .**11** C1
Dutchman Ct NR33 . . . .**114** E7
Dux St IP7 . . . .**65** B1
Dyer Ct IP7 . . . .**149** F5
Dyers La CO10 . . . .**92** E2
Dyers Rd CO9 . . . .**89** C1
Dyke St IP1 . . . .**155** B3
Dyson's Dro CB5 . . . .**44** A7

E

Eades Wlk NR33 . . . .**114** C5
Eagle Ct NR34 . . . .**111** C6
Eagle Dr IP15 . . . .**130** C6
Eagle La CB8 . . . .**59** E5
Eagle St IP4 . . . .**155** C2
Eagle Way IP5 . . . .**98** A8
Eagles Cl IP11 . . . .**152** F4
Earl Soham Prim Sch
IP13 . . . .**54** F2
Earl's Cl IP19 . . . .**118** A2
Earls Cl IP11 . . . .**153** D6
Earls Gn ⑥ CB9 . . . .**132** A6
Earlsbrook IP14 . . . .**52** B1
Earlsfield IP12 . . . .**13** F2
Earlsford Rd Mellis IP23 . . . . .**36** F5
Thornham Parva IP23 . . . . . .**37** A4
Earsham CE VA Fst Sch
NR35 . . . .**7** F4
Earsham Dam NR35 . . . .**110** A3
Earsham Rd NR35 . . . .**7** F2
Earsham St NR35 . . . .**110** A4
Earth La NR32 . . . .**2** F5
Easdale NR33 . . . .**114** D2
Easlea Rd IP32 . . . .**123** E4
East Anglia Transport Mus*
NR33 . . . .**114** A3
East Barton Rd IP31 . . . .**49** B5
East Bergholt CE Prim Sch
CO7 . . . .**151** D6
East Bergholt High Sch
CO7 . . . .**151** B5
East Church St NR16 . . . .**19** B8
East Cl IP33 . . . .**123** C6
East Cliff IP15 . . . .**130** E5
East Dock Rd CO12 . . . .**106** F3
East End La CO7 . . . .**104** E6
East End Rd
East Bergholt CO7 . . . .**151** F4
Stonham Aspal IP14 . . . .**68** C6
East Fen Dro CB7 . . . .**28** F4
East Fen Rd CB7 . . . .**29** D5
East Gn IP19 . . . .**119** D5
East Harling Rd NR16 . . . . . .**18** F8
East La Bawdsey IP12 . . . .**99** F2

East La continued
Dedham CO7 . . . .**104** A2
Middleton IP17 . . . .**58** B6
Ufford IP13 . . . .**85** A7
East Lawn IP4 . . . .**140** C8
East Mill Gn IP9 . . . .**104** F2
East Point Pavillion Visitor
Ctr* NR33 . . . .**115** D8
East Rd CB7 . . . .**28** C3
East Side CO4 . . . .**103** A2
East St ⑦ Harwich CO12 . . . .**107** B2
Southwold IP18 . . . .**119** D5
Sudbury CO10 . . . .**148** D5
East View Carlton IP17 . . . . .**128** D6
Freckenham IP28 . . . .**29** E3
Eastcliff IP11 . . . .**153** E7
Eastern Ave
Haverhill CB9 . . . .**132** A6
⑱ Soham CB7 . . . .**28** D4
Eastern Cl CB8 . . . .**140** F4
Eastern Way
Bury St Edmunds IP32 . . . .**123** C5
Elmswell IP30 . . . .**50** F2
⑱ Mildenhall IP28 . . . .**113** B1
Eastfen Dro IP26 . . . .**5** B2
Eastfield Gdns ⑧ NR33 . . . .**114** E4
Eastgate Sch Ctr IP14 . . . . .**155** C3
Eastgate St IP33 . . . .**154** C2
Eastland Ct IP11 . . . .**152** D7
Eastlands IP21 . . . .**39** B4
Eastlands La IP22 . . . .**52** B8
Eastlands Rd IP16 . . . .**129** D6
Eastlow Hill (Tumulus)*
IP30 . . . .**64** C8
Eastlowhill Rd IP30 . . . .**64** B8
Easton Farm Pk* IP13 . . . . .**70** D6
Easton La
Hacheston IP13 . . . .**70** F5
Reydon IP18 . . . .**27** A1
Easton Prim Sch IP13 . . . . . .**70** F5
Easton Rd
Hacheston IP13 . . . .**71** A4
Woodbridge Airfield IP12 . . .**85** B3
Eastward Ho IP16 . . . .**129** D5
Eastward Pl IP14 . . . .**124** C7
Eastwood Ave NR33 . . . . . .**114** F6
Eaton Cl IP11 . . . .**153** C7
Eaton Gdns IP11 . . . .**153** C7
Eccles Rd IP2 . . . .**138** D2
Economy Rd NR33 . . . .**115** C7
Eddies The NR33 . . . .**114** E4
Eddowes Rd ⑥ IP6 . . . .**82** B5
Edelweiss Cl ⑪ NR33 . . . . . .**114** C4
Eden Rd ⑧ Haverhill CB9 . . .**132** E5
Ipswich IP3 . . . .**140** B5
Edendale NR32 . . . .**112** D2
Edes Paddock ⑧ IP31 . . . . . .**49** A6
Edgar Ave IP14 . . . .**124** D3
Edgar Sewter Prim Sch
IP19 . . . .**118** B5
Edgeborough Cl IP3 . . . .**46** A5
Edgecomb Rd IP14 . . . .**124** C7
Edgefield Ave ⑪ CO11 . . . .**104** D2
Edgerton Rd NR33 . . . .**115** A7
Edgworth Rd CO10 . . . .**148** C4
Edies La CO6 . . . .**102** B7
Edinburgh Cl
⑧ Barnham IP24 . . . .**16** C2
Stowmarket IP14 . . . .**124** E6
Edinburgh Gdns IP6 . . . .**82** B5
Edinburgh Rd
Lowestoft NR32 . . . .**113** D3
Newmarket CB8 . . . .**120** E4
Edith Cavell Way CB9 . . . . . .**88** E3
Edmonton Cl IP15 . . . .**141** A7
Edmonton Rd IP5 . . . .**141** A7
Edmund Cl CB9 . . . .**132** D6
Edmund Moundford Rd ⑪
IP26 . . . .**4** E5
Edmund Rd IP27 . . . .**14** D8
Edmunds Rd IP14 . . . .**65** F4
Edward Cl IP1 . . . .**138** F8
Edward Fitzgerald Ct
IP12 . . . .**146** E6
Edward St ⑥ CO12 . . . .**106** F3
Edwards La IP19 . . . .**41** F5
Edwin Ave IP12 . . . .**146** E4
Edwin Panks Rd IP7 . . . .**149** E6
Edwin Terr IP12 . . . .**146** F6
Egglestone Cl IP2 . . . .**138** F1
Eggshell La CO9 . . . .**88** F1
Eglantine Way ☑ CO6 . . . . .**102** A7
Egremont Cl IP2 . . . .**77** A2
Ehringshausen Way
CB9 . . . .**132** F5
El Alamein Rd IP26 . . . .**4** E5
Elder Crescen ☑ IP7 . . . .**80** D6
Elders The IP7 . . . .**109** E5
Elderstub La IP30 . . . .**49** B1
Eldith Ave CB7 . . . .**29** C1
Eldo Gdns ⑧ IP28 . . . .**29** F6
Eldo Rd IP28 . . . .**29** F6
Eldred Cl
Bury St Edmunds IP32 . . . .**123** E4
Westbourne IP1 . . . .**138** D8
Eldred Dr CO10 . . . .**92** B2
Eleanor Pl ⑥ IP31 . . . .**49** A6
Eley's Cnr IP7 . . . .**94** E8
Elgar Cl NR33 . . . .**115** A6
Elim Terr ⑪ NR12 . . . .**113** D2
Eliot Way ⑪ IP14 . . . .**124** B8
Elizabeth Ave CB8 . . . .**120** E5
Elizabeth Bonhote Cl ⑧
NR35 . . . .**110** C2
Elizabeth Cl NR32 . . . .**113** A3
Elizabeth Ct ⑧ CO10 . . . . . .**148** D6
Elizabeth Dr IP29 . . . .**62** D5

Elizabeth Par CB8 . . . .**120** E5
Elizabeth Rd
Brandon IP27 . . . .**5** F1
⑮ Harwich CO12 . . . .**107** A2
Elizabeth Way
Burrough Green CB8 . . . .**59** F2
Eye IP23 . . . .**117** C3
Felixstowe IP11 . . . .**152** D3
Stowmarket IP14 . . . .**124** E6
Sudbury CO10 . . . .**148** A3
Elizabeth Wlk ☑ NR32 . . . . .**22** D6
Ellenbrook Gn IP2 . . . .**138** D1
Ellenbrook Rd
Ipswich IP2 . . . .**138** D1
Pinewood IP9 . . . .**142** E8
Ellingham VC Prim Sch
NR35 . . . .**9** C2
Ellington Rd ⑪ IP24 . . . .**16** C2
Elliott Ave IP18 . . . .**119** C8
Elliott Cl CB8 . . . .**121** A6
Elliott St IP1 . . . .**139** A6
Ellis Rd CO4 . . . .**102** F2
Ellis St CO10 . . . .**93** C3
Ellison Cl ④ IP30 . . . .**50** F2
Ellough Ind Est NR34 . . . . . .**10** A3
Ellough Rd
Beccles NR34 . . . .**111** D4
Worlingham NR34 . . . .**111** F2
Ellwood Cl NR34 . . . .**111** B7
Ellwood Rd IP29 . . . .**29** C5
Elm Cl
⑯ Bentwaters Airfield IP12 . .**85** E8
⑥ Brantham CO11 . . . .**104** E5
Dullingham CB8 . . . .**59** E5
Haverhill CB9 . . . .**132** D6
Lakenheath IP27 . . . .**109** C7
Lowestoft NR33 . . . .**114** C3
Elm Coppice ⑥ NR33 . . . . . .**114** E4
Elm Ct CB9 . . . .**133** C3
Elm Dr IP31 . . . .**49** F1
Elm Est CO7 . . . .**151** C5
Elm Gdns IP12 . . . .**152** C7
Elm Gr
Garboldisham IP22 . . . .**18** D4
⑤ Nayland CO6 . . . .**102** C5
Elm La
Capel St Mary IP9 . . . .**150** E3
Copdock & Washbrook
IP8 . . . .**95** F4
Elm Lodge Rd ⑦ IP13 . . . . . .**40** B3
Elm Rd
East Bergholt CO7 . . . .**151** B5
Ipswich IP5 . . . .**140** F7
Stowmarket IP14 . . . .**124** C6
Sudbury CO10 . . . .**148** E5
Thetford IP24 . . . .**16** B4
Wickham Market IP13 . . . . .**127** B6
Elm St IP1 . . . .**155** B3
Elm Tree Cl ⑪ IP14 . . . .**51** E1
Elm Tree La ⑤ CO6 . . . .**102** A7
Elm Tree Mid Sch
NR33 . . . .**114** E3
Elm Tree Prim Sch
NR33 . . . .**114** E5
Elm Tree Rd NR33 . . . .**114** E5
Elm Tree Rd W NR33 . . . . . .**114** E5
Elm Way IP14 . . . .**51** F6
Elm Wlk ⑳ IP27 . . . .**13** F2
Elmcroft Cl ⑫ IP28 . . . .**30** A8
Elmcroft La IP11 . . . .**153** C7
Elmcroft Rd IP1 . . . .**135** A2
Elmdale Dr
Lowestoft NR33 . . . .**114** D4
⑳ Mistley CO11 . . . .**104** E2
Elmdon Pl CB9 . . . .**132** F6
Elmers La IP5 . . . .**141** D7
Elmham Dr IP10 . . . .**145** B8
Elmhurst Ave NR32 . . . .**112** E1
Elmhurst Dr IP3 . . . .**132** F5
Elmhurst Dr IP3 . . . .**140** B5
Elmhurst Rd IP12 . . . .**107** B2
Elms Cl ⑥ Earsham NR35 . . . . .**7** F4
Great Barton IP31 . . . .**49** B6
Elms La NR34 . . . .**26** B2
Elms Rd Cowlinge CB8 . . . . . .**75** B7
Freckenham IP28 . . . .**29** F2
Elms The
Framlingham IP6 . . . .**126** C4
④ Horringer IP29 . . . .**63** A8
Elmsett CE Prim Sch
IP7 . . . .**80** F1
Elmsett Cl IP14 . . . .**124** F3
Elmsett Rd IP7 . . . .**81** B3
Elmsley Way IP17 . . . .**57** C8
Elmswell Prim Sch
IP30 . . . .**50** F2
Elmswell Rd
Great Ashfield IP31 . . . .**50** F4
Wetherden IP14 . . . .**51** A1
Elmswell Sta IP30 . . . .**50** E3
Elmtree Bsns Pk IP30 . . . . . .**50** E3
Elsey's Yd IP13 . . . .**154** B3
Elsmere Rd IP1 . . . .**139** C8
Elton Pk IP2 . . . .**138** D6
Elveden CE Prim Sch
IP24 . . . .**15** C2
Elveden Rd IP24 . . . .**15** F2
Elvedon Way CB8 . . . .**120** E5
Ely Cl IP33 . . . .**123** B3
Ely Rd ⑤ Claydon IP6 . . . . . .**82** B5
Soham CB7 . . . .**28** B1
Embry Cres ⑯ IP7 . . . .**80** D6
Emerald Cl IP5 . . . .**141** C8
Emily Frost Cl ④ CB8 . . . . . .**61** E2
Emlen St IP1 . . . .**155** A3
Emmanuel Cl
Ipswich IP2 . . . .**138** F2

Emmanuel Cl *continued*
Mildenhall IP28 ....116 D5
Emmerson Way IP7 ......149 D7
Emperor Circ IP3 ....144 C8
Emsworth Cl 2 IP32 ....123 D6
Endway The CB7 ....88 E4
Engine Rd CB7 ....28 B5
Ennerdale Cl 2 IP11 ....153 D6
Ensign Way IP22 ....20 E2
Enstone Rd NR33 ....115 B6
Enterprise Bsns Pk
IP33 ....154 C4
Entry The IP23 ....52 D8
Epsom Dr IP1 ....135 A4
Erbury Pl CO10 ....90 A8
Eriswell Dr IP27 ....109 D5
Eriswell Rd
Beck Row, Holywell Row
IP28 ....13 E1
Haverhill CB9 ....132 F6
Lakenheath IP27 ....109 D4
Ernleigh Rd IP4 ....140 B6
Erratts Hill CB8 ....61 B1
Errington Way IP30 ....50 B2
Erskine Rd 14 CO11 ......104 C2
Erwarton Wlk IP9 ....106 E6
Eskdale Way NR33 ....113 A4
Esplanade NR33 ....115 D7
Essex Ave CO10 ....148 D7
Essex Rd NR32 ....113 B1
Essex Way IP3 ....140 E1
Estuary Cres 5 IP9 ......107 A4
Estuary Dr IP11 ....153 D7
Estuary Rd IP9 ....107 A4
Ethel Mann Rd 1 NR35 ..110 C2
Ethel Rd NR32 ....113 A1
Ethelreda Dr 1 IP24 .....16 D7
Etna Rd IP33 ....154 B4
Euro Ret Pk IP3 ....140 E1
Europa Rd NR32 ....113 C4
Europa Way
Harwich CO12 ....106 F2
Ipswich IP1 ....138 D8
Euroscope* NR32 ....113 E2
Eustace Rd IP1 ....138 E8
Euston Ave IP4 ....140 F6
Euston Cl IP33 ....154 A1
Euston Ct 4 IP11 ....152 C4
Euston Hall* IP24 ....16 E1
Evans Cl IP18 ....119 C7
Evans Dr NR32 ....113 B2
Evans' Heath CO10 ....93 F4
Eve Balfour Way IP6 ......66 D8
Evelyn Cl IP21 ....38 C7
Everard Cl 5 IP32 ....122 E8
Evergreen La CB8 ....74 C8
Evergreen Rd NR32 ......113 B2
Everitt Rd NR33 ....114 D8
Everton Cres IP1 ....134 F1
Eves Ct 12 CO12 ....106 E1
Evesham Cl IP32 ....122 C8
Exchange Sq 6 NR34 .....111 B5
Exchange St 22 IP20 ......22 D6
Exeter Cres IP27 ....109 F1
Exeter Ct 6 IP19 ....24 C3
Exeter Rd 3 Claydon IP6 ..82 B5
Felixstowe IP11 ....152 E5
Ipswich IP3 ....140 B4
Newmarket CB8 ....121 A4
Exeter Way IP24 ....16 A6
Exmoor Rd IP11 ....152 F6
Exning Prim Sch CB8 .....120 B8
Exning Rd CB8 ....120 D6

F

Factory La
Brantham CO11 ....104 E4
Chevington IP29 ....62 C5
Diss IP22 ....20 B3
Factory St NR32 ....113 D2
Fagbury Rd IP11 ....152 A4
Faiers Cl IP23 ....123 B2
Fair Cl Beccles NR34 ......111 B5
14 Feltwell IP26 ....4 E5
Fair View Rd IP19 ....118 C5
Fairbairn Ave 1 IP41 .....141 D7
Fairey Fox Dr 2 IP28 ....116 B5
Fairfax Cl NR34 ....111 B3
Fairfax Dr IP27 ....5 E4
Fairfax Gdns IP6 ....125 E4
Fairfield Ave IP11 ....153 A5
Fairfield Cres IP13 ....126 D3
Fairfield Dr
Lowestoft NR33 ....114 D2
Saxmundham IP17 ....128 C3
Fairfield Inf Sch IP14 ....124 D6
Fairfield House Gdns
IP17 ....128 C3
Fairfield Inf Sch IP11 ....153 A5
Fairfield Rd
Aldeburgh IP15 ....130 D5
Framlingham IP13 ....126 D2
Ipswich IP3 ....140 A2
Lowestoft NR33 ....114 D6
Reydon IP18 ....119 C8
Saxmundham IP17 ....128 C3

Fairfield Way 12 IP26 ....4 E5
Fairfields IP24 ....16 C7
Fairfoot La CB8 ....120 E5
Fairhead Loke NR33 ......114 B1
Fairlawns Rd CB8 ....120 F2
Fairlight Cl 2 IP14 ....136 A1
Fairmead IP30 ....50 F3
Fairmile Cl 8 NR34 ......111 F4
Fairstead House Sch
CB8 ....121 B4
Fairstead The IP22 ....36 A7
Fairway The
Aldeburgh IP15 ....130 C6
1 Great Yarmouth NR31 ....3 B8
Lowestoft NR33 ....114 F5
Fairways The IP4 ....140 E5
Fakenham Hill IP31 ....33 F5
Falcon Ave IP22 ....20 D3
Falcon Cl CB9 ....133 A6
Falcon Dr IP27 ....6 A1
Falcon Inn Rd NR34 ....26 C7
Falcon La NR35 ....110 B5
Falcon 18 IP26 ....4 E5
Falcon St
Felixstowe IP11 ....152 E6
Ipswich IP1 ....155 B2
Falconer Ave 3 IP14 ......51 E1
Falconer Rd CB9 ....133 A3
Falkenham Rd IP10 ....98 E2
Falklands Dr 21 CO11 ....104 E2
Falklands Rd CB9 ....132 E7
Fallowfield 2 IP30 ....49 F2
Fallowfield Ct 10 CO10 ...132 C5
Fallowfield Wlk IP33 .....122 B1
Fallowfields IP12 ....112 F5
Falmouth Ave CB8 ....120 F3
Falmouth Cl IP5 ....141 B6
Falmouth Gdns CB8 ......121 A6
Falmouth St CB8 ....120 F3
Famona Rd NR33 ....114 C2
Faraday Rd IP3 ....139 F5
Farford Field 6 CO10 ......92 B3
Farina Cl IP8 ....138 F7
Farlingaye High Sch
IP12 ....146 E6
Farlingaves IP12 ....146 F7
Farm Cl Bungay NR35 .....110 D3
Bury St Edmunds IP33 .....123 B1
8 Lowestoft NR33 ....114 C5
Wissett IP19 ....24 C2
Farm Ct St IP20 ....23 E5
Farmerie Rd CO10 ....75 D3
Farmland Cl IP14 ....119 B8
Farnham Cl 5 NR32 ....112 F4
Farnham Rd
Blaxhall IP12 ....71 F5
Snape IP17 ....72 D6
Farrier's Rd IP24 ....124 C3
Farriers Cl
15 Martlesham Heath IP5 ..98 A8
Stradbroke IP21 ....39 B4
Farriers Went IP11 ....152 D7
Farrow Cl IP16 ....129 B6
Farthing Dro
Beck Row, Holywell Row
& Kenny Hill IP27 ....12 E6
Lakenheath IP27 ....13 A6
Farthing Rd Ind Est
IP1 ....138 C7
Farthings The IP28 ....31 D3
Farthings Went IP9 ....150 F4
Fastnet Cl IP9 ....133 B6
Fastoll Cl 4 NR32 ....113 A3
Faulkeners Way IP11 .....152 C7
Faversham Ct NR33 ......115 A4
Fawcett Rd IP15 ....130 E4
Fawley Cl IP4 ....140 C7
Fayrefield Rd IP12 ....147 B7
Feast Cl 7 CB7 ....29 A1
Featherbroom Gdns
IP13 ....127 C5
Feathers Field 3 IP11 ....152 D5
Feilden Way CB8 ....120 E5
Felaw St IP11 ....155 C1
Felix Cl IP5 ....141 B7
Felix Rd
Felixstowe IP11 ....153 B4
Ipswich IP3 ....140 C2
8 Stowupland IP14 ....67 A6
Felixstowe General Hospl
IP11 ....153 B4
Felixstowe Leisure Ctr
IP11 ....152 F3
Felixstowe Mus* IP11 ....107 E2
Felixstowe Rd
Ipswich IP3 ....139 F4
8 Martlesham IP5 ....98 A8
Felixstowe Sta IP11 ....153 A5
Fell Rd CO9 ....89 A4
Fellbrigg Ave IP5 ....140 F6
Fellows Cl IP21 ....21 A1
Felnor Wlk IP11 ....153 B3
Felsham Chase CB5 ....44 B5
Felsham Cl IP14 ....124 F3
Felsham Rd
Bradfield St Clare IP30 .....64 D4
Rattlesden IP30 ....65 C5
Felsham Rise IP17 ....128 C3
Felton Wlk IP32 ....122 D8
Feltons 6 CB7 ....29 A1
Feltwell Elementary Sch
IP26 ....4 E6
Feltwell Rd CB8 ....132 F6
Feltwell Prim Sch IP26 ....4 D5
Fen La Barby NR34 ....10 C4
IP24 ....16 B4
Fir Rd IP24 ....16 B4

Fen Alder Carr Nature
Reserve*** IP6 ....125 D8
Fen Bank CB7 ....29 C6
Fen Cl NR33 ....115 A6
Fen La Ardleigh CO7 ....103 E1
Beccles NR34 ....115 B7
Beck Row, Holywell Row
& Kenny Hill IP28 ....13 D1
Braiseworth IP23 ....37 D3
Creeting St Peter or
West Creeting IP6 ....125 D8
Ditchingham NR35 ....7 E7
Garboldisham IP22 ....18 D3
Hitcham IP7 ....79 E5
Rickinghall Inferior IP22 ...36 A6
Roydon IP21 ....19 F3
Stonham Earl IP6 ....67 D4
Thelnetham IP22 ....18 E1
Fen Meadow IP11 ....152 C8
Fen Pk Prim Sch
NR33 ....115 B6
Fen Rd Blo' Norton IP22 ..18 F2
Pakenham IP31 ....49 F6
Fen St Boxford CO10 ....93 C3
Hinderclay IP22 ....18 F1
Nayland CO6 ....102 D5
Fen View
Halesworth IP19 ....118 A5
Stowmarket IP14 ....124 D3
Fenn La IP12 ....98 D6
Fenstreet Rd IP17 ....58 A7
Fenton Cl CB9 ....132 F6
Fentons Way IP5 ....141 C7
Ferguson Way IP5 ....141 B8
Fern Ave NR32 ....112 E4
Fern Gn Cl 3 8 NR32 .....112 E4
Fern Gr CB9 ....132 C6
Fern Hill CO10 ....77 A4
Ferndale Ave NR32 ....113 B3
Ferndale Cl CB8 ....121 B6
Ferndown Rd 3 IP11 .....153 C6
Ferneley Cres CB8 ....121 A4
Fernhayes Cl IP2 ....139 A3
Fernhill Cl IP12 ....147 A7
Fernlea Rd 4 CO12 ....107 B3
Ferry La
Beck Row, Holywell Row
& Kenny Hill IP28 ....29 F5
Felixstowe IP11 ....152 C3
Ferry Quay IP12 ....147 A4
Ferry Rd Bawdsey IP12 ...99 D1
Felixstowe IP11 ....153 D7
Southwold IP18 ....119 C3
Sudbourne IP12 ....131 C6
Walberswick IP18 ....119 B2
Fersfield Rd IP22 ....19 D5
Festival Cl 4 IP17 ....72 C8
Festival Rd IP3 ....140 C2
Feveryears Yd 1 IP21 .....39 D8
Fiddler's La CO7 ....117 F2
Fiddlers La CO7 ....151 C5
Field Cl 3 IP30 ....49 F2
Field Fuller's IP6 ....135 E4
Field Grange CB8 ....112 F5
Field House Gdns IP22 ...20 D2
Field La NR33 ....11 B1
Field Rd IP20 ....116 C5
Field Stile Rd 2 IP18 .....119 D5
Field Terr Rd CB8 ....120 F5
Field View
Bucklesham IP10 ....98 A4
8 Thurstow IP31 ....49 E4
Field View Gdns NR34 ....111 D3
Field Way
Debenham IP14 ....53 F1
18 Stanton IP31 ....34 E4
Field Wlk IP28 ....116 C5
Fields View CO10 ....148 D6
Fieldview Cl IP18 ....119 B8
Fieldview Dr NR32 ....113 A1
Fife Rd IP4 ....136 B1
Finbars Wlk IP4 ....139 E5
Finborough Cl IP4 ....140 F6
Finborough Rd IP14 ......124 B6
Finch Cl IP7 ....67 A5
Fincham Rd IP28 ....116 B5
Finchingfield Rd
Stambourne CO9 ....89 B1
Steeple Bumpstead CB9 ...88 E3
Finchley Ave IP28 ....116 B6
Finchley Rd IP4 ....139 E6
Findley Cl IP9 ....105 C5
Fingal St IP21 ....39 A1
Finney's Drift IP10 ....145 C5
Finningham Rd
Gislingham IP23 ....36 D1
Old Newton with Dagworth
IP14 ....51 F2
Rickinghall Superior IP22 ..36 A4
Walsham le Willows IP31 ...35 D2
Finsbury Pl IP33 ....154 B1
Finsbury Sq IP33 ....154 C1
Fir Cl Barnby NR34 ....10 C4
Mundford IP26 ....6 B8
Wickham Market IP13 .....127 C6
Fir La NR32 ....113 A2

Fir Tree Cl IP21 ....22 D2
Fir Tree Hill IP9 ....105 F7
Fir Tree La IP14 ....51 C3
Fir Tree Rise IP8 ....138 C2
Fir Wlk IP27 ....113 F2
Fircroft Rd IP1 ....135 A2
Firebrass La IP12 ....85 C2
Firebronds Rd 7 IP9 .....105 E7
Firecrest Dr 2 IP14 ......124 F7
Firefly Way 1 IP3 ....144 B8
Firfield Cl NR34 ....111 B3
Firmin Cl IP1 ....139 A6
Firs The Beccles NR34 ....111 F4
Lakenheath IP27 ....109 C6
Lowestoft NR33 ....114 C3
Southwold IP18 ....119 B8
First Ave
4 Glemsford CO10 ....77 B3
Sudbury CO10 ....148 E7
First Dro Burwell CB5 ......44 B8
Lakenheath IP27 ....109 A8
Firtree Cl IP22 ....122 D7
Fish Pond Hill IP14 ....106 B6
Fishbane Cl 9 IP31 ....128 C2
Fisher Rd IP22 ....20 D3
Fisher Row
Carlton Colville NR32 ......114 B8
Lowestoft NR32 ....112 B1
Fisher's Dro IP22 ....12 D3
Fisher's La
East Bergholt CO7 ....104 E6
Hoxne IP21 ....38 C8
Fisherman's Way 18
NR33 ....11 C1
Fishers The IP5 ....141 C7
Fishpond Rd IP12 ....98 D7
Fishponds Hill CO6 ....102 C3
Fishponds La IP14 ....12 B8
Fishponds Way IP14 ......66 C8
Fiske Cl IP22 ....123 E6
Fison Way IP24 ....16 B7
Fitches La IP16 ....129 D1
Fitches The IP17 ....129 A2
Fitzgerald Cl 4 CO11 ....104 D2
Fitzgerald Rd
Bramford IP8 ....134 A1
Woodbridge IP12 ....147 A6
Fitzgerald Wlk IP3 ....122 B6
Fitzmaurice Rd IP3 ....140 B3
Fitzroy St Ipswich IP1 ....155 B3
Newmarket CB8 ....121 A1
Fitzwilliam Cl
Ipswich IP2 ....138 F2
6 Woodbridge IP12 ....146 E4
Five Acre La NR35 ....7 E3
Five Acres 8 IP9 ....105 E7
Five Cross Ways
Butley IP12 ....98 B4
Sudbourne IP12 ....131 B6
Wetheringsett-cum-Brockford
IP23 ....53 A7
Fiveways IP28 ....116 A3
Flatford Cl IP14 ....124 E3
Flatford La CO7 ....151 D1
Flatford Mill* CO7 ....151 D1
Flatford Rd
East Bergholt CO7 ....151 D2
Haverhill CB9 ....132 A6
Flatts La IP30 ....50 B2
Flavian Cl CB9 ....133 B5
Flax La CO10 ....77 B2
Fleet Dyke Dr NR33 ......114 F5
Fleetwood Ave IP11 ......153 B5
Fleetwood Rd IP11 ....153 B5
Fleming Ave IP28 ....116 C5
Flempton Rd IP28 ....47 D5
Flemyng Rd IP33 ....122 C5
Fletcher Cl 3 IP3 ....140 A1
Fletcher Rd IP3 ....140 A1
Fletcher's La IP5 ....58 B6
Flindell Dr IP14 ....134 A2
Flint Cl IP2 ....139 B2
Flixton Marsh La
NR32 ....112 B6
Flixton Rd
Blundeston NR32 ....112 C8
Bungay NR35 ....110 A1
Flixton NR35 ....7 E2
St Mary, South Elmham
otherwise Homersfield
IP20 ....23 B8
Somerleyton, Ashby &
Herringfleet NR32 ....2 F4
Flora Rd NR33 ....115 A3
Flordon Rd IP6 ....125 E5
Florence Rd NR33 ....115 B3
Florence Way NR35 ....8 D7
Flowerday Cl 4 NR31 .....3 B7
Flowton Rd Elmsett IP7 ...81 A1
Flowton IP8 ....95 B8
Somersham IP8 ....81 C3
Floyd Rd IP32 ....122 D8
Foal's Gn Rd IP21 ....39 D2
Fodderfen Dro
Beck Row, Holywell Row
& Kenny Hill IP28 ....12 C1
Feltwell PE38 ....4 A3
Foden Ave IP1 ....134 C2
Folly End IP15 ....130 D5
Folly La
Bressingham IP22 ....19 F4
Copdock & Washbrook
IP8 ....95 E2
Lawshall IP29 ....63 C3

Folly Rd
Great Waldingfield CO10 ...92 C6
Hundon CO10 ....75 F3
Mildenhall IP28 ....116 A7
Folly The Harleston IP14 ..56 C8
Haughley IP14 ....51 C1
Fonnereau Rd IP1 ....155 B3
Forbes Dr NR34 ....111 B3
Ford Cl
Beck Row, Holywell Row
& Kenny Hill IP28 ....29 F7
Stowmarket IP14 ....124 E4
Ford Hill IP12 ....99 B7
Ford Rd IP13 ....71 C5
Ford View Rd IP14 ....124 E4
Fordham Moor CB7 ....29 A3
Fordham Rd
4 Ipswich IP4 ....140 F5
21 Ixworth IP31 ....34 B1
Fordham Rd
Fordham CB8 ....44 F7
Freckenham IP28 ....29 D2
Mount Bures CO6 ....101 C1
Newmarket CB8 ....120 F7
Snailwell CB8 ....45 A7
7 Soham CB7 ....28 F2
Wormingford CO6 ....101 C2
Fordhams Cl 21 IP31 .....34 E4
Fordley Rd IP17 ....57 F6
Fordson Way NR33 ....114 C3
Fore Hamlet IP3 ....139 E5
Fore St
Framlingham IP13 ....126 D3
Ipswich IP4 ....155 C2
8 Ipswich IP4 ....155 C2
Forest End CB8 ....46 A7
Forest Gdns 9 IP12 ......85 D8
Forest Glade CB8 ....132 D8
Forest La 3 IP5 ....98 A7
Forest Mount NR31 ....2 B7
Forest Prim Sch The
IP27 ....5 F1
Forest Rd IP4 ....66 B6
Forest Ret Pk IP24 ....16 A5
Forester Cl IP8 ....142 E8
Foresters Wlk 6 IP6 ......82 A5
Forfar Cl 2 Benhall IP17 ..72 C8
Ipswich IP4 ....140 B8
Forge Cl 2 Benhall IP17 ..72 C8
Bucklesham IP10 ....98 A4
Palgrave IP22 ....20 C1
Forge End IP28 ....48 B6
Forge Gr NR34 ....9 B6
Forge St CO7 ....104 A3
Forge Way IP22 ....18 D4
Fornham La IP33 ....122 A7
Forties Cl CB9 ....133 B6
Fortress Rd NR33 ....114 E3
Foster Cl IP18 ....119 D6
Foster Rd 7 CO12 ....106 F3
Foundation St IP4 ....155 B2
Foundry La IP1 ....155 B2
Fountain La CB7 ....28 D4
Fountain Rd 4 IP12 ....85 D8
Fountain Way IP18 ....119 C8
Fountain's La NR34 ....10 C4
Fountains Rd
Bury St Edmunds IP33 .....122 D2
Ipswich IP2 ....139 A1
Four Ash Hill CO9 ....89 C4
Four Elms Residential Sch
IP14 ....68 A8
Four Wheel Dr IP30 ....49 B2
Fourth Ave 5 CO10 ....77 A3
Fowe's La CO10 ....90 D4
Fowler's Cres 2 NR32 .....3 D4
Fox And Pin La IP29 ....124 D6
Fox Ct IP41 ....124 D6
Fox Gn CB8 ....74 C8
Fox Hill Hollesley IP12 ....99 F7
St Cross, South Elmham
IP20 ....23 C7
Fox La IP17 ....42 B1
Fox Rd 6 IP26 ....141 E8
Fox Wood N 9 CB7 ....28 D5
Fox Wood S 10 CB7 ....28 D5
Fox Yd IP18 ....119 D5
Foxborough Mid Sch
NR32 ....113 A5
Foxborough Rd NR32 .....113 A4
Foxburrow Cl CB9 ....132 D7
Foxburrow Farm Nature
Reserve*** IP12 ....84 D6
Foxburrow Hill NR32 .....113 A6
Foxburrow Rd 6 IP3 ......140 F1
Foxburrow Wood Nature
Reserve*** NR32 ....113 B6
Foxes La Ashen CO10 ......90 A5
Mendham IP20 ....23 B4
Foxes Rd CO10 ....89 E5
Foxes Wlk NR32 ....112 C2
Foxglade NR32 ....112 C2
Foxglove Ave IP6 ....125 D3
Foxglove Cl
Lowestoft NR33 ....115 A2
1 Worlingham NR34 ....111 E3
Foxglove Cres 3 IP3 ......140 E1
Foxglove Rd IP24 ....16 D6
Foxglove Gdns IP11 ......153 C5
Foxgrove La IP11 ....153 C5

Foxhall Cl CO7 ...151 C6
Foxhall Fields CO7 ...151 C5
Foxhall Rd Foxhall IP10 ...98 A6
Ipswich IP3 ...139 F5
Foxhall Stadium IP4 ...141 A5
Foxtail Rd IP3 ...144 D8
Foxwood Cl CO11 ...104 B1
Foxwood Cres IP4 ...140 F5
Framfield Rd NR33 ...114 C4
Framlingham Cl 4 IP12 ...85 B3
Framlingham Coll IP13 ...126 C4
Framlingham Mere Nature Reserve* IP13 ...126 C4
Framlingham Rd
Dennington IP13 ...39 F2
Easton IP13 ...70 E5
Laxfield IP13 ...40 A2
Framlington Castle (remains of)* IP13 ...126 C4
Framlinham Coll Prep Sch IP13 ...70 A7
Frampton Rd IP3 ...144 A8
Framsden Rd IP14 ...69 E7
Framsden Windmill* IP14 ...69 B6
Francis Cl
Haverhill CB9 ...132 D6
Ipswich IP5 ...141 E8
Francis Rd
13 Kessingland NR33 ...11 B1
8 Sudbury CO10 ...148 C5
Franciscan Way IP1 ...155 B2
Frank Bridges Cl 4 CB7 ...28 D3
Franklin Cl IP15 ...130 D5
Franklin Rd
Aldeburgh IP15 ...130 C5
Ipswich IP3 ...140 B2
Fraser Rd
Bramford IP8 ...134 B2
Ipswich IP1 ...138 F7
Freckenham Rd
Freckenham CB7 ...29 E2
Worlington IP28 ...30 A3
Fred Archer Way CB8 ...121 A3
Fred Dannatt Rd IP28 ...116 A6
Frederick Talbot Cl 14 CB7 ...28 D4
Frederick's Rd 3 NR34 ...111 C4
Free La NR35 ...110 A8
Freehold Rd
Ipswich IP4 ...140 A6
Needham Market IP6 ...125 C6
Freelands IP14 ...52 E4
Freeman Ave 4 IP6 ...82 D6
Freeman Cl IP7 ...149 D7
Freeman Prim Sch The IP14 ...67 B7
Freemantle Rd NR33 ...115 C7
Freewood St IP30 ...64 D6
Freezes Barns CB9 ...88 D4
Frenze Hall La IP22 ...20 D3
Frenze Rd IP22 ...20 D2
Frere Cnr 7 IP22 ...20 A3
Frere Rd 30 IP20 ...22 C6
Freshfields
17 Harwich CO12 ...106 F1
Newmarket CB8 ...120 F4
Fressingfield CE Prim Sch IP21 ...39 D8
Fressingfield Rd IP20 ...23 C1
Freston Hill IP9 ...143 E4
Freston St IP9 ...143 D3
Freston Twr* IP9 ...143 F4
Friar Cl CB9 ...132 D7
Friar's La IP33 ...154 B1
Friars IP9 ...150 F2
Friars Bridge Rd IP1 ...155 A2
Friars Cl
Bury St Edmunds IP33 ...154 B1
7 Felixstowe IP11 ...153 D6
Friars Croft IP21 ...22 D3
Friars Ct Melton IP12 ...147 C7
Sudbury CO10 ...148 C4
Friars Meadow IP21 ...22 D3
Friars Rd IP7 ...149 C6
Friars St Ipswich IP1 ...155 B2
Sudbury CO10 ...148 C5
Friary Meadow IP28 ...48 D5
Friday St
Beck Row, Holywell Row & Kenny Hill IP28 ...29 F6
Rendlesham IP12 ...85 D7
Friday St Farm Maize Maze* IP17 ...72 B7
Friday's Orch IP16 ...129 C5
Friends Field 7 CO8 ...101 C5
Friends Wlk IP5 ...141 D8
Friston Rd IP12 ...85 C2
Fristonmoor La
Knodishall IP17 ...57 E1
Sternfield IP17 ...72 E8
Fritillary Cl IP8 ...142 E8
Fritton Cl Ipswich IP2 ...139 A1
12 Oulton NR32 ...112 F4
Fritton Ct 5 CB9 ...132 C4
Fritton Lake Ctry World* NR31 ...2 C6
Frobisher Rd
21 Harwich CO12 ...106 F1
Ipswich IP3 ...139 E1
Frog Hall La IP7 ...149 F6
Frogmore CB8 ...120 B7
Frogs Alley IP9 ...106 F6
Frogs Alley Vineyard* IP9 ...106 F7
Frogs Hall Rd CO10 ...78 D5
Frogs Hole NR32 ...2 C5
Fronk's Ave 3 CO12 ...107 B1
Fronk's Rd CO12 ...107 A1
Front Rd IP3 ...144 D8
Front St
Mendlesham IP14 ...52 E4
Orford IP12 ...131 B3
Ousden CB8 ...61 E6
Frostenden Cres 1 NR32 ...113 B4
Frowd Cl CB7 ...29 B1
Fryatt Ave 7 CO12 ...107 A2
Fryth Cl CB9 ...132 E7
Fuchsia La IP4 ...140 A5
Fulcher Cl IP33 ...123 D2
Fulchers Field IP13 ...126 B4
Fulford Cl 8 IP28 ...48 C6
Fuller Rd IP20 ...22 D5
Fullers Cl 2 IP7 ...149 E6
Fullers Teasle NR33 ...114 A3
Fulmar Way NR33 ...114 D5
Fulmerston Rd IP24 ...16 B5
Furness Cl IP2 ...142 F8
Further St CO10 ...92 E2
Furthest Dro IP27 ...4 D1
Furze Cl 4 IP31 ...49 D4
Furze Way IP22 ...36 D5
Fyffe Way 12 NR33 ...115 D8
Fynn La IP6 ...136 C5
Fynn Rd IP12 ...146 D3

G

Gables The CB9 ...133 D3
Gaell Cres 5 IP7 ...149 D5
Gage Cl IP32 ...154 A4
Gage's Rd CO10 ...90 C4
Gainsborough Ctr IP3 ...144 B8
Gainsborough Dr
Halesworth IP19 ...118 A2
Lowestoft NR32 ...113 B6
Manningtree CO11 ...104 D2
Gainsborough La IP3 ...143 F8
Gainsborough Rd
Bury St Edmunds IP33 ...122 D5
Felixstowe IP11 ...153 A4
Haverhill CB9 ...132 B7
Ipswich IP4 ...155 C4
Stowmarket IP14 ...124 B6
Sudbury CO10 ...148 C5
Gainsborough St CO10 ...148 C5
Gainsborough's House* CO10 ...148 C5
Galley Cl NR33 ...114 B4
Galley Rd CO10 ...75 D3
Gallow La IP30 ...78 C7
Gallows Hill IP7 ...149 B7
Gallows La IP14 ...66 C7
Galway Ave IP1 ...134 E1
Gandish Cl CO7 ...151 D3
Gandish Rd CO7 ...151 E4
Ganges Rd 1 IP9 ...107 A4
Gannet Cl CB9 ...133 A6
Gannet Rd IP2 ...138 E3
Ganwick Cl CB9 ...132 D8
Gaol La Beccles NR34 ...111 B5
Sudbury CO10 ...148 C5
Gap The NR33 ...114 F6
Garboldisham Rd
Harling NR16 ...18 C7
Kenninghall NR16 ...18 F7
Garboldisham VC Prim Sch IP22 ...18 D4
Garden Cl
Bungay NR35 ...110 C3
5 Great Barton IP31 ...49 A6
Normanston NR32 ...113 B2
Shotley IP9 ...106 F6
Garden Ct 2 CB5 ...44 B6
Garden Field 2 IP11 ...152 E5
Garden Fields IP31 ...33 D3
Garden House La IP30 ...65 C6
Garden La
Beccles NR34 ...111 F4
Westley IP33 ...122 A5
Garden Pl CO10 ...148 B5
Garden Sq IP12 ...85 D8
Gardeners La 21 CB7 ...28 D4
Gardeners Rd IP14 ...53 F1
Gardeners Wlk IP30 ...50 E2
Gardenhouse La IP22 ...36 A6
Gardens The
4 Beyton IP30 ...49 F2
Lowestoft NR33 ...114 C2
Gardiner Cl IP33 ...122 C4
Gardner Rd IP18 ...119 D5
Garfield Cl IP11 ...152 F3
Garfield Rd IP11 ...152 F3
Garland Rd 5 CO12 ...106 F3
Garland St IP33 ...154 B3
Garlic St IP21 ...22 A6
Garnons Chase 3 CO6 ...101 F2
Garrard Pl 12 IP31 ...34 B1
Garrards Rd 3 IP7 ...80 F1
Garrett Cl IP17 ...72 D5
Garrett Cres IP16 ...129 D5
Garrick Way IP1 ...135 A3
Garrison La
Felixstowe IP11 ...152 F4
5 Great Waldingfield CO10 ...92 C6
Garrod App IP12 ...84 E7
Garrods IP9 ...150 F3
Garrods End IP29 ...62 C5
Gas Works Rd NR32 ...113 E2
Gascoigne Dr 3 IP6 ...82 D6
Gashouse Dro IP27 ...5 F1
Gaston End CO7 ...151 C5
Gaston St CO7 ...151 C4
Gatacre Rd IP1 ...139 A7
Gate Farm Rd 2 IP9 ...107 A5
Gatesbury's La IP29 ...62 C2
Gateway The IP33 ...123 C3
Gavell St IP19 ...24 D5
Gawdy Cl 2 IP20 ...22 D6
Gaye Cres IP23 ...117 B3
Gaye St IP1 ...155 A3
Gayfer Ave IP5 ...141 F8
Gayford Sq IP7 ...80 C6
Gaymers La IP11 ...152 B8
Gazeley Rd Ashley CB8 ...46 A1
Kentford CB8 ...46 A5
Gdn Room The* IP6 ...125 D5
Gedding Hill IP30 ...65 B4
Gedding Rd IP30 ...65 B7
Gedge Cl IP33 ...122 C4
Gedgrave Rd IP12 ...131 A1
Geldeston Hill NR34 ...8 F6
Geldeston Rd
Ellingham NR35 ...8 D6
Geldeston NR34 ...9 B6
General Castle Way IP30 ...49 B2
Generals Mews 12 IP11 ...152 D5
Genesta Dr 2 IP31 ...49 D4
Geneva Gdns 4 NR31 ...3 C6
Geneva Rd IP1 ...155 A4
Gentle Ct 3 IP27 ...5 F1
Gents La IP29 ...77 F7
George Baldry Way 2 NR35 ...110 C2
George Brown Way NR34 ...111 C3
George Cl NR32 ...112 E1
George Frost Cl IP4 ...155 C4
George Gent Cl 7 CB9 ...88 D3
George Gibson Cl CB8 ...120 C8
George Hill IP31 ...34 E4
George La 3 CO10 ...77 B2
George Lambpton Ave CB8 ...120 F5
George Rd 3 IP24 ...16 D6
George St Brandon IP27 ...5 F1
Hadleigh IP7 ...149 E6
2 Harwich CO12 ...107 B3
Hintlesham IP8 ...95 C6
George Westwood Way NR34 ...111 C6
Geralds Ave IP4 ...140 A5
Gestingthorpe Rd CO10 ...90 F2
Gibbon Cl IP32 ...123 E5
Gibraltar Cl IP33 ...122 C6
Gibraltar Rd IP6 ...69 B1
Gifford Cl 6 IP9 ...105 E7
Giffords Pl IP4 ...140 F6
Gilbert Cl IP6 ...125 C5
Gilbert Rd 2 CO10 ...90 A8
Giles Way Risby IP28 ...47 E5
4 Witnesham IP6 ...83 A5
Gillingham Rd NR34 ...9 A6
Gillngham Dam NR34 ...111 A7
Gilpin Rd NR32 ...112 D1
Gilray Rd IP22 ...20 D2
Gilstrap Rd IP31 ...48 D5
Gimbert Rd 7 CB7 ...28 D4
Gin La IP13 ...40 C2
Gippeswyk Ave IP2 ...139 A4
Gippeswyk Rd IP2 ...155 A1
Gipping Cl CB9 ...132 C4
Gipping Pl IP14 ...124 D7
Gipping Rd Claydon IP6 ...82 A5
Stowupland IP14 ...67 A7
Gipping Way
Bramford IP8 ...134 B2
Sproughton IP8 ...138 B6
Stowmarket IP14 ...124 D7
Gippingstone Rd IP8 ...134 A1
Gipsy La
Aldringham cum Thorpe IP16 ...129 D1
Frostenden NR34 ...26 D4
Needham Market IP6 ...125 C6
Girling St CO10 ...148 C6
Girton Cl
Mildenhall IP28 ...116 C6
Woodbridge IP12 ...146 D4
Woodditton CB8 ...121 B1
Girton Rd CB9 ...132 F5
Girton Way IP2 ...138 F1
Gisleham Mid Sch NR33 ...114 C1
Gisleham Rd NR33 ...114 B1
Gislingham CE Prim Sch IP23 ...36 C2
Gislingham Rd IP14 ...36 C1
Gissing Rd IP22 ...20 F6
Glade Prim Sch The IP27 ...5 F1
Glade The IP24 ...16 C7
Glades The NR32 ...112 D2
Gladstone Rd
1 Corton NR32 ...3 C4
Ipswich IP3 ...139 F5
6 Woodbridge IP12 ...147 A5
Glamis Cl CB9 ...132 B6
Glamis Ct 26 IP20 ...22 D6
Glamorgan Rd IP2 ...139 B1
Glanely Gdns CB8 ...120 C8
Glanfield Wlk IP33 ...122 C4
Glanville Pl IP5 ...141 B6
Glanville Rd IP7 ...149 E4
Glassfield Rd IP31 ...34 D4
Glastonbury Cl IP2 ...138 F1
Glastonbury Rd IP33 ...122 C3
Glebe Cl Baylham IP6 ...81 E6
Horringer IP29 ...63 A7
Ingham IP31 ...32 F1
Lowestoft NR32 ...113 C5
Sproughton IP8 ...138 B6
1 Tattingstone IP9 ...105 B8
Glebe End IP9 ...150 F4
Glebe La IP9 ...144 B1
Glebe Meadow IP13 ...54 F2
Glebe Rd Bredfield IP13 ...84 C7
Gissing IP21 ...21 A8
Weeting IP27 ...5 E3
Glebe Rd E 15 NR33 ...11 C1
Glebe Rd W 18 NR33 ...11 B1
Glebe The
Haverhill CB9 ...132 E7
Lavenham CO10 ...78 D3
Glebe View NR34 ...111 C3
Glebe Way 1 Claydon IP6 ...82 B5
Mendlesham IP14 ...52 E4
Glebes The IP17 ...72 D5
Glemham Dr IP4 ...140 F4
Glemham Hall* IP13 ...71 E6
Glemham Rd IP17 ...56 E2
Glemsford Cl IP11 ...152 D3
Glemsford Com Prim Sch CO10 ...77 A3
Glemsford Pl 7 CB9 ...132 F6
Glemsford Rd
Lowestoft NR32 ...112 F4
Stowmarket IP14 ...124 E4
Glenavon Rd IP4 ...140 D7
Glenbourne Wlk 2 NR33 ...114 C3
Glencoe Rd IP4 ...136 C1
Gleneagles Cl
4 Bury St Edmunds IP28 ...48 C6
1 Felixstowe IP11 ...153 C6
Gleneagles Dr IP4 ...140 D5
Glenfield Ave IP11 ...153 A6
Glenhurst Ave IP4 ...140 B8
Glenside CO10 ...148 E4
Glenwood Ct CB8 ...120 F3
Glenwood Dr NR34 ...111 E4
Globe Yd 3 CO10 ...148 C6
Gloster Rd IP5 ...98 A8
Gloucester Ave NR32 ...112 F3
Gloucester Pl 4 CO10 ...76 A1
Gloucester Rd
4 Bury St Edmunds IP32 ...122 E8
Haverhill CB9 ...132 D5
Ipswich IP3 ...140 A2
Gloucester Way CO10 ...148 B8
Go Ape* IP27 ...15 C8
Gobbets La IP22 ...35 E7
Gobbett's Rd IP22 ...35 E8
Gobbitts Yd IP12 ...147 A4
Godbold Cl 3 IP5 ...141 D7
Goddard Pl IP14 ...66 B7
Goddard Rd IP1 ...134 C3
Goddard Rd E IP1 ...134 D3
Godetia Ct 6 NR32 ...113 B4
Godfrey's Ct 12 NR32 ...113 D2
Godfrey's Hill IP19 ...40 F8
Godfrey's Wood IP12 ...147 A7
Godolphin Cl IP33 ...122 C3
Godyll Rd IP18 ...119 C5
Goldcrest Rd IP2 ...138 C3
Golden La IP29 ...63 C2
Golden Lion La 5 CO12 ...107 B3
Golden Miller Cl CB8 ...120 D7
Goldenlond CO6 ...102 E7
Golding Way 1 CO10 ...77 A2
Golding's La IP16 ...129 C4
Goldings Cl CB9 ...132 E8
Goldsmith Cl IP32 ...122 D7
Goldsmith Rd IP1 ...134 E3
Goldsmith Way IP21 ...21 F8
Golf La IP15 ...130 C6
Golf Links Rd
Barton Mills IP28 ...30 C3
Worlington IP28 ...116 A1
Golf Rd IP11 ...153 D5
Gondree NR33 ...114 E3
Gonville Cl
Mildenhall IP28 ...116 D6
1 Woodbridge IP12 ...146 E4
Goodall Terr IP5 ...141 E8
Goodchilds Gdns 8 CB7 ...29 C5
Goodlake Cl 9 CO12 ...106 F1
Goodman Gr IP5 ...141 E7
Goodwood Cl IP1 ...135 B4
Goose Gn E NR34 ...111 C5
Goose Gn W NR34 ...111 C5
Gorams Mill La IP13 ...40 B3
Gordon Rd
California IP4 ...140 A6
5 Harwich CO12 ...107 A1
Ipswich IP4 ...140 A7
Lowestoft NR32 ...113 D1
Gordon Richards Cl CB8 ...120 F6
Goring Rd IP4 ...140 C6
Gorleston Rd
Blundeston NR32 ...112 F8
Corton NR32 ...3 B4
Gorse Cl
Lakenheath IP27 ...109 E4
6 Red Lodge IP28 ...30 C1
Gorse Gn NR32 ...113 B3
Gorse Ind Est IP24 ...16 A3
Gorse La IP18 ...119 C7
Gorse Rd Ipswich IP3 ...140 B2
Southwold IP18 ...119 C6
Gorse View IP17 ...58 C8
Gorsehayes IP2 ...139 B3
Gorseland Prim Sch IP5 ...141 F8
Gorselands IP12 ...99 F7
Gorst Cl 7 IP32 ...122 E8
Gosford Cl 4 CO10 ...90 A8
Gosford Rd NR34 ...111 C5
Gosford Way IP11 ...153 C6
Gostling Cl 2 IP22 ...20 B2
Gostling Pl IP5 ...141 E8
Gothic Cl 2 IP20 ...22 D5
Gotsfield Cl 1 CO10 ...92 B7
Gough Pl 9 IP31 ...34 B1
Governors Mews IP33 ...123 C2
Gower St IP2 ...155 B1
Gowers Cl IP5 ...141 E7
Gowers End 6 CO10 ...77 B3
Gowle Rd IP14 ...124 C8
Goyfield Ave IP11 ...152 F4
Gracechurch St IP14 ...53 E2
Graften Way IP1 ...155 A2
Grafton Cl IP33 ...122 D5
Grafton Rd 2 CO12 ...107 B2
Grafton Way IP1 ...155 B2
Graham Ave IP1 ...139 B8
Graham Rd
Felixstowe IP11 ...152 F5
Ipswich IP1 ...155 A4
Grainge Way 3 IP14 ...51 C1
Grainger Cl IP32 ...123 F5
Grammar Sch Pl 11 CO10 ...148 C5
Grampian Way NR32 ...112 D2
Granaries The IP6 ...136 C6
Granary Rd CB8 ...121 B2
Granary The Clare CO10 ...90 A7
Hadleigh IP7 ...149 E5
Granby St CB8 ...121 B3
Grand Ave NR33 ...115 B3
Grange Cl
Felixstowe IP11 ...152 E5
Ipswich IP5 ...141 F8
Grange Ct IP12 ...147 B6
Grange Farm Ave IP11 ...152 D5
Grange La
Barton Mills IP28 ...116 D2
Ipswich IP5 ...141 E8
Grange Mill 3 IP29 ...62 C6
Grange Prim Sch IP11 ...152 D4
Grange Rd
Beccles NR34 ...111 A4
Felixstowe IP11 ...152 D3
Flixton NR35 ...23 E8
16 Harwich CO12 ...107 A2
Ipswich IP4 ...139 E6
Lawford CO11 ...104 C1
Lowestoft NR32 ...112 D2
Wickham Skeith IP23 ...52 D7
Grange View IP17 ...58 B7
Grange Wlk IP33 ...123 A2
Grantchester Pl IP5 ...141 A8
Grantchester Rise CB5 ...44 A7
Grantham Cres IP2 ...155 A1
Granville Gdns 3 IP28 ...116 A4
Granville Rd IP11 ...152 F3
Granville St IP1 ...155 A3
Granworth Cl IP13 ...83 E6
Grasmere Ave 5 IP11 ...153 D6
Gratton Dale NR33 ...114 E2
Gravel Dam NR32 ...112 B2
Gravel Dro IP28 ...29 E6
Gravel Hill CO6 ...102 D5
Gravel Hill Way CO12 ...106 F1
Gravel Pit La CO11 ...104 F5
Gray's La IP19 ...24 D4
Gray's Orch IP10 ...98 E2
Grayling Rd IP8 ...142 E8
Graylings The 10 NR33 ...114 E4
Grays Rd NR34 ...10 C7
Grayson Ave NR33 ...115 A3
Grayson Dr NR33 ...115 A2
Great Back La 4 IP14 ...53 F2
Great Barton Prim Sch IP31 ...49 B6
Great Colman St IP4 ...155 C3
Great Comm La NR34 ...8 E1
Great Cornard Ctry Pk* CO10 ...92 B2
Great Cornard Mid Sch CO10 ...92 B2
Great Cornard Sports Ctr CO10 ...148 F2
Great Cornard Upper Sch CO10 ...148 F2
Great Dro CB7 ...28 A4
Great Eastern Rd CO10 ...148 D5
Great Eastern Sq IP11 ...153 A5
Great Fen Rd CB7 ...28 D8
Great Field IP11 ...152 C8
Great Finborough Prim Sch IP14 ...66 A4
Great Gipping St IP1 ...155 A2
Great Harlings IP9 ...107 A5
Great Heath Prim Sch IP28 ...116 D6
Great Oak Ct CO9 ...90 A1
Great Tufts IP9 ...150 F3
Great Waldingfield VCE Prim Sch CO10 ...92 C6
Great Whelnetham CE Prim Sch IP30 ...63 F6
Great Whip St IP2 ...155 B1
Grebe Cl Ipswich IP2 ...138 E2
Mildenhall IP28 ...116 D3

Grebe Cl continued
Stowmarket IP14 ...... 124 A6
Green Acre 2 CO10 ...... 92 C6
Green Cres IP10 ...... 98 A4
Green Dr NR33 ...... 115 A4
Green Farm La 5 IP29 ...47 A2
Green Fleet Dr NR32 ...112 E4
Green Hill IP6 ...... 68 B1
Green La Boxted CO4 ...102 E3
Burgh St Peter NR34 ...... 10 C8
Cockfield IP30 ...... 64 D2
Creeting St Mary IP14 ...... 67 F5
Ditchingham NR35 ...... 110 C7
6 Feltwell IP26 ...... 4 E5
Frostenden NR34 ...... 26 C4
Great Barton IP31 ...... 49 B5
Hundon CO10 ...... 75 D2
Kessingland NR33 ...... 11 C1
3 Martlesham IP12 ...... 84 A1
Pettistree IP13 ...... 127 D5
Redenhall with Harleston
IP20 ...... 22 E6
Reydon IP18 ...... 26 E1
Shipmeadow NR34 ...... 8 F5
Somerleyton, Ashby &
Herringfleet NR32 ...... 2 E4
Southwold IP18 ...... 119 B8
Starston IP20 ...... 22 D8
Stratford St Mary CO7 ...103 E6
Syleham IP21 ...... 38 E8
2 Tattingstone IP9 ...105 B8
Thelnetham IP22 ...... 35 C6
Thetford IP24 ...... 16 C6
Thrandeston IP21 ...... 37 B6
Troston IP31 ...... 33 C5
Tuddenham St Martin
IP6 ...... 136 C4
Wetheringsett-cum-Brockford
IP14 ...... 53 A6
Green La Cl IP18 ...... 119 B8
Green Man Pl IP12 ...... 71 F2
Green Man Way IP12 ...147 B6
Green Oak Glade IP8 ...142 D8
42 Harleston IP20 ...... 22 D6
Green Pk Brinkley CB8 ...59 E1
42 Harleston IP20 ...... 22 D6
Green Rd Brandon IP27 ...... 6 A1
Newmarket CB8 ...... 121 A2
Thorpe Morieux IP30 ...... 64 F1
Woolpit IP30 ...... 50 D1
Green St IP7 ...... 38 C8
Green The 4 Ashley CB8 ...60 E8
Beck Row, Holywell Row
& Kenny Hill IP28 ...... 29 E7
Chedburgh IP29 ...... 62 C4
6 Earsham NR35 ...... 7 F4
3 Harleston All Saints IP13 ...83 E5
Hadleigh IP7 ...... 149 E6
Hessett IP30 ...... 64 F8
Kersey IP7 ...... 94 A7
Kirtling CB8 ...... 60 E3
Lound NR32 ...... 2 F6
Mendlesham IP14 ...... 52 D2
3 Mistley CO11 ...... 104 F2
North Lopham IP22 ...... 19 A6
Snailwell CB8 ...... 45 A6
Walberswick IP18 ...... 119 E2
Green Willows CO10 ...... 78 C2
Greenacre Cres 1
NR32 ...... 113 A2
Greencares IP14 ...... 51 F1
Greenbank IP19 ...... 118 C5
Greene King Brewing Mus*
IP33 ...... 154 C1
Greene Rd IP33 ...... 122 C4
Greenfield Rd NR33 ...114 F5
Greenfields CB8 ...... 121 C3
Greenfields Way CO10 ...132 C5
Greenfinch Ave IP32 ...138 D3
Greenhills CB7 ...... 28 E3
Greens The
Aldeburgh IP15 ...... 130 C6
Ipswich IP4 ...... 140 F4
Greensmill 2 CO11 ...104 E3
Greenspire Gr IP8 ...138 B2
Greenview IP29 ...... 77 B7
Greenway 4 IP31 ...... 49 A5
Greenway The NR34 ...111 B4
Greenways IP12 ...... 85 C2
Greenways Cl IP11 ...123 B8
Greenways Cres IP32 ...123 E4
Greenwich Bsns Pk
IP3 ...... 139 E2
Greenwich Cl IP3 ...139 E2
Greenwich Rd IP3 ...139 D2
Greenwood Cl CB9 ...132 C6
Greenwood Way 1
NR32 ...... 113 A6
Greenwoods The IP31 ...49 E6
Gregory Rd IP28 ...116 A6
Gregory St CO10 ...148 C5
Grenadier Rd CB9 ...132 A6
Grenville Rd CO10 ...148 D8
Gresham Ave NR32 ...112 F2
Gresham Rd NR34 ...111 C6
Gresley Gdns 3 IP3 ...139 C3
Gretna Gdns IP7 ...... 155 B2
Greville Starkey Ave
CB8 ...... 121 A5
Grey Friars Rd IP1 ...155 B2
Greyfriars*
Dunwich IP17 ...... 43 B1
Ipswich IP1 ...... 155 A2
Woodbridge IP12 ...... 71 A4
Greyfriars Rd IP32 ...123 E4
Greyhound Hill CO4 ...103 C2

Greyhound La IP22 ...... 18 B1
Greyhound Rd 7 CO10 ...77 A2
Greys Cl 5 CO10 ...... 76 E1
Greys La CB9 ...... 75 A3
Grice Cl 3 NR33 ...... 11 C1
Griffith Cl 4 NR33 ...... 11 C1
**Grime's Graves (Flint
Mines)*** IP27 ...... 6 C4
Grimsey Rd IP16 ...129 D5
Grimsey's La IP16 ...129 E5
Grimston La IP11 ...107 C8
Grimwade Cl 9 CO11 ...104 E3
Grimwade St IP4 ...155 C2
Grinder's La IP21 ...... 22 C1
Grindle Gdns IP13 ...123 B3
Grindle The IP8 ...... 95 F8
Grinstead Gdns IP6 ...125 E3
Grinstead Hill IP6 ...125 E3
Gromford La IP17 ...... 72 C5
Groomes Cl 5 NR31 ...... 3 B7
Grosvenor Ave IP4 ...139 E8
Grosvenor Gdns IP33 ...122 F3
Grosvenor House Ct 9
IP28 ...... 116 B5
Grosvenor Rd
Lowestoft NR33 ...115 C4
Sudbury CO10 ...... 148 B8
Grosvenor Yd CB8 ...121 A3
Groton St CO10 ...... 93 B5
**Groton Wood Nature
Reserve*** CO10 ...93 D6
Grove Ave CO10 ...... 92 C6
Grove Cty Prim Sch
NR33 ...... 114 C4
Grove End IP21 ...... 39 B5
Grove Gdns
Carlton Colville NR33 ...114 C4
Fordham CB7 ...... 29 A2
Woodbridge IP12 ...146 E6
Grove Hill Belstead IP8 ...142 C7
Dedham CO7 ...... 103 E2
Langham CO4 ...... 103 C3
Grove La
Ashfield cum Thorpe IP14 ...54 C2
Elmswell IP30 ...... 51 A3
Harkstead IP9 ...... 106 C7
Ipswich IP4 ...... 139 E5
Mendham IP20 ...... 23 A2
Starston IP31 ...... 34 F4
Thetford IP24 ...... 16 C6
Grove Mews 4 NR34 ...111 C4
Grove Pk
Bury St Edmunds IP33 ...154 A3
Fordham CB7 ...... 29 A2
5 Walsham le Willows
IP31 ...... 35 C2
Grove Rd Beccles NR34 ...114 B5
2 Brantham CO11 ...104 E4
Brockdish IP21 ...... 21 F3
Bury St Edmunds IP33 ...154 A3
Felixstowe IP11 ...... 153 A6
Gissing IP21 ...... 21 A8
Knodishall IP17 ...... 72 F7
Lowestoft NR33 ...... 114 D4
Pettistree IP13 ...... 127 A4
Starston IP20 ...... 22 D8
Walsham le Willows IP31 ...35 C2
Woodbridge IP13 ...146 E6
Grove Rd N NR33 ...114 C5
Grove The
Great Glemham IP17 ...... 56 F1
2 Martlesham Heath IP5 ...98 A8
Mildenhall IP28 ...... 29 F4
Stowmarket IP14 ...124 E5
5 Woodbridge IP12 ...147 B6
Grove Wlk IP8 ...... 142 D8
Grove; Henley Rd The
IP1 ...... 135 C2
Grub La IP19 ...... 24 E5
Grundisburgh Cty Prim Sch
IP13 ...... 83 E5
Grundisburgh Rd
Clopton IP13 ...... 83 D8
Great Bealings IP13 ...137 C6
Tuddenham St Martin
IP6 ...... 136 D6
Grundle Cl 6 IP31 ...... 34 E4
**Guildhall Feoffment Cty Prim
Sch** IP33 ...... 154 C1
Guildhall La NR34 ...... 26 D5
**Guildhall of Corpus Christi
The*** CO10 ...... 78 D4
Guildhall St IP33 ...154 B2
Guineas Cl CB8 ...... 120 E6
Gules Gn IP21 ...... 22 F1
Gull Hill IP9 ...... 25 C3
Gull La
Grundisburgh IP13 ...... 83 D6
Thornham Magna IP23 ...37 A2
Gull Rd IP17 ...... 128 B3
Gull The IP13 ...... 70 C2
Gull's La CO7 ...... 104 A2
Gulpher Bsns Pk IP11 ...152 E6
Gulpher Rd IP11 ...152 E6
Gun La Dedham CO7 ...103 D4
Southwold IP18 ...... 119 D4
Gun La NR32 ...... 113 E2
Gunton Ave NR32 ...113 A7
Gunton Church La
NR32 ...... 113 C6
Gunton Cliff NR32 ...113 D5
Gunton Com Prim Sch
NR32 ...... 113 C6
Gunton Dr NR32 ...... 113 D5
Gunton St Peter's Ave
NR32 ...... 113 C6
**Gunton Warren Nature
Reserve*** NR32 ...113 D6

Guntons Cl 12 CB7 ...... 28 D4
Gurdon Rd 5 IP13 ...... 83 E5
Gurlings Cl NR32 ...132 E8
Guscot Cl NR32 ...113 A6
Gusford Prim Sch IP2 ...138 D1
Guston Gdns IP1 ...... 98 E2
Guy Cook Cl CO10 ...... 92 B2
Guyatt Cl CB5 ...... 44 A5
Gwendoline Rd IP4 ...140 E4
Gwynne Rd 4 CO12 ...107 B2
Gymnasium St IP1 ...155 A3

H

Hacheston Rd IP13 ...... 70 F5
Hackney La
Peasenhall IP17 ...... 56 E8
Woodbridge IP12 ...147 B6
Hackney Terr IP12 ...147 B6
Hackney's Cnr IP6 ...81 F5
Haddiscoe Rd NR31 ...... 2 A5
Hadenham Rd NR33 ...114 F1
Hadleigh Bsns Pk IP7 ...94 E4
Hadleigh Dr 2 NR32 ...112 F3
Hadleigh Guildhall*
IP7 ...... 149 D5
Hadleigh High Sch
IP7 ...... 149 F5
Hadleigh Prim Sch
IP7 ...... 149 D5
Hadleigh Railway Walk*
IP7 ...... 94 E3
Hadleigh Rd Aldham IP7 ...94 E8
Bildeston IP7 ...... 79 F3
Boxford CO6 ...... 93 D2
East Bergholt CO7 ...151 B4
Elmsett IP7 ...... 80 F1
Higham CO7 ...... 103 D7
Ipswich IP2 ...... 138 E6
Hadleigh Rd Ind Est
IP2 ...... 138 F7
Hadleigh Swimming Pool
IP7 ...... 149 D6
Hadrian Cl CB9 ...... 133 B5
Haggars Mead IP14 ...67 D7
Hague Cl NR32 ...114 C6
Halcyon Cres NR32 ...113 C1
Hale Cl IP1 ...... 138 D2
Halesowen Cl 2 IP7 ...142 F8
Halesworth & District Mus*
IP19 ...... 118 C4
**Halesworth (Holton) Airfield
Mus*** IP19 ...... 118 D6
Halesworth Gall*
IP19 ...... 118 B3
Halesworth Mid Sch
IP19 ...... 118 C5
Halesworth Rd
Brampton with Stoven
NR34 ...... 25 E3
Heveningham IP19 ...... 40 F3
Linstead Parva IP19 ...... 40 F8
Reydon IP18 ...... 119 B7
St Andrew, Ilketshall
NR34 ...... 25 A6
St Lawrence, Ilketshall
NR34 ...... 24 E1
Sibton IP17 ...... 41 B1
Uggeshall NR34 ...... 25 F3
Walpole IP19 ...... 40 A1
Wenhaston with Mells Hamlet
IP19 ...... 41 A6
Halesworth Sta IP19 ...118 B4
Half Moon La
6 Grundisburgh IP13 ...83 E5
Redgrave IP22 ...... 36 A8
Half Moon St IP30 ...... 65 D5
Halfar Rd 2 IP31 ...... 33 C5
Halfmoon La IP20 ...... 22 E7
Halford Cl IP8 ...... 138 C2
Halford La IP22 ...... 19 D3
Halifax Prim Sch IP2 ...139 A2
Halifax Rd Ipswich IP2 ...139 B2
7 Mildenhall IP28 ...... 30 A8
Halifax St IP27 ...109 F1
Halifax Way CB8 ...120 E5
Haling Way IP24 ...... 16 A6
Hall Barn Rd CB7 ...... 29 A5
Hall Cl IP29 ...... 62 B4
Hall Cl The IP28 ...... 31 C4
Hall Dr 17 Feltwell IP26 ...4 E5
Lakenheath IP27 ...... 109 C7
Lowestoft NR33 ...... 112 C1
Santon Downham IP27 ...... 6 C2
Hall Farm Cl IP12 ...147 B8
Hall Farm La NR34 ...... 10 C1

Hall La continued
Somersham IP8 ...... 81 C3
Spexhall IP19 ...... 24 E4
Wetheringsett-cum-Brockford
IP14 ...... 53 B4
3 Witnesham IP6 ...... 83 A5
Yaxley IP23 ...... 37 B4
Hall Pond Way IP11 ...152 D5
Hall Rd Barnardiston CB8 ...75 B5
Barsham NR34 ...... 8 F3
Bedingfield IP23 ...... 54 A7
Bedingham NR35 ...... 7 C7
Belchamp Walter CO10 ...91 A3
Blundeston NR32 ...... 112 C8
Borley CO10 ...... 91 D5
Brent Eleigh CO10 ...... 79 A3
Brockdish IP21 ...... 22 A3
Buxton & Shimpling IP22 ...20 E7
Carlton Colville NR33 ...114 B2
Charsfield IP13 ...... 69 F3
Chelsworth IP7 ...... 79 E2
Cowlinge CB8 ...... 75 A7
Earsham NR35 ...... 7 E4
Ellingham NR35 ...... 8 C7
Foxhall IP10 ...... 141 E4
7 Hopton on Sea NR31 ...3 B7
Hundon CO10 ...... 75 E4
Kessingland NR33 ...... 11 C1
Lavenham CO10 ...... 78 C4
Little Bealings IP5 ...137 E2
Lowestoft NR32 ...... 112 D1
Marlesford IP13 ...... 71 C5
Mount Bures CO8 ...101 C3
Parham IP13 ...... 71 B7
Pulham St Mary IP21 ...... 22 A8
Stowmarket IP14 ...124 B8
Thornden IP23 ...... 53 C7
Wenhaston with Mells Hamlet
IP19 ...... 42 D5
Hall Rise IP7 ...... 80 D5
Hall St
Long Melford CO10 ...... 91 E8
Soham CB7 ...... 28 D4
Hall Wlk IP8 ...... 81 F1
Hall's La IP15 ...... 50 B5
Hallfields IP27 ...109 C7
Halliday Pl IP7 ...... 77 F7
Halliwell Rd IP4 ...140 B6
Halls Drift IP5 ...141 B6
Hallwong La IP20 ...... 22 D7
Hallwyck Gdns CB8 ...120 F2
Halton Cres IP3 ...140 C1
Hamblin Dr IP12 ...147 A6
Hamblin Rd IP12 ...147 A5
Hambling's Piece NR16 ...18 C8
Hambrook Cl IP30 ...... 63 F7
Hammerton Rd IP31 ...49 D4
Hamilton Cl CB8 ...120 E2
Hamilton Gdns IP11 ...153 A3
Hamilton Rd
Felixstowe IP11 ...153 A4
Ipswich IP3 ...140 B3
Lowestoft NR32 ...113 E1
Newmarket CB8 ...120 D5
Sudbury CO10 ...148 C5
Hamilton St
6 Felixstowe IP11 ...152 E5
4 Harwich CO12 ...106 F3
Hamilton Way
Ditchingham NR35 ...110 C8
Stowmarket IP14 ...124 D7
Hamiltons The CB8 ...120 F2
Hamlet Ct 2 CO8 ...101 C4
Hamlet Dr 2 IP5 ...141 F6
Hammond Cl CB8 ...120 E6
Hammond's Cnr IP14 ...67 C6
Hammonds Wlk IP19 ...42 C6
Hampstead Ave IP28 ...116 B6
Hampton Rd IP1 ...138 F7
Hanchet End CB9 ...... 74 A1
Hanchet End CB9 ...... 132 A7
Hancocks Cl 2 IP16 ...129 D5
Handford Cut IP1 ...155 A3
Handford Hall Prim Sch
IP1 ...... 139 A4
Handford Rd IP1 ...155 A3
Hankin Ave 13 CO12 ...106 C1
Hanmer Ave IP28 ...116 C5
Hanmer Wlk IP33 ...122 B6
Hanover Cl
5 Bury St Edmunds IP32 ...123 A8
Exning CB8 ...... 120 E8
Oulton Broad NR33 ...114 F5
Hanover Ct CO10 ...148 B4
Ha'penny Field IP9 ...105 E7
Ha'penny Pier Visitor Ctr*
CO12 ...... 107 B3
Harbour Cres 7 CO7 ...107 C3
Harbour La IP18 ...... 22 D3
Harbour Rd NR32 ...112 E1
Harbourage The NR34 ...111 C5
Harcourt Ave 1 CO12 ...107 A2
Harding's La IP1 ...... 50 E4
Hardwick Cl IP4 ...140 E5
Hardwick La IP33 ...122 F2
Hardwick Mid Sch
IP33 ...... 123 A5
Hardwick Pk Gdns
IP33 ...... 123 A5
Hardwick Prim Sch
IP33 ...... 123 B2
Hardwick Rd
Haverhill CB9 ...132 F6
Starston IP20 ...... 22 C7
Hardy Cl
8 Brantham CO11 ...104 E4
Lowestoft NR33 ...115 A4
Hardy Cres IP1 ...134 F4

Hardy Ct 1 CO10 ...148 D8
Hare & Hounds Cnr
IP6 ...... 82 F8
Harebell Rd
Ipswich IP2 ...138 F4
Red Lodge IP28 ...... 30 C1
Harefield CO10 ...114 C5
Harefield La IP19 ...... 77 E1
Hares La IP19 ...... 25 B4
Hares Rd IP7 ...... 65 D1
Hares Wlk 1 CO10 ...148 D5
Harewood Terr 7 CB9 ...132 C5
Hargrave Ave IP26 ...125 D3
Hargrave Rd IP29 ...... 62 B6
Harkstead La
Freston IP9 ...... 105 F8
Woolverstone IP9 ...144 A1
Harkstead Rd 3 IP9 ...106 A5
Harland St IP2 ...... 139 C3
Harleston Hill IP17 ...... 39 E8
Harleston Mus* IP20 ...22 D6
Harleston Prim Sch
IP20 ...... 22 D6
Harleston Rd
Metfield IP20 ...... 23 B3
Pulham Market IP21 ...... 21 E8
Scole IP21 ...... 21 D5
Weybread IP21 ...... 22 D4
Harling Dro IP27 ...... 6 E3
Harling Rd
Garboldisham IP22 ...... 18 C6
North Lopham IP22 ...... 19 A6
Harling Way IP16 ...129 B6
Harman's La IP20 ...... 22 C5
Harold Rd NR33 ...115 C6
Harp's Cl Rd NR32 ...113 B3
Harpclose Rd 2 CO10 ...148 D6
Harper's Est 5 IP7 ...94 A2
Harper's Rd 2 CO10 ...77 A2
Harpur's Rd 2 CO10 ...77 A2
Harrier Cl IP3 ...140 B1
Harrier La IP14 ...... 67 A5
Harriers Wlk IP13 ...70 E5
Harrington Ave NR32 ...113 C6
Harrington Cl IP13 ...154 C1
Harris Ave NR32 ...113 C4
Harris Cl 2 IP3 ...... 53 F2
Harris Mid Sch IP32 ...113 C8
Harrison Cl 3 IP18 ...119 D3
Harrison Gr IP5 ...141 C8
Harrison Rd NR32 ...112 E1
Harrison Way IP26 ...... 4 F3
Harrisons La IP19 ...118 C5
Harrold Rd NR33 ...115 C7
Harrop Dale 2 NR33 ...114 E3
Harrow Cl IP4 ...140 E3
Harrow Gn 2 IP29 ...... 63 D1
Harrow La Benhall IP17 ...72 A7
Theberton IP16 ...129 A8
Harrow Rd
Troston IP31 ...... 33 D4
Harrow St CO6 ...102 B8
Harry Palmer Cl 1 CB7 ...29 A1
Hart Cl CB9 ...132 D8
Hart's Cl CO7 ...103 E1
Hartest Hill IP29 ...... 77 C6
Hartest La IP29 ...... 63 C1
Hartest Prim Sch IP29 ...77 A7
Hartest Rd IP29 ...... 63 A1
Hartest Way
Stowmarket IP14 ...124 F3
Sudbury CO10 ...148 F4
Hartfield Rd CB8 ...... 59 F2
Hartington Rd IP15 ...130 E3
Hartismere High Sch
IP23 ...... 117 B3
Hartismere Hospl
IP23 ...... 117 C3
Hartley St IP2 ...155 B1
Hartree Way IP5 ...141 E7
Harvard Rd 6 IP26 ...... 4 F3
Harvest Cl IP14 ...... 51 D1
Harvest Dr NR33 ...114 F2
Harvesters Way
Martlesham IP5 ...141 F6
13 Martlesham Heath IP5 ...98 A7
Harvey Cl 7 CO11 ...104 E2
Harvey La IP21 ...... 21 C5
Harvey's La IP6 ...... 82 C6
Harwich Int Port CO12 ...106 F3
Harwich Rd
Foxash Estate CO11 ...104 A1
Mistley CO11 ...105 A2
Ramsey & Parkeston
CO11 ...... 106 A1
Wrabness CO11 ...105 F1
Harwich Town Sta
CO12 ...... 107 B3
Harwood Ave IP24 ...... 16 C7
Hascot Hill Barking IP6 ...125 A1
Battisford IP14 ...... 81 A8
Haselmere Cl 5 IP32 ...123 D6
Hasketon Rd Burgh IP13 ...83 F6
Woodbridge IP13 ...146 E6
Haskins Wlk IP5 ...141 E7
Haslemere Dr IP4 ...139 E7
Hasse Rd CB7 ...... 28 E8
Hassel Cl CB7 ...122 C4
Hatchley Cl IP12 ...146 E5
Hatfield Rd IP3 ...140 A3
Hatley Dr CB5 ...... 44 A6
Hatter St IP33 ...154 B2

Haugh La
Great Ashfield IP31 .....50 F5
Haughley IP14 .....51 D1
Woodbridge IP12 .....146 F6
Haughgate CI IP14 .....51 C3
Haughley Crawfords CE Prim Sch IP14 .....51 C1
Haughley Dr IP14 .....140 F6
Haughley Pk* IP14 .....51 A1
Haughley Rd IP14 .....66 B7
Hauliers Rd IP11 .....152 D2
Haven Ave NR32 .....113 B3
Haven CI IP11 .....152 D4
Haven Nature Reserve The* IP16 .....130 F6
Haven Rd IP16 .....129 D5
Haven The IP16 .....73 F6
Havens The IP10 .....144 E7
Havergate Island National Nature Reserve* IP12 .....86 F2
Havergate Rd 3 IP3 .....144 D8
Haverhill & District Local History Ctr* CB9 .....132 E5
Haverhill Arts Ctr* CB9 .....132 E5
Haverhill Bsns Pk CB9 .....132 F3
Haverhill Leisure Ctr CB9 .....132 F6
Haverhill Railway Walks Nature Reserve* 133 B4
Haverhill Rd
Haverhill CB9 .....132 F8
Helions Bumpstead CB9 .....88 B5
Kedington CB9 .....133 E8
Steeple Bumpstead CB9 .....88 D5
Haverhill Trade Pk CB9 .....132 F3
Haward St NR32 .....113 C1
Hawbridge IP9 .....150 E4
Hawe's La Norton IP31 .....50 B4
Wicken CB7 .....28 A2
Hawes St IP2 .....155 C1
Hawk End La IP30 .....50 E2
Hawk's La IP29 .....63 A2
Hawke Rd IP31 .....139 E1
Hawker Dr IP5 .....98 A8
Hawkes La IP11 .....152 D6
Hawkins Ct 2 CO10 .....148 D8
Hawkins Rd CO10 .....148 E8
Hawks Mill St IP6 .....125 D5
Hawstead La IP29 .....63 E6
Hawthorn Ave NR33 .....115 A7
Hawthorn Dr
Beccles NR34 .....111 E4
Bury St Edmunds IP32 .....122 D8
Knodishall IP17 .....129 B2
8 Stowupland IP14 .....67 A6
Hawthorn Dr
9 Horringer IP29 .....63 A8
Ipswich IP2 .....138 D2
Hawthorn La 22 IP22 .....13 F2
Hawthorn Pl IP12 .....146 E6
Hawthorn Rd
Haverhill CB9 .....132 B7
Middleton IP17 .....58 A5
Sudbury CO10 .....148 F5
Theberton IP17 .....57 F4
Hawthorn Way CB5 .....44 B6
Hawthorn Wlk 8 IP30 .....30 B8
Hawthorns The 8 IP31 .....49 D4
Hay Barn Meadow 2 IP30 .....50 D1
Haycocks Rd CB9 .....132 A4
Haygate IP23 .....117 C3
Hayhill Rd IP4 .....139 E7
Hayland Dro IP28 .....29 C7
Haylings Gr IP16 .....129 C4
Haylings Rd IP16 .....129 C4
Hayman Rd IP3 .....139 F1
Haynings Mill IP13 .....126 D4
Haysborder Rd IP29 .....46 F3
Hayithill La IP4 .....4 D6
Hayward CI IP23 .....117 D2
Haywards Fields IP5 .....141 D8
Hazel CI
1 Bartrwaters Airfield IP12 .....85 E8
Haverhill CB9 .....132 C5
Mildenhall IP28 .....116 C4
Hazel Covert 4 IP24 .....16 D6
Hazel CI 8 CO10 .....148 D6
Hazel Dr
10 Horringer IP29 .....63 A8
Ipswich IP3 .....140 E1
Hazel Rise IP6 .....134 C8
Hazelcroft Rd IP1 .....135 B2
Hazels La IP17 .....42 D5
Hazelville CI 11 CO12 .....106 F1
Hazelwood 1 IP7 .....80 F1
Hazelwood CI 10 IP31 .....49 D4
Hazelwood Marshes Nature Reserve* IP15 .....73 B4
Hazelwood St IP17 .....130 A7
Hazlitt Rd 6 IP1 .....135 A3
Head La CO10 .....148 F2
Headingham CI 13 IP22 .....139 A2
Headland Ave CB4 .....132 C5
Headland Dro IP26 .....4 A1
Healey CI NR32 .....113 A5
Heasman CI CB8 .....120 F5
Heath CI
East Bergholt CO7 .....151 D5
Hessett IP30 .....64 F8
Polstead CO6 .....93 F3

Heath Ct 12 IP11 .....107 D8
Heath Dr IP2 .....99 C7
Heath Farm Rd IP28 .....30 E1
Heath La Blundeston NR32 .....3 A4
Ipswich IP4 .....140 C5
Pakenham IP31 .....49 D8
Heath La Burwell CB5 .....44 C2
East Bergholt CO7 .....151 D5
Exning CB8 .....120 A4
Fritton & St Olaves NR31 .....2 B5
Geldeston NR34 .....9 A7
Hessett IP30 .....64 F8
Ipswich IP30 .....140 C7
Ixworth IP31 .....33 E2
Kenninghall NR16 .....19 A7
Lowestoft NR33 .....114 F8
Mildenhall IP28 .....116 E5
Mistley CO11 .....105 A2
Newmarket CB8 .....121 C3
Norton IP31 .....50 B4
Polstead CO6 .....93 F2
Sapiston IP31 .....34 B7
Swaffham Prior CB5 .....44 A1
Thurston IP31 .....49 D4
Troston IP31 .....34 A7
Wenhaston with Mells Hamlet IP19 .....42 B7
Woolpit IP30 .....50 D1
Heath The
Dedham CO7 .....104 A2
Great Waldingfield CO10 .....92 C6
Woolpit IP30 .....65 F8
Heath View
Ipswich IP5 .....141 A6
Leiston IP16 .....129 E5
Heath Way CO10 .....92 C6
Heath Wlk IP12 .....72 A4
Heathbell Rd CB8 .....121 C3
Heather Ave IP3 .....140 C2
Heather CI
1 Great Barton IP31 .....49 D4
Martlesham Heath IP5 .....141 F6
Heather Rd IP28 .....113 D4
Heather Way
Brandon IP27 .....6 A1
Worlingham NR34 .....111 F3
Heathercroft Rd IP1 .....135 A3
Heatherhayes IP2 .....139 A3
Heatherset Way IP28 .....30 C1
Heathfield IP5 .....141 F6
Heathfield Mews IP5 .....141 F6
Heathfield Rd 9 IP19 .....105 E2
Heathfields IP11 .....98 D1
Heathgate Piece IP11 .....152 C8
Heathlands Pk IP4 .....140 E4
Heathside Specl Sch IP4 .....140 D6
Hedley La NR43 .....114 A3
Heigham Dr NR33 .....114 F5
Heights The NR34 .....111 C4
Heldhaw Rd IP3 .....123 E5
Helena Rd IP3 .....139 E4
Helens CI 2 IP22 .....36 A8
Helions Bumpstead Rd CB9 .....132 D3
Helions Pk Ave CB9 .....132 E5
Helions Pk Gdns CB9 .....132 E5
Helions Pk Rd 7 CB9 .....132 E5
Helions Rd CB9 .....88 D4
Helions Service Rd 8 CB9 .....132 E5
Helions Wlk CB9 .....132 E5
Helmingham Hall & Gdns* IP14 .....69 A4
Helmingham Prim Sch IP14 .....69 B6
Helmingham Rd IP6 .....69 C2
Helston CI IP5 .....141 B7
Hemmant Way NR34 .....9 B7
Hemplands The 2 NR32 .....113 D2
Hempnall Rd NR35 .....7 A8
Hempstead Rd CB9 .....132 A7
Hen Reed Bed Nature Reserve* IP18 .....43 B8
Hencote La
Horringer IP29 .....63 C8
Nowton IP33 .....123 B1
Henderson CI
Bramford IP8 .....134 A1
Haverhill CB9 .....132 A7
Hengrave CI 1 IP28 .....139 A2
Hengrave Hall* IP28 .....48 A7
Hengrave Rd IP28 .....48 B6
Henham Rd NR34 .....25 A7
Henley Ave IP1 .....135 B3
Henley CI IP17 .....128 C3
Henley Prim Sch IP6 .....82 E6
Henley Rd Henley IP6 .....82 D5
Ipswich IP1 .....155 B4
Henniker Rd
3 Debenham IP14 .....53 F2
Ipswich IP1 .....138 C8
Henny Rd CO8 .....101 A7
Henry CI CB9 .....132 B4
Henry Rd IP3 .....140 B1
Henry St IP2 .....155 A1
Henry Ward Rd 1 IP20 .....22 D6
Henry Watson's Potteries* IP22 .....35 D5
Henslow Rd IP4 .....140 B5
Henstead Gdns IP3 .....140 A2
Hepworth Ave IP33 .....122 D5
Hepworth Rd
Barningham IP31 .....34 F7
Hepworth IP22 .....35 A7
Stanton IP31 .....34 E4

Hepworth Rd continued
Thelnetham IP22 .....35 B7
Herbert CI CO10 .....148 E8
Herbert Human CI 3 CB7 .....28 D4
Herbert Rd IP5 .....141 E8
Hereford Dr 14 IP6 .....82 B5
Hereward Ave IP28 .....116 C5
Hereward Way
6 Feltwell IP26 .....4 D5
Littleport CB7 .....12 B7
Weeting-with-Broomhill IP27 .....5 E3
Heritage Gn 6 NR33 .....11 B1
Heritage Workshop Ctr* NR32 .....113 C3
Herivan CI NR32 .....112 E4
Herivan Gdns 6 NR32 .....112 E4
Hermitage CI IP13 .....126 B3
Hermitage Meadows CO10 .....76 B1
Herolf Way 11 IP20 .....22 D6
Heron CI
5 Mildenhall IP28 .....13 B1
Stowmarket IP14 .....124 A6
Heron Ct CB7 .....28 C5
Heron Hill IP14 .....66 C6
Heron Rd
Bury St Edmunds IP33 .....123 B2
Ipswich IP2 .....138 E3
Saxmundham IP17 .....128 B3
Herons CI NR32 .....112 D2
Herring Fishery Score 2 NR32 .....113 E1
Herring Mkt 14 NR33 .....115 D8
Herringfleet Drainage Mill* NR32 .....1 B4
Herringfleet Rd NR31 .....2 B5
Herringswell
Herringswell IP28 .....30 D2
Kentford CB8 .....46 A6
Hertford CI 16 IP32 .....48 C5
Hertford PI IP15 .....130 E3
Hertford Rd 5 CO10 .....76 A1
Hertfords PI IP12 .....86 D7
Hervey CI 6 IP29 .....107 A5
Hervey Rd IP33 .....122 E3
Hervey St Ipswich IP4 .....155 C4
Lowestoft NR32 .....113 C8
Hessett CI IP14 .....124 F3
Hethersett CI CB8 .....120 E8
Heveningham Long La IP17 .....41 A1
Heveningham Rd IP19 .....40 C5
Hewitt Rd
16 Harwich CO12 .....106 E1
10 Ramsey CO12 .....106 E1
Hexham CI 3 IP2 .....139 A2
Heycroft Way 4 CO6 .....102 C5
Heyford CI 8 IP28 .....116 B5
Heyford Rd 12 IP31 .....33 D5
Heywood Ave IP22 .....20 C3
Heywood CI IP4 .....138 D1
Heywood Rd IP22 .....20 C4
Hibbard Rd IP8 .....134 C2
Hickford Hill CO10 .....90 B7
Hickling Dr IP33 .....123 B1
Hicks Way IP13 .....133 C3
High Baxter St IP33 .....154 B2
High Beach IP11 .....153 C4
High Beech NR32 .....113 B2
High Comm Rd IP22 .....21 C6
High Ct IP20 .....22 E6
High Gn IP29 .....129 C6
High Hall CI IP11 .....107 D8
High House Farm Rd IP12 .....131 D8
High House La IP7 .....79 B5
High La IP14 .....53 B6
High Leas NR34 .....111 C3
High Leas CI 2 NR34 .....111 C3
High Lighthouse Wireless Mus* CO12 .....107 C3
High Lodge Visitor Ctr Thetford Forest Pk* IP27 .....15 C7
High London La IP22 .....20 A8
High Rd Badingham IP13 .....56 C6
Bressingham IP22 .....19 F4
Felixstowe IP11 .....152 B8
Great Finborough IP14 .....66 A2
Kettleburgh IP13 .....55 B2
Leavenheath CO6 .....102 A7
Needham IP20 .....22 B3
Roydon IP22 .....20 A3
Swilland IP6 .....83 A7
Trimley St Martin IP11 .....98 C1
Wortwell IP20 .....23 A7
High Rd E IP11 .....153 B5
High Rd W IP11 .....153 B5
High Row Field IP11 .....153 C5
High St Acton CO10 .....92 B7
Aldeburgh IP15 .....130 E3
Ashley CB8 .....45 A8
Brandon IP27 .....5 B8
Brinkley CB8 .....59 F1
5 Bures CO8 .....101 C5
Burwell CB5 .....44 A5
Cavendish CO10 .....76 E1
Cheveley CB8 .....60 E8
Chippenham CB7 .....45 C8
Clare CO10 .....90 A8
Debenham IP14 .....53 F2
Dedham CO7 .....103 F3
Dunwich IP17 .....43 B1
Felixstowe IP11 .....152 E6
Feltwell IP26 .....4 E5
Flowton IP8 .....81 C1

High St continued
Gislingham IP23 .....36 D2
Great Yeldham CO9 .....90 A1
Hadleigh IP7 .....149 D6
Harwich CO12 .....107 B2
Haverhill CB9 .....132 E5
Hemingstone IP6 .....68 C1
Hitcham IP7 .....79 F4
Hopton IP22 .....18 C2
Ipswich IP1 .....155 B3
Ixworth IP31 .....34 B1
Kessingland NR33 .....11 B1
Lakenheath IP27 .....109 C6
Langham CO4 .....103 B2
Lavenham CO10 .....78 D4
Laxfield IP13 .....40 B3
Leiston IP16 .....129 C6
Long Melford CO10 .....77 E1
7 Lowestoft NR32 .....113 E2
Manningtree CO11 .....104 E2
Mildenhall IP28 .....116 C4
Nayland CO6 .....102 D5
Needham Market IP6 .....125 D5
Newmarket CB8 .....131 C2
Orford IP12 .....131 D4
Pettistree IP13 .....127 C5
Rattlesden IP30 .....65 D6
St Margaret, Ilketshall NR35 .....24 D7
Saxmundham IP17 .....128 D3
Soham CB7 .....28 D4
Southwold IP18 .....119 D5
Stetchworth CB8 .....60 A5
Thelnetham IP22 .....53 E1
Thorndon IP23 .....53 C8
Tuddenham IP28 .....30 F2
Tuddenham St Martin IP6 .....136 B5
Wangford with Henham NR34 .....26 B2
Wicken CB7 .....28 A1
Wickham Market IP13 .....127 C7
Wrentham NR34 .....26 E5
Yoxford IP17 .....57 D8
High St Ex Gall* IP1 .....155 B3
High View Rd IP1 .....134 D1
Higham Rd IP7 .....134 D1
Higham Race Course CO7 .....103 D2
Higham Rd
Higham CO7 .....103 D6
Tuddenham IP28 .....31 A1
Highbridge Gravel Dro IP27 .....109 B7
Highbury Cres IP33 .....122 E5
Highbury Rd IP33 .....122 E5
Highbury Way CO10 .....148 F4
Highclere CI CB8 .....120 D8
Higher Dr NR32 .....112 F2
Highfield
Blythburgh IP19 .....42 F6
Clare CO10 .....90 B8
Highfield App IP23 .....117 C3
Highfield App 1 IP11 .....134 F1
Highfield Ave CO10 .....107 A2
Highfield CI NR33 .....114 B1
Highfield Dr IP6 .....134 D8
Highfield Rd
Felixstowe IP11 .....153 A4
Halesworth IP19 .....118 B2
Ipswich IP1 .....134 F2
8 Stowupland IP14 .....67 A6
Sudbury CO10 .....148 E7
Highfields Bentley IP9 .....104 F7
Great Yeldham CO9 .....90 A1
Lakenheath IP27 .....109 E6
Highfields Dr IP27 .....109 D6
Highgate La IP17 .....70 B2
Highgrove CI NR32 .....113 A3
Highland Dr NR34 .....111 E4
Highland Way NR33 .....114 F6
Highlands IP27 .....109 E6
Highlands CI IP27 .....125 C5
Highlands Rd
Hadleigh IP7 .....149 E5
Monks Eleigh IP7 .....79 C4
Highlands The CB8 .....120 D8
Highview CI CO10 .....148 C8
Highwood Cres CB8 .....46 B2
Highwood La CO10 .....92 E5
Highwood Rd CB8 .....46 B2
Hildesley Ct NR33 .....115 B4
Hill CI
6 Long Melford CO10 .....91 E8
Newmarket CB8 .....120 E3
Hill Cres CB9 .....132 E7
Hill Farm La 9 IP7 .....106 C8
Hill Farm Rd
Grundisburgh IP13 .....83 D6
Halesworth IP19 .....118 C3
Playford IP6 .....137 B4
Reydon IP18 .....56 E4
Hill House Gdns NR33 .....115 C5
Hill House La IP6 .....125 C5
Hill House Rd IP4 .....139 E5
Hill La CB9 .....133 D1
Hill of Health (Tumulus)* IP28 .....32 D2
Hill Rd Lowestoft NR32 .....113 C1
Southwold IP18 .....119 C6
Wangford with Henham NR34 .....26 B1
Westley IP33 .....122 A5
Hill Rise IP14 .....124 D3
Hill St 20 IP26 .....4 E5
Hill The North Cove NR34 .....10 C4

Hill The continued
Shipmeadow NR34 .....8 F4
Tuddenham St Martin IP6 .....136 C5
Westleton IP17 .....58 C8
Hill Top IP31 .....34 E5
Hill View CB8 .....61 C4
Hill View Bsns Pk IP6 .....134 D6
Hillary CI IP4 .....140 A5
Hillcrest IP17 .....129 A3
Hillcrest App IP8 .....134 B2
Hillcrest CI 3 NR34 .....111 E3
Hillcrest Dr NR32 .....113 B4
Hillcrest Gdns NR32 .....113 B3
Hillcrest Rd
Beccles NR34 .....111 B3
Sudbury CO10 .....148 C8
Hillcroft Prep Sch IP14 .....51 D2
Hillrise CI NR34 .....111 C3
Hillside Brandon IP27 .....14 D8
Stowmarket IP14 .....124 D3
Hillside Ave NR34 .....111 C3
Hillside Com Prim Sch IP12 .....139 C3
Hillside Cres 8 IP19 .....140 B3
Hillside CI 1 NR35 .....110 C2
Hillside Meadow CB7 .....29 B1
Hillside Rd
Southwold IP18 .....119 C7
Sudbury CO10 .....148 E5
Hillside Rd 8 NR35 .....110 D3
Hillside Rd W NR35 .....110 B2
Hillside Specl Sch CO10 .....148 D7
Hillside Way IP19 .....118 B5
Hilltop Gn NR32 .....113 A4
Hilltop Rise 2 NR34 .....111 E3
Hilltop Way IP31 .....34 E5
Hilly CI IP31 .....33 F5
Hilly Fields IP12 .....146 E4
Hilton CI 11 CO11 .....104 E2
Hilton Rd Ipswich IP3 .....140 C1
Martlesham Heath IP5 .....98 A8
Hinderclay La IP22 .....18 E1
Hinderclay Rd
Redgrave IP22 .....19 A1
Rickinghall Inferior IP22 .....35 F6
Hines Rd IP3 .....140 A4
Hinesham CI 6 IP4 .....140 F5
Hintlesham & Chattisham CE VCP Sch IP8 .....95 C5
Hintlesham CI 3 IP14 .....124 E3
Hintlesham Dr IP11 .....152 D4
Histon CI IP5 .....140 F7
Hitcham Cswy IP7 .....79 E6
Hitcham Rd
2 Debenham IP14 .....53 F2
Wattisham IP7 .....80 B6
Hitcham's La NR34 .....26 E4
Hitchcock PI CO10 .....148 C7
HMS Ganges Mus* IP9 .....107 B4
Hoad Rd NR32 .....112 E3
Hobart Way IP32 .....123 A8
Hobbies La IP14 .....52 D4
Hobbs Dr CO4 .....103 A3
Hobbs La CO10 .....77 B2
Hobland Rd
Belton with Browston NR31 .....2 F8
Bradwell NR31 .....3 A8
Hocket Cres IP12 .....71 F2
Hockey Hill IP4 .....53 A5
Hockney Gdns IP3 .....144 A8
Hockwold Prim Sch IP26 .....5 A2
Hodgkinson Rd IP11 .....152 C3
Hodson CI 6 IP32 .....122 E8
Hoe La CO10 .....90 F8
Hog La
St Lawrence, Ilketshall NR34 .....24 C7
Wenhaston with Mells Hamlet IP19 .....42 C5
Westhall NR34 .....25 A6
Hogarth Rd IP3 .....139 F1
Hogarth Sq IP3 .....140 A1
Hogarth Wlk NR32 .....113 B6
Hogg La
Bury St Edmunds IP33 .....154 B1
Earsham NR35 .....7 C5
Hoggars Rd IP14 .....52 C4
Hogsty La IP31 .....22 A5
Holbecks La IP7 .....149 C4
Holbein Way 2 NR32 .....113 B6
Holborn Ave IP28 .....116 B6
Holbrook Barn Rd 6 CO10 .....93 C3
Holbrook CI 11 CO10 .....92 C6
Holbrook Cres IP11 .....152 D4
Holbrook High Sch IP9 .....105 E8
Holbrook Prim Sch IP9 .....105 E7
Holbrook Rd
Haverhill CB9 .....132 C4
Holbrook IP9 .....106 A5
Ipswich IP3 .....139 F1
Lowestoft NR32 .....112 F4
Stutton IP9 .....105 D5
Holcombe Cres IP2 .....138 D2
Holdans La IP17 .....56 E2
Holdans Meadow IP17 .....56 E2
Holden CI Ipswich IP2 .....139 D3
Lowestoft NR32 .....112 C1
Holden Rd IP28 .....31 F1
Holderness Rd IP22 .....123 C2
Holeywall La IP31 .....35 A1
Holfen CI IP12 .....84 B1

Holkham Cl **7** IP4 ....140 F5
Holkham Mead **1** CB5 ...44 B5
Holland Pk CB8 ....60 E8
Holland Rd
Felixstowe IP11 ....152 F3
Thurston IP31 ....139 F6
Holland's La NR35 ....7 C7
Hollands Bsns Ctr The
CB9 ....132 C4
Hollands Rd CB9 ....132 E4
Hollands Rd Ind Est
CB9 ....132 C4
Hollesley Ave CB9 ......132 A6
Hollesley Prim Sch
IP12 ....99 F7
Hollesley Rd
Hollesley IP12 ....99 D3
Rendlesham IP12 ....85 D7
Holliday Cl IP32 ....123 F7
Hollingsworth Rd
Lowestoft NR32 ....113 C3
3 Stowmarket IP14 ....124 E5
Hollow Gr Way NR33 ...114 D4
Hollow Hill CB9 ....74 A2
Hollow Hill NR35 ....110 B7
Hollow La
Badingham IP13 ....56 C6
Barningham IP31 ....34 F8
Bures St Mary CO8 .....101 C6
Carlton Colville NR33 ...114 C4
6 Chelmondiston IP9 ...106 C8
Coney Weston IP31 .....18 A1
Earl Soham IP13 ....54 F3
Mendham IP20 ....23 A4
Thurston IP31 ....49 F3
Tostock IP30 ....50 A2
Hollow Rd Ashen CO10 ..89 F5
Bury St Edmunds IP32 ..123 C6
Copdock & Washbrook
IP8 ....95 E4
Hollow Way Hill NR34 ...9 D8
Hollowell Cl **3** NR32 ..112 E4
Hollows The IP6 ....67 F2
Holly Blue Cl IP8 ....142 E8
Holly Bush Cnr CO7 ....103 E7
Holly Cl Beccles NR34 ..111 E3
5 Horringer IP29 ....63 A8
Little Bealings IP13 ....137 D5
6 Red Lodge IP28 ....30 B1
Warren Heath IP3 ......140 F1
Holly End IP5 ....141 F6
Holly Gr NR34 ....111 C4
Holly Hill NR32 ....112 C3
Holly La Wangford IP18 ..142 C7
Great Horkesley CO6 ...102 E2
Lakenheath IP27 ....109 D5
Little Bealings IP13 ....137 D5
Mutford NR34 ....10 E3
Rushmere St Andrew
IP5 ....136 E2
Stutton IP9 ....105 C6
Holly Oaks **2** CO6 ....101 F7
Holly Rd
4 Great Brickett IP7 ...80 C6
Ipswich IP1 ....155 A4
Lowestoft NR32 ....112 E1
Wilbisham IP8 ....81 A5
Holly Wlk **9** IP28 .....30 B8
Hollybush Dr IP11 .....153 D7
Hollybush La IP30 .....64 C6
Hollycroft Cl **5** IP1 ...135 A3
Hollydene Cl **4** NR32 ..112 D2
Holm Cl **4** NR34 ......9 F4
Holme Cl IP22 ....18 C2
Holme's Hill IP17 ......41 A1
Holmere Dr IP19 ......118 A3
Holmes La **5** CB7 ....28 D5
Holmsey Gn
Beck Row, Holywell Row
& Kenny Hill IP28 .....13 C1
Mildenhall IP28 ....30 D8
Holmsey Gn Gdns **7**
IP28 ....30 D8
Holst Cl NR33 ....115 A6
Holst Mead IP14 ......124 C8
Holt Rd CO6 ....93 E2
Holt's La IP6 ....125 F6
Holt's Rd CO6 ....102 A2
Holton Ave NR32 .....112 F4
Holton Rd IP19 ....118 D4
Holton St Peter Postmill*
IP19 ....118 E3
Holton St Peter Prim Sch
IP19 ....118 E4
Holton Terr IP19 ......118 C4
Holy Wells Rd IP3 .....139 E3
Holyhouse Drift **1** IP31 ..49 A6
Holyrood **8** CO12 ....106 F1
Holyrood Cl IP32 .....138 F1
Holywell Cl IP33 ......123 A3
Holywell Dro IP28 .....13 C2
Holywells IP3 ....139 E4
Holywells High Sch
IP3 ....140 C1
Home Cl IP8 ....88 E4
Home Farm La IP33 ...123 B1
Home Farm Rd NR35 ...8 C7
Home Meadow **4** IP13 ..40 B3
Home Piece CO7 ......103 C3
Homefield Boxford CO10 ..93 C3
Capel St Mary IP9 .....150 F3
Homefield Ave
5 Beccles NR34 ......111 B5
Lowestoft NR33 ......114 F6
Homefield Paddock
NR34 ....111 B5

Homefield Rd CB9 .....132 C4
Homefield Rd Ind Est
CB9 ....132 D4
Homeport NR32 ......113 E3
Homer Cl IP1 ....137 D1
Homestall Cres CB9 ....74 A2
Homestead Dr **2** IP28 ..30 B8
Homestead The NR33 ..114 D3
Homey Bridge Rd CO6 ..93 E1
Honey Hill IP33 ....154 C1
Honey La CO6 ....102 B6
Honeymeade Cl CB9 ...34 E4
Honeypot La
Kelsale cum Carlton IP17 ..57 E4
Mendham IP20 ....23 C4
Monewden IP13 ....69 F4
Wattisfield IP22 ....35 D4
Honeypot Meadow **2**
NR35 ....110 B3
Honeysuckle Cl
Haverhill CB9 ....132 C7
1 Lowestoft NR33 ....115 A3
1 Red Lodge IP28 .....46 A8
4 Soham CB7 ....28 D4
Honeysuckle Gdns
IP2 ....138 E4
Honeysuckle Way **4**
IP32 ....123 F6
Honington CE VC Prim Sch
IP31 ....33 F5
Honington Rise IP31 ...33 C5
Hoo La IP12 ....71 E4
Hood Dr IP6 ....81 F5
Hood Rd IP3 ....139 E1
Hood's La NR34 ......25 F4
Hook La IP7 ....149 F4
Hooper Sq IP13 ......122 C6
Hop Meadow CO7 ....151 B4
Hope Cres IP12 ......147 A6
Hopelyns Cl **4** NR32 ..113 B4
Hopper Cl IP22 ......20 E2
Hopton CE VC Prim Sch
IP22 ....18 C1
Hopton Fst Sch NR31 ...3 C6
Hopton Gdns NR31 ....3 B7
Hopton Rd
Barningham IP31 ....34 F8
Thelnetham IP22 ....18 D1
Hopton Rise IP32 .....132 A6
Horham Rd IP21 ....38 E1
Horkesley Cl IP6 ......102 D4
Horkesley Rd CO6 ....102 D4
Horn Hill NR33 ....115 C7
Horn La CB8 ....60 D3
Hornbeam Cl
Beccles NR34 ....111 E4
Rosedale Park NR33 ...114 F4
Hornbeam Dr IP29 ....63 A8
Hornbeam Rd
Mildenhall IP28 ....116 E5
2 Stowupland IP14 ...67 A6
Horringer Ct Mid Sch
IP33 ....122 D3
Horringer Rd IP29 ....122 D2
Horsecroft Cl IP29 ...122 E1
Horsecroft Rd
Bury St Edmunds IP33 ..122 F2
1 Horringer IP29 .....63 C8
Horsefair IP30 ....50 D1
Horsefair Cl IP14 .....52 E4
Horseheath Rd CB9 ...74 A2
Horseshoe Dr IP28 ....30 C1
Horseshoe La CB9 ....132 C5
Horsham Ave IP31 ....140 D3
Horsham Cl CB9 .....132 A7
Hospital Rd
Bury St Edmunds IP33 ..154 A1
Orford IP12 ....131 B6
Hossack Rd IP12 .....144 A8
Hotson Rd IP18 ......119 D6
Houghton Cl
Hopton on Sea NR31 ...3 B6
Oulton NR32 ....112 E4
Houghton Pl **3** IP14 ..140 F5
Houghtons La CB7 ....29 D5
Houldsworth Terr CB8 ..120 F3
Houldsworth Valley Prim Sch
CB8 ....120 E3
How Hill (Tumulus)*
IP27 ....31 B7
Howard Cl
6 Framlingham IP13 ..126 C3
Harleston IP20 ....22 D4
Haverhill CB9 ....132 B5
Howard Com Prim Sch
IP32 ....122 D8
Howard de Walden Way
CB8 ....121 A4
Howard Mid Sch
Bury St Edmunds IP32 ..48 B5
Fornham All Saints IP28 ..122 D8
Howard Rd **1** NR35 ..110 D3
Howard St IP14 ......140 B7
Howards Way IP5 ....141 D8
Howe Ave IP14 ......140 C3
Howe La Cockfield IP30 ..64 C1
Thornham Parva IP23 ..37 A3
Howe Rd CB9 ....132 D7
Howes Ave IP31 ......49 D4
Howlett Cl IP5 ....141 E7
Howlett Way IP24 ....16 B7
Howley Gdns NR32 ...113 A6
Hoxne Cl **5** IP14 ....124 E3
Hoxne Rd Eye IP23 ...117 C2
Hoxne IP21 ....38 D3
Syleham IP21 ....21 F1
Hoxter Way CO10 ....148 C8

Hoylake Cl **6** IP28 ...48 C6
Hubbard's Ave **2** NR32 ..113 C6
Hubbard's Hill IP17 ...41 B1
Hubbard's La IP30 ....64 F8
Hubbard's Loke NR32 ..113 C6
Hubbards Cl IP17 ....128 B4
Hudson Cl
10 Harwich CO12 .....107 A1
Haverhill CB9 ....133 A4
Hudson Way **6** IP29 ..47 A2
Hudsons La CO6 ......103 A7
Huggins La IP29 ......37 B1
Hugh Ager Cl **3** IP14 ..124 D3
Hughes Cnr CO7 .....151 A6
Hughes Rd IP7 ....151 B6
Hull St IP27 ....109 F1
Hulver La IP17 ....72 C6
Hulver Rd NR34 ....9 F2
Humber Doucy La IP4 ..136 A2
Humber Doucy Sports Ctr
IP4 ....140 D7
Hummingbird Cl IP32 ..49 A3
Humphry Rd CO10 ...148 C6
Hundon Cl CB8 ....75 B6
Hundon Pl **6** CB9 ...132 F6
Hundon Prim Sch
CO10 ....75 D3
Hundon Rd
Hundon CO10 ....75 B1
Kedington CB9 ....133 F8
Hundred La
Boxted CO4 ....103 B2
Old Newton with Dagworth
IP14 ....51 F3
Hungate NR34 ....111 B5
Hungate Cl NR34 .....111 B5
Hungate La NR34 ....111 B5
Hungerdown La CO11 ..104 B1
Hunston Rd IP31 ......50 E7
Hunt Cl
5 Redenhall with Harleston
IP20 ....22 D6
Stowmarket IP14 .....124 D3
Hunter Dr
16 Manningtree CO11 ...104 D2
2 Thurston IP31 ....49 D4
Hunter Rd
Bury St Edmunds IP32 ..122 D8
Honington IP31 ....33 D5
2 Ipswich IP3 ....144 C8
Hunter's Chase CO7 ..103 F1
Hunter's La IP22 .....23 A3
Hunters End IP11 ....152 C7
Hunters La IP20 ......23 B2
Hunters Ride **21** IP5 ..98 A8
Huntingdon Cl **9** NR33 ..115 A3
Huntingfield Rd
Cratfield IP19 ....40 D5
Leiston IP16 ....129 C5
Huntley Cres IP19 ...118 C5
Hunts Hill CO10 ......77 A2
Hurdle Dro IP28 ......29 F8
Hurdle Makers Hill IP8 ..95 F6
Hurn Crag Rd IP18 ...119 C7
Hurricane Pl IP2 .....140 B1
Hurstlea Ct IP6 ......125 D5
Hurstlea Rd IP6 .....125 C5
Hurth Way IP14 ......16 C6
Hurts Croft **3** CB7 ...29 A1
Hut Hill (Tumulus)*
IP31 ....17 E3
Hutland Rd IP4 ......139 F7
Hutton Cl IP23 ....117 D3
Hyam's La IP9 ....105 C5
Hyams La IP9 ....105 C5
Hyde Rd CO10 ....148 C5
Hydewood Rd CO9 ...90 A2
Hyem's Cl IP9 ....105 C5
Hyntle Cl IP2 ....138 E5
Hyperion Way IP1 ....120 D8
Hythe Cl **9** CB5 ....44 A6
Hythe La CB5 ....44 A6
Hythe La IP26 ....4 E7

I

Ice House Quay NR32 ..114 E8
Iceni Way CB8 ....120 B8
Icepits Cl IP31 ....49 C6
Ickleton Pl **1** CO10 ..132 F6
Icklingham Rd IP28 ...32 B2
Icknield Cl **3** CB8 ...60 E7
Icknield Cres IP4 ....140 F5
Ickworth Ct **2** IP11 ..152 C3
Ickworth Dr IP33 .....154 A1
Ickworth House Pk & Gdn*
IP29 ....62 E8
Ickworth Pk Prim Sch
IP29 ....63 A8
Ickworth Vineyard*
IP29 ....62 E8
Ilex Cl IP3 ....123 A3
Iliffe Way IP14 ......124 D6
Imperial Mews NR31 ...3 B6
Impson Way IP26 .....6 A8
Ingate NR34 ....111 C4
Ingestre St **1** CO12 ..107 B2
Ingham Rd
Haverhill CB9 ....132 E6
West Stow IP28 ....32 C1
Ingram's Rd IP21 ....21 F3
Ingram's Well Rd
CO10 ....148 D5
Inkerman Dr **4** IP7 ..149 D6

Inkerman Row **4** CO10 ..148 C6
Inkerman Terr **3** IP7 ..149 D6
Innes End **4** IP8 ....138 C2
Inverness Rd IP4 ....136 A2
Inworth La CO6 ......101 B1
Ion Rd **8** IP32 ......122 E8
Ipswich Ave **3** IP27 ..85 B3
Ipswich Cl **1** IP12 ...85 B3
Ipswich Ct IP33 .....154 B3
Ipswich High Sch IP9 ..144 C2
Ipswich Hospl IP4 ....140 C7
Ipswich Mus* IP1 ....155 B3
Ipswich Pre Prep Sch
IP14 ....68 B6
Ipswich Prep Sch IP1 ..155 B4
Ipswich Rd
Brantham CO11 ....104 E5
Charsfield IP13 ....70 B2
Claydon IP6 ....134 C8
Dedham CO4 ....103 D3
East Bergholt CO7 ....151 A6
Eimsett IP7 ....95 A8
Grundisburgh IP13 ...83 E5
Hadleigh IP7 ....149 F7
Harkstead IP9 ....106 A4
Holbrook IP9 ....105 E8
Lowestoft NR32 ......113 C3
Nacton IP10 ....145 A5
Nedging-with-Naughton
IP7 ....80 C4
Needham Market IP6 ..125 E4
Newbourne IP12 ......98 C6
Orford IP12 ....131 B4
Otley IP6 ....69 B2
2 Scole IP21 ....20 F1
Scole NR15 ....21 C7
Stowmarket IP14 .....124 E4
Stratford St Mary CO7 ..103 E4
Tattingstone White House
IP9 ....142 D1
Waldringfield IP12 ...98 D7
Willisham IP8 ....81 B4
Winston IP14 ....53 F1
Witnesham IP6 ....136 A8
Woodbridge IP12 ....146 E3
Yaxley IP23 ....37 B4
Ipswich Sta IP1 .....155 A4
Ipswich St
Bury St Edmunds IP33 ..154 B3
Lakenheath IP27 .....109 F1
Stowmarket IP14 .....124 D6
Ipswich Sta IP1 .....155 A1
Ipswich Transport Mus*
IP3 ....140 C2
Ipswich Way **8** IP6 ..68 E6
Ireland Rd IP3 ....139 F1
Irex Rd NR33 ....115 B3
Iris Cl IP22 ....20 F1
Irlam Rd IP2 ....138 D2
Isaacson Rd CB5 .....44 B8
Isinglass Cl CB8 .....121 E2
Isleham Rd CB7 ......29 B2
Ivry St IP1 ....155 A4
Ivy Cl IP13 ....54 E7
Ivy La NR33 ....114 C7
Ivy Lodge Rd IP12 ...71 D1
Ivytree La **7** IP4 ...94 C7
Ixer La IP30 ....64 B5
Ixworth Abbey IP31 ...34 A1
Ixworth CE Prim Sch
IP31 ....34 B1
Ixworth Mid Sch IP31 ..34 B1
Ixworth Rd
Haverhill CB9 ....132 C4
Honington IP31 ....33 F5
Stowlangtoft IP31 ....50 B6
Troston IP31 ....33 D5
Walsham le Willows IP31 ..35 A1

J

Jack Jarvis Cl **5** CB8 ..121 A3
Jack's Gn Rd IP6 ....125 E6
Jack's La IP14 ....124 A2
Jacks Gn IP6 ....125 E7
Jackson Cl IP5 ....141 F7
Jackson Rd IP12 ....98 C5
Jackson Way IP6 ....125 D8
Jacob Way **1** IP12 ..147 A5
Jacobs Cl **14** IP12 ...34 E4
Jacobs Meadow IP30 ..65 D5
Jacobs St **1** NR32 ...113 D2
Jacqueline Cl
Bury St Edmunds IP33 ..154 A1
7 Grundisburgh IP13 ..83 E5
James Boden Cl **7**
IP11 ....152 E5
James Carter Rd IP28 ..116 A6
Jarman Pl **6** CO10 ..148 C6
Janet Hadenham Cl **11**
NR34 ....9 F4
Janus Cl CB9 ....133 B4
Jaques Cl **3** CO10 ...77 B3
Jarman Pl IP33 ......123 C3
Jarman's La IP28 ....29 F7
Jarrold Cl **1** IP22 ...34 F7
Jarvis Way CB8 .....120 E5
Jasmine Cl
3 Felixstowe IP11 ....107 D8
Ipswich IP2 ....138 F3
Jasmine Gn NR32 ...113 C2
Java Lodge Rd IP13 ..127 B3
Jay Cl IP33 ....123 A5
Jay La NR32 ....3 A6
Jay's Gn IP20 ....22 E6
Jay's Hill Rd
Ellough NR34 ....10 B2

Jay's Hill Rd continued
Willingham St Mary NR34 ..26 A8
Jays Croft Rd **2** IP12 ..85 E8
Jaywick Rd **2** CB9 ...132 E6
Jeaffresons Well IP6 ..126 D4
Jeannie Mann Ct
NR32 ....113 B3
Jeavons La IP5 ......141 E7
Jefferies Rd IP4 .....139 E6
Jellicoe Ave NR33 ...114 D6
Jenkins Gn NR33 ....113 A5
Jenkinsons Pightle
NR35 ....7 B8
Jenner Cl NR35 .....110 C2
Jenners Cl **1** IP12 ..147 B6
Jennings Way IP22 ...20 C3
Jermyn Ave IP32 ....123 F5
Jermyn Way IP19 ...118 A2
Jermyns Cl IP9 ....110 B3
Jermyns Rd IP18 ....119 B8
Jervis Cl **10** IP9 .....105 E7
Jewell View IP5 .....141 D8
Jim Mollison Cl **5** IP28 ..116 A5
Jimmy's Farm* IP9 ...142 E5
Jimmy's La CO11 ....104 F5
Jocelyn Cl **16** IP32 ...48 C5
Jockey's La Combs IP14 ..66 C2
Framsden IP14 ....69 B7
Joes Rd CO10 ....92 C3
John Childs Way
NR35 ....110 C2
John Lawrence Cl
NR34 ....111 B2
John Russell Gall*
IP3 ....155 C2
John Shepherd Rd **1**
IP21 ....39 D8
John St Leiston IP16 ..129 C5
Lowestoft NR33 ......115 C7
Rose Hill IP3 ....139 E4
John Swain Cl IP6 ....125 F6
John Tibauld Ct **4** CB9 ..88 D3
Johnson Cl **3** IP2 ...139 C3
Johnson Rd **7** IP29 ...47 A2
Johnson Way IP32 ..113 A5
Jolly's Way IP31 .....35 C1
Jones Rd CO10 ......76 C3
Jordan Cl IP6 ....125 E7
Jordayn Rise IP7 ....149 E6
Joscelyns The CB7 NR31 ..3 B8
Josselyns The IP11 ...152 B8
Jovian Way IP1 .....138 E8
Joyce Rd NR35 .....110 D3
Jubilee Ave IP14 ....124 D4
Jubilee Cl **11** Claydon IP6 ..82 B5
10 Felixstowe IP11 ....107 D8
16 Isleham CB7 ....29 C5
2 Laxfield IP13 ....40 B3
4 Thetford IP24 ......16 B5
Weeting IP27 ....5 E3
Jubilee Cres IP14 ....67 A7
Jubilee Ct CB8 ....60 A5
Jubilee Ctr IP28 ....116 C3
Jubilee End **5** CO11 ..104 E3
Jubilee La
Bungay NR35 ....110 B2
Lakenheath IP27 .....109 C8
Lowestoft NR33 ......115 A2
Sudbury CO10 ....148 D6
Jubilee Terr **10** IP30 ..50 F2
Jubilee Way
Ipswich IP1 ....113 E2
Mildenhall IP28 ....30 B5
Jubilee Wlk CB9 .....132 E5
Judas La IP23 ....37 B5
Judith Ave IP17 .....129 B2
Julian Cl CB9 ....133 B5
Julian Way **12** NR31 ...3 B7
Julius Martin La CB7 ..28 C4
Junction Rd IP28 ....115 A5
June Ave Ipswich IP1 ..135 B2
Lowestoft NR33 ......113 B3
Juniper Cl IP28 ......116 E5
Juniper Rd IP28 .....30 C1
Jupe's Hill CO7 ......101 B1
Jupes Hill CO7 ......104 B3
Jupiter Cl CB9 ....133 B4
Jupiter Rd IP4 ....140 B7
Justinian Cl CB9 ....133 B4

K

Karen Cl Ipswich IP1 ..135 B4
Kate's La IP14 ....51 A1
Katwijk Way **2** NR32 ..115 D8
Keating Cl **2** CO11 ...104 D2
Keats Cl IP1 ....127 B4
Keats Cres IP1 ......134 F3
Kebbles **2** CO10 ....77 A3
Kedington Hill CO10 ..92 A1
Kedington Prim Sch
CB9 ....133 G8
Kedington Rd CB9 ...133 D3
Keebles Yd **8** CB9 ...132 E6
Keel Cl NR33 ....114 B4
Keens La IP18 ....119 B7
Keep Rose **6** NR35 ..110 B4
Keeper's La
Marlesford IP13 ......71 D5
Stoke-by-Nayland CO6 ..102 C8
Trimley St Mary IP11 ..152 A7
Keightley Way IP6 ...136 B5

Kell's Acres NR34 . . . . . . .8 F7
Kell's Way NR34 . . . . .9 B6
Kelly Rd IP2 . . . . .138 E5
Kelly-Pain Ct NR32 . . . . .113 D3
Kelsale CE VCP Sch
IP17 . . . . .128 C5
Kelso Rd IP33 . . . . .122 D2
Kelvedon Dr IP4 . . . . . . .140 F5
Kelvin Pl IP12 . . . . .16 A4
Kelvin Rd IP1 . . . . .134 F1
Kemball St IP4 . . . . .140 A5
Kembold Cl IP32 . . . . . . .123 E5
Kemps La NR34 . . . . .111 B3
Kempshorne CI NR32 . . .112 E4
Kempson Dr ⑦ CO10 . . . . .92 B3
Kempson Way IP30 . . . . .123 F4
Kempsters The IP11 . . . . .152 D7
Kempton Cl ⑤ IP11 . . . . .135 A3
Kempton Cross NR34 . . . .111 E4
Kempton Rd IP1 . . . . .135 A3
Kemsley Rd IP11 . . . . . . .152 F5
Kendal Gn IP11 . . . . .153 D7
Kendal Rd NR33 . . . . .115 B5
Kennedy Ave IP19 . . . . . .118 A1
Kennedy Cl
Halesworth IP19 . . . . . . .118 B1
Ipswich IP4 . . . . .140 A6
Kennedy Rd ⑨ CB7 . . . . . .29 C5
Kennedy St IP27 . . . . . . .109 E1
Kennel Loke NR31 . . . . . . .3 B8
Kennels La IP13 . . . . .146 C8
Kennels Rd
Brightwell IP10 . . . . .98 A6
Foxhall IP10 . . . . .141 F2
Kennetside CB8 . . . . .61 B1
Kennett Prim Sch CB8 . . . .45 F6
Kennett Rd or Moulton
CB8 . . . . .45 F3
Kennett Sta CB8 . . . . .45 F6
Kenney Cl IP6 . . . . .95 D7
Kenninghall Prim Sch
NR16 . . . . .19 A8
Kenninghall Rd NR16 . . . . .19 A7
Kennyhill Dro IP28 . . . . . .13 A3
Kensington Rd
Ipswich IP1 . . . . .139 A8
Lowestoft NR33 . . . . .115 C5
Stowmarket IP14 . . . . . . .124 D5
Kent Rd Lackford IP28 . . . .31 F1
Lowestoft NR32 . . . . .113 B1
Stowmarket IP14 . . . . . . .124 C7
Kentford Rd ⑤ IP11 . . . . .152 C4
Kenton Rd IP14 . . . . .52 F3
Kents La Bungay NR35 . . .110 D3
Soham CB7 . . . . .28 D4
Kentwell CI IP4 . . . . .140 F4
Kentwell Hall* CO10 . . . . .77 E2
Kentwell Pl ③ CB5 . . . . . .44 A6
Kenyon Cl ⑦ CO7 . . . . . .103 E5
Kenyon Dr ⑨ CO10 . . . . . .92 C6
Kenyon Row NR34 . . . . . . .9 B6
Kenyon St IP2 . . . . .155 B1
Kerridge Way ㉘ IP22 . . . .22 D6
Kerridge's Cut ㉘ CO11 . .105 A2
Kerridges NR16 . . . . .18 C8
Kerrison Con Ctr IP23 . . . .37 D1
Kerrison Rd NR35 . . . . . .110 D2
Kerry Ave IP1 . . . . .134 D1
Kerrys Farm La IP14 . . . . .51 F4
Kersey Ave CO10 . . . . . . .148 F4
Kersey CE Prim Sch
IP7 . . . . .94 A6
Kersey Cl IP14 . . . . .124 E3
Kersey Pottery* IP7 . . . . . .94 A7
Kersey Rd IP11 . . . . .152 D4
Kersley Hall La IP21 . . . . .39 A3
Kesgrave Dr NR32 . . . . . .112 F2
Kesgrave High Sch
IP5 . . . . .141 C8
Kessingland CE VCP Sch
NR33 . . . . .11 C2
Kesteven Rd IP2 . . . . . . .155 A1
Kestrel Cl
① Beck Row, Holywell
Row & Kenny Hill IP28 . . .13 B1
Thetford IP24 . . . . .16 C4
Kestrel Dr IP7 . . . . .67 A5
Kestrel Gn NR33 . . . . . . .114 C6
Kestrel Rd
Bury St Edmunds IP33 . . .123 B2
Haverhill CB9 . . . . .133 A5
Ipswich IP2 . . . . .138 D3
Keswick Cl IP11 . . . . .153 C6
Kettle La IP6 . . . . .67 E1
Kettlebaston Way ③
IP1 . . . . .135 D1
Kettleborrow CI ⑤ IP31 . . .34 B1
Kettleburgh Rd IP13 . . . . .126 C1
Kettlefields CB8 . . . . .59 F5
Kettlefields CP Sch
CB8 . . . . .59 F5
Kevington Dr NR32 . . . . . .112 C2
Key St IP3 . . . . .155 C2
Keynes Way ㉘ CO12 . . . .106 E7
Khartoum Rd IP4 . . . . . . .139 F7
Kidz Kingdom* IP5 . . . . . .98 A8
Kilbourn Rd ⑥ NR33 . . . .115 A3
Kilbrack NR34 . . . . .111 C5
Kilbrack Gdns NR34 . . . . .111 C5
Kildare Ave IP1 . . . . .134 D2
Kilmaine Rd ㉒ CO12 . . . .106 F1
Kiln Bottom IP7 . . . . .149 F8
Kiln Cotts IP14 . . . . .124 C5
Kiln Dr CO10 . . . . .148 E4
Kiln Farm La IP22 . . . . . . .35 F5

Kiln Field ① IP11 . . . . . . .152 D5
Kiln La Benhall IP17 . . . . .128 C1
Boot Street IP13 . . . . . . .137 E6
Buxhall IP14 . . . . .65 F3
Dickleburgh & Rushall
IP21 . . . . .21 C2
Elmswell IP30 . . . . .50 E1
Friston IP17 . . . . .72 D7
① Mistley CO11 . . . . .104 F2
Needham IP20 . . . . .22 A4
Rede IP29 . . . . .62 E4
Stowlangtoft IP31 . . . . . . .34 E1
Kiln La NR34 . . . . .26 C3
Kilverstone Rd IP24 . . . . . .17 A6
Kimberley Rd NR33 . . . . .115 A7
Kimms Belt IP24 . . . . .16 B5
Kirkley High Sch
NR33 . . . . .115 B6
King Edward Ave
IP13 . . . . .127 C7
King Edward Rd
Ipswich IP3 . . . . .140 B3
Leiston IP16 . . . . .129 C6
King Edward VI Sch
IP33 . . . . .154 A3
King Edward VII Dr
IP9 . . . . .107 A4
King Edward VII Rd
CB8 . . . . .120 E5
King George Ave CB8 . . . .120 B8
King George's Ave
③ Harwich CO12 . . . . . . .107 A2
Leiston IP16 . . . . .129 D6
King St Aldeburgh IP15 . . .130 E3
Felixstowe IP11 . . . . .152 E6
Ipswich IP1 . . . . .155 B3
① Mildenhall IP28 . . . . . .116 C4
Sudbury CO10 . . . . .148 C5
Weybread IP21 . . . . .22 D3
King William St ③ IP6 . . .125 D5
King's Ave IP3 . . . . .126 B5
King's Dam NR34 . . . . .9 B6
King's Head St ② CO12 . .107 C3
King's Hill CB9 . . . . .133 E7
King's La Blyford IP19 . . . .42 C8
Gosbeck IP6 . . . . .66 F2
Sotherton NR34 . . . . .25 D2
Tannington IP13 . . . . .55 B7
Walsham le Willows IP31 . .35 C3
Weston NR34 . . . . .9 D1
King's Rd
Bury St Edmunds IP33 . . .154 A2
Harwich CO12 . . . . .107 A2
Topcroft NR35 . . . . .7 A8
King's Theatre CB8 . . . . .120 F3
King's Way IP12 . . . . .140 B2
Kingfisher Ave IP2 . . . . . .138 D3
Kingfisher Cl CB9 . . . . . . .133 A6
Kingfisher Cres IP18 . . . .119 A7
Kingfisher Ct NR33 . . . . . .114 C6
Kingfisher Dr
⑬ Burwell CB5 . . . . .44 A6
Claydon IP6 . . . . .81 F5
⑱ Harwich CO12 . . . . . .106 F1
Kingfisher Leisure Ctr
CO10 . . . . .148 D4
Kingfisher Rd IP32 . . . . . .123 F7
Kingfisher Rise IP17 . . . . .128 C4
Kingfisher Way
Mildenhall IP28 . . . . .116 D4
⑧ Stowmarket IP14 . . . . .67 A5
Kings Ave IP6 . . . . .139 E5
Kings CI ① Acton CO10 . . .92 B7
① Manningtree CO11 . . . .104 E2
Mildenhall IP28 . . . . .116 D5
Woodbridge IP12 . . . . . . .146 E4
Kings Dr CB8 . . . . .121 B1
Kings Fleet Prim Sch
IP11 . . . . .153 C6
Kings Fleet Rd IP11 . . . . .152 E3
Kings Head La IP22 . . . . . .19 A6
Kings Hill CO10 . . . . .148 E4
Kings Mead CB8 . . . . .60 E8
Kings Meadow
Great Cornard CO10 . . . . .148 E4
Kedington CB9 . . . . .133 E7
Kings Parade CB7 . . . . . . .28 D3
Kings Pk IP29 . . . . .62 D5
Kings Rd Bungay NR35 . . .110 C2
Glemsford CO10 . . . . .77 A3
Leiston IP16 . . . . .129 C5
Kingsbury Rd IP11 . . . . . .152 C7
Kingsfield Ave IP1 . . . . . .139 D8
Kingsgate Dr IP4 . . . . . . .139 F8
Kingshall St IP30 . . . . .64 D8
Kingsland IP9 . . . . .106 F5
Kingsland La ③ CO6 . . . .102 A7
Kingsley CI ⑧ IP1 . . . . . .135 A3
Kingsmead CB8 . . . . .121 C1
Kingsmead Rd IP14 . . . . .124 C7
Kingston Ave IP12 . . . . . .146 F7
Kingston Ct NR34 . . . . . . .123 A3
Kingston Ct NR34 . . . . . . .111 D5
Kingston Dr NR34 . . . . . .111 C5
Kingston Farm Rd
IP21 . . . . .147 A4
Kingston Pas ③ CB8 . . . .121 A3
Kingston Rd
Ipswich IP1 . . . . .138 F8
Woodbridge IP12 . . . . . . .147 A4
Kingsway ④ Earsham NR35 . .7 A7
⑨ Harwich CO12 . . . . . .107 B2
Mildenhall IP28 . . . . .116 C4
Newmarket CB8 . . . . .120 F4
Woodbridge IP12 . . . . . . .147 B5
Kingswood Ave NR33 . . . .114 D4
Kingswood CI IP18 . . . . . .119 B7
Kinross Rd IP4 . . . . .136 B1
Kipling CI ⑤ NR33 . . . . . .11 C1
Kipling Rd IP14 . . . . .134 F3

Kipling Way IP14 . . . . . . .124 B8
Kirby Cane Wlk NR32 . . . .113 A3
Kirby Cl IP4 . . . . .140 A6
Kirby St IP4 . . . . .140 A7
Kirkdale Ct ④ NR33 . . . . .115 B4
Kirkham Cl ② IP2 . . . . . . .139 A2
Kirkley Cliff Rd NR33 . . . .115 C5
Kirkley Gdns NR33 . . . . . .115 B6
Kirkley High Sch
NR33 . . . . .115 A6
Kirkley Mid Sch NR33 . . . .115 B6
Kirkley Pk Rd NR33 . . . . .115 B6
Kirkley Run NR33 . . . . . . .115 A7
Kirkley Sports & Fitness Ctr
NR33 . . . . .115 B7
Kirkley St NR33 . . . . .115 B6
Kirkstead Rd IP33 . . . . . . .122 D3
Kirkstone Way ④ NR32 . .113 A4
Kirkton Cl IP9 . . . . .107 A5
Kirtling Cl ⑨ IP1 NR33 . . .114 C3
Kirtling Pl ③ CB9 . . . . . . .132 F6
Kirtling Rd CB8 . . . . .60 E5
Kirton Rd IP11 . . . . .107 D8
Kitchen Hill CO10 . . . . . . .91 D4
Kitchener Rd
Ipswich IP1 . . . . .138 F8
Leiston IP16 . . . . .129 C6
Kitchener Way ⑤ IP9 . . . .107 A5
Kitson Meadows IP33 . . . .122 A5
Kittiwake CI
Ipswich IP2 . . . . .138 E3
Lowestoft NR33 . . . . .114 D5
Klondyke IP32 . . . . .122 F8
Knaves Acre Dro CB7 . . . . .29 B6
Knettishall Heath Ctry Pk*
IP31 . . . . .17 E3
Knight Rd ① IP12 . . . . . . .85 D8
Knights Cl
⑦ Debenham IP14 . . . . . . .53 F2
⑥ Felixstowe IP11 . . . . . .153 D6
⑥ Manningtree CO11 . . . .104 E2
④ Old Newton with Dagworth
IP14 . . . . .51 E1
Knights Ct
⑱ Haverhill CB9 . . . . . . .132 C5
Roman Hill NR32 . . . . . . .113 C1
Knights La ⑤ IP5 . . . . . . .141 D7
Knights Yd NR34 . . . . .111 B6
Knightsdale Rd IP1 . . . . . .135 A1
Knightswood ⑧ NR32 . . . .113 B5
Knoll The IP13 . . . . .126 D3
Knowle The ⑦ IP31 . . . . . .34 E4
Knox La IP12 . . . . .34 C4
Knutsford CI IP8 . . . . .138 C1
Kreswell Gr ⑦ CO12 . . . .107 A1
Kylborne CI IP33 . . . . . . .122 C4
Kyson Hill* IP12 . . . . .146 F2
Kyson Prim Sch IP12 . . . .146 D4

L

La Salle CI IP7 . . . . .139 B3
Laburnum Ave IP28 . . . . .116 E5
Laburnum Cl
③ Ipswich IP8 . . . . .138 C2
Mildenhall IP28 . . . . .140 D2
Red Lodge IP28 . . . . .30 B1
Worlingworth IP13 . . . . . . .54 E7
Laburnum Dr IP14 . . . . . . .80 C8
Laburnum Gdns IP5 . . . . .136 E1
Laburnum La ⑪ CB5 . . . . .44 A6
Laburnum Rd ③ NR35 . . .110 B3
Laburnum Way ② CO6 . . .102 C5
Lacewing CI ⑬ IP8 . . . . . .142 D8
Lacey St IP4 . . . . .139 E6
Lacey's La CB8 . . . . .120 B7
Lachlan Gn IP12 . . . . .146 F7
Lackford CI IP4 . . . . .140 F4
Lackford La IP28 . . . . .47 D6
Lackford Pl ⑦ IP3 . . . . . .144 D8
Lackford Wildfowl Nature
Reserve* IP28 . . . . .31 F1
Lacon Rd ⑧ IP3 . . . . .134 A2
Ladbrooke CI IP7 . . . . .80 E1
Lady La Hadleigh IP7 . . . .149 E7
Ipswich IP1 . . . . .155 A3
Lady La Ind Est IP7 . . . . .149 E7
Lady Margaret Gdns
IP12 . . . . .146 D4
Lady St ⑥ CO10 . . . . .78 D4
Lady's La IP22 . . . . .19 F5
Lady's Meadow NR34 . . . .111 B6
Ladyfield IP14 . . . . .66 D8
Ladygate ① CB9 . . . . .132 C4
Ladywell Rd IP14 . . . . .51 F7
Ladywood Rd IP14 . . . . . .140 C7
Lagonda Dr IP1 . . . . .134 C1
Lake Ave IP32 . . . . .48 C5
Lake Side IP14 . . . . .124 C6
Lake View Rd NR33 . . . . .114 E8
Lakeland ③ IP26 . . . . .5 A3
Lakeland Dr NR32 . . . . . . .112 F1
Lakeside Ave IP16 . . . . . . .73 E6
Lakeside CI IP18 . . . . .119 B7
Lakeside Pk Dr IP18 . . . . .119 B6
Lakeside Rd IP2 . . . . .138 E2
Lakeside Rise NR32 . . . . .112 C8

Lakforth ④ CO10 . . . . . . .91 E8
Lamarsh Hill ① CO8 . . . . .101 C5
Lamarsh Rd CO8 . . . . . . .101 A6
Lamb Ct IP28 . . . . .116 D2
Lambert Cl
Halesworth IP19 . . . . . . .118 B3
Weeting IP27 . . . . .5 E4
Lambert Dr CO10 . . . . . . .92 B7
Lambert's La
Mendlesham IP14 . . . . . . .52 C3
Sudbourne IP12 . . . . .73 B1
Lambert's Way NR35 . . . .110 C6
Lamberts CI ② IP26 . . . . . .4 E5
Lamberts La IP35 . . . . . . .136 C2
Lambeth CI ① IP1 . . . . . .139 A7
Lambeth Way IP14 . . . . . . .67 F7
Lamble CI IP28 . . . . .20 B8
Lambourne ③ IP32 . . . . .123 E6
Lambourne Rd IP1 . . . . . .135 B4
Lambourne Rd IP1 . . . . . .63 D1
Lambseth Meadow
IP17 . . . . .128 D4
Lambseth St IP23 . . . . . . .117 C3
Lamdin Rd IP32 . . . . .48 C5
Lammas CI IP31 . . . . .34 C4
Lanark Rd IP4 . . . . .136 B1
Lancaster Ave IP32 . . . . . .122 F6
Lancaster CI IP32 . . . . . . .122 F6
Lancaster Dr ⑧ IP5 . . . . . .98 A7
Lancaster Rd
Feltwell IP26 . . . . .4 E5
Ipswich IP4 . . . . .139 E6
⑦ Mildenhall IP28 . . . . . .30 A8
Sudbury CO10 . . . . .148 B8
Lancaster Way
⑫ Claydon IP6 . . . . .82 B5
Stradishall CB8 . . . . .75 C7
Lancers The IP2 . . . . .146 E3
Lancewood Wlk ㉗ IP27 . . .13 F2
Lancing Ave IP4 . . . . .140 E6
Landguard Fort*
IP11 . . . . .107 E2
Landguard Nature Reserve*
IP11 . . . . .107 E2
Landguard Rd CO10 . . . . .148 E4
Landsdown Rd CO10 . . . .148 C7
Landseer CI IP3 . . . . .140 A1
Landseer Rd ① IP3 . . . . .132 D4
Landseer Rd IP3 . . . . .139 E2
Landspring La IP14 . . . . . .114 E6
Landwade Rd CB8 . . . . . . .44 D6
Lane The
Creeting St Peter or West
Creeting IP6 . . . . .67 B5
③ Mistley CO11 . . . . .104 F2
Wrentham NR34 . . . . .26 E5
Yoxford IP17 . . . . .57 C8
Lanercost Way IP2 . . . . . .139 A1
Lang Gate Way NR35 . . . . .7 D6
Langdale CI IP3 . . . . .153 D6
Langdale Pk NR32 . . . . . .113 A4
Langer Prim Sch IP11 . . . .152 E2
Langer Rd IP11 . . . . .152 E2
Langford CI IP14 . . . . .124 B8
Langham CI CO4 . . . . .103 B1
Langham Rd
Blaxhall IP12 . . . . .72 B4
Boxted CO4 . . . . .102 F1
Langham Way IP4 . . . . . . .74 A1
Langley Ave IP11 . . . . . . .152 E4
Langley CI IP11 . . . . .152 E5
Langley Gdns NR34 . . . . . .25 E4
Langley Hill CO8 . . . . . . .101 B6
Langmere Rd IP21 . . . . . . .21 C4
Langridge The IP31 . . . . . .34 B2
Langstons IP11 . . . . .152 C7
Langton Rd ④ IP33 . . . . . .22 C2
Lanman Mus* IP13 . . . . . .126 D4
Lansbury Rd IP19 . . . . . . .118 B3
Lansdowne Rd
Felixstowe IP11 . . . . .153 B6
Ipswich IP4 . . . . .140 A5
Lanwades Bsns Pk CB8 . . .46 A5
Lapwing CI ④ IP28 . . . . . .30 B1
Lapwing CI ④ IP28 . . . . . .16 D2
Lapwing Rd ④ IP2 . . . . . .138 D3
Lapwing Way CB7 . . . . . . .28 C5
Larch CI IP27 . . . . .109 D7
Larch Gr ⑥ CO6 . . . . . . .102 C5
Larch Rd NR32 . . . . .113 B3
Larchcroft CI IP1 . . . . .135 B2
Larchcroft Rd IP1 . . . . . . .135 A2
Larches The NR34 . . . . . . .26 E5
Larchwood CI IP8 . . . . . . .138 C5
Largent Gr IP5 . . . . .141 E8
Lark CI
④ Stowmarket IP14 . . . . . .67 A5
Worlington IP28 . . . . .30 A8
Lark Hill CB8 . . . . .45 F3
Lark Rd IP28 . . . . .116 D4
Lark Rise
⑥ Martlesham Heath IP5 . .98 A8
Sudbury CO10 . . . . .148 B3
Lark Valley Dr ⑨ IP28 . . . .48 C6
Larkhall Rd CB7 . . . . .28 F1
Larkhill Rise IP14 . . . . . . .140 E5
Larkhill Way ⑧ IP1 . . . . . .152 D5
Larks CI ③ CB9 . . . . .133 A5
Larks Gate IP28 . . . . .48 C6
Larks Rise IP19 . . . . .118 A5
Larksfield Cres ⑤ CO12 . .107 A2
Larksfield Rd IP9 . . . . . . .105 D5
Larkspur CI
Red Lodge IP28 . . . . .30 B1
Worlingham NR34 . . . . . . .111 F3
Larkspur Rd IP2 . . . . .138 F3
Larksway IP11 . . . . .152 D3

Larters La IP14 . . . . .67 D8
Lathbury Ct IP33 . . . . .154 B3
Latimer Sq ④ NR32 . . . . .113 C2
Lattice Ave IP4 . . . . .140 C6
Laud Mews IP3 . . . . .140 A2
Laud's CI IP11 . . . . .152 B8
Laundry La
Bury St Edmunds IP33 . . .123 B3
Huntingfield IP19 . . . . .41 A4
Laureate Com Prim Sch
CB8 . . . . .120 E6
Laureate Gdns CB8 . . . . .120 E6
Laureate Paddocks
CB8 . . . . .120 E6
Laureate Sch Rd CB8 . . . .120 E6
Laurel Ave
① Harwich CO12 . . . . . . .106 F1
Ipswich IP5 . . . . .141 A7
Laurel CI Haverhill CB9 . . .132 B7
② Red Lodge IP28 . . . . . .30 C2
⑩ Thurstow IP31 . . . . . . .49 D4
Laurel Cr ③ IP30 . . . . .50 F2
Laurel Dr ⑱ Claydon IP6 . .82 A5
⑥ Long Melford CO10 . . . .91 E8
Laurel Rd NR33 . . . . .115 B6
Laurel Way ⑤ IP6 . . . . . .134 C8
Laurelhayes IP2 . . . . .139 A3
Laurels The
⑧ Hopton on Sea NR31 . . .3 B7
Worlingham NR34 . . . . . . .111 F3
Lavender CI ③ IP28 . . . . . .30 B1
Lavender Hill IP2 . . . . .138 F4
Lavenham Guildhall of
Corpus Christi* CO10 78 E4
Lavenham Prim Sch
CO10 . . . . .78 D4
Lavenham Rd
Great Waldingfield CO10 . .78 D1
Ipswich IP2 . . . . .138 E5
Lavenham Way
⑤ Lowestoft NR32 . . . . . .112 F3
④ Stowmarket IP14 . . . . .124 E3
Law's Drift IP10 . . . . .98 B2
Lawn Gr NR32 . . . . .112 F5
Lawn Way IP11 . . . . .152 E5
Lawns The IP4 . . . . .140 C8
Lawrence Dr NR32 . . . . . .112 A4
Lawrence Rd ② IP24 . . . . .16 D7
Lawshall Rd
Hartest IP29 . . . . .77 B8
Lawshall Row IP29 . . . . . . .63 D4
Lawson Ct ② NR33 . . . . . .115 C7
Lawson Pl IP32 . . . . .48 C7
Lawson Rd NR33 . . . . . . .115 C7
Laxfield & District Mus*
IP13 . . . . .40 B3
Laxfield Rd
Badingham IP13 . . . . .56 B8
Dennington IP13 . . . . .55 E6
Fressingfield IP21 . . . . . . .39 F7
Laxfield IP13 . . . . .40 C1
Stradbroke IP21 . . . . .39 E4
Laxfield Way NR33 . . . . . .114 F4
Layer Rd CB9 . . . . .132 C5
Layham Dr ④ IP33 . . . . . .123 A8
Layham Gdns IP14 . . . . . .124 F3
Layham Rd IP7 . . . . .149 D4
Layhill CI IP32 . . . . .123 B5
Laywood CI ① IP32 . . . . .123 D6
Layzell Croft CO10 . . . . . . .92 B2
Le Grice Wlk IP32 . . . . . . .122 E7
Lea The IP18 . . . . .119 B2
Lea's Drift ① NR33 . . . . . .114 C5
Leabrook CI IP32 . . . . . . .123 B6
Leader's Way CB8 . . . . . . .120 E4
Leas The NR32 . . . . .112 F5
Leather La
Great Yeldham CO9 . . . . . .90 A1
Haverhill CB9 . . . . .132 C5
Leathes CI NR32 . . . . . . .112 F1
Leathes Ham Nature
Reserve* NR32 . . . . .113 A1
Lee CI CB9 . . . . .132 D8
Lee Rd Aldeburgh IP15 . . .130 E3
Harwich CO12 . . . . .107 B2
Ipswich IP3 . . . . .139 F3
Leech Wlk IP32 . . . . .122 E8
Leeks CI IP1 . . . . .149 D7
Leeks Hill IP12 . . . . .147 A7
Leggatt Dr IP4 . . . . .134 A2
Leicester CI IP2 . . . . .138 F1
Leighton Rd IP3 . . . . .144 A8
Leighton Sq ⑧ IP3 . . . . . .144 A8
Leiston Abbey* IP16 . . . . . .58 C3
Leiston High Sch IP16 . . .129 E5
Leiston Leisure Ctr
IP16 . . . . .129 E5
Leiston Mid Sch IP16 . . . .129 C5
Leiston Prim Sch
IP16 . . . . .129 C5
Leiston Rd
Aldeburgh IP15 . . . . .130 D3
Coldfair Green IP17 . . . . .129 B3
Haverhill CB9 . . . . .132 C5
⑨ Lowestoft NR32 . . . . . .113 D1
Theberton IP16 . . . . .58 B5
Leisure Way NR32 . . . . . .113 B7
Lely Rd IP1 . . . . .143 F8
Lemons Hill IP9 . . . . .105 B8
Lentins The IP14 . . . . .68 C6
Leona Cres NR33 . . . . . . .114 C2
Leonard Dr ② NR32 . . . . .113 A6
Leonard's La IP26 . . . . .4 D5
Leopold Gdns IP4 . . . . . . .140 B8
Leopold Rd
Felixstowe IP11 . . . . .153 A3
Ipswich IP4 . . . . .140 B7

Leslie Rd IP3 ....140 C1
Lester Piggott Way CB8 ....120 F6
Letton Cl IP 150 E3
Leverett's La IP18 ....119 B2
Levington Ct NR33 ....115 D8
Levington La IP10 ....98 A3
Levington Rd
Felixstowe IP11 ....152 E1
Ipswich IP3 ....140 A4
Nacton IP10 ....145 C4
Lewis Cl IP3 ....140 E3
Lewis Cl
Ditchingham NR35 ....110 C8
Hopton IP22 ....18 C2
Lewis La IP9 ....105 B5
Ley Rd Barrow IP29 ....47 A2
Stetchworth CB8 ....60 A5
Leys La IP23 ....37 B5
Leys Rd IP30 ....50 B2
Leyton Ave IP28 ....116 B6
Liberty Cl IP32 ....123 F6
Liberty Intermediate Sch IP27 ....14 A3
Lidgate Ct **1** IP11 ....152 C4
Lidgate Rd CB8 ....60 A1
Lighthouse Score **2** NR32 ....113 E3
Lilac Cl IP27 ....14 D8
Lilac Dr
Lakenheath IP27 ....109 D6
Lowestoft NR32 ....113 B3
Lilac Wlk IP6 ....125 D3
Lilley Cl IP3 ....122 C3
Lily La NR34 ....10 A7
Lily Way NR14 ....114 C5
Lime Ave
Harwich CO12 ....107 A2
Lowestoft NR32 ....112 D2
Lime Cl Burwell CB5 ....44 B5
7 Harleston IP20 ....22 D5
Lakenheath IP27 ....109 D5
Mildenhall IP28 ....116 F5
8 Ufford IP13 ....84 F7
Wickham Market IP13 ....127 B6
Lime Gr CO10 ....148 A3
Lime Kiln Quay IP12 ....147 B5
Lime Kiln Quay Rd IP12 ....147 B5
Lime Tree Ave IP16 ....129 C5
Lime Tree Cl **3** IP30 ....64 F8
Lime Tree Pl IP14 ....124 D5
Lime Wlk IP30 ....65 A3
Limecroft Cl **1** IP1 ....134 C8
Limekiln Cl **7** IP6 ....134 C8
Limerick Cl IP1 ....134 E2
Limes Ave IP8 ....134 C2
Limes The
Framlingham IP16 ....126 B4
Halesworth IP19 ....118 A3
6 Framlingham IP20 ....63 A8
Long Melford CO10 ....91 E8
Rushmere St Andrew IP5 ....136 D1
Limestone Cl **12** CB7 ....29 C5
Limetree Cl IP6 ....125 E4
Limmer Ave IP21 ....21 C5
Lincoln Ave IP21 ....128 B2
Lincoln Cl IP1 ....135 B1
Lincoln Gdns **8** IP6 ....82 B5
Lincoln Gn IP23 ....123 B2
Lincoln La CO6 ....102 E1
Lincoln Rd IP28 ....30 A8
Lincoln Terr IP12 ....152 F3
Linda Cl **11** NR32 ....3 D4
Lindbergh Rd IP1 ....140 C1
Linden Cl
Aldeburgh IP15 ....130 D6
20 Manningtree CO11 ....104 D2
Linden Rd IP15 ....130 C5
Linden Wlk IP30 ....13 B1
Lindisfarne Cl IP9 ....139 A1
Lindisfarne Sch IP33 ....122 D2
Lindsey Ave CO10 ....148 F4
Lindsey Rd IP4 ....140 C7
Lindsey Way IP14 ....124 E3
Ling Rd Palgrave IP22 ....20 B2
Wortham IP22 ....19 F2
Ling's La IP6 ....106 B7
Lingfield Rd IP1 ....135 B4
Lingheath Rd IP27 ....6 A1
Lings Field IP13 ....70 C7
Lingside **1** IP25 ....98 A7
Link La IP9 ....104 E7
Link Rd
Capel St Mary IP9 ....150 E3
7 Shotley Gate IP9 ....107 A5
Link The IP9 ....104 E7
Links Ave IP11 ....153 B6
Links Cl
Bury St Edmunds IP33 ....123 B1
Lowestoft NR33 ....114 F5
Worlington IP28 ....30 B4
Links Dr
Great Yarmouth NR31 ....3 B8
Lowestoft NR32 ....113 D5
Links The Flempton IP28 ....32 E1
Woodditton CB8 ....59 E8
Links View CO10 ....92 D3
Linksfield IP5 ....140 E2
Linksfield Gdns IP5 ....140 E7
Linkwood Rd IP30 ....64 B7
Linnet Cl IP14 ....67 A5
Linnet Pl IP3 ....154 C1
Linnet Rd
Bury St Edmunds IP33 ....122 E4

Linnet Rd *continued*
Ipswich IP2 ....138 D4
Linnetts La CB8 ....133 E2
Linstead Rd IP19 ....40 F5
Linton Cl CB8 ....120 F5
Linton Gdns IP23 ....122 E3
Linton Pl **2** CB9 ....132 F6
Linx The **6** IP13 ....40 B3
Lion La IP6 ....125 E3
Lion Meadow CB9 ....88 D4
Lion Rd Glemsford CO10 ....77 A3
Palgrave IP22 ....20 B2
Wortham IP22 ....36 F8
Lion St IP1 ....155 B3
Lionel Hurst Cl **15** CO10 ....92 B3
Lisburn Rd IP4 ....121 B3
Lister Rd Hadleigh IP7 ....149 F5
Ipswich IP1 ....134 F1
Litchfield CO10 ....91 D7
Lithgo Paddock **8** IP31 ....49 A6
Little Back La IP13 ....53 F2
Little Fen Dro CB5 ....44 A7
Little Gipping St IP1 ....155 A3
Little Gn Cheveley CB8 ....60 E6
Earl Soham IP13 ....54 F1
Elmswell IP30 ....50 E2
Little Gn Cl IP23 ....36 C3
Little Gr IP9 ....150 E2
Little Gulls IP9 ....150 D3
Little Hall* CO10 ....78 E4
Little Hasse Dro CB7 ....28 E6
Little Horkesley Rd CO6 ....102 A2
Little Hyde Cl IP9 ....90 A1
Little Hyde Rd CO9 ....90 A1
Little London Hill IP14 ....53 E3
Little London La CB7 ....29 B5
Little Lumpkid IP7 ....149 E8
Little Meadows Dr IP6 ....69 C2
Little Mill La IP29 ....47 D8
Little Oulsham Dro IP26 ....4 B6
Little St IP17 ....57 C8
Little St John's St **8** IP12 ....147 A5
Little St Mary's CO10 ....91 E7
Little Tufts IP7 ....150 F3
Little Whip St IP2 ....155 B2
Little Yeldham Rd CO9 ....90 B2
Little's Cres IP2 ....155 B1
Littlemoor IP17 ....57 E6
Livermere Drift IP31 ....48 E6
Livermere Rd
Great Barton IP31 ....49 A6
Troston IP31 ....33 D2
Llewellyn Drift **8** IP5 ....141 C7
Lloyd Rd **3** IP7 ....107 A4
Lloyds The IP1 ....155 B3
Lloyds The IP11 ....11 B1
Loam Pit La IP19 ....118 C4
Locarno Rd IP4 ....140 D2
Loch Rannoch Cl IP30 ....50 E2
Lock Cl **14** IP14 ....53 F2
Lock's La
6 Leavenheath CO6 ....102 A7
Shipmeadow NR34 ....26 F6
Wrentham NR34 ....26 E4
Lock's Rd NR34 ....25 C5
Lockhart Rd NR35 ....8 D7
Lockington Cl **4** IP14 ....124 E5
Lockington Cres IP14 ....124 D5
Lockington Rd IP14 ....124 D5
Lockington Wlk IP14 ....124 D5
Lockwood Cl **11** IP12 ....147 A5
Loddon Rd
Ditchingham NR35 ....110 C7
Gillingham NR34 ....9 B6
Kirby Cane NR35 ....8 E8
Lode Cl CB7 ....28 D3
Lode La CB7 ....28 A1
Lodge Cl IP14 ....51 E1
Lodge Farm Dr IP11 ....153 C5
Lodge Farm La
Barsham NR34 ....9 B4
8 Melton IP12 ....84 E6
Lodge Farm Rd CO10 ....77 B1
Lodge La Claydon IP6 ....134 A8
Riddlesworth IP22 ....18 A3
Sheifanger IP22 ....20 B5
Lodge Way IP4 ....16 B7
Lofft Cl **10** IP31 ....14 D6
Loftus Ave IP13 ....119 C7
Loganberry Rd **4** IP3 ....144 C7
Loggers La IP22 ....18 E1
Loke The
Blundeston NR32 ....3 A4
Ditchingham NR35 ....110 B7
Lombardy Rd CO10 ....148 B8
Lombarn Hill CO11 ....105 D1
London City Rd IP21 ....39 C3
London La
Harleston IP20 ....66 C7
4 Mundford IP26 ....6 B8
London Rd
Beccles NR34 ....111 B2
Blythburgh IP19 ....42 E5
Brampton with Stoven NR34 ....25 E6
Brandon IP27 ....14 E8
Capel St Mary IP9 ....150 F2

London Rd *continued*
Copdock & Washbrook IP8 ....138 A1
24 Elveden IP24 ....15 C2
Great Horkesley CO6 ....102 C1
Halesworth IP19 ....118 A2
Harleston IP20 ....22 D5
Icklingham IP27 ....31 E8
Ipswich IP1 ....155 A3
Kessingland NR33 ....11 B2
Lowestoft NR33 ....114 D8
Pinewood IP8 ....138 B2
Thetford IP24 ....16 A5
Westley Waterless CB8 ....59 A4
Weston NR34 ....9 D2
Wrentham NR34 ....26 E4
London Rd N NR32 ....113 D1
London Rd Pakefield NR33 ....115 A2
London Rd S NR33 ....115 C5
Lone Barn Cl IP1 ....138 D8
Lonely Rd IP21 ....21 C6
Long Acre
Lowestoft NR33 ....115 B3
Southwold IP18 ....119 B7
Long Ave IP17 ....128 B4
Long Bessels IP7 ....149 D6
Long Brackland IP33 ....154 B3
Long Dolver Dro CB7 ....28 D6
Long Field IP12 ....152 D6
Long Marsh Cl IP18 ....119 C7
Long Meadow Wlk NR33 ....114 D5
Long Meadows CO10 ....106 F1
Long Melford CE Prim Sch CO10 ....91 E8
Long Pastures **2** CO10 ....77 B2
Long Perry IP7 ....150 F3
Long Rd
Lowestoft NR33 ....114 E3
Mannicgtree CO11 ....104 D1
Long Rd E CO7 ....104 A2
Long Rd W CO7 ....103 F2
Long Row IP6 ....129 D6
Long Shop Mus* IP16 ....129 C6
Long St IP3 ....139 E5
Long Thurlow Rd IP31 ....51 A7
Longacre Gdns IP33 ....122 E3
Longbeach IP9 ....114 D3
Longcroft IP21 ....152 E6
Longden Ave NR32 ....112 F2
Longfield Rd IP9 ....150 E4
Longfield Way **6** NR32 ....112 D2
Longfulans La NR31 ....3 B6
Longmeadow IP33 ....122 D7
Longmere La CB7 ....28 C5
Longrigg Rd NR33 ....110 C7
Lonsdale Cl IP4 ....139 F7
Looe Rd IP11 ....153 C5
Looms La IP33 ....154 B2
Lopham Rd NR16 ....18 D8
Lophams Cl CB9 ....132 D8
Loraine Way IP8 ....134 A1
Lord Rd IP22 ....20 D2
Lord's Croft La CB9 ....132 E5
Lord's Highway The IP14 ....67 E5
Lord's La CB8 ....61 E5
Lord's Wlk IP13 ....13 F2
Lorne Pk Rd NR33 ....115 C6
Lorne Rd
Lowestoft NR33 ....115 C6
Southwold IP18 ....119 D5
Lothing St NR32 ....112 F1
Lothingland Cl NR32 ....112 F5
Lothingland Mid Sch NR32 ....3 A5
Lotus Cl IP1 ....134 C1
Loudham Hall Rd IP13 ....127 D3
Loudham La IP13 ....85 A7
Louie's La IP22 ....20 C3
Lound Dam NR14 ....2 A3
Lound Rd
Belton with Browston NR31 ....2 E8
Blundeston NR32 ....63 D3
Rattlesden IP30 ....65 D3
Louvain Rd **16** CO12 ....107 A1
Lovat Cl IP22 ....22 E6
Love La Lowestoft NR33 ....114 F4
Thorndon IP23 ....53 B8
Westleton IP17 ....58 C7
Love Rd NR32 ....113 C1
Lover's La IP16 ....129 C8
Lovers La IP9 ....106 B6
Lovetofts Dr IP1 ....134 D1
Lovewell Rd NR33 ....115 C6
Low Comm IP19 ....19 B3
Low Comm La NR34 ....2 A1
Low Comm Rd IP22 ....19 B3
Low Farm Dr NR33 ....114 C3
Low La Brandeston IP13 ....70 A7
Creeting St Mary IP6 ....125 B8
Low Lighthouse Maritime Mus* CO12 ....107 C3
Low Rd Alburgh IP20 ....7 A1
Bramfield IP19 ....42 A5
Brampton with Stoven NR34 ....25 D5
Burwell CB5 ....44 A5
Carlton IP17 ....128 D6
Cransford IP17 ....56 C4
Darsham IP17 ....57 F8

Low Rd *continued*
Debenham IP14 ....53 E1
Denham IP21 ....38 C2
Denton IP20 ....7 B1
8 Dickleburgh & Rushall IP21 ....20 F2
Earl Soham IP13 ....54 E2
Eyke IP13 ....85 B7
1 Fressingfield IP21 ....39 E8
Friston IP17 ....72 F6
Great Glemham IP17 ....56 C1
Harwich CO12 ....106 F1
Hasketon IP13 ....146 B8
Hedenham NR35 ....7 D8
Marlesford IP13 ....71 C5
Mettingham NR35 ....110 F5
Monk Soham IP13 ....54 D3
Redenhall with Harleston IP20 ....22 F5
St John, Ilketshall NR34 ....8 D2
Starston IP20 ....22 C7
Stratford St Andrew IP17 ....71 F7
Swefling IP17 ....56 E3
Ubbeston IP19 ....40 D3
Wenhaston with Mells Hamlet IP19 ....42 C7
Wortham IP20 ....23 A7
Low St Badingham IP13 ....56 A7
Bardwell IP31 ....34 C3
Glemsford CO10 ....77 B3
Hoxne IP21 ....38 B8
Kettleburgh IP13 ....70 B7
St Margaret, Ilketshall NR35 ....24 B8
Low Water La IP22 ....20 A1
Low's La IP22 ....20 C1
Lower Baxter St IP33 ....154 B2
Lower Brook St IP4 ....155 B2
Lower Broom Rd IP30 ....50 C1
Lower Byfield IP7 ....79 C2
Lower Coney Gr IP8 ....81 A4
Lower Cres IP9 ....150 E2
Lower Dales View Rd IP1 ....139 A8
Lower Drag Way IP22 ....19 A4
Lower Downs Slade **5** CB9 ....132 E6
Lower Farm Rd
Boxted CO4 ....103 A4
Ringshall IP27 ....80 E6
Lower Harlings **4** IP9 ....107 A4
Lower House La IP12 ....98 C5
Lower Houses Rd IP9 ....106 B5
Lower Marine Par CO12 ....107 B1
Lower N St CO10 ....75 D3
Lower Oakley IP17 ....38 F4
Lower Olland St NR35 ....110 B4
Lower Orwell St IP4 ....155 C2
Lower Pk Wlk IP19 ....118 E4
Lower Rd Borley CO10 ....91 D6
Coddenham IP6 ....68 B1
Falkenham IP10 ....98 F1
Glemsford CO10 ....77 B1
Grundisburgh IP13 ....83 B5
Hemingstone IP6 ....68 C1
Hundon CO10 ....75 D3
Lavenham CO10 ....78 D4
Little Blakenham IP8 ....81 D3
Melton IP13 ....84 F6
Mount Bures CO8 ....101 D3
Onehouse IP14 ....66 B5
Westerfield IP6 ....135 D4
Wicken CB7 ....28 A2
Lower Rose La IP21 ....20 D1
Lower St Bayham IP6 ....81 E7
Cavendish CO10 ....76 E1
Great Bealings IP13 ....137 E6
Rattlesden IP30 ....65 D6
Sproughton IP8 ....138 A6
Stansfield CO10 ....76 A6
Stanstead CO10 ....77 C3
Stratford St Mary CO7 ....103 E5
Stutton IP9 ....105 D5
Ufford IP13 ....85 A6
Wickham Market IP13 ....127 B6
Lower Ufford Rd IP13 ....127 D3
Lower Ufford Rd IP13 ....127 C1
Lowes Hill IP17 ....128 E7
Lowestoft & E Suffolk Maritime Mus* NR32 ....113 A3
Lowestoft Coll NR32 ....113 C2
Lowestoft Hospl NR32 ....113 D1
Lowestoft Mus* NR33 ....114 D8
Lowestoft Porcelain* NR32 ....113 E8
Lowestoft Rd
Beccles NR34 ....111 E4
Blundeston NR32 ....112 E8
Hopton on Sea NR31 ....3 B6
Lowestoft NR33 ....114 D3
Reydon IP18 ....119 C8
Worlingham NR34 ....10 A4
Lowestoft Sta NR32 ....115 D8
Lowestoft War Meml Musuem* NR32 ....113 B3
Lowgate St IP23 ....117 D2
Lowlands Cl **17** NR33 ....11 C1
Lowry Cl CB9 ....132 B7
Lowry Gdns **6** IP3 ....144 A8
Lowry Way
Lowestoft NR32 ....113 C5
Stowmarket IP14 ....124 B7
Lowther St CB8 ....120 F3

Loxley Rd NR33 ....114 E6
Lucas Rd CO10 ....148 D5
Lucena Ct IP14 ....124 C6
Lucerne Cl
Lowestoft NR33 ....114 C5
5 Red Lodge IP28 ....30 B1
Ludbrook Cl IP6 ....125 C5
Ludgate Cswy IP23 ....117 E2
Ludlow Cl IP1 ....135 B4
Luff Meadow IP6 ....125 D5
Lugano Ave IP12 ....98 B8
Lulworth Ave IP3 ....140 D3
Lulworth Dr **14** IP30 ....132 C6
Lulworth Pk **8** NR32 ....113 A4
Lummis Vale IP5 ....141 C7
Lundy Cl CB9 ....133 B5
Lunnish Hill CO12 ....106 C2
Lupin Cl IP18 ....119 B6
Lupin Rd IP2 ....138 E4
Lupin Way IP6 ....125 D3
Lushington Rd **5** CO11 ....104 E2
Luther Rd IP17 ....155 B1
Lutus Cl CO10 ....90 A7
Lydgate Cl
1 Bury St Edmunds IP32 ....48 C5
14 Lawford CO11 ....104 D2
Lydgate Rd IP14 ....124 C7
Lyle Cl IP5 ....141 E7
Lymingster Cl **6** IP22 ....123 C6
Lymm Rd NR32 ....113 B5
Lyncroft Rd NR33 ....115 B3
Lyndhurst Ave IP4 ....140 C5
Lyndhurst Rd IP4 ....113 D4
Lyng La IP22 ....18 F5
Lyngate Ave NR33 ....114 F5
Lynn's Hall Cl CO10 ....92 C5
Lynnbrook Cl IP22 ....138 E1
Lynton Gdns NR32 ....113 C3
Lynwood Ave IP11 ....153 B5
Lynx Bsns Pk CB8 ....44 F7
Lyon Cl IP23 ....37 C4
Lysander Dr **3** IP3 ....144 C8

M

MacAulay Rd IP1 ....134 F3
MacKenzie Dr IP5 ....141 B8
MacKenzie Pl IP24 ....78 C8
MacKenzie Rd IP24 ....16 C5
Maconochie Way NR33 ....115 C7
MacPherson Robertson Way **3** IP28 ....116 B5
Mafeking Pl IP1 ....134 F3
Magdalen Cl **3** NR32 ....113 A3
Magdalen Ct IP23 ....117 C2
Magdalen Dr IP12 ....146 D3
Magdalen Rd IP7 ....149 D6
Magdalen St IP23 ....117 C2
Magdalene Cl IP4 ....138 F2
Magingley Cres IP4 ....140 F6
Magnolia Cl
8 Beck Row, Holywell Row & Kenny Hill IP28 ....13 B1
3 Red Lodge IP28 ....30 B1
Magnolia Ct **3** NR32 ....113 C3
Magnolia Dr **7** IP12 ....85 D8
Magpie Cl
8 Ipswich IP8 ....138 C2
Ramsey CO12 ....106 F1
Magpie Cl IP20 ....22 D6
Magpie Hill IP22 ....19 E1
Maid Marion Ct IP33 ....122 F3
Maiden Way IP7 ....149 D6
Maidenhall App IP2 ....139 B2
Maidenhall Sports Ctr IP2 ....139 A2
Maids Cross Hill IP27 ....109 E6
Maids Cross Way IP27 ....109 D6
Maidscross Hill Nature Reserve* IP27 ....109 F5
Maidstone Cty Inf Sch IP11 ....152 E5
Maidstone Rd
Felixstowe IP11 ....152 E5
Ipswich IP2 ....113 C1
Main Rd Benhall IP17 ....72 C8
Buckelsham IP10 ....141 F1
Chelmondiston IP9 ....106 B8
Darsham IP17 ....42 A1
Hacheston IP13 ....127 D8
Harwich CO12 ....106 F1
Henley IP6 ....82 D6
Ipswich IP5 ....141 A8
Kelsale cum Carlton IP17 ....128 C8
Marlesford IP13 ....71 D4
Martlesham IP12 ....146 C4
Parham IP13 ....70 F8
Pettistree IP13 ....127 B3
3 Ramsey & Parkeston CO12 ....106 D1
Somersham IP8 ....81 C3
Tuddenham St Martin IP6 ....136 B4
Woolverstone IP9 ....143 F2
Wormingford CO6 ....101 F2
Main St
Hockwold cum Wilton IP26 ....4 F3
Leiston IP16 ....129 C6
Maine St **4** IP24 ....16 A5
Maisie's Meadow IP13 ....54 D7
Maitland Rd IP3 ....125 E3

Major La IP23 ....37 A2
Major's CI IP29 ....62 C5
Makins Rd 2 CO12 ......106 F3
Malcolm Way C88 .....121 A5
Maldon Ct CO10 ......148 F5
Malin CI C89 ....133 B5
Mallard Rd IP18 ......119 B7
Mallard Way
  Brandon IP27 ....6 A1
  Hollesley IP12 ....99 F7
  Ipswich IP2 ....138 F3
  Stowmarket IP14 ......124 A6
  Sudbury CO10 ....92 B3
Mallards The IP27 .....109 D5
Mallets La IP12 ....131 C2
Mallow Rd 1 IP24 ......16 D6
Mallow WIk 4 C89 ....132 A6
Mallowhayes CI IP2 ...139 B3
Malmesbury La IP32 ...139 A2
Malt CI 5 Laxfield IP13 ...40 B3
  Newmarket C88 ......121 B3
Malt Office Ave IP19 ..24 B4
Malt Office La IP19 ...24 A4
Malt's La IP22 ....4 F3
Malthouse Ct 24 IP20 ..22 D6
Malthouse La
  Bury St Edmunds IP32 ..154 B4
  Gissing IP22 ....20 F8
Malthouse Rd 22 CO11 ..104 E2
Malting End CO8 ....60 E2
Malting Farm La CO7 ..103 E1
Malting La 6 Clare CO10 ..90 B8
  Iskham C87 ....29 C5
Malting Row IP11 ....33 F5
Maltings 52 D3
Maltings CI
  2 Bures Hamlet CO8 ...101 C5
  1 Chevington IP29 ....62 C6
  Halesworth IP19 .....118 B4
  Moulton C88 ....45 F3
Maltings Dr 6 IP20 .....22 D6
Maltings Garth 3 IP31 ..49 D4
Maltings La IP31 ....32 F1
Maltings Mews IP7 ....149 D5
Maltings The
  Beccles NR34 ....111 B7
  Bungay NR35 ....110 C4
Maltsters' Way NR32 ..114 D8
Maltsters WIk IP14 ...124 C3
Maltward Ave IP33 ....122 C5
Malvern CI Ipswich IP3 ..140 B3
Malvern Rd IP33 ....122 D3
Malvern Rise IP32 .....113 B3
Malyon Rd IP7 ....149 E8
Manchester Rd IP12 ...138 D2
Manderston Rd C88 ...120 E3
Manderville Rd IP33 ...122 C4
Mandeville 14 C85 .....44 A5
Mandy CI IP4 ....140 A6
Mannall WIk IP5 ......141 E8
Manners Rd IP31 ......48 D5
Manning Rd
  Bury St Edmunds IP32 ..123 F7
  Felixstowe IP11 ......152 E2
Manning's La IP22 .....35 D5
Mannings La IP9 ......104 F5
Mannington CI 3 IP4 ..140 F5
Manningtree High Sch
  CO11 ....104 D2
Manningtree Mus*
  CO11 ....104 E2
Manningtree Rd
  Dedham CO7 ....104 A3
  East Bergholt CO7 ...151 F3
  Stutton IP9 ....105 C5
Manningtree Sports Ctr
  CO11 ....104 D2
Manningtree Sta
  CO11 ....104 D3
Manor Ash Dr IP32 ....123 E6
Manor CI 9 Beccles NR34 ..9 F4
  3 Cavendish CO10 .....76 E1
  Walberswick IP18 .....119 A2
  Worlingham NR34 ......9 F4
Manor Farm CI
  Haverhill CO9 ....132 F5
  10 Southwold IP18 ....119 D5
Manor Farm Rd
  St John, Ilketshall NR34 ..8 D3
  1 Thistley Green IP28 ..29 F6
Manor Garth IP31 ......49 E6
Manor Gdns
  7 Hopton on Sea NR31 ..3 B4
  Saxmundham IP17 ....128 C2
Manor House Mus*
  IP33 ....154 C1
Manor La Gosbeck IP6 ..68 D2
  14 Harwich CO12 .....107 A2
  Horringer IP29 ....122 B1
  Stutton IP9 ....105 C5
Manor Pk Rd
  Corton NR32 ....3 C4
  5 Southwold IP18 ....119 D5
Manor Rd 10 Bildeston IP7 ..79 F4
  Brandon IP27 ....5 E1
  Bungay NR35 ....110 B2
  Clopton IP13 ....69 E1
  Elmsett IP7 ....80 F2
  Felixstowe IP11 ......152 B8
  Harwich CO12 ....107 A2
  Hasketon IP13 ....146 D6
  Haverhill CO9 ....132 F5

Manor Rd continued
  Hessett IP30 ....64 F7
  Hopton on Sea NR31 ...3 B6
  Ipswich IP4 ....139 D8
  11 Martlesham Heath IP5 ..98 A8
  Mendlesham IP14 .....116 B4
  Roydon IP22 ....20 B3
  Sudbury CO10 ......148 C7
  Trimley St Martin IP11 ..153 111
Manor Terr IP11 ......107 F3
Manor View IP28 .....116 D2
Manor WIk 20 NR33 ...11 B1
Manorhouse La 8
  NR34 ....111 B6
Mansbrook Bvd 5 IP3 ..144 C7
Manse La IP19 ....40 C6
Mansfield Ave IP1 ....134 F2
Manthorp CI IP12 ....147 B8
Manwick Rd IP11 .....152 E2
Maple CI
  6 Great Brickett IP7 ..80 D6
  Ipswich IP2 ....139 A3
  12 Lakenheath IP27 ..13 F2
  Rendlesham IP12 .....85 D8
  Yaxley IP23 ....37 B5
Maple Covert 5 NR32 ..112 F5
Maple Ga 3 IP31 ......49 A6
Maple Gr IP6 ....82 A6
Maple Hill CO10 ......75 E1
Maple Rd
  8 Lowestoft NR33 ....114 F7
  Stowupland IP14 .....67 A6
  Sudbury CO10 ......148 F3
Maple Way
  Beccles NR34 ....111 C5
  Eye IP23 ....117 D3
  Leavenheath CO6 ...102 B7
  Maples The IP5 ......140 E8
Marbella Gn NR33 ....114 E5
Marbled White Dr IP9 ..142 E8
March PI 2 CO10 ......76 A1
Marcus CI C89 ....133 B5
Marcus Rd IP11 ......153 D5
Mardle Rd Reydon NR34 ..43 B8
  Wangford with Henham
  NR34 ....26 C1
Mardle The NR33 ....114 C2
Mare Hill CO10 ....75 D3
Margaret Rd 2 IP4 ...124 C7
Margaret St IP11 .....152 E5
Margate Rd IP3 ......140 B3
Marham Rd 4 NR32 ..113 B2
Maria St 6 CO10 ......91 B7
Marigold Ave IP2 .....138 E3
Marigold Dr 3 IP28 ...46 A8
Marina 6 NR32 ......113 E1
Marina Gdns IP11 ...152 E2
Marina Theatre 11
  NR32 ....113 D1
Marine CI 3 IP31 ......3 B8
Marine Par
  12 Harwich CO12 ....107 B2
  Lowestoft NR33 .....115 D7
Mariner's CI 2 NR31 ..3 B8
Mariners Pk CI 11 NR31 ..3 B7
Mariners St NR32 ....113 E2
Mariners Way IP11 ...130 D5
Marion CI 8 NR34 ....111 C3
Mark Jennings La
  IP33 ....154 C3
Mark La IP27 ....6 C2
Markant CI IP32 .....123 E6
Market Cross PI IP15 ..130 F4
Market Gr CO9 ....90 A1
Market Hill 2 Clare CO10 ..90 A8
  Clopton IP13 ....83 D8
  Framlingham IP13 ...126 C3
  Haverhill C89 ....132 E6
  Orford IP12 ....131 C2
  6 Sudbury CO10 .....148 C5
Market La
  Blundeston NR32 ......3 B4
  Burston & Shimpling IP22 ..20 E5
  Somerleyton, Ashby &
  Herringfleet NR32 ....2 D6
Market PI 11 Bildeston IP7 ..79 F4
  Hadleigh IP7 ....149 D5
  2 Halesworth IP19 ...118 A3
  22 Harleston IP20 ...22 D6
  8 Kessingland NR33 ..11 B1
  11 Lavenham CO10 ...78 D4
  Saxmundham IP17 ...128 D3
  Southwold IP18 .....119 D5
  Stowmarket IP14 ...124 D6
Market Row NR34 ....111 B5
Market Sq C88 ......121 A3
Market St
  1 Beccles NR34 .....111 B5
  Fordham C87 ....29 A1
  3 Harwich CO12 .....107 C3
  Laxfield IP13 ....40 B3
  5 Mildenhall IP28 ...116 C4
  2 Newmarket C88 ...121 A3
  24 Soham C87 ....28 D4
Market Thoroughfare
  IP33 ....154 B2
Market Weston Rd
  IP22 ....35 A7
Markhams CI C89 ....132 D7
Marlborough Ct
  4 Haverhill C89 ......132 C5
  Lowestoft NR32 .....112 F1
Marlborough Dr 4
  CO10 ....148 D6
Marlborough Rd
  Ipswich IP4 ....140 A5
  Lowestoft NR32 .....112 F1
  Saxtead IP13 ....55 A4

Marlborough Rd continued
  Southwold IP18 .....119 D6
Marlesford Rd IP13 ...71 B5
Marlow Rd IP1 ....134 D1
Marriott's WIk 3 IP14 ..124 D5
Marsden CI 5 NR33 ..115 A3
Marsh La Aldeby NR34 ..10 C7
  Carlton Colville NR33 ..114 A4
  3 Earsham NR35 ......7 F4
  Felixstowe IP11 .....153 C8
  26 Kessingland NR33 ..11 C1
  Kessingland NR33 .....27 C8
  North Cove NR34 .....10 B5
  Reydon IP18 ....26 D2
  Somerleyton, Ashby &
  Herringfleet NR32 ....2 C4
  Worlingham NR34 ......9 F5
  Wortham IP22 ....20 A1
Marsh Rd Boxford CO10 ..93 C3
  Fritton & St Olaves NR31 ..2 B7
  Lowestoft NR33 .....114 B5
  Stoke-by-Nayland CO6 ..103 C7
Marsh View IP14 .....111 D5
Marsh Way IP33 .....154 A4
Marshall CI IP5 ......141 D8
Marshalls Meadow 3
  IP14 ....67 A6
Marshams Piece 4
  NR33 ....114 C5
Marshy La IP14 ....90 B4
Martello La IP11 .....153 D5
Martello Rd NR32 ...113 B4
Marten's La CO10 ...102 F8
Martin CI Brandon IP27 ..6 A1
  Lowestoft NR33 .....114 D3
  Mildenhall IP28 .....116 D3
Martin Rd 8 Burwell C85 ..44 A6
  Harleston IP20 ....22 E6
  Ipswich IP2 ....155 B1
Martin's Ave NR33 ..115 B6
Martin's Meadow Nature
  Reserve* IP13 ....69 E4
Martinet Gn IP3 .....140 C1
Martins La IP13 ......82 F5
Martins Meadow 6 IP29 ..36 D2
Martins Mews 2 C89 ..132 A7
Martins Rd CO10 ....148 F7
Martinsyde 9 IP5 ....98 A8
Martlesham Beacon Hill Prim
  Sch IP12 ....98 A8
Martlesham Heath Control
  Twr Mus* 11 IP5 ......98 A8
Martlesham Rd IP13 ..137 F3
Martyns Rise 5 CO10 ..91 E7
Mary La CO10 ....75 C3
Mary's La IP19 ....40 E6
Maryday CI IP6 ....68 B1
Maryon Rd IP1 ......140 B1
Masefield Rd Diss IP22 ..20 D2
  Stowmarket IP14 ....124 B8
Mashay Rd CO10 .....90 B3
Maskell's La IP7 ......80 E4
Mason CI 1 IP6 ......82 A5
Mason Gdns 2 IP28 ..29 F6
Mason Rd C85 ....44 A7
Mason's La 5 IP30 ...50 D1
Masons CI IP4 ....139 F6
Masters La IP7 ......141 C6
Masterford Ind Est
  IP16 ....129 B6
Masterson Gr IP5 ...141 C6
Mat Dawson CI C88 ..120 F6
Mather La IP20 ....22 B5
Mather Way IP2 .....155 C1
Matlock Ct 18 IP8 ...138 C2
Mattock Dale 8 NR33 ..114 E3
Matson Rd IP1 ......138 F8
Matthews La IP8 .....74 C7
Maude St IP3 ....139 E4
Maudslay Rd IP1 ....134 C2
Maulkin CI IP32 .....123 F7
Mautby Way NR33 ...114 F5
May Rd Ipswich IP3 ..140 C2
May's La CO7 ....103 F2
Maybird Rd IP14 ....140 B1
Maybush La IP11 ....153 C5
Maycroft CI 2 IP21 ..135 A3
Mayes La CO12 .....106 D1
Mayfair Rd NR35 ...110 C3
Mayfield CO6 ....102 B7
Mayfield Ave 12 NR33 ..11 C1
Mayfield La IP7 ......91 C1
Mayfield Rd
  Bury St Edmunds IP33 ..123 B1
  Ipswich IP4 ....140 C7
  Lowestoft NR33 .....114 C4
Mayfield Way IP5 ....52 E5
Mayfields
  Lakenheath IP27 .....109 C7
  6 Martlesham Heath IP5 ..98 A7
Mayflower Ave
  8 Harleston IP20 .....22 D5
  Saxmundham IP17 ..128 D2
Mayflower Way
  14 Harleston IP20 ...22 D5
Mayfly CI 2 IP8 .....148 D8
Mayhew PI 4 IP8 ....142 E8
Mayhem Adventure Play
  Area* NR33 ....115 E8
Maynewater La IP33 ..154 C1
Maynewater Sq IP33 ..154 C1
Maypole La C85 .....60 C6
McCalmont Way C88 ..121 E2
McIntyre WIk IP32 ..122 C7
McLaren CI 1 NR34 ..111 C3
McLean Dr 18 NR34 ..11 B1

Mead Dr IP5 ....141 C7
Mead The CO10 .....148 F2
Mead Way IP14 ....52 E5
Meadow Barn IP14 ...66 C2
Meadow CI
  Bury St Edmunds IP33 ..122 E3
  8 Felixstowe IP11 ...107 D8
  Felsham IP30 ....65 A4
  Lavenham CO10 ......78 D3
  Westhall IP19 ....25 B4
Meadow Cres 3 IP3 ..140 F1
Meadow Ct
  8 Great Yarmouth NR31 ..3 B8
  10 Stanton IP31 ......34 E4
Meadow Dr
  Horringer IP29 ....63 A8
  Lakenheath IP27 ....109 D7
Meadow Gdns NR34 ..111 A3
Meadow La
  Newmarket C88 .....121 C1
  Sudbury CO10 ......148 C4
  Thurston IP31 ....49 E4
Meadow Prim Sch
  NR33 ....115 B6
Meadow Rd
  8 Barrow IP29 ....47 A2
  Bungay NR35 ....110 D2
  Ipswich IP4 ....112 F4
  Lowestoft NR33 .....114 C2
Meadow Rise IP12 ...129 D2
Meadow Sh Ctr The
  IP14 ....124 D6
Meadow Valley IP7 ...80 D5
Meadow View
  Needham Market IP6 ..125 C5
  Woolpit IP30 ....65 B8
Meadow View Rd
  CO10 ....148 B6
Meadow Way
  Assington CO10 ......92 F1
  Lowestoft NR33 .....114 C2
Meadow WIk 3 IP17 ..72 C8
Meadowlands
  11 Blundeston NR32 ..3 A4
  11 Burwell C85 ....44 A5
  Kirton IP10 ....98 D2
  4 Woolpit IP30 ....50 D1
Meadowlands CI IP17 ..57 C8
Meadows The
  Drinkstone IP30 ......65 B7
  Worlington IP28 ......30 B4
Meadows Way IP7 ...149 D6
Meadowside
  Bilo' Norton IP22 .....18 E2
  Wickham Market IP13 ..127 C7
Meadowside Gdns
  IP4 ....140 E8
Meadowsweet CI
  Haverhill CO9 ....132 C7
  3 Lowestoft NR33 ...114 D5
Meadowvale CI
  Beccles NR34 ....111 B2
  Ipswich IP4 ....139 F8
Meads The NR32 ....113 F8
Meadway 22 CO11 ..104 D2
Mear CI IP17 ....85 C2
Mechanical Music Mus &
  Bygones* IP14 ......91 C1
Meekings Rd CO10 ..148 F6
Meeting Field 10 CO10 ..91 E8
Meeting La
  Grundisburgh IP13 ...83 E5
  Ridgewell CO9 ....89 D4
Meeting WIk C89 ....132 F5
Melbourne Dr IP28 ..116 B5
Melbourne Rd
  Ipswich IP4 ....140 D7
  Lowestoft NR33 .....114 D3
Melford CI 2 Burwell C85 ..44 A5
  8 Ipswich IP4 ....140 F5
Melford Hall* CO10 ..77 E1
Melford Rd Acton CO10 ..92 A8
  Cavendish CO10 ......76 F1
  Lawshall IP29 ....63 D1
  Stowmarket IP14 ...124 F4
  Sudbury CO10 ......148 B2
Melford Way IP11 ...152 D3
Mellis CI C89 ....74 A1
Mellis Ct 18 IP11 ...152 D5
Mellis Rd
  Gislingham IP23 .....36 D3
  Thrandeston IP21 ....36 F4
  Wortham IP22 ....37 B5
  Yaxley IP23 ....37 B5
Mellisash Rd IP23 ...36 F5
Melplash CI IP3 .....140 E4
Melplash Rd IP3 ....140 E4
Melrose CI NR32 ...112 F5
Melrose Gdns
  Ipswich IP4 ....140 B8
  Newmarket C88 .....120 E4
Melton CI C88 ......121 B2
Melton CP Sch IP12 ..147 C7
Melton Grange Rd
  IP12 ....147 B6
Melton Hill IP12 ....147 C7
Melton Meadow Rd 4
  IP12 ....147 B6
Melton Rd
  Hollesley IP12 ....99 F8
  Woodbridge IP12 ...147 B6
Melton Sta IP12 ....147 D7
Melville Rd IP4 .....139 F5
Mendham CI 28 IP20 ..22 D6
Mendham La
  38 Harleston IP20 ...22 D6

Mendham La continued
  St Cross, South Elmham
  IP20 ....23 C6
Mendham Prim Sch
  IP20 ....23 A6
Mendham Rd IP20 ...23 A4
Mendip Dr IP5 ......140 F6
Mendip Rd IP32 ....112 E2
Mendlesham Prim Sch
  IP14 ....52 D4
Mendlesham Rd IP14 ..52 B5
Mercers Rd IP32 ...123 D7
Mere CI IP31 ....49 C6
Mere Gdns IP4 .....140 F4
Mere La IP28 ....48 A6
Mere Manor Ct 20 C2
Mere Side C87 ....28 C4
Meredith Rd IP1 ....134 E2
Meriton Rise IP7 ...149 F4
Merivale Rd 17 CO11 ..104 D2
Merlewood IP12 ......21 C5
Merlin Rd IP2 ......138 C3
Mermaid CI IP32 ...123 A8
Merriam CI 5 CO11 ..104 E4
Merrifield Rd NR33 ..114 F3
Merrion CI 12 IP8 ...138 C2
Merrylees NR34 ....111 C4
Mersey Rd IP3 ......139 F2
Merville 9 NR33 ....114 E5
Messenger CI NR35 ..110 B2
Metfield Rd IP20 .....23 D3
Metfield St IP20 .....23 C3
Methersgate Hall Dr
  IP12 ....84 E1
Meynell Gdns IP30 ..121 A5
Micawber Mews 4 NR32 ..3 A4
Michaelhouse Way 12
  IP31 ....48 A5
Michaels Mount 3 IP3 ..137 D5
Michaelstowe CI 11
  CO12 ....106 E1
Michigan CI IP5 ....141 B7
Mickfield Mews 18
  IP11 ....152 D5
Micklegate Rd IP4 ..152 E2
Micklesmere Dr 28 IP31 ..34 E1
Mid Suffolk Leisure Ctr
  IP14 ....124 B7
Middle Dro C87 ......28 B4
Middle Gn CO6 .....101 B1
Middle La NR34 .....10 D8
Middle Rd
  Blo' Norton IP22 .....18 F2
  4 Clopton IP13 ....7 C4
Middle Way CO10 ...91 E8
Middle WIk NR32 ...113 C5
Middlefield Dr 3 IP14 ..66 B4
Middlefield Rd 10 CO11 ..105 A2
Middleton CI IP2 ...138 D2
Middleton Prim Sch
  IP17 ....58 B6
Middleton Rd
  Sudbury CO10 ......148 B4
  Yoxford IP17 ....57 F7
Midhurst CI 3 IP32 ..123 D6
Midmeadow 4 NR34 ..111 B5
Mid-Suffolk Light Rly Mus
  The* IP14 ....53 B4
Milano Ave IP12 ....99 B8
Milburn Dro C88 .....45 F3
Milden CI 6 IP14 ...124 E3
Milden Rd
  Brent Eleigh CO10 ...79 A2
  Ipswich IP2 ....138 E5
Mildenhall Airfield
  IP28 ....30 B7
Mildenhall Coll of Tech
  IP28 ....116 E4
Mildenhall Dro IP28 ..12 F3
Mildenhall Ind Est
  IP28 ....116 B6
Mildenhall Mus*
  IP28 ....116 C4
Mildenhall Pl 11 C89 ..132 F6
Mildenhall Rd
  Barton Mills IP28 ...116 C2
  Beck Row, Holywell
  Row & Kenny Hill IP28 ..116 C8
  2 Bury St Edmunds IP28 ..123 A8
  Fordham C87 ....29 C1
  Icklingham IP28 ......31 A5
  Littleport C87 ....12 A8
Mildenhall Stadium
  IP28 ....29 D8
Mildmay Rd IP3 ....140 B1
Mile End IP27 ....14 E8
Mile End Rd C87 ....12 A7
Miles Hawk Way IP28 ..116 A5
Miles Paddock IP14 ..52 A6
Military Rd C87 ......12 A7
Military Way 5 CO12 ..106 E1
Mill Bank 4 NR32 ...112 F2
Mill Broadway IP12 ..131 C4
Mill Chase 88 E3
Mill CI 6 Burwell C85 ..44 B5
  Capel St Mary IP9 ...150 C3
  Exning C88 ....120 B8
  Felixstowe IP11 .....152 D4
  Kirby Row NR35 ......8 E7
  18 Walsham le Willows
  IP31 ....35 C2
  Woolpit IP30 ....50 D1
Mill Cnr C87 ....28 C3
Mill Croft 9 C87 .....28 D3
Mill Drift 5 A3
Mill Dro C87 ....28 C3
Mill End La IP14 .....67 C2

Mill Field
3 Aldeburgh IP15 .... 130 E5
Bramford IP8 .... 134 B2
Pettaugh IP14 .... 68 E6
Mill Fields IP14 .... 51 D1
Mill Gdns
Bedingham NR35 .... 7 B8
Elmswell IP30 .... 50 F2
Mill Hill (Tumulus)*
NR31 .... 2 C8
Mill Hill Burgh IP13 .... 83 F6
Capel St Mary IP9 .... 150 C3
Cotton IP14 .... 54 E1
Earl Soham IP13 .... 53 E1
Hadleigh IP7 .... 94 B7
Haverhill CB9 .... 132 D5
Lawford CO11 .... 104 B2
Leiston IP16 .... 129 C2
Manningtree CO11 .... 104 E2
Mettingham NR35 .... 8 D5
Newmarket CB8 .... 121 A4
Peasenhall IP17 .... 56 F8
Rattlesden IP30 .... 65 D6
Sudbury CO10 .... 148 B5
Wormingford CO6 .... 101 F3
Mill Hill IP19 .... 118 A4
Mill Hill Est IP16 .... 129 C2
Mill Hoo IP12 .... 99 E4
Mill La
All Saints & St Nicholas,
South Elmham IP20 .... 23 E5
Barnham IP24 .... 16 B2
Barrow IP29 .... 47 A2
Baylham IP6 .... 81 F7
Benhall IP17 .... 72 C8
Boyton IP12 .... 86 B2
Bradfield CO11 .... 105 B1
Bramford IP8 .... 134 B1
Brandeston IP13 .... 70 A7
Bruisyard IP17 .... 56 C5
7 Burwell CB5 .... 44 B5
Butley IP12 .... 86 B6
Campsey Ash IP13 .... 127 F6
Cavendish CO10 .... 90 D8
Chelmondiston IP9 .... 106 B8
Coddenham IP6 .... 68 B1
Combs IP14 .... 124 B1
Copdock & Washbrook
IP8 .... 138 A1
Corton NR32 .... 3 D4
Cowlinge CB8 .... 75 B8
Creeting St Peter or
West Creeting IP6 .... 125 D8
Dedham CO7 .... 103 F4
Dennington IP13 .... 55 D5
Ellingham NR35 .... 8 E7
Exning CB8 .... 120 B8
Felixstowe IP11 .... 152 F4
Fordham CB7 .... 29 B1
Garboldisham IP22 .... 18 D3
9 Great Blakenham IP6 .... 82 A5
Great Yeldham CO9 .... 90 A2
Hasketon IP13 .... 146 A7
Henley IP6 .... 82 D6
Hockwold cum Wilton IP26 .... 5 A3
Hoo IP13 .... 70 C6
Hopton IP22 .... 18 C3
Hundon CO10 .... 75 D7
Kersey IP7 .... 94 A7
Layham IP7 .... 149 E2
Leiston IP16 .... 129 C2
18 Manningtree CO11 .... 104 E2
Marlesford IP13 .... 71 C5
Metfield IP20 .... 23 C3
North Cove NR34 .... 10 C4
Polstead CO6 .... 102 E8
Pulham St Mary IP21 .... 21 F8
4 Redgrave IP22 .... 36 A8
St John, Ilketshall NR34 .... 8 E2
Shadingfield NR34 .... 25 D7
Somersham IP8 .... 81 C3
Southwold IP18 .... 119 D5
Stetchworth CB8 .... 59 F5
Stoke Ash IP23 .... 52 F8
Stonham Earl IP14 .... 67 D5
Stradbroke IP21 .... 39 C5
Sudbury CO10 .... 148 A5
Thetford IP24 .... 16 B1
Thurston IP31 .... 49 D5
Tunstall IP12 .... 72 B1
Weybread IP22 .... 22 C3
Wickham Market IP13 .... 127 C6
2 Witnesham IP6 .... 83 A5
Woodbridge IP12 .... 147 A5
Woolpit IP30 .... 50 D1
Wrentham NR34 .... 26 F5
Mill Piece IP10 .... 145 C6
Mill Pool La NR35 .... 8 D6
Mill Pouch IP11 .... 152 C8
Mill Rd (South) IP14 .... 154 A1
Mill Rd
Aldeby/Wheatacre/Burgh
St Peter NR34 .... 10 B8
Ashley CB8 .... 45 F1
Badingham IP13 .... 56 A7
Barningham IP31 .... 34 E7
Battisford IP14 .... 80 B8
Beccles NR34 .... 111 C2
Birdbrook CO9 .... 89 C5
Botesdale IP22 .... 36 B6
Boxted CO4 .... 102 F2
Brockish IP21 .... 21 E3
Brockley IP29 .... 63 A1
Burston & Shimpling IP21 .... 20 E6
Bury St Edmunds IP33 .... 154 A2
Buxhall IP14 .... 65 F4
Chevington IP29 .... 62 C6
Clare CO10 .... 90 B8

Mill Rd *continued*
Coldfair Green IP17 .... 129 A2
Cotton IP14 .... 52 A6
East Bergholt CO7 .... 151 E4
Ellingham NR35 .... 8 D7
Foxearth CO10 .... 91 B7
Friston IP17 .... 72 E6
Gazeley CB8 .... 46 B3
Great Barton IP31 .... 49 A6
Halesworth IP19 .... 118 E3
Haverhill CB9 .... 132 E5
Hemley IP12 .... 98 E5
Hargrave IP28 .... 48 A7
Honington IP31 .... 33 F5
Hundon CO10 .... 75 D4
Ipswich IP3 .... 140 F1
Kedington IP28 .... 133 E8
Kirtling CB8 .... 60 F3
Lakenheath IP27 .... 109 D6
Laxfield IP13 .... 40 B2
Lowestoft NR33 .... 115 C7
Mendlesham IP14 .... 52 D4
Moulton CB8 .... 46 A1
Mutford NR34 .... 10 D3
Newbourne IP12 .... 98 D5
Occold IP23 .... 37 F1
Peasenhall IP17 .... 56 E8
Redlingfield IP23 .... 38 C2
Ridgewell CO9 .... 89 D3
Rumburgh IP19 .... 24 B4
Saxmundham IP17 .... 128 C3
Stambourne CO9 .... 89 B2
Swefling IP17 .... 56 E3
Thelnetham IP22 .... 18 E1
Westleton IP17 .... 58 C7
Weybread IP21 .... 22 C2
Winfarthing IP22 .... 20 B8
Wissett IP19 .... 118 A5
Worlingworth IP13 .... 54 D7
Wyverstone IP14 .... 51 D6
Mill Rd S IP22 .... 36 B6
Mill Reef Cl CB8 .... 120 D7
Saxmundham IP17 .... 128 C2
Mill Rise 11 Holbrook IP9 .... 105 E7
Saxmundham IP17 .... 128 C2
Mill St Gislingham IP23 .... 36 B2
Isleham CB7 .... 29 C7
Middleton IP17 .... 58 A6
Mildenhall IP28 .... 116 B3
Stowupland IP14 .... 67 A6
Westleton IP17 .... 58 C7
Mill Tye CB8 .... 86 A3
Mill View CB8 .... 46 B3
Mill View Cl IP12 .... 146 E5
Millbank CB8 .... 120 F4
Millennium Grandstand
CB8 .... 120 C1
Millennium Way
Kesgrave IP5 .... 141 E7
Lowestoft NR32 .... 113 A4
Miller Cl Elmswell IP30 .... 50 F2
Lowestoft NR33 .... 115 B5
Millers Cl Bungay NR35 .... 110 C3
Hadleigh IP7 .... 149 E6
Stowmarket IP14 .... 124 C3
Millers Ct 5 IP6 .... 82 A5
Millers Dr IP21 .... 21 B5
Millers Gn 44 IP20 .... 22 D6
Millers View IP1 .... 138 F7
Millfield IP23 .... 117 B3
Millfield Ave IP14 .... 124 C5
Millfield Cl
Ditchingham NR35 .... 110 C8
1 Saxmundham IP17 .... 128 C2
Millfield Dr IP14 .... 65 F4
Millfield Gdns IP14 .... 140 A7
Millfield Rd
6 Barningham IP31 .... 34 F7
Walberswick IP18 .... 119 A2
Millfields
2 Peasenhall IP17 .... 56 F8
Wangford NR34 .... 26 B2
Millfields Way CB8 .... 132 F6
Millmarsh Dro IP27 .... 109 A7
Mills Dr NR32 .... 3 D1
Mills La CO10 .... 91 E6
Mills Meadow IP13 .... 126 D3
Mills Rd CO10 .... 148 E6
Mills The
Framlingham IP13 .... 126 C3
Ipswich IP4 .... 140 E8
Millside IP23 .... 37 C4
Millway NR34 .... 10 C4
Millway Ave IP22 .... 20 C5
Millway La
Palgrave IP22 .... 20 A1
Wortham IP22 .... 19 F1
Millwood Rd CO6 .... 94 A3
Milner Rd Chilton CO10 .... 92 B4
Sudbury CO10 .... 148 F6
Milner St IP4 .... 155 C4
Milnes Way NR33 .... 114 B3
Milnrow 10 IP9 .... 138 C2
Milton Cl IP17 .... 128 B4
Milton Rd CO11 .... 104 D1
Milton Rd E
Lowestoft NR32 .... 113 D1
Stowmarket IP14 .... 124 E6
Milton Rd N 4 NR34 .... 124 D6
Milton Rd S IP14 .... 124 E6
Milton Rd W NR32 .... 113 D1
Milton St IP4 .... 140 B7
Mimosa Wlk NR32 .... 113 B2
Mincarlo Trawler*
NR33 .... 115 D8
Minden Dr
Bury St Edmunds IP33 .... 122 D5

Minden Dr *continued*
Leiston IP16 .... 129 D5
Minden Rd
Lowestoft NR32 .... 113 C2
Sudbury CO10 .... 148 D5
Minerva Cl IP3 .... 133 B4
Minos Rd NR32 .... 113 C4
Minos Way IP1 .... 138 D8
Minsmere House Hospl
IP4 .... 140 C6
Minsmere Nature Reserve*
IP17 .... 58 E6
Minsmere Rd IP14 .... 53 F8
Minsmere Rise IP17 .... 58 A6
Minsmere Way CO10 .... 92 B3
Minster Rd CB9 .... 132 D7
Minton Ent Pk CB8 .... 120 E7
Mirbeck's Cl 6 NR34 .... 9 F4
Misburgh Way NR31 .... 3 C6
Mission La CO7 .... 104 D6
Mission Rd IP22 .... 20 D2
Mistley Sta CO11 .... 104 F2
Mistley Way IP14 .... 146 F6
Mitchell Ave IP32 .... 48 C5
Mitchery La NR34 .... 65 E4
Mitford Cl IP7 .... 135 A4
Mitford Rd IP17 .... 72 B8
Mitre Cl 8 IP30 .... 50 D1
Mitre Way IP3 .... 139 E4
Moat Farm Cl IP14 .... 80 F1
Moat La
Alphamstone CO8 .... 101 A6
Rushbrooke with Rougham
IP30 .... 49 D1
Moat Rd Birdbrook CO9 .... 89 B4
Theberton IP16 .... 57 F4
Moat Wlk 8 CB9 .... 132 C6
Mobbs Way IP32 .... 112 E3
Mockbeggars Hall*
IP8 .... 134 C6
Moffat Ave IP14 .... 136 B1
Moles La NR34 .... 8 D1
Moll's La NR34 .... 25 D5
Monarch Cl CB9 .... 132 A6
Monarch Way
Carlton Colville NR33 .... 114 A3
Pinewood IP8 .... 142 D8
Monastery Ct IP7 .... 149 E7
Monastery Hill IP17 .... 43 B1
Monckton Ave NR32 .... 112 F2
Monckton Cres NR32 .... 112 F2
Monet Sq IP1 .... 133 B5
Moneweden Rd IP13 .... 70 A3
Moneyhole Cnr CO10 .... 78 E5
Moneypiece Cl CB9 .... 73 A2
Moneypot La IP22 .... 19 B1
Monk's La CO7 .... 103 E2
Monks Cl IP11 .... 153 D6
Monks Gate IP8 .... 138 A6
Monksgate IP24 .... 16 B6
Monkshood Cl NR34 .... 114 F2
Monmouth Cl IP3 .... 139 B1
Montagu Dr IP27 .... 5 E4
Montague Rd IP11 .... 153 A4
Montana Rd IP5 .... 141 A7
Montessori Sch The
IP7 .... 94 E6
Montfort Cl CB5 .... 44 B6
Montfort Ct 11 CB9 .... 132 D5
Montgomery Ave
NR32 .... 113 B4
Montgomery Rd IP2 .... 139 B1
Monton Rise IP2 .... 138 D2
Montpelier Dr IP2 .... 16 A5
Monument Farm La
IP10 .... 141 C3
Monument Farm Rd
IP10 .... 141 B4
Moo Play Farm* IP24 .... 25 C5
Moon Hall La CB9 .... 132 E3
Moor Rd
Burston & Shimpling IP21 .... 21 B6
Langham CO4 .... 103 B2
Middleton IP17 .... 57 F6
Moor's Way IP14 .... 146 E5
Moorbridge La IP14 .... 66 B8
Moore Rd Ipswich IP1 .... 134 F3
Rushbrooke with Rougham
IP30 .... 49 B2
Moore's Cl 7 IP14 .... 53 F2
Mooreland Dr IP31 .... 49 C6
Moorfield Rd IP31 .... 49 C6
Moorhall Cswy IP23 .... 117 C1
Moorsfield CO10 .... 148 F2
Moreton Hall Prep Sch
IP32 .... 123 D5
Morgan Cl 3 IP6 .... 134 C8
Morgan Dr IP1 .... 134 C1
Morgan Meadow IP24 .... 124 C2
Morland Prim Sch
IP3 .... 144 A8
Morland Rd 1 IP3 .... 144 A8
Morley Ave IP3 .... 146 F4
Morley Cl 3 IP28 .... 30 B8
Morleys La IP3 .... 36 D2
Mormor La IP21 .... 21 F4
Mornington Ave 2 IP1 .... 134 F1
Morris Way IP6 .... 125 D4
Mors End 2 CO7 .... 103 E5
Morston Hall Rd IP11 .... 98 B1
Mortimer La IP28 .... 29 E3
Mortimer Pl 3 CO10 .... 76 A1
Morton Peto Cl NR32 .... 2 D3
Morton Rd NR33 .... 115 B4
Moss La IP6 .... 135 F4
Mother Quy's IP24 .... 15 C5

Mottram Cl 14 IP8 .... 138 C2
Moulton Ave CB8 .... 46 A5
Moulton CE Prim Sch
CB8 .... 45 F3
Moulton Cl 5 CO10 .... 148 D6
Moulton Packhorse Bridge*
CB8 .... 45 F3
Moulton Paddocks
CB8 .... 121 F7
Moulton Rd
Cheveley CB8 .... 121 D4
Gazeley CB8 .... 46 B3
Kentford CB8 .... 46 A5
Lowestoft NR32 .... 113 C4
Mount Cl 8 IP30 .... 64 F8
Mount Dr IP3 .... 140 F1
Mount Pleasant
Framlingham IP13 .... 126 B4
Halesworth IP19 .... 118 B5
Lowestoft NR32 .... 113 C3
1 Peasenhall IP17 .... 56 F8
Southwold IP18 .... 119 C8
Mount Rd
Bury St Edmunds IP32 .... 123 D6
Haverhill CB9 .... 132 E5
Rushbrooke with Rougham
IP30 .... 49 A3
Mount St IP22 .... 20 C3
Mountbatten Cl CO10 .... 148 D8
Mountbatten Ct IP1 .... 139 A7
Mountbatten Rd
Bungay NR35 .... 110 B2
Lowestoft NR32 .... 113 B4
Sudbury CO10 .... 148 D8
Mounts The IP17 .... 56 F8
Mouse La IP30 .... 49 C2
Moverley Way 1 IP15 .... 130 E5
Mow Hill IP6 .... 83 A5
Mowbrays The IP13 .... 126 B4
Mowlands IP9 .... 150 F3
Mowness Hall La IP14 .... 68 A6
Moyes Rd NR32 .... 112 D1
Moyse Ave 4 IP18 .... 119 C8
Moyse's Hall Mus*
IP33 .... 154 B2
Mulberry Cl
Beccles NR34 .... 111 C5
18 Feltwell IP26 .... 4 E5
Mildenhall IP28 .... 116 E4
Mulberry Gdns 11 IP6 .... 82 A5
Mulberry Rd 3 IP3 .... 144 C7
Mumford Rd IP1 .... 138 E8
Munday's La CO10 .... 131 B3
Mundford Prim Sch
IP26 .... 6 A8
Mundford Rd
Brandon IP27 .... 5 F2
Thetford IP24 .... 16 B7
Weeting-with-Broomhill
IP27 .... 6 A4
Mundy's Rd IP20 .... 23 A5
Munnings Cl
Haverhill CB9 .... 132 B7
3 Lowestoft NR33 .... 114 C3
Newmarket CB8 .... 121 A5
Munnings Way CO11 .... 104 D3
Munson's La IP26 .... 4 E6
Munson's Pl IP26 .... 4 E6
Murfitt's La CB7 .... 29 A2
Muriel Cl 4 IP17 .... 149 E6
Murillo Dr 1 NR32 .... 113 C6
Murray Rd IP3 .... 140 A3
Murrayfield Prim Sch
IP3 .... 140 A3
Murrills Rd IP3 .... 140 E1
Murton Cl 10 CB8 .... 45 A4
Museum of E Anglian Life*
IP14 .... 124 D5
Museum St IP1 .... 155 B3
Musgrave St IP4 .... 155 C4
Mustards Gapp CB9 .... 133 A5
Mustow St IP33 .... 154 C2
Mutford Cl NR32 .... 113 C4
Mutford Gn IP27 .... 109 C2
Mutford Wood NR33 .... 10 D4
Mutfordwood La
NR33 .... 114 A2
Mutton La IP30 .... 70 A8
Mylford Cl IP32 .... 123 D4
Mylodon Rd IP3 .... 133 C3
Myrtle Cl
Bury St Edmunds IP33 .... 154 A3
20 Eriswell IP27 .... 113 F2
Lowestoft NR32 .... 113 B4
Myrtle Rd IP3 .... 139 E4

N

Nacton CE VC Prim Sch
IP10 .... 145 C5
Nacton Cl 5 IP2 .... 138 B3
Nacton Cres IP3 .... 140 B2
Nacton La 2 IP3 .... 149 A6
Nacton Rd
Felixstowe IP11 .... 152 E1
Ipswich IP10 .... 144 D7
Levington IP10 .... 145 E3
Nan Hazle's La IP22 .... 36 B4
Nansen Rd IP3 .... 140 B2
Napier Pl IP24 .... 16 B5
Naples Cl 5 NR31 .... 3 C6
Narrow Way IP19 .... 42 C6
Nash Cl CO11 .... 104 D3
Nash Gdns 2 IP3 .... 144 B8
Nat Flatman St CB8 .... 121 B3
National Horseracing Mus*
CB8 .... 121 A3

National Stud* CB8 .... 59 B8
Nato Pl IP27 .... 109 F1
Naughton Gdns 8 IP14 .... 124 E3
Naughton Rd IP7 .... 80 C5
Naunton Rd IP12 .... 146 E5
Navarre St IP1 .... 155 B3
Naverne Meadow
IP12 .... 147 A5
Nayland Prim Sch
CO6 .... 102 D5
Nayland Rd
Bures St Mary CO8 .... 101 D4
1 Felixstowe IP11 .... 152 C3
Great Horkesley CO6 .... 102 D2
Haverhill CB9 .... 132 C4
Little Horkesley CO6 .... 102 C3
Naylor Ct IP14 .... 124 B7
Neale Cl IP16 .... 129 B6
Neale St IP1 .... 155 B3
Neath Dr IP2 .... 139 A1
Neaves La IP21 .... 39 B4
Nedging Rd IP7 .... 79 F3
Needham La IP7 .... 79 F4
Needham Lake Nature
Reserve & Visitor Ctr*
IP6 .... 125 C4
Needham Mkt Mid Sch
IP6 .... 125 D4
Needham Mkt Sta IP6 .... 125 C4
Needham Rd
Coddenham IP6 .... 67 F1
Needham IP20 .... 22 C5
Stowmarket IP14 .... 124 E4
Needham Rd W IP14 .... 124 F4
Needle Cnr IP9 .... 106 C6
Nelson Cl IP6 .... 83 A8
Nelson Cres 2 IP24 .... 16 B5
Nelson Rd
Bury St Edmunds IP33 .... 154 A2
Ipswich IP4 .... 140 A7
1 Lowestoft NR33 .... 115 A3
Sudbury CO10 .... 148 E7
Nelson Wharf IP3 .... 144 D7
Nene Dr IP3 .... 144 D7
Neptune Quay IP4 .... 155 C2
Neptune Sq IP4 .... 155 C2
Neptune St NR32 .... 115 C8
Ness Rd Arwarton IP9 .... 106 D5
Burwell CB5 .... 44 B7
Nether Hall Mus & Gall*
CO10 .... 76 E2
Nether Hill CO9 .... 90 E2
Nether Rd 2 CO10 .... 76 E1
Nethergate St
Bungay NR35 .... 110 A5
Clare CO10 .... 90 A7
Hopton IP22 .... 18 B2
Netherhall Cl IP14 .... 52 A1
Netley Cl IP7 .... 142 F8
Netley Rd IP33 .... 122 D3
Nettlestead Rd IP8 .... 81 D4
Neve Gdns IP28 .... 30 A6
New Cangle Com Prim Sch
CB9 .... 133 A2
New Cardinal St IP1 .... 155 A2
New Cheveley Rd CB8 .... 121 C3
New Comm Rd IP22 .... 35 B8
New Cut 5 Bures CO8 .... 101 C4
8 Glemsford CO10 .... 77 A2
Hadleigh IP7 .... 149 E6
Halesworth IP19 .... 118 E3
Newmarket CB8 .... 121 A3
Sawmundham IP17 .... 128 D3
New Cut E IP3 .... 155 C1
New Cut W IP3 .... 155 C1
New Dro
Beck Row, Holywell Row
& Kenny Hill IP28 .... 12 E1
Soham CB7 .... 28 A4
New England Way 2
IP24 .... 16 A5
New Gn Ave 18 IP31 .... 49 E4
New Hampshire Way 5
IP24 .... 16 A5
New House La CO10 .... 76 B3
New La IP9 .... 105 F6
New Mkt NR34 .... 26 B2
New Path IP14 .... 29 A1
New Quay Ct IP12 .... 147 B5
New Quay La IP12 .... 147 B5
New Quay Terr IP12 .... 147 B5
New Queens Rd CO10 .... 148 C7
New Rd Ampton IP31 .... 33 A1
Aspall IP14 .... 53 E4
Badingham IP13 .... 56 B8
Barnby NR34 .... 10 C8
Barrow IP29 .... 47 B3
Beccles NR34 .... 111 B7
Brettenham IP24 .... 17 B6
5 Burwell CB5 .... 44 A6
Chevington IP29 .... 62 C7
Dickleburgh & Rushall
IP21 .... 21 A4
Elmswell IP30 .... 50 E2
Exning CB8 .... 120 B8
Felixstowe IP11 .... 152 C7
Framlingham IP13 .... 126 C5
Fritton & St Olaves NR31 .... 2 B7
Gissing IP22 .... 20 F8
Great Glemham IP17 .... 71 E8
Helmingham IP14 .... 69 A5
18 Ixworth IP31 .... 34 B1

New Rd continued
Little Livermere IP31 . . . . . . .33 A2
Long Melford CO10 . . . . .91 D8
Manningtree CO11 . . . . .104 E2
Marlesford IP13 . . . . .71 C6
Melton IP12 . . . . .84 D6
Mettingham NR35 . . . . .110 F2
Nedging-with-Naughton
  IP7 . . . . .80 C3
Rumburgh IP19 . . . . .24 C4
Rushbrooke with Rougham
  IP30 .49 D1
St Cross, South Elmham
  IP20 .23 D5
Sibton IP17 . . . . .41 D1
Thelnetham IP22 . . . . .35 B7
Thrandeston IP21 . . . . .37 C8
Timworth IP31 . . . . .48 E8
Tivetshall St Mary NR15 . . . .21 B8
Tostock IP30 . . . . .50 B2
Troston IP31 . . . . .33 C4
Worlingworth IP13 . . . . .54 F8
New River Gn CB8 . . . . . . .120 B8
New St Chippenham CB7 . . .29 E1
Framlingham IP13 . . . . .126 A4
Fressingfield IP21 . . . . .39 D8
Glemsford CO10 . . . . .77 A3
4 Mildenhall IP28 . . . . . . .116 C4
Stradbroke IP21 . . . . .39 A4
Sudbury CO10 . . . . .148 C6
9 Woodbridge IP12 . . . . . .147 A5
New St Cl IP21 . . . . .39 A4
New Way IP2 . . . . .138 F6
New Wolsey Theatre★
  IP1 .155 A3
Newall Rd 2 IP24 . . . . .16 C2
Newark Cl IP27 . . . . .138 F1
Newark Rd
  3 Lakenheath IP27 . . . . . . .13 F2
  Lowestoft NR33 . . . . .115 B6
Newberry Rd 7 IP7 . . . . . . .79 F4
Newbourn Rd IP10 . . . . .98 C4
Newbourne Gdns
  IP11 . . . . .152 D3
Newbourne Rd
  Brightwell IP10 . . . . .98 A6
  Martlesham IP12 . . . . .84 B1
  Waldringfield IP12 . . . . .98 C7
**Newbourne Springs Nature
  Reserve★** IP12 . . . . .98 D6
Newbury Rd IP4 . . . . .140 C6
Newby Cl IP19 . . . . .118 A3
Newby Dr IP4 . . . . .140 F5
Newcastle Cl 6 IP27 . . . . . . .13 F2
Newcombe Dr 10 IP26 . . . . .4 E5
Newcombe Rd NR32 . . . . . .113 E1
Newdelight Rd IP22 . . . . . . .35 F2
Newell Rise IP6 . . . . .134 C8
Newfen Gravel Dro
  IP27 . . . . .109 A8
Newgate Beccles NR34 . . . .111 B5
  Kirby Row NR35 . . . . .8 E7
Newgate La NR35 . . . . .8 E7
Newhaven Way IP7 . . . . . .149 E7
Newland Ave NR34 . . . . . . .111 E4
Newlands 2 Elmsett IP7 . . .80 F1
  Otley IP6 . . . . .69 D2
Newlands Cl
  46 Harleston IP20 . . . . . . .22 D6
  Lowestoft NR33 . . . . .114 F3
Newlands La CO6 . . . . .102 D5
Newman's Rd CO10 . . . . . .148 C6
Newmarket Coll CB8 . . . . .120 F4
Newmarket Com Hospl
  CB8 . . . . .120 E3
**Newmarket Lawn Tennis
  Club** CB8 . . . . .120 E3
Newmarket Leisure Ctr
  CB8 . . . . .120 F4
Newmarket Racecourse
  CB8 . . . . .120 B1
Newmarket Rd
  1 Ashley CB8 . . . . .60 F8
  Barton Mills IP28 . . . . .116 D1
  Burwell CB5 . . . . .44 B5
  Bury St Edmunds IP33 . . . . .122 D6
  Cowlinge CB8 . . . . .61 B2
  Fordham CB7 . . . . .44 E8
  Moulton CB8 . . . . .45 F3
  Newmarket CB8 . . . . .121 B8
  Red Lodge IP28 . . . . .30 C2
  Risby IP28 . . . . .47 C5
  Snailwell CB8 . . . . .45 A5
Newmarket Sports Ctr
  CB8 . . . . .121 A4
Newmarket Sta CB8 . . . . .121 A2
Newmarket Swimming Pool
  CB8 . . . . .120 F4
Newmarket Upper Sch
  CB8 . . . . .120 F4
Newmill La CO11 . . . . .105 A5
Newnham Ave IP14 . . . . . .146 D4
Newnham Cl IP28 . . . . . . .116 D5
Newnham Ct IP22 . . . . . . .138 E1
Newnham Dro CB5 . . . . . . .44 A6
Newnham La 14 CB5 . . . . . .44 A6
Newport Ave CB7 . . . . .29 C1
Newport Cl 8 IP27 . . . . . . .13 F2
Newquay Cl IP5 . . . . .140 F6
Newry Ave IP11 . . . . .152 F4
Newson Ave NR34 . . . . . . .10 C3
Newson St IP1 . . . . .155 A4
Newson's Meadow 1
  NR32 . . . . .113 C2
Newthorpe IP30 . . . . .49 D1

Newton Croft CO10 . . . . . .148 E5
Newton Pl 4 CB9 . . . . .132 F6
Newton Rd
  17 Harwich CO12 . . . . . . .107 A2
  Ipswich IP1 . . . . .140 A4
  Stowupland IP14 . . . . .124 D8
  Sudbury CO10 . . . . .148 D5
Newton St IP4 . . . . .155 C3
Nicholas Dr IP18 . . . . .119 C7
Nicholas Everitt Pk
  NR33 . . . . .114 D8
Nicholl Pl IP11 . . . . .152 C4
Nicholas's St IP22 . . . . .20 C3
Nicholls Cl 7 IP13 . . . . .84 F7
Nichols Cl 2 CO11 . . . . . . .104 D2
Nicholson Dr NR34 . . . . . .111 C2
Nicholson Sq 2 NR32 . . . . .113 C2
Nicholsons Ct CO10 . . . . . . .92 D3
Nick's La IP23 . . . . .117 B6
Nidderdale 8 NR33 . . . . . .114 E3
Nightall Rd 5 CB7 . . . . .28 D4
Nightingale Ave IP18 . . . . .119 B7
Nightingale Cl
  Bury St Edmunds IP33 . . . . .154 A1
  3 Harwich CO12 . . . . . . .106 F1
  8 Mildenhall IP28 . . . . . .116 D4
  5 Stowmarket IP14 . . . . . .67 A5
Nightingale Hill CO10 . . . .103 C3
Nightingale La 9 IP26 . . . . .4 E5
Nightingale Piece
  IP12 . . . . .131 C3
Nightingale Rd
  Ipswich IP3 . . . . .144 A8
  Lowestoft NR33 . . . . .115 B3
Nightingale Sq 5 IP3 . . . . .144 A8
Nimbus Way CB8 . . . . .120 E8
Nine Acres IP2 . . . . .138 D6
Ninfield Cl NR33 . . . . .114 D4
No Man's Meadow★
  IP33 . . . . .123 C4
Noahs Ark Pl CO11 . . . . . . .148 B5
Noahs Dr 5 NR33 . . . . .11 B1
Noaks Rd IP7 . . . . .94 F1
Nock Gdns IP5 . . . . .141 C6
Noel Cl NR31 . . . . .3 B7
Noel Murless Dr CB8 . . . . .120 F6
Noel Rd NR32 . . . . .112 C1
Noel's Wlk NR34 . . . . .111 B6
Noller's La IP14 . . . . .24 F4
Nonsuch Meadow 2
  CO10 . . . . .148 C4
Norbury Rd IP4 . . . . .140 B7
Nordalls The 16 NR33 . . . . .11 C1
**Norfolk & Suffolk Aviation
  Mus★** NR35 . . . . .7 D2
Norfolk Cl CB8 . . . . .120 E5
Norfolk Cres 1 IP13 . . . . . .126 C3
Norfolk Rd
  Bury St Edmunds IP32 . . . . .123 A8
  8 Honington IP31 . . . . . . .33 D5
  Ipswich IP4 . . . . .155 C3
  Thetford IP24 . . . . .16 C6
  Wangford NR34 . . . . .26 C3
Norgate La IP21 . . . . .21 B2
Norman Cl
  Felixstowe IP11 . . . . .153 D6
  Woodbridge IP12 . . . . .147 A7
Norman Cres IP3 . . . . .140 A2
Norman Rd
  6 Bury St Edmunds IP32 . . .48 C5
  Bury St Edmunds IP32 . . . . .122 F8
  26 Manningtree CO11 . . . .104 E2
Norman Way 1 CO10 . . . . .78 D4
Normandie Way 8 CO8 . . .101 C4
Normandy Cl IP11 . . . . .124 D3
Normandy Rd NR32 . . . . . .113 B4
Normanhurst Cl NR32 . . . .113 A2
Normanston Dr 5 NR32 . . .113 B2
Nornea La CB7 . . . . .28 A8
Norse Ave IP29 . . . . .64 A3
North Acres IP8 . . . . .81 A6
North Cl Bacton IP14 . . . . . .51 F6
  Ipswich IP3 . . . . .135 E1
  9 Stanton IP31 . . . . .34 E4
North Cres CB9 . . . . .88 D4
North Dr
  Newmarket CB8 . . . . .120 F5
  1 Soham CB7 . . . . .28 D5
North End CB8 . . . . .120 B8
North End Ave IP6 . . . . .73 F6
North End Rd CO9 . . . . .90 C2
North Entrance IP17 . . . . .128 D3
North Gate Ave IP24 . . . . .16 B5
North Gn Rd 3 NR32 . . . . .112 F5
North Gn IP18 . . . . .119 D6
North Gn Rd
  Cratfield IP19 . . . . .40 C7
  Pulham St Mary IP21 . . . . . . .22 A8
North Hill IP17 . . . . .146 F6
North Hill Gdns IP18 . . . . .139 E6
North Hill Rd IP4 . . . . .139 E6
North Lawn IP6 . . . . .140 B8
North Lopham Rd
  NR16 . . . . .19 A7
North Par Bungay IP18 . . . .119 E6
North Parade
  Lowestoft NR32 . . . . .113 D4
  Southwold IP18 . . . . .119 D4
North Pl IP28 . . . . .116 C4
North Rd
  Great Yeldham CO9 . . . . .90 A1
  Lakenheath IP27 . . . . .109 E4
  Southwold IP18 . . . . .119 D4
North Rise CO10 . . . . .148 E4
North St Burwell CB5 . . . . . .44 A6
  Freckenham IP28 . . . . .29 E3
  Hundon CO10 . . . . .75 D4

North St continued
  11 Manningtree CO11 . . . .104 E2
  Steeple Bumpstead CB9 . . . .88 D4
  Sudbury CO10 . . . . .148 C6
  Wicken CB7 . . . . .28 A1
North St Parade 5
  CO10 . . . . .148 C5
North Terr IP28 . . . . .116 C5
North Warren IP15 . . . . . . .130 C8
**North Warren Nature
  Reserve★** IP15 . . . . .73 D6
Northacre IP31 . . . . .11 B1
Northcroft 1 CO10 . . . . . . .148 C5
Northern Rd CO10 . . . . . . .148 C6
Northern Rose Cl
  IP32 . . . . .123 F7
Northern Way IP32 . . . . . . .48 C5
Northfield Ct IP15 . . . . . . .130 E5
Northfield La IP15 . . . . .130 E5
Northfield Pk CB7 . . . . .28 C5
Northfield Rd
  Onehouse IP14 . . . . .66 C6
  Soham CB7 . . . . .28 C5
**Northfield St Nicholas CP
  Prim Sch** NR32 . . . . .113 C3
Northgate
  Beccles NR34 . . . . .111 B6
  11 Harleston IP20 . . . . . . .22 D5
  Lowestoft NR32 . . . . .113 B2
Northgate Ave IP32 . . . . . .154 B4
Northgate Cty High Sch
  IP4 .136 A1
Northgate Lodge IP33 . . . .154 B3
Northgate Sports Ctr
  IP4 .136 A2
Northgate St
  Bury St Edmunds IP33 . . . . .154 C3
  Ipswich IP4 . . . . .155 B3
Northgate St Bsns Pk
  IP33 . . . . .154 C3
Northumberland Ave
  IP32 . . . . .122 E8
Northwood Cl NR33 . . . . . .114 F6
Norton CE Prim Sch
  IP31 .50 B5
Norton Rd
  Haverhill CB9 . . . . .132 C4
  Hunston IP31 . . . . .50 E5
  11 Thurstow IP31 . . . . . . .49 D4
  Tostock IP30 . . . . .50 B2
Norway Cres 2 CO12 . . . . .106 F2
Norwich La
  Bardwell IP31 . . . . .34 C8
  Coney Weston IP31 . . . . .17 E2
Norwich Rd Barham IP6 . . .82 A6
  Claydon IP6 . . . . .134 C8
  Denton IP20 . . . . .7 B3
  5 Dickleburgh & Rushall
  IP21 .20 F1
  Ditchingham NR35 . . . . .110 A8
  Earsham NR35 . . . . .7 E5
  Gillingham NR34 . . . . .111 A8
  Halesworth IP19 . . . . .118 C5
  Ipswich IP1 . . . . .155 A3
  5 Lakenheath IP27 . . . . . . .13 F2
  Lakenheath IP27 . . . . .109 F1
  Lowestoft NR32 . . . . .113 C1
  Newmarket CB8 . . . . .121 D6
  Pulham St Mary IP21 . . . . . . .21 F8
  Scole IP21 . . . . .20 D1
  Stockton NR34 . . . . .9 A8
  Thetford IP24 . . . . .16 C6
Norwich Rd Sch IP24 . . . . .16 C6
Norwood Rd IP27 . . . . .14 E8
Notcutts CO7 . . . . .151 E3
Notley Dr CB8 . . . . .132 A7
Notley Ent Pk CO7 . . . . . . .95 A2
Nottage Rd IP8 . . . . .134 D6
Nottidge Rd IP4 . . . . .139 E6
Nova Scotia La IP7 . . . . . . .79 B4
Nowton Ctry Pk★ IP33 . .63 E8
Nowton Pk Rd IP29 . . . . . .123 D1
Nowton Rd
  Bury St Edmunds IP33 . . . . .123 C1
  Nowton IP29 . . . . .63 E8
Noyes Ave IP13 . . . . .40 B3
Nuffield Hospl (Private)
  IP33 . . . . .154 C1
Nunn Cl 1 IP22 . . . . .84 A1
Nunn Sq IP32 . . . . .122 D8
Nunn's Hill IP19 . . . . .24 C3
Nunn's La IP19 . . . . .23 E1
Nuns' Bridges Rd IP24 . . . .16 B5
Nuns Wlk CO9 . . . . .89 F1
Nursery Cl Isleham CB7 . . . .29 B4
  Mildenhall IP28 . . . . .116 D4
Nursery Gn 2 CB8 . . . . .45 F2
Nursery Rd CO10 . . . . .148 F2
Nursery Wlk IP11 . . . . .152 F4
Nursey Cl NR35 . . . . .8 D7
Nuttery Vale IP23 . . . . .38 B6

O

Oak Ave NR34 . . . . .111 F5
Oak Cl
  Bury St Edmunds IP28 . . . . . .48 C6
  Felixstowe IP11 . . . . .152 E4
  4 Great Finborough IP14 . .66 B4
Oak Cres IP23 . . . . .117 C3
Oak Dr Diss IP22 . . . . .20 E2
  6 Mildenhall IP28 . . . . . . .30 B8
Oak Eggar Chase IP8 . . . .142 D8
Oak Farm La IP14 . . . . .52 D6
Oak Gn IP19 . . . . .118 B2

Oak Gr
  Fornham St Martin IP31 . . . .48 D5
  Sproughton IP8 . . . . .138 A6
Oak Hill Cl NR34 . . . . .26 E5
Oak Hill La IP22 . . . . .139 B3
Oak La Beccles NR34 . . . . . .111 D2
  Cheveley CB8 . . . . .60 E6
  Elmswell IP30 . . . . .50 F3
  Ipswich IP1 . . . . .155 B3
  Lakenheath IP27 . . . . .13 F2
  Rushbrooke with Rougham
  IP30 .64 D8
  Woolpit IP30 . . . . .65 E8
Oak Meadow Cl IP19 . . . . .42 C6
Oak Rd 5 Sudbury CO10 . . .92 B3
  Sudbury CO10 . . . . .148 F4
Oak St IP26 . . . . .4 E5
Oak Tree Way 6 IP20 . . . . .22 D5
Oak Way IP19 . . . . .118 A1
Oakdene IP10 . . . . .98 D2
Oakes Cl IP32 . . . . .122 E7
Oakes Rd IP32 . . . . .122 E7
Oakey Field Rd 6 IP31 . . . .49 E4
Oakey Ley IP30 . . . . .64 D6
Oakfield Rd Bacton IP14 . . .52 A6
  Copdock & Washbrook
  IP8 .142 A6
**Oakfield Wood Nature
  Reserve★** CO11 . . . . .105 E3
Oakland Rd 16 CO12 . . . . .107 B2
Oaklands CO6 . . . . .102 B8
Oaklands Dr IP27 . . . . .14 D8
Oakley Church La IP21 . . . .37 F8
Oakley La IP21 . . . . .106 E1
Oakley Sq IP15 . . . . .130 E4
Oaks Bsns Pk CB8 . . . . . . .120 E7
Oaks Com Prim Sch
  Chantry IP2 . . . . .138 E3
  Ipswich IP2 . . . . .138 E3
Oaks Dr CB8 . . . . .120 F7
Oaks La NR34 . . . . .2 B1
Oaks The
  7 Horringer IP29 . . . . .63 A8
  Martlesham Heath IP5 . . . . .141 F6
  Soham CB7 . . . . .28 D3
  Wattisfield IP22 . . . . .35 C5
  Woolpit IP30 . . . . .65 F8
Oaksmere Gdns 8 IP22 . . .139 A2
Oakwood Pk IP17 . . . . .57 D7
Oakwood Rd NR33 . . . . . . .114 F5
Oasis Camelid Ctr★
  IP19 .40 C8
Oast Cl IP33 . . . . .154 C1
Oast La IP13 . . . . .39 D8
Oatlands 8 IP12 . . . . .84 A8
Oatlands Cl 4 NR33 . . . . . .114 E4
Oban St IP1 . . . . .155 A4
Occold Prim Sch IP23 . . . . .37 F1
Occold Rd IP23 . . . . .38 B2
O'feld Terr IP11 . . . . .153 C6
Off Sea View Rd IP18 . . . .119 C7
Offton Rd Elmsett IP7 . . . . .80 F5
  Great Bricett IP7 . . . . .80 D5
Ohio Cl 9 NR33 . . . . .114 E3
Old Barn Rd CO8 . . . . .101 C3
Old Barningham Rd 1
  IP31 .34 E4
Old Barrack Rd IP12 . . . . .146 E4
Old Brandon Rd IP26 . . . . .4 F5
Old Brewery Yd IP19 . . . . .118 A3
Old Buckenham Hall Sch
  IP7 . . . . .79 B7
Old Bungay Rd NR35 . . . . . .8 D8
Old Bury Rd
  Alpheton CO10 . . . . .78 A6
  Lackford IP28 . . . . .31 F1
  Palgrave IP22 . . . . .37 A8
  Stanton IP31 . . . . .34 E4
  Stuston IP21 . . . . .20 D1
  Wortham IP22 . . . . .36 F8
Old Cattle Mkt IP2 . . . . . .155 B2
Old Church La
  Bulmer CO10 . . . . .91 C1
  Westley IP33 . . . . .122 A6
Old Church Rd 1 NR31 . . . .3 B6
Old Clements La 5
  CB9 . . . . .132 D5
Old Coll Cl NR34 . . . . .111 B5
Old Convent Orch
  IP33 . . . . .154 B1
Old Dairy Bsns Pk IP31 . . .49 B5
Old Farm Rd
  Beccles NR34 . . . . .111 C5
  4 Lowestoft NR33 . . . . . .114 D5
Old Forge Cl IP22 . . . . .36 D8
Old Forge Ct IP21 . . . . .22 A2
Old Foundry Pl IP16 . . . . .129 C6
Old Foundry Rd IP4 . . . . . .155 C3
Old Gram La NR35 . . . . . . .110 B3
Old Hall Cl 2 IP26 . . . . .82 D6
Old Hall La Bentley IP9 . . . .95 F2
  Bury St Edmunds IP28 . . . . . .48 D5
  Cockfield IP30 . . . . .64 B3
  Westleton IP17 . . . . .58 B8
Old Hall Meadow IP30 . . . .65 D6
Old Harleston Rd NR35 . . . .7 E3
Old Haverhill Rd CB9 . . . . .74 F2
Old High Rd
  Roydon IP22 . . . . .20 B3
  Yoxford IP17 . . . . .57 F8
Old Homes Rd 7 IP16 . . . . .73 F6
Old House Ca CO4 . . . . . . .103 A1
Old House Rd CO6 . . . . . . .102 D2
Old Ipswich Rd IP6 . . . . . .134 C7
Old Kirton Rd IP11 . . . . . . .107 D8
Old La
  Bradfield Combust with
  Stanninghield IP29 . . . . .63 F3

Old La continued
  Corton NR32 . . . . .113 B8
  Thelnetham IP22 . . . . .35 C6
Old London Rd IP9 . . . . . . .150 D1
Old Maids' La IP13 . . . . .70 A7
Old Maltings App
  IP12 . . . . .147 B6
Old Maltings Ct IP12 . . . . .147 B5
Old Methwold Rd IP26 . . . .4 E6
Old Mill Dr IP21 . . . . .21 F8
Old Mill La
  Barton Mills IP28 . . . . .116 F2
  Beccles NR34 . . . . .111 B4
Old Mill Rd CO4 . . . . .103 B3
Old Mill Terr 2 NR34 . . . . .111 B4
Old Mkt 6 NR34 . . . . .111 B6
Old Mkt Pl
  21 Harleston IP20 . . . . . . .22 D6
  19 Sudbury CO10 . . . . . . .148 C5
Old Mkt Plain 8 NR32 . . . .113 C2
Old Mkt St IP12 . . . . .84 D6
Old Nelson St 6 NR32 . . . .113 C1
Old Newton CE Prim Sch
  IP14 .52 A1
Old Norwich Rd
  Whitton IP1 . . . . .134 D5
  Yaxley IP23 . . . . .37 C5
Old Orch IP7 . . . . .149 F1
Old Orch Cl IP19 . . . . .118 A2
Old Paper Mill La 8
  IP6 .134 C8
Old Post Office La
  Blaxhall IP12 . . . . .72 A4
  Kirby Row NR35 . . . . .8 E7
  Sutton IP12 . . . . .99 A8
Old Post Office Rd
  IP29 .62 C6
Old Priory Gdns NR34 . . . .26 E2
Old Rd The CO6 . . . . .102 B8
Old Rectory Cl
  2 Claydon IP6 . . . . .82 B5
  6 Roydon IP22 . . . . .20 A3
Old Rectory Gdns 3
  IP23 .37 F1
Old Rectory La IP29 . . . . . .77 E6
Old Rectory Rd IP13 . . . . . .56 A6
Old Rectory Sch The
  IP7 . . . . .65 C1
Old Rectory Wlk IP9 . . . . .150 D3
Old Rly Rd Alburgh IP20 . . . .7 B1
  Bungay NR35 . . . . .110 A4
Old Rope Wlk CB9 . . . . . . .132 C5
Old Sch Cl
  Brampton with Stoven
  NR34 . . . . .25 E5
  5 Burwell CB5 . . . . .44 B6
  Leiston IP16 . . . . .129 C6
  4 Soham CB7 . . . . .28 D5
Old Sch Dr IP28 . . . . .26 E1
Old Sch Hall The★
  IP3 .154 B3
Old Sch La CB8 . . . . .59 F1
Old Sch Rd IP29 . . . . .63 A5
Old Sch The NR34 . . . . .10 E1
Old Schools Ct IP30 . . . . . . .50 E2
Old St IP14 . . . . .51 C1
Old St The IP9 . . . . .150 F3
Old Sta Rd
  Ellingham NR35 . . . . .8 D6
  Halesworth IP19 . . . . .118 B5
  Mendlesham IP14 . . . . .52 E3
  Newmarket CB8 . . . . .121 B4
Old Stores Cl IP13 . . . . . . .54 E7
Old Stowmarket Rd
  IP6 . . . . .50 D1
Old Town La IP13 . . . . .53 C1
Old Vicarage Dr IP31 . . . . .50 E7
Old Vicarage Rd 13
  CO12 . . . . .107 A2
Oldfield Rd IP18 . . . . .138 B1
Oldhall Rd IP9 . . . . .106 F6
Olding Rd IP33 . . . . .122 D6
Olive Cl 2 IP27 . . . . .13 F2
Olive Ct NR32 . . . . .113 B3
Oliver Cl NR33 . . . . .114 D2
Oliver Ct IP27 . . . . .5 E4
Oliver Rd IP33 . . . . .122 C6
Olivers Cl CO10 . . . . .91 E8
Olland Ct 5 NR35 . . . . .110 B3
Olle Cl IP33 . . . . .123 C1
Olympus Cl IP1 . . . . .134 C2
One Eyed La IP21 . . . . .22 D3
Onehouse La IP1 . . . . .135 C1
Onehouse Rd IP14 . . . . . . .124 B6
Onner's La IP16 . . . . .58 C4
Ontario Rd NR33 . . . . .115 C6
Opal Ave 1 Ipswich IP1 . . .134 D1
  Ipswich IP1 . . . . .138 D8
Orchard Ave NR34 . . . . . . .114 E4
Orchard Cl Beyton IP30 . . . .49 F1
  2 Blundeston NR32 . . . . . . .3 A4
  Elmswell IP30 . . . . .50 F3
  Great Livermere IP31 . . . . . .33 C2
  6 Haverhill CB9 . . . . .132 D5
  Lidgate CB8 . . . . .61 C4
  2 Ramsey & Parkeston
  CO12 . . . . .106 D1
  Ridgewell CO9 . . . . .89 D3
  Risby IP28 . . . . .47 D5
  Rushbrooke with Rougham
  IP30 .64 D8
  Woodbridge IP12 . . . . .147 A7
Orchard Croft NR33 . . . . .114 D4
Orchard Dr IP14 . . . . .65 F4
Orchard End 10 IP13 . . . . .83 E5
Orchard Farm Barns 2
  IP29 .47 A2

Orchard Farm Bsns Pk
CB7 ....28 C7
Orchard Gate
Ipswich IP2 ....138 C5
🚺 Needham Market IP6 ..125 D5
Orchard Gdn NR33 ....114 E7
Orchard Gr NR34 ....111 C4
Orchard Gr
Claydon IP6 ....134 C7
Ipswich IP5 ....141 A7
Orchard La
🔳 Blundeston NR32 ....3 A4
Thurston IP31 ....49 E5
Orchard Pl
Sudbury CO10 ....148 B4
Wickham Market IP13 ....127 B6
Orchard Rd
🔟 Bramford IP8 ....134 A2
Leiston IP16 ....129 C5
Orchard Rise
Badingham IP13 ....56 A7
Beccles NR34 ....111 F4
Redisham NR34 ....85 A7
Orchard Row CB7 ....28 E2
Orchard St
Bury St Edmunds IP33 ....154 B3
Ipswich IP1 ....155 C3
Orchard Terr 🔳 NR32 .....115 C7
Orchard The 🔁
🔳 Ashley CB8 ....60 F8
🔳 Brandon IP30 ....65 A4
Redisham NR34 ....85 A7
Orchard Valley IP19 .....118 D4
Orchard Way 🔳
IP29 ....63 A8
Orchards The 🔳 IP13 ....40 B3
Orchid Cl
Halesworth IP19 ....118 C4
Ipswich IP2 ....138 E4
Orchid Way IP6 ....125 D3
Orchids Cl NR35 ....110 D3
Oregon Rd IP9 ....141 A6
Orford Castle Mus & Visitor
Ctr* IP12 ....131 B2
Orford CE VA Prim Sch
IP12 ....131 B3
Orford Dr NR32 ....112 F3
Orford Ness* IP12 ......131 C1
Orford Ness National Nature
Reserve* IP12 ....87 C3
Orford Rd
Bromeswell IP12 ....147 F7
Butley IP12 ....86 A6
Felixstowe IP11 ....152 A6
Haverhill CB9 ....132 D4
Tunstall IP12 ....71 F2
Orford St IP1 ....155 A4
Oriel Cl CO10 ....148 F4
Original Factory Shop The
IP32 ....123 D7
Orkney Cl CB9 ....133 B5
Orkney Rd 🔳 IP4 ....136 A1
Orttewell Rd IP32 ....123 E6
Orvis Cl 151 E3
Orwell Ave IP17 ....128 D4
Orwell Cl IP12 ....146 E3
Orwell Ctry Pk* IP3 ...139 F3
Orwell Dr NR32 ....112 F3
Orwell High Sch IP11 ...152 A4
Orwell Pk Sch IP10 .....145 B3
Orwell Pl 🔟 IP4 ....155 C2
Orwell Rd
Felixstowe IP11 ....152 E3
🔟 Harwich CO12 ....107 B2
Ipswich IP3 ....140 A4
Stowmarket IP14 ....124 D4
Orwell Ret Pk IP2 ....139 A5
Orwell Rise 🔟 IP9 ......106 C8
Orwell View Rd IP9 .....106 F6
Osborne Rd IP3 ....140 A4
Osborne St 🔳 NR32 ....113 E3
Osier Cl IP17 ....147 B6
Osier Rd IP23 ....154 B3
Osiers The IP14 ....124 D7
Osmund Wlk IP33 ....122 C4
Osprey Gn NR33 ....114 C6
Osprey Rd CB9 ....133 A5
Oswyn Cl IP32 ....123 D4
Otley Coll Otley IP6 .....69 C1
Otley IP6 ....85 E8
Otley Ct 🔳 IP11 ....152 D5
Otley Hill IP6 ....69 C3
Otley Prim Sch 69 C2
Otley Rd IP12 ....85 C2
Otten Rd CO10 ....90 D5
Otter Trust The* NR35 ..7 E3
Oulton Broad N Sta
NR32 ....112 F1
Oulton Broad Prim Sch
NR32 ....112 C2
Oulton Broad S Sta
NR33 ....114 D2
Oulton Broad Wr Sports Ctr
NR33 ....112 F1
Oulton Cl IP2 ....138 D4
Oulton Ct NR32 ....106 F2
Oulton Ind Est NR32 ....112 E3
Oulton Rd Flixton NR32 .112 F7
Ipswich IP3 ....139 F2
Lowestoft NR32 ....113 A4
Oulton Rd N NR32 ....112 F5
Oulton St NR32 ....112 F4

Ound Farm Nature Reserve*
IP17 ....56 C1
Ousden Ct IP29 ....62 A6
Out Northgate IP33 .....154 B4
Out Risbygate IP33 .....122 C6
Out Westgate IP33 ......154 B1
Outney Meadow Cvn Pk
NR35 ....110 A5
Outney Rd NR35 ....110 A4
Overbury Hall Rd IP7 ...149 D1
Ovington Pl 🔳 CB9 ......132 F6
Owell The IP31 ....49 E6
Oxer Cl IP30 ....50 F2

Oxford Cl
Mildenhall IP28 ....116 A4
Sudbury CO10 ....148 E4
Oxford Dr Hadleigh IP7 ..149 D8
Woodbridge IP12 ....146 D3
Oxford Rd 🔳 Feltwell IP26 ..4 E5
Ipswich IP4 ....139 E5
Lowestoft NR33 ....113 D3
🔳 Manningtree CO11 ....104 E2
Oxford St CB8 ....120 B8

P

Packard Ave IP3 ....140 B2
Packard Pl IP8 ....134 B2
Packards La
Fordham CO6 ....102 A1
Wormingford CO6 ....101 F1
Packway La IP31 ....50 A5
Packway The IP20 ....23 A7
Paddock Cl IP33 ....122 C5
Paddock Hill IP33 ....34 D8
Paddock Rd 🔳 IP20 .....117 E7
Paddock St CB7 ....28 D4
Paddock The 🔟 IP31 ....34 B1
Paddock Way
Chedburgh IP29 ....62 C4
Troston IP31 ....33 D3
Paddock Wood Cl 🔳
NR33 ....114 C4
Paddocks Cty Prim Sch
CB8 ....120 E4
Paddocks Dr CB8 ....121 A2
Paddocks Rd NR34 ......111 F4
Paddocks The
Ashen CO10 ....89 C5
Badwell Ash IP31 ....50 F7
🔳 Bures CO8 ....101 C4
🔟 Burwell CB5 ....44 A5
Halesworth IP19 ....118 A3
🔳 Martlesham Heath IP5 .98 A8
Tuddenham St Martin
IP6 ....136 B5
Worlington IP28 ....30 B4
Padstow Rd IP5 ....141 A6
Page Gdns IP33 ....141 E8
Pageant Pl IP13 ....126 C2
Page's Cl IP14 ....124 C6
Pages Hill Rd IP29 ....63 B6
Paget Cl IP6 ....125 C5
Paget Pl CB8 ....121 A6
Paget Rd IP1 ....155 A4
Pains Cl IP8 ....134 F3
Pains Hill IP14 ....67 F6
Pakefield Mid Sch
NR33 ....115 A3
Pakefield Prim Sch
NR33 ....115 C5
Pakefield St NR33 ....115 B4
Pakenham Pl CB8 ....132 F5
Pakenham Rd IP31 ....49 D6
Pakenham Watermill*
IP31 ....49 F8
Pakenham Windmill*
IP31 ....49 E8
Palace La CB7 ....45 B8
Palace St 🔳 CB8 ....121 A3
Palfrey Height CO11 ....104 E4
Palgrave VC Prim Sch
IP22 ....20 C1
Palmcroft Cl 🔟 IP1 .....135 A3
Palmcroft Rd IP1 ....135 A3
Palmer Cl IP14 ....113 B6
Palmer Dr IP27 ....109 C7
Palmer St IP31 ....35 C1
Palmer's La IP18 ....119 A2
Palmerston Rd IP4 ......139 E6
Palmerswood Cl CO10 .148 C1
Pamment's La IP28 ....29 F6
Pannels Cl 🔳 CO10 ....77 A2
Pantile La 🔟 CB5 ....44 A6
Papeley Meadow IP29 ...47 B2
Paper Mill La IP8 ....134 B4
Parade Dr 🔳 CO12 .....106 E1
Parade Rd IP4 ....139 F7
Parade Rd N 🔳 NR33 ..115 D7
Parade Rd S NR33 ......115 D7
Parade The IP19 ....133 F8
Paradise Pl IP16 ....129 C5
Pardoe Pl IP4 ....140 C7
Park Cl
🔳 Bentwaters Airfield
IP12 ....85 D8
🔟 Lowestoft NR33 ....114 D4

Park Cl continued
🔳 Martlesham Heath IP5 ..98 A8
🔳 Moulton CB8 ....45 F3
Sudbury CO10 ....148 E6
Park Cotts CB8 ....121 B2
Park Dr CB8 ....121 B2
Park Dr NR34 ....111 E4
Park End IP17 ....128 C2
Park Farm Dr
Barton Mills IP28 ....30 C2
Stanton IP31 ....34 E3
Park Farm La
Euston IP24 ....33 E8
Hoxne IP21 ....38 E6
Park Hill IP16 ....129 C6
Park La Aldeburgh IP15 ..130 E4
Bulmer CO10 ....91 C2
Charsfield IP13 ....70 C3
Eye IP23 ....117 D1
Glemsford CO10 ....77 B2
Hawstead IP29 ....63 D7
Kirton IP10 ....98 E3
Langham CO4 ....107 B3
Newmarket CB8 ....121 B3
Southwold IP18 ....119 D4
Thornham Parva IP23 ....37 A3
Park Meadows NR32 ....112 F6
Park N IP1 ....139 D8
Park Pl IP17 ....57 D7
Park Rd
Aldeburgh IP15 ....130 D4
Benhall IP17 ....72 A7
Boot Street IP13 ....137 D8
Burwell CB5 ....44 A5
Bury St Edmunds IP33 ..122 D4
Cheveley CB8 ....60 D7
Combs IP14 ....124 B2
Diss IP22 ....20 C2
East Bergholt CO7 ....104 D5
Great Horkesley CO6 ...102 D4
Grundisburgh IP13 ....83 E5
Halesworth IP19 ....118 A5
🔳 Harwich CO12 ....107 B2
Haverhill CB9 ....132 B7
Ipswich IP1 ....139 C8
Lavenham CO10 ....78 D4
Letheringham IP13 ....70 D4
Lowestoft NR32 ....113 D3
Needham Market IP6 ....125 D4
St Cross, South Elmham
IP20 ....23 C7
Southolt IP23 ....54 A8
Stoke-by-Nayland CO6 ..102 F6
Sudbury CO10 ....148 D5
Wetherden IP14 ....51 A1
Park St CO6 ....102 E7
Park The
🔳 Great Barton IP31 .....49 A5
Tannington IP13 ....104 E2
Park View
Botesdale IP22 ....36 B7
Wetherden IP27 ....5 E3
Wetherden IP21 ....51 A1
Park View Rd IP1 ....135 B1
Park Wlk IP19 ....118 E5
Parker Ave IP11 ....152 B4
Parker's Dro 🔳 IP28 ...29 F6
Parker's La IP24 ....52 A5
Parker's Way CO6 ....102 D5
Parkers Pl 🔳 IP5 ....98 A8
Parkers Wlk CB8 ....120 E8
Parkeston Rd
Felixstowe IP11 ....152 D4
Harwich CO12 ....107 A2
Parkhill NR32 ....112 F5
Parkington Wlk IP12 ...122 D7
Parklands 🔳 IP5 ....84 F7
Parklands Cl 🔟 CO10 ...77 B3
Parklands Dr 🔟 IP28 ...48 C6
Parklands The NR34 ....114 D4
Parklands Way 🔼 IP20 ..22 D6
Parkside
Chippenham CB7 ....45 C8
Haverhill CB9 ....132 D4
Mildenhall IP28 ....30 C8
🔳 Stanton IP31 ....34 E3
Parkside Ave IP14 ....155 C4
Parkside Dr NR32 ....113 A2
Parkway
Bury St Edmunds IP33 ..154 A2
Wickham Market IP13 ...127 C2
Parkway Mid Sch CB8 ..132 B6
Parkwood Dr CO10 .....148 B8
Parliament Rd IP4 ....140 B5
Parliament Sq IP4 ....140 B5
Parmenter Rd IP7 ....92 B3
Parnell Cl IP1 ....134 F3
Parnell La IP30 ....50 D3
Parnell Rd IP1 ....134 F3
Parnham Pl 🔳 IP7 ....140 F5
Parr Rd CB9 ....132 B4
Parrington Way 🔳
CO11 ....104 D2
Parry Cl IP19 ....118 B5
Parsonage Cl
🔳 Burwell CB5 ....44 A5
Felixstowe IP11 ....152 D4
Parsonage Gr IP7 ....104 A3
Parsonage La
Burwell CB5 ....44 A5
Chelsworth IP7 ....79 E3
Parson's Field CO4 .....104 A3
Parson's La IP16 ....125 B2
Parsons Ct IP33 ....122 A6
Parsons Field 🔳 IP15 ..130 E5
Parsons Hill IP12 ....99 F7

Parsons Yd 🔳 CO11 .....104 E2
Partridge Cl
Boxford CO10 ....93 C4
🔳 Thurston IP31 ....49 D4
Partridge Rd IP2 ....138 D3
Pashford Cl IP27 ....109 D6
Pashford Pl IP3 ....144 C8
Paske Ave IP32 ....132 D5
Pastures The
Ipswich IP4 ....140 F5
Oulton NR32 ....112 F6
Patricia Cl NR32 ....112 D2
Patrick Stead Hospl
IP19 ....118 C5
Patten La NR15 ....21 B7
Patterdale Gdns 🔳
NR32 ....113 A4
Pattern Bush Cl 🔳
CO11 ....104 E4
Patteson Rd IP3 ....139 E4
Patticroft 🔟 CO10 ....77 A3
Paul's Rd IP2 ....138 C3
Pauline St IP2 ....155 B1
Pavilion Ct IP9 ....132 F5
Paxton Chadwick Cl 🔳
IP16 ....129 D5
Payne St NR33 ....115 C7
Payne's La IP26 ....4 E5
Peach Maltings IP33 ....154 B4
Peacock Cl
Hockwold cum Wilton IP26 ..4 F3
🔳 Thurston IP31 ....49 D4
Lowestoft NR32 ....114 C2
Peacock Rise 🔳 IP31 ...34 B1
Peacock St IP5 ....141 E7
Peacock's Pyghtle
IP12 ....131 C3
Peacocks Cl 🔟 CO10 ....76 E1
Peacocks Rd CO10 ....76 E2
Peak Dale NR33 ....114 F4
Pear Cl 🔟 IP23 ....36 D2
Pearce Rd IP3 ....140 A4
Pearce's Cl 🔳 IP26 ......5 A3
Pearcroft Rd IP1 ....135 B3
Pearl Cl IP6 ....69 C2
Pearl Rd IP1 ....134 F3
Pearmain Wlk 🔳 CB9 ...132 A6
Pearse Way IP3 ....140 E1
Pearson Rd IP4 ....140 C5
Pearsons Way IP8 ....95 F5
Peart Gr IP5 ....141 D6
Peartree Cl IP17 ....128 C6
Peartree Hill CO8 ....101 D2
Peasecroft Rd 🔳 IP31 ..34 B1
Peasenhall Cl 🔳 IP12 ...85 E3
Peasenhall Prim Sch
IP17 ....56 E8
Peasenhall Rd IP19 .....141 C6
Peasey Gdns IP5 ....141 C6
Peasey La IP5 ....141 C6
Pebble Cl NR32 ....113 A3
Pebble View Wlk 🔳 NR33 ..3 C6
Peckham St IP33 ....154 B3
Pecockes Cl 🔟 CO10 ...92 B3
Peddars Cl 🔳 IP31 ....34 B1
Peddars La NR34 ....111 B4
Peddars Way NR32 ....113 B4
Peel St IP1 ....155 B3
Peel Yd 🔳 IP5 ....98 A8
Peewit Hill IP1 ....152 D3
Pegasus Mews 🔳 NR32 ..112 D1
Pegg's Hill IP29 ....22 F2
Pelham 🔳 CO12 ....106 F1
Pelican Cl IP4 ....138 E3
Pemberton Rd IP20 .....22 D5
Pemberton Wlk IP33 ...123 C4
Pembroke Ave IP12 ...146 E4
Pembroke Cl
Ipswich IP2 ....139 B3
Mildenhall IP28 ....116 C5
Newmarket CB8 ....148 B8
Pembroke Pl CO10 .....148 B8
Pembroke Rd
Bury St Edmunds IP33 ..122 D3
Framlingham IP13 ....126 B3
Pembrooke Way 🔳
NR32 ....113 A4
Pendleton Rd IP2 ....138 D1
Penfold Rd IP11 ....153 A4
Penn Cl IP7 ....150 F4
Pennine Way NR32 .....112 E2
Pennings Nature Reserve
The* IP23 ....117 E2
Penny La 🔳 Ipswich IP3 ..140 F1
Lowestoft NR33 ....112 E3
Penny Meadow 🔳 IP3 ..150 E3
Pennycress Dr 🔳 IP4 ..16 D7
Pennyfields NR35 ....110 B2
Pennygate Dr IP14 .....114 E6
Pennyroyal Gdns IP2 ..138 E4
Penryn Rd IP5 ....141 A7
Penshurst Rd IP3 ....140 D4
Pentland Wlk 🔳 NR32 ..113 A4
Pentlow Cr CO10 ....76 E1
Pentlow Hawke Cl
CB9 ....133 A5
Pentlow Hill CO10 ....91 A8
Penzance Rd IP5 ....141 A6
Pepper La IP31 ....49 E3
Pepper Pl IP5 ....141 D6
Pepper's Rd CO4 ....102 F1
Peppercorn Way 🔳 IP2 ..139 C3
Peppers Cl IP7 ....5 E3
Peppers Wash IP13 .....126 B6
Pepys Ave 🔳 NR34 ....9 F4
Percy Ruse Cl CO10 ....148 F5
Peregrine Way 🔳 NR33 ..11 C1

Periwinkle Cl 🔳 NR33 ..114 C5
Perkins Rd IP30 ....49 B2
Perkins Way
Ipswich IP3 ....139 F1
Tostock IP30 ....50 B3
Perry La CO4 ....103 D2
Perrydown La IP30 ......64 C1
Perryfields CO10 ....148 F2
Persimmon Wlk CB8 ...120 A7
Pesthouse La IP6 ....82 A6
Petch Cl IP33 ....154 B3
Peter Dr 🔳 IP24 ....16 D7
Peter's Gr 🔳 IP4 ....150 E3
Peterhouse Cl
Ipswich IP2 ....138 F2
Mildenhall IP28 ....116 D4
Peterhouse Cres IP12 ..146 D4
Peterhouse Dr CB8 ....121 A2
Petingo Cl CB8 ....120 D7
Pett Couronne Way
NR34 ....111 A1
Peto Way NR32 ....113 A1
Pets Cnr NR33 ....114 D7
Pettaugh La IP6 ....68 C2
Petticoat La
🔳 Barrow IP29 ....47 A2
Bury St Edmunds IP33 ..154 A1
Pettits La IP21 ....20 E3
Petunia Way IP27 ....14 E8
Pheasant Cl 🔁 IP21 .....49 D4
Pheasant Rd IP2 ....138 E3
Pheasant Rise IP8 ....95 F4
Pheasant Way IP27 ....6 A1
Pheasants Wlk NR35 ....7 E4
Philip Ave IP11 ....152 E3
Philip Rd
Bury St Edmunds IP32 ..122 F8
Ipswich IP2 ....155 B1
Philipps Cl CB8 ....120 D4
Philipps Rd 🔳 IP5 ....82 B5
Phillips Cres IP6 ....125 E3
Phillips Field Rd CO10 ..148 E3
Phoenix Day Hospl
IP33 ....154 A4
Phoenix Rd IP4 ....140 A7
Phoenix Way IP4 ....124 F7
Phoenix Yd CB9 ....132 E3
Picketts Rd IP11 ....153 C5
Pickwick Cres IP33 .....154 C3
Pickwick Dr 🔳 NR32 .....3 A4
Pickwick Rd IP2 ....138 E6
Picton Ave 🔳 IP3 ....135 D1
Pier Ave IP18 ....119 D6
Pier Terr NR33 ....115 D8
Pig La NR34 ....111 B6
Pigeon La IP28 ....48 B6
Pigeon's La IP9 ....138 A3
Pightle Cl IP30 ....50 E2
Pightle The
Capel St Mary IP9 ....150 F4
Haverhill CB9 ....132 E6
🔳 Martlesham IP6 ....125 D5
North Cove NR34 ....10 B4
Pilgrim's Way 🔳 IP20 ...22 D6
Pilgrims Way
Bungay NR25 ....110 C3
🔳 Great Finborough IP14 ..66 B4
🔳 Thorpeness IP16 ....73 F6
Pimpernel Rd IP2 ....138 F3
Pin Mill Cl IP8 ....138 C1
Pin Mill Cliff* IP9 ....106 D8
Pinbush Cl NR33 ....114 F2
Pinbush Rd NR33 ....114 F2
Pine Ave IP1 ....135 B1
Pine Bank IP5 ....141 F6
Pine Cl
🔳 Brantham CO11 ....104 E4
Eye IP23 ....117 D3
🔳 Harleston IP20 ....22 D5
🔳 Kenleheath IP27 ....13 F2
Rendlesham IP12 ....85 D8
Pine Gr 🔟 IP13 ....83 E5
Pine Leys IP32 ....122 F8
Pine Sq IP7 ....80 D6
Pine Tree Cl NR34 ......111 F4
Pine Tree Ct IP22 ....18 C2
Pine Trees Ave IP28 ...116 F4
Pine View IP4 ....52 A6
Pine View Rd IP1 ....139 B8
Pinecroft Rd IP1 ....135 A2
Pinecroft Rd CO10 .....148 B3
Pinecroft Way IP4 ......125 E4
Pines Ind Est The CB8 ..44 F6
Pines The Claydon IP6 ..134 C8
Felixstowe IP11 ....153 C6
Pinetree Cl IP5 ....140 F7
Pinetrees NR31 ....2 B7
Pineview Cl IP14 ....148 D5
Pineview Cl 🔳 IP29 .....63 A1
Pinewood Cl IP4 ....146 E3
Pinewood Ave NR33 ...114 F6
Pinewood Dr IP27 ......114 F8
Pinewood Gdns NR34 ..10 B4
Pinhoe Dr 🔳 CB9 ....132 A6
Pinkney's La 🔟 IP18 ...119 C5
Pinkuah La CO10 ....90 F7
Pinmill Rd IP9 ....106 C8
Pinners La IP13 ....146 B7
Pintail Cl IP2 ....138 E3
Pintail Rd IP14 ....67 A5
Pinza Cl CB8 ....120 E8
Piperell Way CB9 ....132 E3
Pipers Cl IP18 ....133 A4
Pipers Meadow IP13 ....54 E7

Pipers Vale Cl IP3 ....**139** E1
Pipers Vale Com Prim Sch
  Gainsborough IP3 ....**139** F1
  Ipswich IP3 ....**139** F1
Pipers Vale Nature Reserve*
  IP3 ....**143** F7
Pipney Hill IP17 ....**156** F4
Pipp's La IP6 ....**135** E6
Pippin Cl 2 IP32 ....**123** E6
Pippin Post Cl CO10 ....**76** C6
Pippins The
  Blundeston NR32 ....**3** A4
  Glemsford CO10 ....**77** B2
Pirnhow St NR35 ....**110** D5
Pit Rd NR34 ....**10** B8
Pitcairn Rd IP1 ....**138** E8
Pitman's Gr IP19 ....**42** A4
Pitmire La CO8 ....**101** A7
Pits The CB7 ....**29** C4
Pitts End CO7 ....**151** D5
Place Farm Com Prim Sch
  CB9 ....**132** D6
Place for Plants The*
  CO7 ....**151** F3
Plampin Cl CO10 ....**92** D3
Plantation The IP15 ...**130** D5
Plantation Way IP14 ....**66** C1
Planters Gr 3 NR33 ....**114** F7
Plash Rd IP23 ....**53** F7
Plashwood Rd IP14 .....**51** B8
Platers Wlk IP16 ....**129** C5
Platten Cl IP6 ....**125** C5
Platters Cl IP3 ....**144** A7
Platters Rd IP11 ......**152** E2
Playfield Rd IP9 ......**150** F3
Playford La IP5 ....**136** E2
Playford Mount IP13 ...**137** C6
Playford Rd
  Ipswich IP4 ....**140** E8
  Playford IP5 ....**137** B2
Pleasant Pl NR34 ......**111** B3
Pleasant Row IP14 .....**155** C2
Pleasurewood Cl 5
  NR32 ....**113** B5
Pleasurewood Hill
  NR32 ....**113** A7
Pleasurewood Hills Leisure
  Pk* NR32 ....**113** C8
Plough Hill CO10 ....**76** C7
Plough La
  Leavenheath CO6 ......**102** B7
  Sudbury CO10 ....**148** B5
Plough Rd
  Capel St Mary IP9 .....**150** D3
  Woolpit IP30 ....**50** D1
Plough St IP3 ....**139** E4
Ploughman's Dro IP26 ..**4** B5
Plover Cl
  4 Mildenhall IP28 .....**13** B1
  11 Stowmarket IP14 .....**67** A5
Plover Rd IP2 ....**138** E2
Plovers Way
  Bury St Edmunds IP33 ...**123** C1
  Hockwold cum Wilton IP26 ..**4** F3
  Lowestoft NR33 ....**114** D5
Plum St CO10 ....**77** A3
Plum Tree Rise 3 IP7 ...**80** D6
Plummer Cl 22 IP31 ....**34** B1
Plummers Dell 10 IP6 ...**82** A5
Plumpton Ave IP28 .....**116** C5
Plumtrees 8 NR32 ......**112** D2
Plymouth Rd
  Felixstowe IP11 ....**152** F6
  4 Troston IP31 ....**33** D5
Pole Hill (Tumulus)*
  IP10 ....**141** F5
Police Sta Rd 6 NR31 ..**3** D3
Pollard Piece NR33 ....**114** E5
Pollards La IP29 ....**29** F7
Polls La NR34 ....**9** C2
Polstead St CO10 ....**76** E1
Pooley St IP22 ....**19** C3
Pope's Gn La IP7 ....**94** B2
Popes Ct CB9 ....**133** C3
Poplar Cl 1 Barrow IP29 ..**47** A2
  4 Claydon IP6 ....**134** C8
  Haverhill CB9 ....**132** B7
  Mildenhall IP28 ....**116** C6
Poplar Farm La IP31 ....**49** E5
Poplar Farm Rd IP22 ....**73** A2
Poplar Hill IP14 ....**124** E4
Poplar La IP8 ....**138** B3
Poplar Rd
  Lowestoft NR33 ....**114** D3
  Sudbury CO10 ....**148** F5
Poplars Cl 1 CB5 ....**44** A5
Poplars The
  Beck Row, Holywell Row
  & Kenny Hill IP28 ....**13** D1
  3 Brantham CO11 ......**104** E5
  Spexhall IP19 ....**24** F5

Poppy Cl
  Bury St Edmunds IP32 ...**123** C4
  Ditchingham NR35 ......**110** B7
  Ipswich NR3 ....**138** F5
  Worlingham NR34 ......**111** F3
Poppy Fields 9 CB7 .....**28** D5
Popson St NR35 ....**110** A4
Port La IP23 ....**37** C3
Port of Felixstowe Rd
  IP11 ....**152** C3
Portal Ave IP5 ....**84** A1
Portal Cl 4 Barnham IP24 ..**16** C2
  7 Feltwell IP26 ....**4** D5
Porter Rd 3 IP3 ....**140** F1
Porthole Cl NR33 ......**114** B4
Portland Ave 6 CO10 ....**107** B2
Portland Cl 18 IP27 .....**13** F2
Portland Cres 4 IP12 ...**146** E4
Portland Pl 3 IP24 .....**16** A5
Portland Rd CB8 ....**120** E3
Portlight Cl 3 CO11 ....**105** A2
Portman Rd IP1 ....**155** A2
Portman's Wlk IP1 .....**139** A5
Portsch Rd NR33 ......**114** E3
Portsmouth Cl 1 IP27 ...**13** F2
Portsmouth Rd 3 IP1 ....**33** D5
Post Mill Cl IP4 ....**139** F6
Post Mill Cres 12 IP13 ..**83** E5
Post Mill Gdns 10 IP13 ..**83** E5
Post Office La
  Gestingthorpe CO10 ....**77** A3
  Martlesham IP12 ....**146** C1
Post Office Rd IP17 ....**129** A3
Posters La IP31 ....**35** A2
Posting House Pottery The*
  CO10 ....**91** D8
Pot Kiln Chase CO9 .....**90** F1
Pot Kiln Prim Sch
  CO10 ....**148** E4
Pot Kiln Rd CO10 ......**148** F4
Pot Kilns The CO10 .....**92** B3
Potash La Bentley IP9 ..**104** F8
  Eye IP23 ....**117** B5
  Polstead CO6 ....**93** F4
  Wyverstone IP14 ......**51** D7
Potkins La IP12 ....**131** B3
Potland La 18 CO10 .....**78** D4
Pott Hall Rd IP28 ......**30** A6
Potter's La
  Rickinghall Superior IP22 ..**36** B5
  Stanton IP31 ....**34** E4
Potter's St IP16 ....**58** C4
Potters Brook IP6 ......**126** B3
Potters Dr NR31 ....**3** B7
Potters Vale IP22 ....**35** E7
Pouch Mill IP11 ....**152** B8
Poulter's La IP19 ....**62** F6
Poultry Rd IP27 ....**13** A7
Pound Cl 4 Burwell CB5 ..**44** A5
  Halesworth IP19 ......**118** B3
  4 Harleston IP20 ....**22** D6
  4 Walsham le Willows
  IP31 ....**35** C2
Pound Farm Dr
  8 Harwich CO12 ....**107** A2
  Lowestoft NR32 ....**112** F2
Pound Farm Parade 7
  NR32 ....**112** F4
Pound Fm Nature Reserve*
  IP17 ....**56** C1
Pound Gn Rd IP13 ....**56** C7
Pound Hill Bacton IP14 ..**51** E6
  Dallinghoo IP13 ....**70** C1
Pound Hill Cl IP14 .....**51** F6
Pound La
  Blundeston NR32 ....**3** A4
  Bramford IP8 ....**81** F3
  Capel St Mary IP9 .....**150** D1
  Dallinghoo IP13 ....**70** C1
  Ditchingham NR35 ......**110** B7
  Hadleigh IP7 ....**149** C6
  Isleham CB7 ....**29** C5
  Stowmarket IP14 ......**124** D7
Pound Meadow 3 IP28 ...**48** B6
Pound Pl NR34 ....**111** B6
Pound Rd
  3 Beccles NR34 ....**111** B6
  Creeting St Peter or West
  Creeting IP6 ....**67** B4
  Sotterley NR34 ....**26** A7
  Pound Wlk NR34 ......**111** B6
Pouy St IP17 ....**41** B1
Powling Rd IP3 ....**140** A2
Powney St IP7 ....**93** B8
Pratt St CB7 ....**29** C4
Pratt's La IP9 ....**144** A2
Prentice Rd IP14 ......**124** E6
Prentice St 8 CO10 .....**78** D4
Prentices La IP13 .....**146** D6
Prescott Dr 11 IP30 ....**50** F2
Presland St IP27 ......**109** B7
Presmere Rd IP13 .....**127** A4
Preston Dr IP1 ....**134** F2
Preston Rd CO10 ....**78** D4
Prestwick Ave 2 IP11 ..**153** C6
Pretty Dr IP21 ....**21** A2
Pretty Rd IP16 ....**58** A4
Pretyman Ave IP14 .....**51** F6
Pretyman Rd
  Felixstowe IP11 ....**152** E1
  Ipswich IP3 ....**140** B3
Prevetts Way IP15 .....**130** E5
Prickwillow Rd CB7 .....**12** A2
Priestly Cl IP14 ......**124** B8
Priestly Rd IP6 ......**125** D4
Prigg Wlk IP32 ....**122** E7
Primes La Blyford IP19 ..**42** B8

Primes La continued
  Holton IP19 ....**118** F5
Primrose Alley IP18 ...**119** D4
Primrose Cl NR33 .....**114** F2
Primrose Hill
  Haverhill CB9 ....**132** D5
  Ipswich IP2 ....**138** F4
Royal Hospital School
  IP9 ....**105** E6
Primrose La
  Frostenden NR34 ....**26** B4
  Ramsey & Parkeston
  CO11 ....**106** A1
  10 Soham CB7 ....**28** D8
Primrose Rise NR34 ....**111** E3
Primrose Way IP6 .....**125** D3
Prince Charles Ave 17
  IP32 ....**48** C5
Prince Charles Cl
  CO10 ....**148** D6
Prince Cl CB8 ....**120** B8
Prince of Wales Cl
  IP33 ....**122** E5
Prince of Wales Dr 9
  IP2 ....**139** A2
Prince St CO10 ....**148** C6
Prince's Rd NR35 ......**110** C6
Princedale Cl IP11 ....**135** A1
Princel La CO7 ....**158** F3
Princes Gdns IP11 ....**152** F4
Princes' Gdns IP6 .....**81** C3
Princes Ga IP19 ....**118** A2
Princes Rd
  Felixstowe IP11 ....**152** F4
  13 Harwich CO12 ....**107** A2
  Lowestoft NR32 ....**113** C2
Princes St
  Bury St Edmunds IP33 ..**154** A2
  Ipswich IP1 ....**155** A1
  Lowestoft NR32 ....**113** A2
Princess Rd 3 IP18 ....**119** C8
Princess Way
  5 Earsham NR35 ....**7** F4
  Haverhill CB9 ....**132** B6
  Newmarket CB8 ....**120** E4
Princethorpe Rd IP3 ...**140** C4
Prior Stephen Way
  IP24 ....**16** B5
Prior's Ave IP33 ......**122** E4
Priors Cl
  Lowestoft NR32 ....**113** C5
  Rushbrooke with Rougham
  IP30 ....**64** D8
Priors' Hill Rd IP15 ...**130** D3
Priors Way IP15 ....**130** E4
Priory Ave 1 CB9 ......**132** E5
Priory Cl 7 Burwell CB5 ..**44** A5
  Ingham IP31 ....**32** F1
  Palgrave IP22 ....**20** C1
  St Olaves NR31 ....**2** A3
  Stradbroke IP21 ....**39** B4
Priory Cres IP21 ....**39** D8
Priory Gdns
  Isleham CB7 ....**29** C5
  St Olaves NR31 ....**2** A3
  Sudbury CO10 ....**148** B4
Priory La Bungay NR35 ..**110** B4
  Carlton Colville NR33 ...**114** A2
  Darsham IP17 ....**42** B1
  Debenham IP14 ....**53** F2
Priory Pk IP10 ....**144** C6
Priory Rd Beccles NR34 ..**111** B3
  Blythburgh IP19 ....**42** F6
  Felixstowe IP11 ....**153** C5
  Fressingfield IP21 .....**39** D7
  Fritton & St Olaves NR31 ..**2** A4
  Palgrave IP22 ....**20** C1
  Snape IP17 ....**72** E5
  Sudbury CO10 ....**148** B4
  Wrentham NR34 ....**26** E5
Priory Speci Sch IP32 ..**123** C5
Priory Stadium CO10 ...**148** B4
Priory Wlk CO10 ......**148** B4
Prittlewell Cl IP2 ....**138** F1
Private Rd Earsham NR35 ..**7** D4
  4 Oulton Broad NR33 ..**114** A7
Privet Gn IP4 ....**135** A7
Progress Way IP23 ....**117** B5
Promenade
  Harwich CO12 ....**107** A1
  Southwold IP18 ....**119** D4
Prospect Hill CO10 .....**92** B2
Prospect Pl
  Leiston IP16 ....**129** D6
  Lowestoft NR33 ....**115** B3
Prospect Rd
  Ipswich IP1 ....**139** A6
  Lowestoft NR32 ....**113** D3
  Norton IP31 ....**50** C4
Prospect Row IP33 ....**154** B2
Prospect Terr CB9 ....**133** F8
Providence La 1 IP5 ...**139** A7
Providence Stree IP1 ..**155** B3
Provost Rd CO10 ......**148** D5
Prussia La IP3 ....**140** A3
Puddingmoor NR34 ....**111** A5
Puddleduck La NR34 ...**111** F3
Pug St IP21 ....**21** A6
Pump Cl IP13 ....**84** C7
Pump Ct 9 CO10 ....**78** D4
Pump House La IP17 ....**57** A8
Pump La IP13 ....**154** B2
Pump St
  Needham Market IP6 ...**125** E4
  Orford IP12 ....**131** C2
Punchard Way IP11 ....**152** C8
Purcell Rd IP14 ......**124** B8

Purdis Ave IP3 ....**140** F2
Purdis Farm La
  Foxhall IP10 ....**141** C2
  Ipswich IP3 ....**140** F2
  Purdis Farm IP10 ......**141** B2
Purdis Rd IP10 ....**141** D2
Purplett St IP2 ....**155** C1
Putney Cl IP27 ....**14** E8
Puttocks La CO7 ......**151** E5
Pyes Meadow 1 NR30 ...**50** F2
Pykenham Way IP7 ....**149** D6
Pytches Cl 2 IP12 ....**147** B6
Pytches Rd IP12 ......**147** A6**

Q

Quadling St IP1 ......**155** B2
Quail Cl IP14 ....**124** F7
Quaker La Bardwell IP31 ..**34** C4
  Beyton IP30 ....**49** F1
Quaker's La 2 CB9 .....**132** E5
Quakers' Rd IP18 ......**119** C5
Quakers Way 3 IP16 ...**129** D5
Quantock Cl IP5 ....**140** F7
Quantrill Terr IP5 ....**141** D6
Quarries Cross IP14 ....**66** C8
Quaves La NR35 ....**110** B4
Quay La Reydon IP18 ...**26** D1
  Sudbury CO10 ....**148** C4
Quay Side IP12 ....**147** A4
Quay St
  Halesworth IP19 ......**118** B4
  8 Manningtree CO11 ...**104** E2
  Orford IP12 ....**131** C2
  Woodbridge IP12 ......**147** A4
Quay The 1 CO12 ......**107** B3
Quay Theatre The*
  CO10 ....**148** C4
Quay View NR32 ....**113** A1
Quay's Rd IP9 ....**47** E5
Quayside CIP27 ....**109** C2
Quebec Dr IP5 ....**141** B8
Queech La IP9 ....**105** B4
Queech The IP9 ....**150** F4
Queen Edith Dr CB9 ....**88** E3
Queen Elizabeth Cl
  IP16 ....**129** C4
Queen Elizabeth Dr
  NR34 ....**111** D3
Queen St Cowling CB8 ..**61** B1
  6 Hadleigh IP7 ....**149** D6
  Haverhill CB9 ....**132** E6
  Ipswich IP1 ....**155** B2
  Newmarket CB8 ....**121** B3
  Southwold IP18 ....**119** C5
  Stradbroke IP21 ....**39** B5
Queen's Cl IP33 ....**122** E5
Queen's Dr IP28 ....**116** B4
Queen's Head La IP12 ..**146** F5
Queen's Head Rd CO4 ...**102** F1
Queen's Highway
  NR32 ....**112** C2
Queen's Rd
  Beccles NR34 ....**111** B6
  Bungay NR35 ....**110** B4
  Bury St Edmunds IP33 ..**154** A2
  Felixstowe IP11 ....**153** A3
  4 Harwich CO12 ....**107** A1
  Lowestoft NR32 ....**113** D3
  Southwold IP18 ....**119** D4
Queens' Way IP3 ......**140** B2
Queens Ave 1 IP27 ....**14** E8
Queens Cl Combs IP14 ..**124** A1
  Halesworth IP19 ......**118** A2
  Saxmundham IP17 .....**128** C3
  Sudbury CO10 ....**148** C6
Queens Ct CB9 ....**132** C6
Queens La CB9 ....**132** E5
Queens Ln IP29 ....**62** D5
Queens Rd Brandon IP27 ..**14** E8
  1 Southwold IP18 .....**119** C5
  Sudbury CO10 ....**148** C6
Queens Sq 2 CB9 ......**132** E6
Queens St CB9 ....**74** B2
Queens View CB8 .....**120** A8
Queensberry Rd
  5 Ipswich IP3 ....**144** B8
  Newmarket CB8 ....**121** A3
Queenscliffe Rd IP2 ...**139** A3
Queensdale Cl IP1 .....**135** B1
Queensdale Rd IP1 .....**135** B1
Queensgate Dr IP4 ....**139** F8
Queensland IP2 ....**138** F1
Queensway 3 Acton CO10 ..**92** B7
  7 Earsham NR35 ....**7** F4
  Exning CB8 ....**120** B8
  Haverhill CB9 ....**132** E6
  8 Manningtree CO11 ...**104** E2
  2 Mildenhall IP28 .....**116** B4
  8 Soham CB7 ....**28** D4
  Sudbury CO10 ....**148** F3
  Thetford IP24 ....**16** B3
Queensway Com Jun Sch 7
  IP24 ....**16** B3
Queensway Inf Sch
  IP24 ....**16** B5
Quendon Pl CB9 ....**132** F6
Quentin Cl IP1 ....**134** F2
Quilter Dr Ipswich IP8 ..**138** C1
Quilter Rd IP11 ......**152** C8
Quilter Rd IP11 ......**153** A4
Quince Cl 3 CO11 .....**104** E5
Quinnell Way 5 NR32 ..**113** A6
Quinton Cl IP7 ....**149** C4
Quinton's La CO7 .....**151** C5
Quintons Cnr CO7 .....**151** D6

Quintons Rd CO7 ......**151** C5
Quoits Field 2 IP6 ....**134** C8
Quoits Meadow IP14 ....**68** B6**

R

Rackham Cl 1 NR31 .....**3** B7
Radcliffe Dr IP2 .....**138** D2
Radcliffe Rd 8 IP27 ...**14** A2
Radiator Rd CO10 .....**148** E3
Radleys La CO6 ....**102** B6
Radnor Cl IP23 ....**128** C4
Raeburn Rd IP3 ....**139** F1
Raeburn Rd S IP3 .....**139** E1
Redwald Dr IP13 ......**123** D5
Raedwald Way IP14 ....**53** F1
Rag's La IP30 ....**50** D1
Raglan Rd 2 NR32 ....**113** D1
Raglan St NR32 ......**113** D5
Raile Wlk CO10 ....**91** E8
Railway App IP11 .....**153** A5
Railway Cl CB5 ....**44** A4
Railway Hill CO10 .....**22** C6
Railway St CO11 .....**104** E2
Railway Terr CB9 .....**133** E7
Raine Ave CB9 ....**132** B6
Rainey Ct 37 IP20 .....**22** D6
Raingate St IP33 .....**154** C1
Raleigh Cl CO10 ......**148** E8
Raleigh Inf Sch 1 IP24 ..**16** C7
Raleigh Rd CO10 .....**148** E8
Ram La NR35 ....**21** C8
Rampart Way IP24 .....**16** C5
Rampling Cl IP27 .....**149** D7
Ramsey Cl IP2 ....**139** A1
Ramsey Rd
  Hadleigh IP7 ....**149** F7
  Harwich CO12 ....**106** D1
Ramsgate Dr IP3 .....**140** B3
Randall Cl
  2 Hopton on Sea NR31 ..**3** B7
  Ipswich IP1 ....**141** E7
Randolph Cl IP14 .....**140** B5
Rands Rd IP7 ....**149** B1
Rands Way IP3 ....**140** B4
Randwell Cl IP4 ......**140** B5
Ranelagh Prim Sch
  IP2 ....**138** F5
Ranelagh Rd
  Felixstowe IP11 ....**153** A4
  Ipswich IP2 ....**155** A1
Ransom Rd 2 IP12 .....**146** E6
Ransome Ave IP21 .....**21** A2
Ransome Cl IP8 ....**138** A6
Ransome Cres IP3 .....**140** B2
Ransome Rd IP3 ......**140** B2
Ransomes Europark
  IP10 ....**144** F7
Ransomes Way IP3 ....**140** D1
Ranson Rd IP6 ....**125** C4
Rant Score NR32 ......**113** E2
Ranville NR33 ....**114** E3
Ranworth Ave NR33 ...**114** E5
Raphael Wlk 18 IP2 ...**113** B6
Rapier St 6 IP2 ......**139** C3
Rare Breeds Farm*
  CO7 ....**151** A1
Rat Hill IP9 ....**106** C5
Rattla Cnr IP16 ....**58** C5
Rattler's Rd IP27 ......**14** A2
Rattlerow Hill IP21 ....**39** B6
Rattlesden CE Prim Sch
  IP30 ....**65** D6
Rattlesden Cl 2 IP14 ..**124** D3
Rattlesden Rd IP30 ....**65** C6
Raven Cl
  Mildenhall IP28 ....**116** D3
  Stowmarket IP14 ......**124** F7
Raven Rd NR33 ....**123** C1
Raven Way IP7 ....**149** D4
Raveningham Rd NR34 ...**9** E8
Ravens La IP8 ....**134** A2
Ravens Way 6 IP12 ....**84** A1
Ravensfield Rd IP1 ...**134** E1
Ravensmere NR34 .....**111** B6
Ravensmere Cty Inf Sch
  NR34 ....**111** B7
Ravensmere E NR34 ...**111** B6
Ravenswood Ave IP3 ...**144** C8
Ravenswood Com Prim Sch
  IP3 ....**144** C8
Ravenswood Mews
  NR33 ....**115** A5
Ravine NR34 ....**115** C5
Rawlings Way 22 IP26 ..**4** E5
Ray Ave CO12 ....**107** A2
Ray La 8 CO12 ....**106** F3
Raydon Croft IP14 ....**124** F3
Raydon La IP7 ....**131** D3
Raydon Rd CO7 ....**150** A4
Raydon Way CO10 ......**92** B3
Rayes La CB8 ....**121** A4
Rayleigh Rd IP1 ......**134** C1
Rayment Drift 5 IP5 ..**141** C7
Rayner's La NR35 ....**8** D8
Raynham Rd IP32 .....**154** A4
Raynsford Rd IP30 .....**63** F7
Reach Rd CB5 ....**44** A5
Reade Rd 5 IP9 ....**105** E7
Reading Gn IP21 ....**38** D4
Reading Rd IP4 ......**140** B7
Reading's La IP31 .....**35** A2
Rebow Rd 6 CO12 .....**107** A1
Reckford Rd IP17 ......**58** B6
Recreation La IP11 ...**152** F6
Recreation Rd
  Haverhill CB9 ....**132** D5

Recreation Rd continued
Stowmarket IP14 . . . . .124 C6
Recreation Way
Ipswich IP3 . . . . .140 C2
Mildenhall IP28 . . . . .116 C4
Recreation Wlk CO10 . . .148 F3
Rectory Cl
Beccles NR34 . . . . .111 F4
3 Glemsford CO10 . . . . . . .77 F3
Ousden CB8 . . . . .61 E6
Raydon IP7 . . . . .94 F1
Rectory Gdns IP30 . . . . . .49 F1
Rectory Gr IP19 . . . . .118 A4
Rectory Gr IP29 . . . . .63 B5
Rectory Hill
Botesdale IP22 . . . . .35 F6
East Bergholt CO7 . . . . . . .151 C4
Polstead CO6 . . . . .102 E8
Rickinghall Superior IP22 . .36 A5
Rectory La Beccles NR34 . .9 F3
Brantham CO11 . . . . .104 F5
Hintlesham IP8 . . . . .7 D8
Hintlesham IP8 . . . . .95 C6
Kettlebaston IP7 . . . . .79 B5
Kirton IP10 . . . . .98 D2
Mettingham NR35 . . . . .110 F3
4 Ramsey & Parkeston
CO12 . . . . .106 C3
Scole IP21 . . . . .21 C5
Stuston IP21 . . . . .37 D8
Whatfield IP7 . . . . .80 C1
3 Woolpit IP30 . . . . .50 D1
Rectory Meadow **5** IP28 . .88 B6
Rectory Pk **3** CO10 . . . . . .93 C3
Rectory Pl IP29 . . . . .47 A1
Rectory Rd
Aldeby/Wheatacre/Burgh
St Peter NR34 . . . . .10 A8
Bacton IP14 . . . . .51 E5
Blaxhall IP12 . . . . .71 F4
Brome & Oakley IP23 . . . . .117 B7
Broome NR35 . . . . .8 B7
Burston & Shimpling IP22 . .20 E6
Dickleburgh IP21 . . . . .21 B5
Gillingham NR34 . . . . .9 B7
Gissing IP22 . . . . .20 F8
Great Waldingfield CO10 . . .92 D6
Harkstead IP9 . . . . .106 B6
Hemingstone IP6 . . . . .68 C1
Hollesley IP12 . . . . .99 F7
Ipswich IP2 . . . . .155 A1
Kedington CB9 . . . . .133 F8
Langham CO4 . . . . .103 C3
6 Lowestoft NR33 . . . . . . .115 C6
Mellis IP23 . . . . .36 F5
Middleton CO10 . . . . .148 C2
Newton CO10 . . . . .92 D2
Orford IP12 . . . . .131 C3
Shelfanger IP22 . . . . .20 B6
Sotterley NR34 . . . . .26 A7
Tivetshall St Mary NR15 . . .21 C8
Whepstead IP29 . . . . .63 B4
Wortham IP22 . . . . .19 F1
Wrabness CO11 . . . . .106 A2
Wyverstone IP14 . . . . .51 D6
Rectory St IP19 . . . . .118 B4
Red Barn Rd **4** CO6 . . .102 C4
Red Barn Piece **1** IP13 . .83 E5
Red Dock La CB8 . . . . . . .61 C1
Red Hall Cl IP11 . . . . . . .153 C4
Red Hill IP7 . . . . .94 D7
Red Hill Rd IP7 . . . . .149 D8
Red House **5** IP15 . . . . .130 C6
Red House Cl
3 Felixstowe IP11 . . . . . . .107 D8
Lowestoft NR32 . . . . .112 F6
Red House La
Leiston IP16 . . . . .129 D4
Sudbury CO10 . . . . .148 E2
Red House Rd IP13 . . . . . .56 B8
Red House Wlk IP10 . . . .145 E4
Red La
Capel St Mary IP9 . . . . .150 F7
Sternfield IP17 . . . . .72 D8
Red Lion Cl IP21 . . . . .38 C7
Red Rose Cl IP12 . . . . .99 E4
Red Sleeve IP9 . . . . .150 D3
Redan St IP1 . . . . .155 A4
Redbarn La IP17 . . . . .72 D7
Redcastle Furze Prim Sch **3**
IP24 . . . . .16 B5
Reddells Cl CO10 . . . . . . .148 D5
Rede La IP6 . . . . .134 F8
Rede Rd IP29 . . . . .62 F4
Rede Way CO10 . . . . .92 B3
Rede Wood Nature Reserve *
IP6 . . . . .134 E8
Redenhall Rd IP20 . . . . . . .22 D6
Redgate IP7 . . . . .124 C6
Redgate La IP9 . . . . .143 D5
Redgrave & Lopham Fen National Nature Reserve *
IP22 . . . . .19 C2
Redgrave & Lopham Fen Visitor Ctr * IP22 . . . . . . .19 C3
Redgrave Rd IP22 . . . . .19 B3
Redhouse Gdns **6** CB7 . .28 D3
Redhouse La
Bawdsey IP12 . . . . .101 E1
Boxted CO4 . . . . .102 E1
1 Sudbury CO10 . . . . . . .148 C5
Redisham Cl NR32 . . . . . .113 A5
Redisham Rd
Redisham NR34 . . . . .25 B6
Weston NR34 . . . . .9 C1
Redlingfield Rd
Horham IP21 . . . . .38 D2

Redlingfield Rd continued
Occold IP23 . . . . .37 F2
Redshank Cl CB9 . . . . . . .133 A5
Redwald Rd IP12 . . . . .85 E8
Redwing Cl IP2 . . . . .138 D3
Redwing Rd IP33 . . . . . . .123 C1
Redwings Horse Sanctuary (Caldecott) * NR31 . . . . . .2 C8
Redwings Horse Sanctuary (Stonham) * IP14 . . . . . . .68 C6
Redwold Cl IP12 . . . . .146 C1
Redwood Gdns IP33 . . . .154 C2
Redwood La **2** IP27 . . . .13 F2
Reed's Bldgs IP33 . . . . . . .154 C3
Reedland Way **4** IP11 . . .152 D5
Reeds La CB9 . . . . .132 E6
Reeds Way IP14 . . . . .67 A7
Reet **1** NR32 . . . . .115 D8
Reeve Cl
2 Bury St Edmunds IP32 . .48 C5
Scole IP21 . . . . .21 A2
Reeve Gdns IP5 . . . . .141 C8
Reeve St NR32 . . . . .113 D2
Reeve's Cl NR35 . . . . .110 C3
Reeves La IP26 . . . . .5 A3
Refinery Rd CO12 . . . . . . .106 F3
Regal Dr CB7 . . . . .28 C3
Regal La CB7 . . . . .28 E3
Regan Cl NR32 . . . . .113 A5
Regent Pl **3** CB7 . . . . .28 D3
Regent Rd NR32 . . . . .113 D1
Regent St
20 Manningtree CO11 . . . .104 E2
Stowmarket IP14 . . . . .124 D7
Regent Theatre * IP4 . . . .155 C3
Regents Ct **6** CB8 . . . . . .121 A4
Regimental Mus *
IP33 . . . . .122 E6
Regimental Way
18 Harwich CO12 . . . . . . .106 E1
9 Ramsey CO12 . . . . .106 E1
Regina Cl IP4 . . . . .140 B5
Reigate Cl IP3 . . . . .140 B3
Rembrandt Cl IP3 . . . . . . .140 B5
Rembrandt Ct NR32 . . . . .113 C6
Rembrandt Gdns **4**
IP3 . . . . .122 F3
Rembrandt Way IP23 . . . . .123 A3
Rembrow Rd IP9 . . . . .150 E3
Remembrance Rd
IP16 . . . . .73 F6
Remercie Rd IP14 . . . . . . .105 A2
Rendall La IP30 . . . . .67 A8
Rendham Hill IP17 . . . . . . .56 F7
Rendham Rd
Bruisyard IP17 . . . . .56 D4
Kelsale cum Carlton
IP17 . . . . .128 A6
Peasenhall IP17 . . . . .56 F7
Rendlesham Est * IP12 . .85 D6
Rendlesham Forest Ctr *
IP12 . . . . .85 F3
Rendlesham Rd
6 Felixstowe IP11 . . . . . . .152 D5
9 Ipswich IP1 . . . . .139 A7
Renfrew Rd IP4 . . . . .136 B1
Renoir Pl **2** NR32 . . . . . .113 B5
Renson Cl IP30 . . . . .64 F8
Reydon Bsns Pk IP18 . . . .119 C8
Reydon Cl **2** IP30 . . . . . .132 A6
Reydon La IP18 . . . . .26 D1
Reydon Mews NR32 . . . . .113 A6
Reydon Prim Sch
IP18 . . . . .119 C8
Reydon Wood Nature Reserve * IP34 . . . . .26 C2
Reynolds Ave **2** IP13 . . .144 A8
Reynolds Ct **6** IP11 . . . . .152 D5
Reynolds Rd IP3 . . . . .140 A1
Reynolds Way CO10 . . . . .148 E8
Reynolds Wlk
Bury St Edmunds IP33 . . . .122 B6
Gunton NR32 . . . . .113 B6
Ribblesdale NR33 . . . . . . .114 E3
Riby Rd IP11 . . . . .152 F3
Richard Burwin Way
CO10 . . . . .148 C8
Richard Crampton Rd
NR34 . . . . .111 A4
Richard Easter Rd IP24 . . .16 C7
Richards Dr IP13 . . . . .137 D5
Richard's Cl NR33 . . . . . .114 E6
Richardson Rd CO7 . . . . . .151 F5
Richardsons La IP10 . . . .106 B8
Richer Cl IP31 . . . . .50 F7
Richer Rd IP31 . . . . .50 F7
Richmond Cres **8** CO4 . .107 A1
Richmond Pl **8** NR33 . . .115 C6
Richmond Rd
Brandon IP27 . . . . .14 C6
Ipswich IP1 . . . . .138 F7
7 Lowestoft NR33 . . . . . .115 C6
Riddlesworth Hall Sch
IP22 . . . . .17 F4
Rider Haggard La **7**
NR33 . . . . .11 C1
Rider Haggard Way
NR35 . . . . .110 C2
Ridgeville **9** NR33 . . . . . .114 F3
Ridgeway IP2 . . . . .124 B6
Ridgeway The **10** CO12 . .107 A2
Ridgeways The IP14 . . . . . .51 A7
Ridgewell Rd CO10 . . . . . .89 D5
Ridings The
3 Beccles NR34 . . . . .111 F4
Leavenheath CO6 . . . . .102 B8
Ridley Rd IP3 . . . . .122 C6
Rigbourne Hill NR34 . . . . .111 C3

Rigbourne Hill La **6**
NR34 . . . . .111 C2
Rigby Ave CO11 . . . . .105 A2
Riley Cl IP1 . . . . .134 C1
Rimmer Cl IP10 . . . . .148 E8
Ringham Rd IP4 . . . . .140 A6
Ringsfield CE VCP Sch
NR34 . . . . .9 B2
Ringsfield Rd
Beccles NR34 . . . . .111 A4
6 Lowestoft NR32 . . . . . .113 A3
Ringsfield NR34 . . . . .9 A1
Ringshall Prim Sch
IP14 . . . . .80 E6
Rio Cl **3** NR32 . . . . .114 C5
Risbridge Dr CB9 . . . . . . .133 E8
Risby Barn Antique & Craft Ctr * IP28 . . . . .47 D5
Risby CE VC Prim Sch
IP28 . . . . .47 D5
Risby Cl IP4 . . . . .140 B6
Risbygate St IP33 . . . . . . .154 B2
Risewaye Cl IP33 . . . . . . .123 B1
Rishton Rd IP27 . . . . .109 C2
Rising Sun Hill IP30 . . . . . .65 D5
Rissemere La E IP18 . . . .119 C8
Ritabrook Rd IP2 . . . . .138 E1
Rivendale NR33 . . . . .114 D3
River Gdns IP14 . . . . .124 E4
River Hill IP8 . . . . .138 A5
River La Fordham CB7 . . . . .29 A1
Halesworth IP19 . . . . .118 B3
River View NR34 . . . . .111 B7
River View Rd **1** IP9 . . . .106 A5
Riverbank Cl CO10 . . . . . . .90 B8
Rivers St IP4 . . . . .139 F7
Riverside
4 Framlingham IP13 . . . . .126 C3
Haskerton IP13 . . . . .146 A7
Palgrave IP22 . . . . .20 B2
Riverside Ave E **6**
CO11 . . . . .104 E3
Riverside Ave W **4**
CO11 . . . . .104 E3
Riverside Bsns Ctr
NR33 . . . . .115 C8
Riverside Cl IP28 . . . . .116 B4
Riverside Ct IP32 . . . . . . .123 A8
Riverside Ind Est IP12 . . .127 C7
Riverside Ind Pk IP2 . . . .139 D3
Riverside Mid Sch
IP28 . . . . .116 B4
Riverside Rd
Ipswich IP1 . . . . .138 F7
Lowestoft NR33 . . . . .115 B8
Riverside Theatre The *
IP12 . . . . .147 A4
Riverside View IP13 . . . . .127 C8
Riverside Way IP27 . . . . . . .5 F2
Riverview IP27 . . . . .147 C7
Riverwalk Sch IP33 . . . . .154 A1
Rivish La CO10 . . . . .91 E8
Rixon Cres IP3 . . . . .84 E6
Roamwood Gn La IP14 . . .53 C3
Robeck Rd IP3 . . . . .139 E1
Robert Boby Way
IP33 . . . . .154 B2
Robert's Hill CO8 . . . . . . .101 C2
Robin Cl Haverhill CB9 . . .133 A5
Mildenhall IP28 . . . . .116 D4
18 Stowmarket IP14 . . . . .67 A5
12 Thurstow IP31 . . . . . . .49 D4
Robin Dr IP2 . . . . .138 D3
Robin Rd NR32 . . . . .113 A2
Robin Rd IP33 . . . . .123 B1
Robin Way CO10 . . . . .148 A3
Robins Cl **16** CB7 . . . . . . .29 C5
Robinson Cl IP33 . . . . . . .122 D6
Robinson Rd **7** IP21 . . . . .20 F1
Robinson Wlk IP32 . . . . . .122 D7
Robletts IP3 . . . . .84 D7
Rochdale Wa **1** CO6 . . . . .61 F3
Rochdale **3** NR33 . . . . . . .114 F3
Rochester Rd NR33 . . . . . .115 B4
Rochester Way CO10 . . . .148 B8
Rochford Ave CB8 . . . . . . .120 E5
Rock Rd NR32 . . . . .112 D1
Rockall Cl CB8 . . . . .61 B6
Rockall Cl CB8 . . . . .133 B5
Rockalls Rd CO6 . . . . .102 E8
Rockingham Rd IP33 . . . . .123 B3
Rockstone La IP19 . . . . . . .41 C7
Rodber Way IP30 . . . . . . .113 A6
Rodbridge Hill CO10 . . . . . .91 B6
Rodney Ct IP2 . . . . .146 F7
Roebuck Dr IP27 . . . . .109 E4
Roebuck The IP27 . . . . . . .109 E1
Roger's Cl NR31 . . . . .3 B7
Roger's La CO10 . . . . .92 F4
Rogerson Cl CO10 . . . . . . .75 D3
Rogers Cl IP11 . . . . .152 F6
Rogue's La IP13 . . . . .127 C5
Rokewood Pl IP29 . . . . . . .64 A3
Roman Cl **2** CB5 . . . . .44 A5
Roman Hill Mid Sch
NR32 . . . . .113 C1
Roman Hill Prim Sch
NR32 . . . . .113 C1

Romany Rd NR32 . . . . . . .114 C8
Romany Way IP33 . . . . . . .123 D3
Romney Pl **6** NR32 . . . . . .113 B4
Romney Rd IP3 . . . . .140 A1
Romsey Rd IP33 . . . . .122 D3
Ronald La IP17 . . . . .128 D5
Ronden Cl NR34 . . . . .111 B2
Rook's La IP2 . . . . .111 B5
Rookery Chase CO7 . . . . .103 F1
Rookery Cl NR33 . . . . .114 F7
Rookery Dro **2** IP28 . . . . .13 B1
Rookery La IP19 . . . . .23 F4
Rookery Rd Elmsett IP7 . . .80 E2
Moneweden IP13 . . . . .69 F5
Rookery Sth Cir CB8 . . . . . .121 B4
Rookery The
Brandon IP27 . . . . .5 D1
Eye IP23 . . . . .117 D2
4 Mannington CO11 . . . . .104 E2
Newmarket CB8 . . . . .121 B3
Rookery Way IP14 . . . . . . .51 F1
Rookery Wlk IP27 . . . . . . .109 B7
Rookwood La CO10 . . . . . . .78 F6
Rookwood Way CO10 . . . .132 E4
Roosevelt Wlk **5** NR33 . .114 C5
Rope Wlk
Carlton Colville NR33 . . . . .114 B4
Ipswich IP4 . . . . .155 C2
Roper's Ct **3** CO10 . . . . . .91 D7
Ropers La CO10 . . . . .78 D4
Ropes Dr IP5 . . . . .141 B8
Rosbrook Cl **1** IP33 . . . .122 D4
Rose Acre CO7 . . . . .103 F7
Rose Ave IP22 . . . . .20 A3
Rose Ct Lowestoft NR32 . .113 B2
Shotley IP9 . . . . .106 F6
Rose Gn CO10 . . . . .101 F8
Rose Gn La **4** IP28 . . . . . .30 B8
Rose Hall Gdns NR35 . . . .110 B3
Rose Hill
Grundisburgh IP13 . . . . .83 E5
Withersfield CB9 . . . . .74 B3
Witnesham IP6 . . . . .135 F7
Rose Hill Prim Sch
IP3 . . . . .140 A4
Rose La Botesdale IP22 . . . .36 A7
Bungay NR35 . . . . .110 B3
Diss IP22 . . . . .20 D1
Elmswell IP30 . . . . .50 E2
Ipswich IP4 . . . . .155 B2
Wickham Skeith IP23 . . . . . .52 D8
Rose La Cl IP22 . . . . .20 C1
Rose Wlk IP6 . . . . .125 D3
Rosebay Gdns **1** CB7 . . . .28 C4
Rosebery Rd
Felixstowe IP11 . . . . .153 B4
Ipswich IP4 . . . . .139 F5
Rosebery Way CB8 . . . . . .120 E5
Rosecroft Rd IP1 . . . . .135 A2
Rosecroft Way IP24 . . . . . .16 D6
Rosedale Gdns **8** NR33 . .114 D3
Rosefinch Cl CB9 . . . . .133 A5
Rosehill Cres IP3 . . . . .139 F4
Rosehill Rd IP3 . . . . .139 F4
Rosemary Ave IP11 . . . . . .153 B5
Rosemary Cl **4** IP28 . . . . .30 C1
Rosemary Gdns CO10 . . . .148 D8
Rosemary La
Ipswich IP4 . . . . .155 B2
Kelsale cum Carlton
IP17 . . . . .128 C6
Rosemary Musker Cty High Sch IP24 . . . . .16 C7
Rosemary Rd **5** IP32 . . . . .48 C5
Rosery La IP17 . . . . .137 F6
Rosewood NR33 . . . . .115 A5
Rosewood Cl **22** IP27 . . . .13 F2
Ross Cl CB9 . . . . .132 A6
Ross Peers Sports Ctr The
CB7 . . . . .28 D3
Ross Rd IP4 . . . . .136 B1
Rosyth Rd **5** IP31 . . . . . . .33 D5
Rotheram Rd IP7 . . . . .79 F4
Rotten Row CO10 . . . . .92 D2
Rotterdam Rd NR32 . . . . .113 B1
Rougham CE Prim Sch
IP30 . . . . .49 D1
Rougham Control Twr Museum * IP30 . . . . .49 B3
Rougham Hill IP33 . . . . . .123 D3
Rougham Ind Est IP30 . . . .49 B2
Rougham Rd
Bradfield St George IP30 . . .64 D7
Bury St Edmunds IP33 . . . .123 C3
Roughhams IP27 . . . . .109 D6
Roundridge Rd IP30 . . . . .150 F4
Roundwood Rd IP4 . . . . . .140 A7
Rous Meml Ct CB8 . . . . . .121 B3
Rous Rd CB8 . . . . .121 B3
Rousies Cl **6** IP7 . . . . .149 E6
Routh Ave IP3 . . . . .140 C4
Row The Bramford IP8 . . . .134 A2
Gipsy Row CO7 . . . . .150 A4
Stratford St Mary CO7 . . . . .103 E5
Rowan Cl Haverhill CB9 . . .132 C7
Priory Heath IP3 . . . . .140 D2
Rowan Dr Brandon IP27 . . .14 F8
Bury St Edmunds IP32 . . . .123 F6
Rowan Gn **7** IP30 . . . . . . .50 F2
Rowan Way
Beccles NR34 . . . . .111 E3
Lowestoft NR33 . . . . .114 D6
5 Thurstow IP31 . . . . .49 D4
Rowan Wlk IP28 . . . . .116 E5
Rowanhayes Cl IP2 . . . . . .139 B3
Rowans Way **1** CO6 . . . . .102 A7
Rowarth Ave IP5 . . . . .141 C7
Rowe's Hill IP13 . . . . .40 C2

Rowell Cl CB9 . . . . .132 E8
Rowell's La IP14 . . . . .51 D4
Rowley Cl **7** CO11 . . . . . .104 E3
Rowley Ct
Newmarket CB8 . . . . .120 E3
Sturmer CB9 . . . . .133 C3
Rowley Dr CB8 . . . . .120 F3
Rowley Hill CB9 . . . . .133 B8
Rowntree Cl NR32 . . . . . . .113 A6
Rows The CB8 . . . . .120 E3
Roxburgh Rd IP4 . . . . .136 B1
Roy Ave IP4 . . . . .140 B5
Roy Cl IP5 . . . . .141 B7
Royal Ave NR32 . . . . .113 D4
Royal Hospl Sch IP9 . . . . .105 E6
Royal Naval Patrol Service Mus * 113 E3
Royal Pal Cl CB8 . . . . .120 D7
Royal Plain NR33 . . . . .115 D8
Royal Terr NR33 . . . . .115 D7
Roydon Fen IP22 . . . . .20 B2
Roydon Prim Sch IP22 . . . .20 B3
Roydon Rd IP22 . . . . .20 C3
Roydon Way **10** IP22 . . . .112 F4
Roylands La CO10 . . . . .93 D3
Royston Dr IP2 . . . . .138 D2
Rozlyne Cl **1** NR33 . . . . . .114 E4
Rubens Rd IP3 . . . . .140 A1
Rubens Wlk
Gunton NR32 . . . . .113 B6
Sudbury CO10 . . . . .148 E8
Ruby Cl **9** NR32 . . . . .3 D4
Rudlands IP8 . . . . .138 C1
Rudlands Cl **6** CB7 . . . . . .29 C5
Rue's La IP11 . . . . .153 C8
Ruffles Rd CB9 . . . . .133 A5
Rugby Rd CO10 . . . . .148 F2
Rumburgh La NR35 . . . . . .24 D6
Rumburgh Rd
Lowestoft NR32 . . . . .113 B5
Rumburgh IP19 . . . . .24 B3
Run Meadow NR33 . . . . . .114 C6
Run The NR34 . . . . .26 A7
Runce's La NR32 . . . . .114 C3
Runnacles Way IP11 . . . . .152 D5
Runnymede Gn IP33 . . . . .123 A3
Rush Cl IP4 . . . . .140 E4
Rushall Rd IP20 . . . . .22 B6
Rushbrooke La IP33 . . . . .123 C4
Rushbury Cl IP4 . . . . .140 D3
Rushford Rd
Coney Weston IP31 . . . . .17 E1
Euston IP24 . . . . .16 D4
Rushlake Way **7** NR33 . . .114 C6
Rushmeadow Way **1**
IP11 . . . . .153 D7
Rushmere Hall Prim Sch
IP4 . . . . .136 A1
Rushmere Pl CB7 . . . . .132 F6
Rushmere Rd
Gisleham NR33 . . . . .114 B1
Ipswich IP4 . . . . .140 A4
Rushmere NR33 . . . . .10 F3
Rushmere St IP5 . . . . .136 E1
Rushton Dr NR33 . . . . . . .114 B3
Ruskin Cl IP4 . . . . .122 B8
Ruskin Rd IP4 . . . . .139 F5
Russell Baron Rd IP31 . . . .48 D5
Russell Cl IP12 . . . . .146 E6
Russell Rd
Felixstowe IP11 . . . . .152 F2
Ipswich IP1 . . . . .155 A3
Russell's Gn NR34 . . . . .9 C2
Russet Cl
1 Beccles NR34 . . . . .111 C3
Great Barton IP32 . . . . .123 E7
Russett Cl CB9 . . . . .132 A6
Rutland Cl **15** CB9 . . . . . .132 C5
Rutland Sq CO10 . . . . .154 C1
Rydal Ave IP11 . . . . .153 D7
Rydal Cl IP14 . . . . .124 B6
Rydal Wlk IP3 . . . . .140 C2
Ryders Way **8** IP22 . . . . . .36 A6
Rye Cl Ipswich IP3 . . . . . . .140 D4
3 Lowestoft NR33 . . . . . .114 D4
Rye Ct **8** CB9 . . . . .132 C5
Ryeburn Cl **1** NR33 . . . . . .11 B1
Ryedale IP14 . . . . .124 B6
Ryefields IP31 . . . . .49 E4
Ryes La CO10 . . . . .91 D1
Ryes Sch The
Bulmer Tye CO10 . . . . .91 E1
Kesgrave IP5 . . . . .137 E3
Rylands IP4 . . . . .150 E4
Rylands Cl **1** IP31 . . . . . . .49 E4

S

Sackville St CB8 . . . . .121 B4
Sackville St IP14 . . . . .53 E1
Saddlemakers La
IP12 . . . . .147 C8
Saddlers Meadow **2**
IP13 . . . . .83 E5
Saddlers Pl **15** IP5 . . . . . . .98 A8
Saddlers Yd IP31 . . . . .34 B1
Saffron Sq NR33 . . . . .115 A2
Saffrons Cl IP30 . . . . .50 D1
Sagehayes Cl IP2 . . . . . . .139 B3
Sages End Rd CB9 . . . . . . .88 A4
St Agnes Way IP5 . . . . . . .140 F6
St Alban's Cath High Sch
IP4 . . . . .140 D7
St Albans CB8 . . . . .121 A6

St Andrew **2** C88 ....121 A4
St Andrew Cl **1** NR31 ....3 C7
St Andrew's Church Cl
IP5 ....136 D1
St Andrew's Cl IP12 ....147 D7
St Andrew's Ct **4** IP33 .154 B2
St Andrew's Dr **3** IP9 .106 C8
St Andrew's Pl IP17 ....147 D8
St Andrew's Rd
Beccles NR34 ....111 C2
Coldfair Green IP17 .....129 B2
Felixstowe IP11 ....153 A5
St Andrew's St IP28 ...116 C4
St Andrew's St N IP3 ....153 B4
St Andrew's St S IP33 ..154 B2
St Andrews CE VA Prim Sch
IP22 ....19 A5
St Andrews Cl
2 Barningham IP31 .....34 E7
3 Great Finborough IP14 .66 B4
Ipswich IP4 ....140 D5
3 Isleham CB7 ....29 C5
St Andrews Dr **7** IP28 .48 C6
St Andrews Mead 68 B8
St Andrews Rd
Scole IP21 ....21 A1
Sudbury CO10 ....148 E4
St Anne's Cl NR34 .....111 C4
St Anne's Dr IP28 ......116 C4
St Anne's Rd NR34 ....111 C4
St Annes Cl IP12 ....146 D3
St Anthony **3** C88 ....121 A4
St Anthonys Cres 139 F6
St Aubyn's Rd **5** NR33 .115 C6
St Aubyns Rd IP4 ......140 A5
St Audrys Pk Rd **5** IP12 .84 E6
St Audrys Rd IP12 ......84 E6
St Augustine Rd **3** ..140 D4
St Augustine's Gdns
IP3 ....140 D3
St Austell Cl IP5 ......141 A6
St Austin's La **1** CO12 .107 C3
St Barbara's Cl IP18 ..148 C5
St Bartholomews La
CO10 ....148 B7
St Benedict's Rd NR34 .111 B6
St Benedicts Cath Sch
IP32 ....122 F8
St Benedicts Rd IP27 ....6 A1
St Benet's Dr NR34 ....111 C3
St Benet's RC Minst
NR34 ....111 A4
St Benets RC Prim Sch
NR34 ....111 A5
St Botolph's La IP33 ...154 C1
St Botolph's Way C89 .132 D6
St Botolphs CE VC Prim Sch
IP22 ....36 B7
St Botolphs Pl **18** C89 .132 D5
St Catherine's Cl
NR33 ....114 E4
St Catherine's Ct IP2 .138 E1
St Catherine's Rd **11**
CO10 ....91 E8
St Catherines Cl IP28 .116 D6
St Clare Ct **15** NR31 ...3 B7
St Clement Mews **13** NR31 .3 B7
St Clement's Hospl
IP3 ....140 C4
St Clements Church La
IP4 ....155 C2
St Cross Rd IP20 ....23 B8
St David **4** C88 ......121 A4
St David's Cl **5** NR34 .111 C2
St David's Rd **7** IP33 .140 B3
St Denis Cl IP12 ......107 A1
St Denys **3** C88 ......121 A4
St Domonic's Dr IP9 ....6 A1
St Edmund Cl **5** IP31 ..34 B1
St Edmund Rd IP27 ......5 E4
St Edmund's Cl **1** IP21 .85 A5
St Edmund's Dr IP30 ...50 F2
St Edmund's Hill 101 B7
St Edmund's Pl IP1 ...139 C8
St Edmund's Rd
Felixstowe IP11 ....152 E2
Ipswich IP1 ....139 B8
Southwold IP18 ....119 D6
St Edmunds Cl
2 Beccles NR34 ....111 C2
12 Haverhill CO12 ......107 A1
Stowmarket IP14 ....124 C8
3 Woodbridge IP12 ....146 E4
St Edmunds Cres **1**
NR33 ....11 C1
St Edmunds Gate **11**
IP31 ....33 D5
St Edmunds La CO8 ....101 D5
St Edmunds Pl IP33 ...154 B3
St Edmunds Prim Sch
IP21 ....38 C6
St Edmunds RC Prim Sch
NR35 ....154 B1
St Edmunds Rd IP14 ...124 C7
St Edmunds Sq IP30 ...50 F2
St Edmundsbury Cath*
IP33 ....154 C2
St Edmundsbury CE VA Prim
Sch IP33 ....154 A3
St Edmundsbury Mews
IP33 ....154 B1
St Edmundsbury Ret Pk
IP32 ....123 E4

St Etienne IP14 ....69 E6
St Fabians Cl CB8 .....120 F5
St Fabians Ct CB8 .....120 E5
St Felix CE VE Mid Sch
CB8 ....120 F6
St Felix Cl **2** CB7 ....28 D5
St Felix RC Prim Sch
CB9 ....132 B5
St Felix Sch IP18 .....119 A6
St George **1** CB8 ....121 A4
St George's Ave **2**
CO12 ....107 B1
St George's Rd
Beccles NR34 ....111 B4
Felixstowe IP11 ....153 C6
Lowestoft NR33 ....115 B4
Stowlangtoft IP31 ......50 B7
St George's St IP1 ....155 B3
St Georges Sch IP18 ..119 A7
St Gotthards Ave IP12 ..98 B8
St Gregory Ct CO10 ...148 B6
St Gregorys CE VC Prim Sch
IP4 ....139 E6
St Gregorys La **5** IP12 .85 E8
St Helena Wlk IP28 ....116 C6
St Helen's St IP4 .....155 C3
St Helens Prim Sch
IP4 ....139 E6
St Helens Way IP24 ....16 B7
St Isidores IP5 ....141 E7
St Ives Cl IP5 ....141 A6
St James **8** CB8 .....121 A4
St James Ct **8** C89 ..132 C6
St James' Gn **2** IP18 .119 D5
St James La IP33 .....154 A2
St James' La
Chediston IP19 ....24 A3
St James, South Elmham
IP19 ....23 F4
St James Mid Sch
IP33 ....123 C5
St James St
All Saints & St Nicholas,
South Elmham IP19 ......24 A5
St James, South Elmham
IP19 ....23 F4
St James's St IP17 ....43 B1
St John's Cl IP28 .....116 D6
St John's Hill
Bungay NR35 ....110 C2
4 Woodbridge IP12 ....147 A5
St John's Pl IP33 .....154 B3
St John's Rd
Bungay NR35 ....110 B3
Ipswich IP4 ....140 A6
Lowestoft NR33 ....115 D7
Saxmundham IP17 ....128 C3
St John's St
Beck Row, Holywell Row
& Kenny Hill IP28 ......30 C8
Bury St Edmunds IP33 ..154 B3
Woodbridge IP12 ....147 A5
St John's Terr **5** IP12 .147 A5
St John's Way
18 Feltwell IP26 ......4 E5
Thetford IP24 ....16 A5
St Johns Ave CB8 .....121 A4
St Johns CE Prim Sch
IP4 ....140 A7
St Johns Ct IP11 .....153 A4
St Johns Meadow IP20 ..23 C3
St Josephs Coll IP2 ...139 A3
St Josephs RC Prim Sch
CO10 ....148 B6
St Lawrence Cl NR34 ..111 C2
St Lawrence Gn IP5 ...141 A7
St Lawrence Prim Sch
NR34 ....24 F6
St Lawrence Sch IP1 ..155 B3
St Lawrence Way IP5 ..141 B8
St Leonard's Rd **1**
NR33 ....115 C7
St Leonards Cl IP21 ...21 A1
St Leonards Hospl
CO10 ....148 D5
St Leonards Rd **2** IP3 .140 B3
St Leonards St IP26 ....6 B8
St Louis Cath Mid Sch
IP33 ....154 B1
St Louis RC Prim Sch
CB8 ....121 A4
St Margaret's Cres
Leiston IP16 ....129 B6
8 Thetford IP24 ......16 B5
St Margaret's Gn IP4 ..155 C3
St Margaret's Pl CB8 ..75 E7
St Margaret's Rd
Bungay NR35 ....110 B1
1 Lowestoft NR32 .....113 E3
St Margaret's St IP4 ..155 C3
St Margaret's Way **3**
NR31 ....3 B7
St Margarets CE VA Prim Sch
IP4 ....155 C3
St Margarets Com Prim Sch
NR32 ....113 C3
St Margarets Plain
IP4 ....155 B3
St Marks RC Prim Sch
IP2 ....138 F3
St Martin's Cl CB8 ....120 C7
St Martin's La IP24 ....16 B2
St Martin's St IP33 ...154 B3
St Martin's Way IP33 ..16 B5
St Martins Ct IP5 .....141 E7
St Martins Gn **14** IP11 .107 D8
St Mary's Ave **5** IP14 ..51 C1
St Mary's Cl Bacton IP14 .51 F6

St Mary's Cl continued
Bramford IP8 ....134 B1
Felixstowe IP11 ....152 B7
Flixton NR35 ....7 E1
Harleston IP20 ....22 E6
Horham IP21 ....38 F3
Mildenhall IP28 ....116 C3
Sudbury CO10 ....148 F8
St Mary's Cres
Badwell Ash IP31 ....50 E7
Felixstowe IP11 ....152 F6
St Mary's Gdns IP6 ...125 E5
St Mary's Rd
Aldeby NR34 ....10 A7
Beccles NR34 ....111 A5
Creeting St Mary IP6 ..125 E5
Stowmarket IP14 ....124 B7
St Mary's Sq IP33 ....154 C1
St Mary's St **7** NR35 ..110 B4
St Mary's Wlk C89 .....88 D3
St Marys Cath Prim Sch
IP4 ....139 F6
St Marys CE Aided Prim Sch
IP22 ....146 E5
St Marys CE VA Prim Sch
IP28 ....116 C5
St Marys Cl **1** IP23 ...36 D2
St Marys Pk IP10 ......98 A4
St Marys Prim Sch
IP7 ....149 E6
St Marys RC Prim Sch
NR33 ....115 C5
St Marys Rd IP4 ......139 F6
St Marys Sq **9** C88 ..121 A4
St Marys View IP31 ....49 E6
St Marys Way IP6 .....135 F4
St Mathew's St Service Rd
IP1 ....155 A3
St Matthew's Ave **3**
NR34 ....111 C2
St Matthew's CE VA Prim Sch
IP1 ....155 A3
St Matthew's St IP1 ...155 A3
St Michael's Cl
1 Beccles NR34 ....111 C2
Ipswich IP5 ....141 A6
Lowestoft NR32 ....112 C1
St Michael's Rd **4** CO12 .107 B2
St Michael's Way IP19 .42 C6
St Michaels Cl IP6 ...126 C4
St Michaels Ct **16** CO11 .104 C2
St Nicholas Cl
Bury St Edmunds IP32 .123 C6
Rattlesden IP30 ....65 D5
St Nicholas Ct IP1 ...155 B2
St Nicholas Dr **25** IP26 ...4 E5
St Nicholas St IP1 ....155 B2
St Olaves Prec IP32 ..122 D8
St Olaves Precinct
IP32 ....122 E8
St Olaves Rd
Bury St Edmunds IP32 .122 E8
Herring Fleet NR32 ......2 D4
Ipswich IP5 ....141 D8
St Osyth Cl IP2 ......142 F8
St Pancras Cath Prim Sch
IP1 ....134 F2
St Patrick **7** CB8 ....121 A4
St Paul's Cl
4 Beccles NR34 ....111 C2
Brockdish IP21 ....21 F2
St Pauls Ct IP15 .....104 C2
St Peter & Paul CE VA Prim
Sch IP23 ....117 D2
St Peter's Ave **1** IP6 .134 C8
St Peter's Brewery & Visitor
Ctr* NR35 ....24 A8
St Peter's Cl
Brockdish IP21 ....21 F2
8 Claydon IP6 ....82 A5
Stowmarket IP14 ....124 B6
Woodbridge IP12 ....146 D4
St Peter's Ct **16** CO10 ..148 C5
St Peter's Hall* NR35 ..24 A8
St Peter's Rd
Lowestoft NR33 ....115 C6
Stowmarket IP14 ....124 B6
St Peter's St
Ipswich IP1 ....155 B2
4 Lowestoft NR32 .....113 D2
St Peter's Wlk IP26 ....4 F3
St Peters Ave CB8 .....45 F2
St Peters Ct
Charsfield IP13 ....70 B3
6 Moulton CB8 ....45 F2
St Peters Dr IP33 ....154 B1
St Peters Path IP19 ...21 E3
St Peters Pl CB7 ......29 B1
St Peters Rd
Aldeburgh IP15 ....130 E5
Lowestoft NR33 ....114 C3
St Peters Way **11** IP31 .49 E4
St Philips Rd IP2 ....120 F5
St Quinton's Ct NR33 .115 B5
St Stephens Cl IP33 ..123 C6
St Stephens La IP1 ...155 B2
St Vincent Wlk **14** NR31 ...3 B7
St Wendred's Way
Salehurst Rd IP33 ....140 E3
Salisbury Cl IP29 .....63 E8
Salisbury Gn IP23 ....123 B3
Salisbury Rd
Ipswich IP3 ....140 A3
Lowestoft NR33 ....115 C7
1 Southwold IP18 .....119 D5

Salisbury Terr **1** CO10 .148 C6
Sallows Cl IP1 ....138 F7
Sally Wood's La IP6 ...125 F6
Salmet Cl IP22 ....139 A3
Salmon Wlk IP32 ......122 D7
Salmond Dr **5** IP24 ...16 C2
Salter Cl IP32 ....123 E4
Salter's Ct **6** IP13 ...83 E5
Salters Hall Mews
CO10 ....148 B5
Saltgate **5** NR34 .....111 B6
Salthouse La IP4 ......155 C2
Saltwater Way NR33 ..114 E8
Samford Cl IP9 ....105 E8
Samford Ct **8** NR34 ...111 F4
Samford Rd IP9 ....138 B6
Sampson Dr IP10 ......91 E8
Samson Cl **14** IP32 ...48 C5
Samson's La IP22 ......19 F4
Samuel Cl IP4 ....155 C3
Samuel St Wlk IP33 ...154 B2
Samuel Vince Rd **2**
IP21 ....39 D8
Samuel Ward Arts & Tech
Coll CB9 ....132 F7
San Francisco Wlk **3**
NR33 ....114 C5
Sancroft Way
3 Fressingfield IP21 ...39 D8
Wortwell IP20 ....23 A7
Sancroft Wlk IP33 ....122 B6
Sanctuary Gdns **4**
NR32 ....112 F5
Sanctuary The IP6 .....73 F6
Sanctuary Way IP33 ...111 B1
Sand Acre Cl IP28 ....116 D5
Sand Hill CO10 ....93 C3
Sand St CB7 ....28 D3
Sandbank Rd NR33 ....114 E4
Sandbanks Ct IP17 ...129 B2
Sanderling Cl **3** IP28 .116 D4
Sanders Cl **3** NR32 ...112 F4
Sandford Rd IP14 ......52 A1
Sandgalls Rd IP27 ....109 D6
Sandholme Cl IP33 ...123 B2
Sandhurst Ave IP33 ..139 F4
Sandling Cres IP4 ....140 E5
Sandlings Prim Sch
IP12 ....85 C3
Sandlings The
Aldeburgh IP15 ....130 C6
Ipswich IP3 ....140 D1
Sandown Cl **3** IP1 ...135 A3
Sandown Rd IP1 ......135 A3
Sandpiper Cl IP21 .....39 E8
Sandpiper Ct C89 .....133 A6
Sandpiper Rd
Bury St Edmunds IP33 .123 C2
Ipswich IP2 ....138 E2
1 Stowmarket IP14 .....124 F7
Sandpit Cl IP4 ....140 F5
Sandpit Dr **31** IP31 ...49 E4
Sandpit Hill IP20 .....23 B3
Sandpit La
Thurston IP31 ....49 A4
Worlingham NR34 ....9 F4
Sandringham Dr IP22 .138 F2
Sandringham Rd
NR32 ....113 A1
Sandsift Cl **9** NR31 ...3 C6
Sandy Cl **4** NR34 ....132 D2
Sandy Cl **5** IP11 .....107 D8
Sandy Dro IP28 ....30 F3
Sandy Hill Barham IP6 ..82 A6
Wormingford CO6 ....101 E3
Sandy La Barham IP6 ..82 A6
Barningham IP31 ....34 E8
Barsham NR34 ....9 A4
2 Bromeswell IP12 ....85 A8
Buxhall CO10 ....91 D3
Diss IP22 ....20 D2
Gisleham NR33 ....11 A1
Holton IP19 ....118 E4
Hoo IP13 ....70 B4
Iken IP12 ....72 E2
Little Bealings IP13 ...137 D4
Marlesford IP13 ....71 C5
Rendham IP17 ....56 F3
Ringshall IP14 ....80 D8
St Mary, South Elmham
otherwise Homersfield
IP20 ....23 B7
Sternfield IP17 ....72 C8
Stowlangtoft IP31 .....50 A7
Sudbury CO10 ....148 A4
Tostock IP14 ....99 B8
Waldringfield IP12 ....98 E8
Westerfield IP6 ....135 E5
Wickham Market IP13 ..127 D5
Witnesham IP6 ....136 B8
Woodbridge IP12 ....146 D2
Sandyhill La IP13 .....139 E1
Sapiston Rd IP31 ......33 F5
Sapling Pl IP4 ....138 D3
Saracens House Bsns Ctr
IP4 ....155 C3
Sarah Ct CB9 ....132 E3
Sarsen Cl IP19 ....42 C6
Sascombe Vineyard*
CB8 ....60 F2
Saturn Cl NR32 ....113 D4
Sawmill La IP32 ......145 B6
Sawmills Rd IP22 ......20 E2
Sawston Cl **10** IP22 ..139 A2
Sawyers IP7 ....80 F1
Sawyers Cl IP9 ....150 E2
Saxham Bsns Pk IP29 ..47 E4

Saxmundham Mid Sch
IP17 ....128 C2
Saxmundham Mus*
IP17 ....128 D3
Saxmundham Prim Sch
IP17 ....128 C3
Saxmundham Rd
Aldeburgh IP15 ....130 C5
Framlingham IP13 ......126 E3
Friston IP17 ....72 E7
Knodishall IP17 ....57 F1
Theberton IP16 ....58 A2
Saxmundham Sports Club
IP17 ....128 C4
Saxmundham Sta
IP17 ....128 C3
Saxon Cl Exning CB8 ..120 D8
1 Felixstowe IP11 .....153 D6
Saxon Cres **7** IP31 ...33 D5
Saxon Dr **9** CB5 ......44 A5
Saxon La IP9 ....66 A4
Saxon Pl **1** Thetford IP24 .16 B5
Weeting IP27 ....5 E3
Saxon Rd
Lowestoft NR33 ....115 B3
Saxmundham IP17 ......128 B3
Saxon Rise IP23 ......122 E3
Saxon St Rd CB8 ......60 E6
Saxon Way IP12 ......147 A7
Saxon Wlk IP26 ....6 A8
Saxonfields IP17 ......72 D5
Saxons Way IP19 .....116 C4
Saxstead Gn Postmill*
IP13 ....55 B3
Saxtead Rd
Dennington IP13 ....55 D5
Framlingham IP13 ......126 A5
Scales St NR35 ....110 A4
Scalesbrook La IP19 ..118 E7
Scaltback Cl CB8 .....120 E6
Scaltback Mid Sch
CB8 ....120 E5
Scama La IP22 ....36 C6
Scarlin Rd IP33 ......122 C3
Schneider Rd **3** IP11 .153 H11
Scholars Wlk IP22 ....20 C3
School Ave IP30 ......50 E2
School Cl
1 Capel St Mary IP9 ..150 E3
Cheveley CB8 ....60 E8
Hadleigh IP7 ....149 E5
Kenninghall NR16 ......19 A8
North Cove NR34 ....10 C4
Norton IP31 ....50 B4
Orton IP31 ....34 E4
School Cres C89 ......133 E8
School Farm La CO10 ..78 C2
School Hill
Boxford CO10 ....93 C3
Copdock & Washbrook
IP8 ....95 F4
Kettleburgh IP13 ......70 C7
Nacton IP10 ....145 B4
School La Bardwell IP31 .34 C1
Bawdsey IP12 ....99 E2
Benhall IP17 ....72 C8
3 Brantham CO11 .....104 E5
16 Burwell CB5 ....44 A5
Dedham CO7 ....103 F4
East Bergholt CO7 ....151 B5
Elmswell IP30 ....70 E3
Fornham St Martin IP31 .34 D6
Great Barton IP31 .....49 B6
Great Horkesley CO6 ..102 C1
Halesworth IP19 ....118 A4
17 Harleston IP20 .....22 D6
Haverhill CB9 ....132 B5
Hollesley IP12 ....99 F7
Little Horkesley CO6 ..102 B3
Long Melford CO10 ....101 D1
Manningtree CO11 .....104 D1
Martlesham IP12 ......146 C1
Metfield IP20 ....23 C3
4 Mistley CO11 ......104 F2
Reydon IP18 ....26 E1
Stratford St Mary CO7 .103 E5
Thelnetham IP22 ......18 E1
7 Thurstow IP31 .....99 E4
Ufford IP13 ....84 F7
School Meadow
1 Stowmarket IP14 ....124 E3
4 Wetherden IP14 .....51 A1
School Rd Alburgh NR35 ...7 A1
Bedingham NR35 ....7 B7
Blaxhall IP12 ....72 A3
Bressingham IP22 ....19 E1
Coddenham IP6 ....68 B1
Coldfair Green IP17 ...129 A3
Earsham NR35 ....7 F4
Elmswell IP30 ....50 E2
Great Ashfield IP31 ...50 F6
Great Barton IP31 .....49 B6
Great Wratting CB9 ....74 F3
Hinderclay IP22 ....18 F5
Hollesley IP12 ....99 F7
Kedington CB9 ....133 E8
Kirby Cane NR35 ....8 E8
Knodishall IP17 ....73 A8
Langham CO4 ....103 C2
Little Horkesley CO6 ..102 B2
Little Yeldham CO9 ....90 B2
Lowestoft NR33 ....114 F8
Monk Soham IP13 ......54 D4
Pentlow CO10 ....90 F7
Ringsfield NR34 ....9 B1
Risby IP28 ....47 E5
St Andrew, Iketshall
NR34 ....8 E2

School Rd *continued*
  🟨 Shotley Gate IP9 ....107 A4
Sudbourne IP12 ....87 A8
Tattingstone IP9 ....142 D1
Thurstow IP31 ....49 E4
Tunstall IP12 ....71 F2
Waldringfield IP12 ....98 D7
Woodditton CB8 ....60 D6
School St Foxearth CO10 ......91 B7
Needham Market IP6 ....125 D4
Stoke-by-Nayland CO6 ....102 F1
Sudbury CO10 ....148 C5
School View NR34 ....24 F5
Schoolhall La IP33 ....154 B3
Schreiber Rd IP4 ....140 B7
Scofield Ct CO10 ....148 E4
Scole Comm IP21 ....20 F3
Scole Comm Rd IP21 ....21 A2
Scole Prim Sch IP21 ....21 A2
Scole Rd IP21 ....21 F2
Sconch Beck Rd IP20 ....23 A6
Scopes Rd IP5 ....141 C8
Scotland La IP33 ....154 B3
Scotland End CO8 ....29 E1
Scotland St CO6 ....103 A7
Scotred Cl CB5 ....44 A4
Scott Ave IP8 ....116 C5
Scott Rd Ipswich IP3 ....140 B1
  🔢 Ixworth IP31 ....34 B1
Scott's Hill IP14 ....66 B6
Scott's La IP13 ....84 C7
Scotts Cl 🔢 NR33 ....11 B1
Scrivener Dr IP8 ....115 B2
Scudamore Pl NR35 ....110 B7
Scuffin's La IP14 ....52 A6
Sea Lake Rd NR32 ....114 E8
Sea Rd IP11 ....152 F2
Sea View NR33 ....1 C1
Sea View Rise IP3 ....3 C6
Sea View Wlk NR33 ....115 B4
Seabreeze Rd IP14 ....124 D5
Seafield Ave 🟨 CO11 ....105 A2
Seafield Rd 🟨 CO12 ....107 A1
Seafields Dr 🟨 NR31 ....3 B6
Seago St NR32 ....113 D1
Sealodes Rd CB7 ....28 A5
Seaman Ave IP17 ....128 B2
Seaton Cl 🔢 CO11 ....104 D2
Seaton Rd IP11 ....152 D5
Seavert Cl 🟨 NR33 ....114 E3
Seaview Rd IP18 ....119 C7
Seaward Ave 🟨 IP16 ....129 D5
Sebert Rd IP32 ....122 E3
Sebert Wood Cty Prim Sch
  IP32 ....123 D5
Seckford Almshouses
  IP12 ....146 F5
Seckford Cl 🔢 IP4 ....140 F5
Seckford Hall La
  IP12 ....146 D3
Seckford St IP12 ....146 F5
Second Ave
  Felixstowe IP11 ....152 B7
  🟨 Glemsford CO10 ....77 B3
  Sudbury CO10 ....148 E2
Second Dro IP27 ....13 C7
Sedan Wlk IP1 ....155 A2
Sedge Way IP33 ....154 A4
Sedgefen Rd IP27 ....12 C3
Seescombe Rd 🟨
  NR33 ....114 D5
Sefton Way CB8 ....120 D5
Selby St NR32 ....113 C1
Self's La IP22 ....18 F3
Selkirk Rd IP4 ....136 C1
Selvale Way IP11 ....152 E4
Selwyn Cl Ipswich IP2 .....155 B1
  Mildenhall IP28 ....23 A6
  Newmarket CB8 ....121 A1
Semer Cl IP14 ....124 E3
Semere Gn La IP21 ....21 D6
Semere La IP21 ....21 D8
Sergeants Wlk IP33 ....154 B3
Serpentine Rd IP3 ....140 B2
Seven Acres IP33 ....115 A2
Seven Cotts La IP5 ....136 C1
Seven Gdns Rd IP13 ....83 F6
Seven Hills (Barrow
  Cemetery)*
  Brettenham IP24 ....16 F4
  Little Livermere IP31 .....33 A4
Sevenhills La IP31 ....33 A4
Several Rd IP13 ....55 B3
Severalls La IP13 ....55 D6
Severals The CB8 ....121 B4
Severn Rd
  Bury St Edmunds IP32 .....48 C5
  Ipswich IP3 ....139 F3
Sewell Wontner Cl
  IP5 ....141 C8
Sewell's La CO10 ....90 D5
Sewells IP7 ....79 E6
Sewells The IP33 ....123 A2
Sexton Rd NR35 ....7 D6
Sextons Manor Prim Sch
  IP33 ....122 C6
Sextons Md IP33 ....154 C1
Sextons Meadow IP33 ......123 B3
Sextons Mews IP33 ....154 C1
Seymore Dr CB9 ....132 B5
Seymour Ave IP27 ....14 D8
Seymour Cl CB8 ....121 C3
Seymour Rd IP2 ....155 B1
Shackleton Cl 🔢 CO12 ....106 F1
Shackleton Rd IP3 ....140 B3
Shackleton Sq 🔢 IP3 ......140 B3
Shaddick Rd IP18 ....119 B8
Shade The CB7 ....28 C5

Shadingfield Cl NR32 ......113 A5
Shadowbush Cl CB9 ....132 D7
Shadwell Cl IP27 ....5 E3
Shadwell Wlk IP33 ....122 B6
Shaftesbury Ave 🟨
  CO12 ....107 A2
Shaftesbury Sq IP4 ....155 C2
Shafto Rd IP1 ....134 E1
Shaker's La IP33 ....123 C5
Shaker's Rd IP29 ....47 B4
Shakers' Rd
  Brandon IP27 ....15 A5
  Wangford IP27 ....14 E4
Shakespeare Rd
  Ipswich IP1 ....134 E3
  Stowmarket IP14 ....124 B8
Shamrock Ave IP4 ....138 E4
Shannon Cl CB9 ....133 B5
Shannon Rd 🟨 IP3 ....144 A8
Shardlow Cl CB9 ....132 A7
Sharman's Rd IP4 ....29 A1
Sharon Dr NR32 ....113 B3
Sharon Rd IP33 ....122 D5
Sharp Rd IP23 ....122 F2
Sharp's Gn 🔢 IP29 ....63 A8
Sharpe's Hill IP29 ....47 B2
Sharpe's La IP29 ....63 A7
Sharpe's Row IP30 ....65 E8
Sharper's Cnr IP27 ....109 B8
Shaw Ave NR33 ....114 D3
Shaw Rd CO10 ....91 E8
Shaw Valley Rd 🔢 IP12 ....84 A1
Shawlands Ave CO10 ......148 F5
Shawsgate Vineyard*
  IP13 ....126 F6
Shearman Rd IP7 ....149 F5
Sheepdrift Rd IP12 ....85 B5
Sheepgate NR34 ....111 B5
Sheepgate La
  Badwell Ash IP31 ....51 B7
  Falkenham IP10 ....98 F1
Sheepshead Hill 🟨 CO10 ..77 B3
Sheepwash La IP17 ....58 E6
Sheerwater 🟨 IP14 ....67 A5
Sheerwater Cl IP30 ....123 F6
Shelbourne Cl 🟨 IP5 ....141 D7
Sheldrake Dr IP2 ....138 E1
Sheldrick's Rd CB7 ....29 D5
Shelley Ave CO10 ....148 F4
Shelley Cl IP14 ....124 F3
Shelley Rd
  🟨 Bury St Edmunds IP32 .48 C5
  Layham IP7 ....149 E1
Shelley St IP2 ....155 B1
Shelley Way
  Bacton IP14 ....51 E5
  Thetford IP24 ....16 C7
Shelterhouse Cnr IP27 ......32 C8
Shelton Hill IP21 ....39 B5
Shelton Rd 🟨 NR33 ....114 C3
Shenley Rd IP3 ....140 B1
Shenstone Dr IP1 ....135 A3
Shepherd Dr IP8 ....138 C2
Shepherds Cr 🟨 CB9 ......132 E5
Shepherds Dr 🟨 IP29 ......63 D1
Shepherds Gr Ind Est
  IP22 ....35 B4
Shepherds La
  Burgate IP22 ....36 D7
  Glemsford CO10 ....77 A3
  Onehouse IP14 ....124 A8
Sheppards Way IP5 ....141 D7
Sherborne Ave IP4 ....136 A2
Sherborne Rd IP33 ....122 D3
Sherbourne St CO10 ....93 B4
Sheridan Cl IP14 ....124 E3
Sheridan Wlk NR34 ....111 E4
Sheriffs Cl CB9 ....59 F2
Sherrington Rd IP1 ....139 A8
Sherwood Fields 🟨 IP5 ....141 C7
Shetland Cl
  🟨 Ipswich IP4 ....136 A1
  Ipswich IP4 ....140 A8
Shetland Rd CB8 ....133 B5
Shetlands 🔢 IP31 ....33 A4
Shickle Pl IP22 ....18 C2
Shilling St 🔢 CO10 ....78 D4
Shillitoe Cl IP33 ....154 A2
Shimpling Cl 🟨 IP21 ....21 B8
Shimpling Rd IP21 ....21 B5
Shingle Hill IP21 ....38 C4
Ship Gdns IP28 ....116 B3
Ship La Bradfield CO11 ....105 C2
  Bramford IP8 ....134 B1
Ship Launch Rd IP3 ....139 E3
Ship Rd NR33 ....115 A4
Shippea Hill Sta CB7 ......12 C7
Shire Ct 🔢 CB9 ....132 C5
Shire Hall Yd IP14 ....155 C2
Shires The NR32 ....113 B8
Shirley Cl 🟨 IP1 ....135 A3
Shoals Wlk NR33 ....114 E6
Shoe Devil La NR35 ....24 C8
Shoebridge's Hill CO7 ....103 F3
Shop Hill CB8 ....61 E1
Shop La IP13 ....71 E5
Shop Rd IP13 ....69 E1
Shop St IP17 ....54 D7
Shore La
  Bradfield CO11 ....105 C2
  Harkstead IP9 ....106 A5
  Nacton IP10 ....145 B3
Shores Cl IP28 ....29 E2
Short Beck 🔢 IP26 ....4 A1
Short Brackland IP33 ......154 B2
Short La Feltwell IP26 ....4 D5
  Lowestoft NR33 ....114 C2

Short La *continued*
  Walberswick IP18 ....43 C5
Short Rd
  Belton with Browston NR31 .2 D8
  Blundeston NR32 ....3 A4
  Snailwell CB8 ....12 A5
Short St 🟨 NR33 ....115 B4
Shortlands IP20 ....138 D1
Shotford Rd IP20 ....22 D5
Shotley Cl
  Felixstowe IP11 ....152 D4
  Ipswich IP8 ....138 C2
Shotley Mews 🟨 IP12 ......85 B3
Shotley Prim Sch IP9 .....106 F5
Shotley Wlk IP9 ....106 E7
Shrimpling Rd IP29 ....77 C6
Shrub House Cl 🔢 IP28 ....30 B8
Shrubberies The IP28 .....121 D1
Shrubbery Cl IP11 ....152 F4
Shrubbery Rd IP13 ....146 B7
Shrubland Ave IP4 ....134 E1
Shrubland Dr IP4 ....140 F5
Shrubland Pk Gdns*
  IP6 ....82 A6
Shrubland Rd 🔢 CO11 .....105 A2
Shrublands 🟨 IP28 ....116 C4
Siam Pl 🟨 CO10 ....148 C5
Siamhall La CO10 ....92 F3
Sicklesmere Rd
  Bury St Edmunds IP33 ....123 D2
  Newton IP33 ....63 E8
Sidegate Ave IP4 ....140 A8
Sidegate La IP4 ....136 A1
Sidegate La W IP4 ....135 F1
Sidegate Prim Sch
  IP4 ....140 A8
Sidegate Rd NR31 ....3 A8
Siding Rd NR34 ....111 A4
Silent St IP4 ....155 B2
Silhalls Cl 🔢 CB8 ....60 F8
Silk Mill Cl 🟨 IP27 ....149 D5
Silver Dr IP15 ....130 C6
Silver Hill IP8 ....95 D6
Silver Leys IP9 ....104 F7
Silver St Burwell CB5 ......44 A6
  Kedington CB9 ....133 F7
  Old Newton with Dagworth
    ....51 E2
  South Lopham IP22 ....19 C3
  Withersfield CB9 ....74 A2
Silverdale Ave IP14 ....124 C7
Silverdale Cl IP1 ....135 A1
Silverley Way 🟨 CB8 ....60 F8
Silverwood Cl NR33 ....115 A4
Sim's La CB9 ....133 F7
Simon's Cross IP13 ....127 B7
Simons Rd IP21 ....147 A7
Simpers Drift IP17 ....56 D1
Simpson Cl IP14 ....139 F1
Sinclair Dr IP2 ....139 C3
Singleton Ct CO10 ....148 E3
Sir Alf Ramsey Way
  IP4 ....155 A2
Sir John Leman High Sch
  NR34 ....111 A4
Sir John Leman Rd
  NR34 ....111 A4
Sir Robert Hitcham CE VA
  Prim Sch IP14 ....53 E2
Sir Robert Hitchams CE VAP
  Sch IP13 ....126 B4
Sirdar Rd IP1 ....139 A6
Siskin Gn 🔢 NR33 ....114 D5
Sitwell Cl 🔢 CO11 ....104 D2
Sitwell Gdns 🔢 IP13 ......126 C3
Sizewell Belts Nature
  Reserve* IP16 ....58 E2
Sizewell Gap IP16 ....58 F2
Sizewell Power Sta
  IP16 ....58 F2
Sizewell Rd IP16 ....129 D5
Sizewell Visitor Ctr*
  IP16 ....58 F2
Skamacre Cres NR32 ......113 B6
Skate's Hill CO10 ....77 F8
Skeaping Cl IP14 ....121 A5
Skelton Cl 🟨 CO11 ....104 E2
Skelton Rd IP22 ....20 D2
Skoulding's Cl 🔢 NR33 ....114 F7
Sky Hall Hill CO4 ....103 B4
Skylark Cl IP32 ....49 A4
Slade Cl 🟨 IP2 ....138 C2
Slade La IP22 ....22 B8
Slade St IP4 ....155 C2
Slade The IP6 ....134 D8
Slades Cl 🔢 CO10 ....77 B3
Slaters Dr CB9 ....132 C8
Slaughden Rd IP15 ....130 E2
Sleaford Cl IP2 ....139 A3
Slough La IP17 ....129 A4
Slough Hill IP29 ....77 E7
Slough La Acton CO10 .....78 C1
  Horringer IP29 ....122 A2

Smaley La 🔢 CO10 ....91 E8
Smallbridge Entry
  CO8 ....101 E4
Smallbridge Hall*
  CO8 ....101 E4
Smallworth La IP22 ....18 E3
Smart St IP4 ....155 C2
Smear La IP18 ....26 D2
Smear La E IP18 ....26 F1
Smeetham Hall La
  CO10 ....91 C3
Smith Cres 🔢 NR33 ....11 B1
Smith Wlk IP33 ....123 D2
Smith's Wlk NR33 ....114 C6
Smithbrook La IP27 ....77 A8
Smithers Cl 🟨 IP9 ....150 E3
Smithfield IP12 ....147 B6
Smiths Cl IP14 ....54 E7
Smiths Dr IP21 ....21 A2
Smiths Pl 🟨 IP5 ....141 D7
Smithy Cl
  Bradfield Combust with
    Stanningfield IP29 ......64 A3
  Rushbrooke with Rougham
    IP30 ....64 D8
Smock Meadow 🟨 IP7 .....79 F4
Snab Hill NR33 ....11 A1
Snailwell Rd
  Fordham CB8 ....44 F7
  Newmarket CB8 ....121 B7
Snailwell Short Rd CB8 ...44 F5
Snake's La Lound NR32 .....7 A8
  Topcroft NR35 ....7 A8
Snape Com Prim Sch
  IP17 ....72 D5
Snape Dr NR32 ....113 A4
Snape Hill IP22 ....35 F6
Snape Maltings IP17 ....72 D4
Snape Rd Friston IP17 .....129 A2
  Sudbourne IP12 ....131 A7
  Tunstall IP12 ....72 A2
Snare Dro IP28 ....12 E3
Snipe Farm Rd IP13 ....69 E1
Snow Hill CO10 ....76 A1
Snow Hill La CO6 ....103 B7
Snowberry Way 🟨 CB7 ....28 D5
Snowcroft IP9 ....150 E3
Snowdens Yd 🔢 IP18 .....119 D5
Snowdon Ct 🔢 CB9 ....132 C4
Snowdon Hill IP13 ....127 C7
Snowdon Rd IP2 ....139 B2
Snowdrop Cl IP32 ....123 F5
Soames Cl IP14 ....124 F3
Soane St IP4 ....155 C3
Soft Rd CO10 ....90 F3
Soham Rd IP28 ....28 A8
Soham Town Cnr IP13 .....54 F3
Solace Cl NR35 ....110 D3
Solomon Rd 🔢 IP11 ....11 C1
Somerleyton Hall & Gdns*
  NR32 ....2 D4
Somerleyton Prim Sch
  NR32 ....2 D4
Somerleyton Rd NR32 ....112 F4
Somerleyton Sta NR32 ....2 C3
Somerset Ct 🟨 CB9 ....132 C5
Somerset Rd IP4 ....139 F8
Somersham Prim Sch
  IP8 ....81 C3
Somersham Rd IP8 ....81 F2
Somerton Rd NR32 ....113 C3
Somerton Rd IP27 ....77 A7
Somerville Lea 🟨 IP11 ...130 E5
Sorrel Cl IP2 ....138 F3
Sorrel Wlk CB9 ....132 B7
Sorrell Gn IP14 ....51 D6
Sorrell Wlk IP5 ....141 F7
Sotterley Cl IP2 ....139 A2
Sotterly Rd
  🟨 Lowestoft NR32 ....112 F4
  Sotterley NR34 ....10 C1
  Willingham St Mary NR34 ..25 F7
Sound The NR33 ....114 E5
South Cl Beccles NR34 ....111 A3
  Bury St Edmunds IP33 ...154 A1
  Ipswich IP4 ....139 E8
  Leiston IP16 ....129 D5
  🔢 Melton IP12 ....84 E6
South Coast National Nature
  Reserve* IP17 ....43 B4
South Dr CB8 ....120 F4
South Elham Hall*
  IP20 ....23 D6
South Elmham Terr
  NR33 ....114 E8
South Entrance IP17 ......128 D2
South Gn IP9 ....119 D4
South Hill IP11 ....152 F3
South Lee Sch IP33 ....123 C2
South Leet Cl NR32 ....112 E4
South Lodge Dr IP8 ....48 C6
South Lowestoft Ind Est
  NR33 ....114 E2
South Pk IP27 ....5 E3
South Rd Beccles NR34 ...111 A3
  Lakenheath IP27 ....109 E3
South St
  Hockwold cum Wilton IP26 .4 F2
  🔢 Ipswich IP1 ....155 A4
  🔢 Manningtree CO11 ....104 E2
  Risby IP28 ....47 D4
South Strand 🔢 CO11 ....104 E3
South View Cl 🔢 NR32 ...113 B2
South View Gn IP9 ....104 F7
Southend Rd 🔢 NR35 .....110 B3
Southern
  Southern Belle Cl
    IP32 ....123 F7
Southern La IP22 ....19 A1

Southery Rd IP26 ....4 B6
Southfield Dr IP16 ....129 C5
Southfield Gdns NR33 ....114 F6
Southfields C07 ....103 F3
Southfields Cl CB8 ....120 E4
Southgate 🔢 IP20 ....22 D5
Southgate Ave IP28 ....116 B7
Southgate Gdns
  Bury St Edmunds IP33 ....123 C3
  🟨 Long Melford CO10 .....91 E7
Southgate Rd IP8 ....138 B1
Southgate St
  Bury St Edmunds IP33 ....154 C1
  🔢 Long Melford CO10 .....91 E7
Southolt Rd
  Athelington IP21 ....38 F1
  Bedfield IP13 ....54 D6
Southwell La NR34 ....26 A6
Southwell Rd NR33 ....115 B7
Southwold & District Hospl
  IP18 ....119 D6
Southwold Lighthouse*
  IP18 ....119 D5
Southwold Maze*
  IP18 ....43 C7
Southwold Mus*
  IP18 ....119 D5
Southwold Pier*
  IP18 ....119 E6
Southwold Prim Sch
  IP18 ....119 D5
Southwold Rd
  Blyford IP19 ....42 B8
  Brampton with Stoven
    NR34 ....25 E5
  Holton IP19 ....118 F3
  Wrentham NR34 ....26 E5
Southwold Sailors Reading
  Rm* IP18 ....119 D5
Southwood IP17 ....128 D2
Spalding's Chair Hill
  IP24 ....17 B3
Spanbies Rd 🟨 C07 ....103 E5
Sparhawk St IP33 ....154 C1
Sparkes Cl 🟨 CB7 ....29 C5
Sparks La CO9 ....89 D3
Sparrow Ct 🔢 IP11 ....53 F2
Sparrow Rd CO10 ....148 F4
Sparrowhawk Rd
  IP19 ....118 C7
Sparrows Croft Rd 🟨
  IP12 ....85 E8
Spartan Cl 🔢 CB9 ....132 A6
Spashett Rd 🔢 NR32 .....113 B4
Speckled Wood Cl
  IP8 ....142 D8
Speed La CB7 ....28 B8
Speedwell Rd 🔢 NR33 ...113 A3
Speedwell Rd IP2 ....138 F4
Speedwell Way 🔢 IP20 ....22 D5
Spencer Dr IP1 ....133 B6
Spencer Dro CB7 ....28 C4
Spencer Rd 🟨 IP28 ....116 B8
Spencer Way IP14 ....124 B7
Spenser Rd IP1 ....134 E3
Sperling Dr CB9 ....132 C8
Spexhall Way NR32 ....113 B5
Spicers La 🟨 CO10 ....91 E8
Spiers Way IP22 ....20 B2
Spike's La IP14 ....66 E7
Spindle Rd CB9 ....132 B7
Spindler Cl IP5 ....141 D7
Spinks' La NR33 ....115 A3
Spinnel's Hill CO11 ....105 D1
Spinnel's La CO11 ....105 E1
Spinner Cl IP21 ....138 D8
Spinners La 🔢 IP18 ......119 D5
Spinney Cl NR34 ....10 B4
Spinney Gdns NR33 ....114 C4
Spinney Hill IP7 ....81 A1
Spinney Rd IP31 ....33 B3
Spinney The
  Beccles NR34 ....111 D4
  Ipswich IP4 ....140 F4
Spinning Cl IP17 ....128 D5
Spire Chase CO10 ....148 E8
Spirkett's La IP20 ....22 D5
Spitfire Cl IP3 ....140 B1
Spong La IP30 ....50 E2
Spong The IP20 ....23 C3
Spooners La CB8 ....54 E4
Spooners Cl 🟨 IP7 ....59 F4
Spooners La 🔢 IP7 ....149 D6
Spout La CO10 ....101 B8
Spring Cl
  🔢 Bentwaters Airfield
    IP12 ....85 D8
  Burwell CB5 ....44 A5
Spring La
  Bury St Edmunds IP33 ...154 A4
  Crowfield IP6 ....68 B3
  Dennington IP13 ....55 B5
  🔢 Glemsford CO10 ....78 D4
  Polstead CO6 ....93 D2
  Ufford IP13 ....127 B1
  Wickham Market IP13 ....127 D7
Spring Meadow
  🔢 Glemsford CO10 ....77 A3
  Playford IP6 ....137 B4
Spring Pk IP6 ....69 C2
Spring Rd Bardwell IP31 ..34 C5
  Copdock & Washbrook
    IP8 ....95 E5
  Ipswich IP4 ....139 F6
Spring Row IP14 ....124 D7

Spring St **6** CO10 ......78 D4
Spring Wood Nature
  Reserve* IP9 ......142 E7
Springbank Ave **18**
  CO11 ......104 D2
Springett's Hill CO8 ......101 B5
Springfield IP18 ......119 A7
Springfield Ave
  Bury St Edmunds IP33 ......154 A3
  Felixstowe IP11 ......153 A5
Springfield Dr IP27 ......109 D6
Springfield Gdns
  NR33 ......114 F5
Springfield Inf Sch
  IP1 ......138 F8
Springfield Jun Sch
  IP1 ......138 F8
Springfield La IP1 ......138 F8
Springfield Rd
  Aldeburgh IP15 ......130 C5
  Bury St Edmunds IP33 ......154 A3
  4 Somersham IP8 ......81 C3
  Sudbury CO10 ......148 C7
Springhurst Cl IP4 ......139 F6
Springland Cl IP4 ......140 A6
Springlands Way
  CO10 ......148 D8
Springtail Rd IP8 ......142 E8
Sprites End IP11 ......152 D7
Sprites La IP8 ......138 C1
Sprites Prim Sch IP2 ......138 C2
Spriteshall La IP11 ......152 D7
Sproughton Bsns Pk
  IP8 ......138 B6
Sproughton CE Prim Sch
  IP8 ......138 B6
Sproughton Ct IP8 ......138 A6
Sproughton Rd IP1 ......138 C7
Spruce Cl **14** IP27 ......13 F2
Spruce Ct CO13 ......113 C3
Spruce Ct IP27 ......5 F1
Spur End IP12 ......147 C7
Spurgeon Score **12**
  NR32 ......113 E2
Spurling Cl **2** CB8 ......60 E7
Square The IP14 ......124 E4
Squires Ct **21** CB9 ......132 C5
Squires La **4** IP5 ......98 A8
Squires Wlk NR32 ......113 C5
Squirrells Mill Rd **3** IP7 ......79 F4
Squirrels The IP9 ......150 E4
Stackwood Rd CO6 ......93 F3
Stafford Cl NR32 ......112 E4
Staithe Cl **4** NR35 ......110 B4
Staithe Rd
  Bungay NR35 ......110 B4
  Burgh St Peter NR34 ......10 C7
Staithe The NR33 ......114 E6
Stambourne Rd CO9 ......89 E2
Stamford Cl IP2 ......142 F8
Stamford Ct IP33 ......122 F3
Stamford St CB8 ......121 B2
Stammers Pl IP5 ......141 E8
Stanford St **3** NR32 ......113 C1
Stanhope Cl IP17 ......72 D5
Stanley Ave IP3 ......140 A4
Stanley Drapkin Prim Sch **8**
  CB9 ......132 B5
Stanley Rd Diss IP22 ......20 B2
  Felixstowe IP11 ......153 A3
  Lowestoft NR33 ......114 E7
  Newmarket CB8 ......121 C3
  Sudbury CO10 ......148 C6
Stanley Rd NR32 ......113 D1
Stanley Wood Ave
  CO10 ......148 D7
Stannard Way CO10 ......148 E4
Stanningfield Rd IP30 ......63 F5
Stansfield Cl NR33 ......114 E6
Stanton Cl
  Beccles NR34 ......111 C4
  Lowestoft NR32 ......113 C5
Stanton Com Prim Sch
  IP31 ......34 E4
Stanton Hughes Way **10**
  CO11 ......104 D2
Stanton Pl **12** CB9 ......132 F6
Stanton Postmill*
  IP31 ......34 F4
Stanton Rd IP31 ......34 C4
Stanway Cl CO10 ......77 B3
Staple Cl IP31 ......35 C1
Staplehurst Cl **22** NR33 ......114 C4
Staples La IP7 ......80 D2
Star And Garter La CB8 ......60 E8
Star La IP4 ......155 C2
Starfield Cl IP14 ......140 B6
Starhouse La IP14 ......66 C5
Starre Rd IP33 ......122 C5
Starston La IP20 ......22 C5
Station App
  Newmarket CB8 ......121 A2
  Saxmundham IP17 ......128 D3
Station Gate CB5 ......44 A4
Station Hill
  1 Bures CO8 ......101 C4
  Bury St Edmunds IP33 ......154 B4
  Harleston IP20 ......22 D6
  Little Whelnetham IP30 ......64 B6
  Thurstow IP31 ......49 D4
Station La **18** CO12 ......107 B2
Station Rd Alburgh IP20 ......7 A1
  Bacton IP14 ......52 A6
  Barnham IP24 ......16 B2
  Beccles NR34 ......111 B5

Station Rd *continued*
  Bentley IP9 ......104 E7
  Birdbrook CO9 ......89 B4
  Blaxhall IP12 ......71 E3
  Bradfield CO11 ......105 B2
  Brampton with Stoven
    NR34 ......25 C5
  Burston & Shimpling IP21 ......20 F6
  Clare CO10 ......90 B8
  Claydon IP6 ......134 B8
  8 Corton NR32 ......3 D4
  Corton NR32 ......113 C8
  Diss IP22 ......20 D2
  Ditchingham NR35 ......110 C6
  Dullingham CB8 ......59 E5
  2 Earsham NR35 ......7 F4
  Ellingham NR35 ......8 D7
  Elmswell IP30 ......50 F2
  Felixstowe IP11 ......152 C7
  Fordham CB7 ......29 A1
  Framlingham IP13 ......126 C2
  Geldeston NR34 ......8 F6
  Haddiscoe NR31 ......2 A5
  Hadleigh IP7 ......149 E5
  Halesworth IP19 ......118 B4
  Harleston IP20 ......22 D6
  1 Harwich CO12 ......106 F3
  Haughley IP14 ......124 E6
  4 Haverhill CB9 ......132 E6
  Hopton on Sea NR31 ......3 B6
  Islenham CB7 ......29 F4
  Kennett CB8 ......45 F7
  Lakenheath IP27 ......109 C7
  Laxfield IP13 ......39 F4
  Leiston IP16 ......129 C6
  Long Melford CO10 ......91 E7
  Lowestoft NR32 ......113 D4
  Mildenhall IP28 ......116 B3
  Manningtree CO11 ......104 E3
  Pulham Market IP21 ......21 E8
  Pulham St Mary IP21 ......22 A8
  Ramsey & Parkeston
    CO12 ......106 F3
  Soham CB7 ......28 C4
  Somerleyton, Ashby &
    Herringfleet NR32 ......2 C3
  Southwold IP18 ......119 C6
  Sudbury CO10 ......148 C5
  Tattingstone IP9 ......105 A7
  Thetford IP24 ......16 B6
  Wetheringsett-cum-Brockford
    IP14 ......53 B4
  Woodbridge IP12 ......147 A4
  Wrabness CO11 ......105 F2
Station Rd W IP14 ......124 C6
Station Sq **11** NR32 ......115 D8
Station St IP17 ......139 C3
Station Terr IP13 ......126 C2
Station Yd
  Hadleigh IP7 ......149 E5
  Mildenhall IP28 ......116 B3
  Needham Market IP6 ......125 E4
Staverton Cl IP12 ......85 B6
Stayngate Wlk **7** NR32 ......112 E4
Stearn Dr IP14 ......66 C6
Stearn's La IP14 ......67 D6
Stebbings La IP14 ......99 E7
Stedman Terr IP18 ......119 C8
Steeds Meadow **7** CO10 ......91 E8
Steeles Rd IP30 ......50 D1
Steeple Bumpstead Pottery*
  CB9 ......88 B4
Steeple Bumpstead Rd
  CB9 ......88 B4
Steeple End IP19 ......118 B3
Steeplechase CO10 ......75 C4
Steggall Cl IP14 ......124 B7
Stella Maris IP2 ......138 D5
Stennetts Cl IP2 ......152 B8
Stephen Cl
  Haverhill CB9 ......132 D6
  Long Melford CO10 ......91 E7
Stephen Rd IP5 ......141 E8
Stephen's Ct IP4 ......140 B6
Stephenson Way IP24 ......16 A4
Stephensons Wlk
  NR32 ......113 D4
Stepping Hill **3** NR34 ......111 B5
Stetchworth Rd
  Dullingham CB8 ......59 F4
  Stetchworth CB8 ......60 A4
Stevens St NR32 ......113 C1
Stevenson Rd IP1 ......155 A3
Steward Rd IP33 ......123 C2
Stewards Field CB7 ......29 A1
Stewart Young Gr
  IP5 ......141 D7
Stimpson Cl **3** NR32 ......113 A6
Stirling Cl
  Lowestoft NR32 ......112 F4
  7 Thistley Green IP28 ......29 F6
Stirling Gdns CB8 ......120 E4
Stirling Rd **3** IP26 ......4 E5
Stirrups La NR32 ......3 C5
Stobart Cl NR34 ......111 D3
Stockley Cl IP13 ......133 A5
Stockmers End **8** IP9 ......150 E3
Stocks La IP10 ......119 A2
Stockton Cl IP7 ......149 F4
Stockton Rd NR34 ......9 A7
Stoke Ash Prim Sch
  IP23 ......52 F8
Stoke Coll CO10 ......89 E6
Stoke Hall* IP2 ......155 B1
Stoke Hall Rd IP2 ......155 B1
Stoke High Sch IP2 ......139 C3

Stoke Pk Dr IP2 ......139 A1
Stoke Quay IP2 ......155 C1
Stoke Rd Clare CO10 ......90 A7
  Layham IP7 ......149 D1
  Leavenheath CO6 ......102 B8
  Nayland-with-Wissington
    CO6 ......102 D5
  Stoke Ash IP23 ......37 D1
  Stoke-by-Clare CO10 ......89 F7
Stoke St IP2 ......155 B1
Stoke-by-Nayland CE VC
  Prim Sch CO6 ......102 E7
Stoke-by-Nayland Mid Sch
  CO6 ......102 D7
Stollery Cl IP5 ......141 B7
Stonalls IP30 ......50 C1
Stone Hall Rd IP23 ......36 A2
Stone La
  Bressingham IP22 ......19 F6
  Wrabness CO11 ......105 F2
Stone Lodge La IP2 ......139 B3
Stone Lodge La W
  IP2 ......138 F3
Stone Lodge Wlk IP2 ......139 B3
Stone Pl IP2 IP2 ......147 A5
Stone St Boxford CO6 ......93 C3
  Crowfield IP6 ......68 C3
  Hadleigh IP7 ......149 B8
  Spexhall IP19 ......118 C8
Stone St Rd **2** CO10 ......89 E6
Stonebridge Ave IP33 ......122 F3
Stonebridge La IP7 ......67 A8
Stonechat Rd IP2 ......138 C3
Stonegrove Rd IP11 ......152 D1
Stonehouse Rd IP2 ......138 D2
Stonewell Hill IP6 ......68 D1
Stoney La Barrow IP29 ......47 B2
  Thurston IP31 ......49 F4
Stoney Rd IP13 ......83 D6
Stonham Aspal CE Prim Sch
  IP14 ......68 B6
Stonham Barns Leisure
  Complex* IP14 ......68 C6
Stonham Rd IP14 ......52 B4
Stony La
  2 Aldringham cum Thorpe
    IP16 ......73 F6
  Debenham IP14 ......53 D2
  Wortwell IP20 ......22 F8
Stopford Ct **8** IP1 ......139 A7
Store St IP22 ......20 C3
Stour Ave IP11 ......152 E3
  4 Harwich CO12 ......106 E1
  Saxmundham IP17 ......128 C3
Stour Gdns CO10 ......148 E2
Stour Rd CO12 ......107 B3
Stour St Cavendish CO10 ......90 D8
  17 Manningtree CO11 ......104 E2
  Sudbury CO10 ......148 B5
Stour Vale CO9 ......89 B5
Stour Valley Rd CB9 ......132 F5
Stour Wood Nature
  Reserve* CO12 ......106 B2
Stourdale Cl **27** CO11 ......104 D2
Stourmead Cl CB9 ......133 E8
Stourside IP9 ......107 A4
Stourview Ave **4** CO11 ......105 A2
Stourview Cl **6** CO11 ......105 A2
Stoven Cl NR32 ......113 B5
Stow Rd NR34 ......25 F3
Stow La IP31 ......50 A8
Stow Rd IP31 ......34 B1
Stowmarket High Sch
  IP14 ......124 B7
Stowmarket Mid Sch
  IP14 ......124 C6
Stowmarket Rd
  Badley IP6 ......125 A8
  Great Blakenham IP6 ......81 F6
  Old Newton with Dagworth
    IP14 ......51 C1
  Rattlesden IP30 ......65 C6
  Stonham Aspal IP14 ......68 A6
  Wetherden NR15 ......9 A7
Stowmarket Sta IP14 ......124 C6
Stowupland High Sch
  IP14 ......67 A7
Stowupland Rd IP14 ......124 F7
Stowupland St IP14 ......124 D6
Stradbroke CE Prim Sch
  IP21 ......39 A5
Stradbroke High Sch
  IP21 ......39 A4
Stradbroke Rd
  Fressingfield IP21 ......39 D7
  Ipswich IP4 ......140 A7
  Lowestoft NR33 ......115 A4
  Southwold IP18 ......119 D5
Stradishall Rd CO10 ......75 E5
Straight La **19** IP20 ......22 D6
Straight Rd
  Battisford IP14 ......66 D1
  Boxted CO4 ......103 E8
  Bradfield CO11 ......105 B1
  Foxhall IP10 ......141 C1
  Polstead CO6 ......93 F3
  Whepstead IP29 ......63 C5
Strand The IP2 ......143 C8
Strasbourg Sq **11** CB9 ......132 F6
Stratford Rd
  Dedham CO7 ......103 E4
  Ipswich IP1 ......134 F2
Stratford St Mary Prim Sch
  CO7 ......103 D5
Strattonhall Drift
  IP10 ......145 F2
Straw La CO10 ......148 B5

Strawberry Fields
  CB9 ......132 B5
Strawberry La IP19 ......25 D8
Street Farm La **4** IP31 ......34 B1
Street Farm Rd IP17 ......128 D3
Street The Aldeby NR34 ......9 F5
  Alderton IP12 ......99 E3
  Aldham IP7 ......148 B8
  Ashbocking IP6 ......68 C2
  Ashfield cum Thorpe IP14 ......54 C1
  Assington CO10 ......92 F1
  Bacton IP14 ......51 E5
  Badwell Ash IP31 ......50 E7
  Barnham IP24 ......16 B2
  Barrow IP29 ......47 A2
  Barton Mills IP28 ......116 E2
  Bawdsey IP12 ......99 E8
  Beck Row, Holywell Row
    & Kenny Hill IP28 ......30 C8
  Belchamp Otten CO10 ......90 E4
  Belstead IP8 ......142 C6
  Benacre NR34 ......27 A7
  Birdbrook CO9 ......89 A3
  Blo' Norton IP22 ......18 E2
  Blundeston NR32 ......3 A4
  Botesdale IP22 ......36 A6
  Boxted IP29 ......77 A6
  Bradfield CO11 ......105 C1
  Bradfield Combust with
    Stanningfield IP30 ......64 B4
  Bramfield IP19 ......41 F5
  Bramford IP8 ......134 A2
  Brampton with Stoven
    NR34 ......25 E4
  Brandon IP27 ......5 E1
  Brantham CO11 ......105 A5
  Bredfield IP13 ......84 C8
  Bressingham IP22 ......19 D6
  Brettenham IP7 ......65 C1
  Bridgham NR16 ......17 E8
  Brockdish IP21 ......21 E2
  Brome & Oakley IP23 ......117 D8
  Bruisyard IP17 ......56 D4
  Brundish IP13 ......39 D1
  Bulmer CO10 ......91 C3
  Burrough Green CB8 ......59 E3
  12 Bury St Edmunds IP28 ......48 C6
  Capel St Mary IP9 ......150 D3
  Cavenham IP28 ......47 A8
  Charsfield IP13 ......70 B3
  Chattisham IP8 ......95 C4
  Chedburgh IP29 ......62 C4
  Chelsworth IP7 ......79 D3
  Coney Weston IP31 ......17 E1
  Copdock & Washbrook
    IP8 ......95 F5
  Corton NR32 ......3 D4
  Cratfield IP19 ......40 D5
  Cretingham IP13 ......69 E7
  Culford IP28 ......48 B8
  Dalham CB8 ......61 B8
  Darsham IP17 ......42 B1
  Dennington IP13 ......55 C6
  Dickleburgh IP21 ......21 B5
  Drinkstone IP30 ......65 B8
  Earl Soham IP13 ......54 C2
  Earsham NR35 ......7 F4
  East Bergholt CO7 ......151 B4
  Easton IP13 ......70 C5
  Elmsett IP7 ......80 F1
  Eriswell IP27 ......13 F1
  Eye IP21 ......38 B4
  Eyke IP12 ......85 B6
  Farnham IP17 ......72 A7
  Flixton NR35 ......8 C5
  Foxearth CO10 ......91 B7
  Framsden IP14 ......69 B6
  Freckenham IP28 ......29 E8
  Gazeley CB8 ......46 B3
  Geldeston NR34 ......9 A7
  Great Barton IP31 ......49 B5
  Great Bricett IP7 ......80 D5
  Great Livermere IP31 ......33 C2
  Great Waldingfield CO10 ......92 D6
  Great Wratting CB9 ......74 F3
  Grundisburgh IP13 ......83 E5
  Hacheston IP13 ......70 F1
  Halesworth IP19 ......118 E3
  Harkstead IP9 ......106 A5
  48 Harleston IP20 ......22 D6
  Hessett IP30 ......64 F8
  Hinderclay IP22 ......35 C7
  Holbrook IP9 ......105 E7
  Hollesley IP12 ......99 F7
  Horham IP21 ......38 E3
  Horninger IP29 ......122 B1
  Huntingfield IP19 ......41 A4
  Icklingham IP28 ......31 D4
  Kersey IP7 ......93 F7
  Kettleburgh IP13 ......70 C7
  Kirtling CB8 ......60 E3
  Lawshall IP29 ......63 D3
  Layham IP7 ......149 E2
  Letheringham IP13 ......70 D4
  Lidgate CB8 ......61 B4
  Little Bealings IP13 ......137 D4
  Little Thurlow CB9 ......74 E5
  Little Waldingfield CO10 ......92 E8
  Lound NR32 ......2 F6
  Market Weston IP22 ......35 A8
  Martlesham IP12 ......146 C1
  Middleton CO10 ......148 C1
  Mildenhall IP28 ......30 B8
  Monks Eleigh IP7 ......79 C2
  Moulton CB8 ......45 F3
  Nacton IP10 ......145 C5

Street The *continued*
  Newbourne IP12 ......98 D6
  North Cove NR34 ......10 B4
  North Lopham IP22 ......19 A6
  Norton IP31 ......50 B4
  Occold IP23 ......37 F1
  Pakenham IP31 ......49 E6
  Parham IP13 ......71 A7
  Peasenhall IP17 ......56 F8
  Pettistree IP13 ......127 C4
  Poslingford CO10 ......76 A3
  Preston St Mary CO10 ......79 A5
  Ramsey & Parkeston
    CO12 ......106 D1
  Raydon IP7 ......94 E1
  Redenhall with Harleston
    IP20 ......22 F5
  1 Redgrave IP22 ......36 A8
  Riddlesworth IP22 ......18 A3
  Rumburgh IP19 ......24 C4
  Rushmere NR33 ......10 C1
  St James, South Elmham
    IP19 ......23 F4
  Shotley IP9 ......106 F6
  Shottisham IP12 ......99 B7
  Snailwell CB8 ......45 A6
  Somerleyton, Ashby &
    Herringfleet NR32 ......2 D4
  South Lopham IP22 ......19 B4
  Southolt IP23 ......54 B7
  Stanton IP31 ......34 E5
  Stanton IP20 ......72 C7
  Sternfield IP17 ......72 D8
  Stoke Ash IP23 ......52 F8
  Stoke-by-Clare CO10 ......89 D6
  Stonham Aspal IP14 ......68 B6
  Stowlangtoft IP31 ......50 B6
  Stradishall CB8 ......75 E6
  Stratford St Mary CO7 ......103 E4
  Sturmer CB9 ......133 D3
  Thornton IP23 ......53 B8
  Thornham Magna IP23 ......37 A2
  Troston IP31 ......33 D3
  Tuddenham St Martin
    IP6 ......136 C5
  Ubbeston IP19 ......40 F3
  Walberswick IP18 ......119 A2
  Wattisfield IP22 ......35 C4
  Wenhaston IP19 ......42 C6
  Westleton IP17 ......58 C7
  Wetheringsett-cum-Brockford
    IP14 ......52 F6
  Weybread IP21 ......22 D2
  Whatfield IP7 ......80 C1
  Wherstead IP9 ......143 A6
  Winfarthing IP22 ......20 B8
  Wissett IP19 ......24 D2
  Witnesham IP6 ......136 A8
  Woodbridge IP12 ......147 C7
  Woodditton CB8 ......60 D5
  Woolpit IP30 ......50 D1
  Worlington IP28 ......30 B4
  Worlingworth IP23 ......55 D1
Stretham Rd CB7 ......77 F7
Stretton Ave CB8 ......121 B2
Strickland Manor Hill
  IP17 ......57 C8
Strickland Pl **18** IP18 ......119 D5
Stricklands Rd **1** IP14 ......124 E5
Strickmere CO7 ......103 E5
Strollers Way CB8 ......60 A5
Strowger's Way **6** NR33 ......11 C1
Struggler's La IP6 ......136 A8
Stuart Cl
  5 Felixstowe IP11 ......153 D7
  Ipswich IP4 ......139 F7
Stuart Dr NR34 ......111 C4
Stubbin's La CB8 ......46 B3
Stubbing's La IP22 ......22 C3
Stubbs Cl Ipswich IP3 ......140 A1
  3 Manningtree CO11 ......104 D2
Stubbs Wood NR32 ......113 B6
Studio Cl IP17 ......58 C8
Studlands Pk Ave
  CB8 ......120 D6
Stump St IP13 ......127 A3
Stump's Cross CO9 ......89 D1
Sturdee Ave IP3 ......140 B3
Sturgeon Way **22** IP31 ......34 E4
Sturmer End Ind Est
  CB9 ......133 A3
Sturmer Rd CB9 ......133 D5
Sturston Cl IP26 ......16 C7
Stuston La IP21 ......117 B8
Stuston Rd IP21 ......20 E1
Stutton CE Prim Sch
  IP9 ......105 D5
Stutton Cl IP9 ......105 D5
Stutton Gn IP9 ......105 E5
Stutton La IP9 ......105 B7
Stutton Rd CO11 ......105 A5
Sub-station Rd IP11 ......152 D2
Suckling Yd CB9 ......88 E4
Sudbourne Rd
  16 Felixstowe IP11 ......152 D5
  Orford IP12 ......131 B5
Sudbury Arts Ctr
  CO10 ......148 D7
Sudbury Common Lands
  Nature Reserve* CO10 ......148 B6
Sudbury Rd Acton CO10 ......92 B7
  Bulmer CO10 ......91 C3
  Bures St Mary CO8 ......101 C5
  3 Felixstowe IP11 ......152 C4
  Gestingthorpe CO9 ......90 F1
  Great Whelnetham IP30 ......64 A6
  Lavenham CO10 ......78 D3

Sudbury Rd *continued*
Long Melford CO10 . . . . .91 D6
Newton CO10 . . . . .92 C4
Stoke-by-Nayland CO6 . . . .102 D7
Sudbury Ret Pk CO10 . . . .148 F6
CO10 . . . . .148 C1
Sudbury Sports Ctr
CO10 . . . . .148 D5
Sudbury Sta CO10 . . . . . .148 D5
Sudbury Upper Sch & Arts
Ctr CO10 . . . . .148 D7
Sue Ryder Foundation Mus*
CO10 . . . . .11 D5
Suffolk Ave IP31 . . . . . . .123 F4
Suffolk Bsns Pk IP30 . . .123 F4
Suffolk Coast National
Nature Reserve*
IP19 . . . . .43 A5
Suffolk Coll IP4 . . . . .139 E5
Suffolk Ct IP27 . . . . .5 F1
Suffolk Dr IP12 . . . . .85 D8
Suffolk Horse Mus*
IP12 . . . . .147 A5
Suffolk Nuffield Hospl The
IP10 . . . . .141 B4
Suffolk Odyssey Llamas*
IP19 . . . . .41 C5
Suffolk Owl Sanctuary*
IP14 . . . . .68 C6
Suffolk Pl IP12 . . . . .147 B5
Suffolk Rd
2 Bury St Edmunds IP32 . .122 E4
Ipswich IP4 . . . . .155 C4
Lowestoft NR32 . . . . .115 D8
Sudbury CO10 . . . . .148 C6
Suffolk Ret Pk IP4 . . . . . .139 A6
Suffolk Ski Ctr* IP2 . . . .143 B7
Suffolk Sq 5 CO10 . . . . . .148 C6
Suffolk Way CB8 . . . . . . .120 E5
Suffolk Wildlife Pk*
NR33 . . . . .11 B1
Suffolk Wr Pk* IP8 . . . . .134 A5
Sulleys Hill IP7 . . . . .103 D8
Sullivan Pl IP12 . . . . .98 D7
Summer La IP12 . . . . .85 A6
Summer Rd 8 NR32 . . . . .113 D1
Summerfield Cl IP4 . . . . .140 D8
Summerfield Gdns
NR33 . . . . .115 A6
Summerhill Sch IP16 . . . .129 C7
Summers Rd IP32 . . . . . . .122 E8
Summit Bsns Pk IP11 . . . .152 E1
Sumner Rd IP22 . . . . .35 A4
Sun La Newmarket CB8 . .121 A3
Woodbridge IP12 . . . . .147 A5
Sun Rd NR35 . . . . .110 D8
Sun St 4 IP27 . . . . .29 C5
Sunbeam Cl NR33 . . . . . . .114 A3
Sunderland Rd
IP11 . . . . .153 H11
Sunfield Cl IP4 . . . . .140 B4
Sunley Cl NR33 . . . . .110 E8
Sunningdale Ave
Ipswich IP4 . . . . .140 D5
Lowestoft NR33 . . . . .115 B4
Mildenhall IP28 . . . . .116 B4
Sunningdale Dr IP11 . . . .153 B6
Sunningdale Rd NR33 . . . .115 B4
Sunnyhill IP12 . . . . .98 D7
Sunnyside
Bedingham NR35 . . . . .7 C8
Diss IP22 . . . . .20 C3
Sunray Ave IP11 . . . . . . .153 B6
Surbiton Rd IP1 . . . . .138 F7
Surrey Cl 8 IP19 . . . . .126 C3
Surrey St
6 Lowestoft NR32 . . . . . . .113 D1
4 Lowestoft NR32 . . . . . . .115 D1
Sussex Crof 9 IP12 . . . . . .85 B3
Sussex Rd NR32 . . . . .113 D3
Sutton Cl
Bury St Edmunds IP32 . . . .123 E5
Woodbridge IP12 . . . . .147 B5
Sutton Hoo* IP12 . . . . . .147 D5
Sutton Hoo Maze Adventure
Pk* IP12 . . . . .146 D5
Sutton Rd IP2 . . . . .147 F5
Sutton Rd 10 NR34 . . . . . . .9 F4
Swaffham Heath Rd
CB8 . . . . .59 A7
Swaffham Rd
Burwell CB5 . . . . .44 A3
Mundford IP26 . . . . .6 B8
Swainston Way IP13 . . . .55 D5
Swallow Cl
Felixstowe IP11 . . . . .153 C7
2 Harwich CO12 . . . . .106 F1
3 Stowmarket IP14 . . . . . . .67 A5
Swallow Dr Brandon IP27 . .6 A1
3 Stowmarket IP14 . . . . . . .67 A5
Swallow Rd IP2 . . . . .138 C3
Swallowfields NR33 . . . .114 D3
Swallowtail Cl IP8 . . . . . .142 E8
Swamp La IP22 . . . . .20 A3
Swan Cl
Halesworth IP19 . . . . .118 B3
26 Martlesham Heath IP5 . .98 A8
Stowmarket IP14 . . . . .124 B4
Swan Ct 5 CO11 . . . . . . .105 A2
Swan Gn La IP19 . . . . .40 C5
Swan Gr CB8 . . . . .120 B8
Swan Hill IP8 . . . . .138 A2
Swan La
Bury St Edmunds IP33 . . . .154 C1
Coney Weston IP31 . . . . . . .34 D8
Cretingham IP13 . . . . .69 E8

Swan La *continued*
Exning CB8 . . . . .120 B8
Halesworth IP19 . . . . .118 B3
Haverhill CB9 . . . . .132 E6
8 Long Melford CO10 . . . . .91 D8
North Cove NR34 . . . . .10 C4
Redenhall with Harleston
IP20 . . . . .22 D6
Westerfield IP6 . . . . .135 E4
Swan Meadow CO7 . . . . . .103 E5
Swan Rd IP13 . . . . .54 E7
Swan St CO10 . . . . .91 E8
Swanfield CO10 . . . . .91 E8
Swansea Ave IP31 . . . . . . .139 B1
Swatchway Cl 3 IP3 . . . . .144 B8
Swaynes 1 CO7 . . . . .103 E5
Sweden Cl 1 CO12 . . . . . .106 F2
Swift Cl NR33 . . . . .114 D3
Swift Dr NR34 . . . . .9 F4
Swithub La IP14 . . . . .52 A4
Swinburne Rd IP1 . . . . . . .134 E3
Swine's Gn NR34 . . . . .111 C4
Singleton Hill IP7 . . . . . . .79 C2
Swinton Cl IP7 . . . . .138 D1
Swonnell's Wlk 2 NR32 . .112 D1
Swonnells Cl NR32 . . . . . .114 D8
Swonnells Ave NR33 . . . . .114 D7
Sycamore Cl
Beccles NR34 . . . . .111 E3
1 Great Brickett IP7 . . . . . .80 E6
Ipswich IP8 . . . . .138 C1
Leiston IP16 . . . . .129 C5
Sycamore Dr
8 Beck Row, Holywell
Row & Kenny Hill IP28 . . . .13 B1
5 Mildenhall IP28 . . . . .30 A8
Rendlesham IP12 . . . . .85 D8
Sycamore Rd
Stowupland IP14 . . . . .67 A4
Sudbury CO10 . . . . .148 F4
Sycamore Way
Brantham CO11 . . . . .104 E5
Diss IP22 . . . . .20 D2
Sycamore Wlk IP27 . . . . . .13 F2
Syleham Hall La IP21 . . . . .22 C1
Syleham Rd
Brockdish IP21 . . . . .22 A2
Syleham IP21 . . . . .38 D8
Sylvester Rd IP16 . . . . . . .129 D5
Symonds Rd IP31 . . . . . . .123 C4

T

Tacket St IP4 . . . . .155 C2
Tacon Cl IP23 . . . . .117 C2
Tacon Rd IP11 . . . . .152 E1
Takers La IP14 . . . . .124 E4
Talbot Rd CO10 . . . . .90 D8
Tallboys Cl IP5 . . . . .141 C8
Tallyho Cnr 8 CO7 . . . . . .103 E5
Talmash Gdns IP22 . . . . . .139 A4
Tamage Rd CO10 . . . . .92 B7
Tan House La CB5 . . . . .44 A4
Tan Office La
Chevington IP29 . . . . .62 C5
Mendlesham IP14 . . . . .52 E1
Tanners La CB7 . . . . .28 D3
Tanners View IP1 . . . . . . .138 F7
Tannersfield Way CB8 . . .120 F4
Tannery Bsns Ctr The
IP14 . . . . .66 E2
Tannery Dr IP33 . . . . .123 B3
Tannery Rd IP13 . . . . .138 F4
Tannington Long Rd
IP13 . . . . .39 D1
Tanns La IP22 . . . . .19 A6
Tansy Cl 5 NR33 . . . . .114 F3
Tansy Meadow 3 IP21 . . .39 D8
Tarn Hows Cl 1 IP11 . . . .153 D6
Tasman Rd CB9 . . . . .133 A5
Tasmania Rd IP4 . . . . .140 D6
Tassel Rd IP32 . . . . .123 F6
Tattingstone CE Prim Sch
IP9 . . . . .105 B8
Taunton Cl IP1 . . . . .135 B4
Taunton Rd IP1 . . . . .152 F5
Tavern La IP33 . . . . .154 B2
Tavern St Ipswich IP1 . . .155 B3
Stowmarket IP14 . . . . .124 D6
Tavneys Ride 2 CO8 . . . . .101 D4
Tayberry Pl IP3 . . . . .144 C7
Tayfen Rd IP33 . . . . .154 B3
Tayfen Terr IP33 . . . . .154 B3
Tayler Cl 4 IP7 . . . . .149 D5
Tayler Rd IP7 . . . . .149 E5
Tayler Dr 8 CO11 . . . . . . .104 E2
Taylor Rd 8 IP27 . . . . .20 B2
Taylors Farm IP14 . . . . . . .66 C6
Taylors Farm Rd CB9 . . . . .75 A2
Taylors Field CB8 . . . . . . .59 F4
Tea Kettle La CB8 . . . . . . .59 F5
Teal Ave CB7 . . . . .28 C5
Teal Cl IP2 . . . . .138 D3
Teal Wlk IP27 . . . . .6 A1
Teasel Cl CB9 . . . . .132 B7
Tedder Cl 3 IP24 . . . . .16 C2
Tedder Rd NR32 . . . . .113 B4
Teesdale IP7 . . . . .153 C5
Telesia CB8 . . . . .32 A4
Telesia Ct NR32 . . . . .113 B4
Temperance Pl 8 NR34 . . .111 B5
Templars Cl 6 CB9 . . . . . .132 C5
Temple Cl IP28 . . . . .31 C4
Temple End CO9 . . . . .74 C5
Temple Pattle 1 CO11 . . .104 E4
Temple Rd Ipswich IP1 . .140 C4
Isleham CB7 . . . . .29 B4

Temple Rd *continued*
Stowmarket IP14 . . . . .124 D5
Ten Bell La 12 CB7 . . . . . . .28 C4
Tenby Rd IP1 . . . . .139 B1
Tennyson Cl IP12 . . . . . . .146 E6
Tennyson Rd
15 Bury St Edmunds IP32 . .48 C5
Lowestoft NR32 . . . . .113 D2
Saxmundham IP17 . . . . . . .128 B4
Tennyson Way IP24 . . . . . .16 C4
Tenter Field 4 CO7 . . . . . .103 E5
Tenter Piece CO10 . . . . . . .78 D4
Tenterden Cl 6 NR33 . . . .114 D5
Tenth Rd CO10 . . . . .98 A3
Tentree Rd CO10 . . . . .92 C7
Terence Airey Ct 25 IP20 . .22 D6
Tern Cl CB9 . . . . .133 A5
Tern Rd Ipswich IP2 . . . . .138 E2
Stowmarket IP14 . . . . .124 F6
Terr The
Aldeburgh IP15 . . . . .130 E4
Newmarket CB8 . . . . .121 A3
Snape IP17 . . . . .72 D5
Terry Gdns IP5 . . . . .141 E7
Tewkesbury Pl 7 IP31 . . . .49 A5
Thackeray Gr IP14 . . . . . .124 B7
Thackeray Rd IP1 . . . . . . .134 E3
Thanet Rd IP4 . . . . .140 B6
Tharp Way CB7 . . . . .29 E1
Thatchers Wlk 4 IP14 . . . .124 D3
Theatre Royal* IP33 . . . .154 C1
Theatre St IP12 . . . . .146 F5
Theberton Rd IP16 . . . . . .129 D5
Thedwastre Cl 8 IP30 . . . . .50 F2
Thedwastre Rd IP31 . . . . . .49 E3
Theinetham Fen Nature
Reserve* IP22 . . . . .18 C3
Thellusson Rd 3 IP22 . . . . .85 E8
Thelnetham Rd IP22 . . . . . .18 E2
Thelnetham Windmill*
IP22 . . . . .18 E1
Theobald Cl 6 IP6 . . . . . .125 D4
Thetford Adult Ed Ctr 8
IP24 . . . . .16 B5
Thetford Cl 10 IP27 . . . . . .13 F2
Thetford Cottage Hospl
IP24 . . . . .16 C6
Thetford Gram Sch
IP24 . . . . .16 B6
Thetford Heath National
Nature Reserve*
IP24 . . . . .16 A2
Thetford Mus* IP24 . . . . .16 C6
Thetford Rd Brandon IP27 . .5 F1
Coney Weston IP31 . . . . . . .34 D8
Euston IP24 . . . . .16 E2
Fakenham Magna IP24 . . . . .33 E8
Fornham St Martin IP31 . . . .48 B5
Garboldisham IP22 . . . . . . .18 C4
2 Ipswich IP1 . . . . .139 A7
Ixworth IP31 . . . . .34 A2
Ixworth Thorpe IP31 . . . . . .33 F3
Mildenhall IP28 . . . . .116 E4
Santon Downham IP27 . . . . .6 B1
South Lopham IP22 . . . . . . .19 A4
Thetford Sta IP24 . . . . .16 B5
Thieves La IP31 . . . . .49 F8
Thingoe Hill IP32 . . . . .154 B4
Third Ave CO10 . . . . .77 B3
Thirlmere Cl IP11 . . . . .153 D6
Thirlmere Dr IP14 . . . . .124 B6
Thirlmere Wlk IP24 . . . . . . .113 A4
Thirlwall Dr CB7 . . . . .29 C1
Thistle Cl IP27 . . . . .6 A1
Thistledown NR33 . . . . .114 D4
Thistledown Dr IP31 . . . . . . .34 B2
Thixendale NR33 . . . . .114 E2
Thomas Arne Cl IP4 . . . . . .124 C8
Thomas Ave IP11 . . . . .152 D8
Thomas Bardwell Dr 4
NR35 . . . . .110 C2
Thomas Bole Cl IP22 . . . . . .18 D4
Thomas Gn IP27 . . . . .34 B1
Thomas La IP31 . . . . .154 B1
Thomas Mills High Sch
IP13 . . . . .126 A5
Thomas Walls Cl 3 IP31 . . .83 C5
Thomas Wolsey Specl Sch
IP1 . . . . .134 E3
Thomas Young Cl 3
IP14 . . . . .124 D3
Thompson Cl IP31 . . . . .51 D1
Thompson Rd IP1 . . . . .138 F8
Thompson Wlk IP32 . . . . . .122 D7
Thomsons La IP14 . . . . .69 A2
Thong Hall Rd IP13 . . . . . . .127 A5
Thorington Rd IP19 . . . . . . .42 A5
Thorn Cl CB7 . . . . .28 D8
Thorn Way IP11 . . . . .152 E4
Thorn Wlk IP12 . . . . .85 C2
Thornbush La IP8 . . . . .138 A8
Thorndon CE Prim Sch
IP23 . . . . .53 B8
Thorney Gn Rd IP14 . . . . . . .67 A6
Thorney Hall Cl IP14 . . . . . .124 E6
Thorney Rd IP9 . . . . .150 E4
Thornham Cl 8 NR33 . . . . .114 F4
Thornham Rd IP23 . . . . .36 D2
Thornham Walled Gdn*
IP23 . . . . .37 A2
Thornhayes Cl IP2 . . . . . . .139 A3
Thornhill Rd IP6 . . . . .82 B5
Thornley Dr IP4 . . . . .140 C8
Thornley Rd IP11 . . . . .153 B4
Thorns Cl 8 CB8 . . . . .61 E2
Thornton Cl IP18 7 . . . . . . .119 D7
Thornton Rd IP33 . . . . .122 E2

Thornycroft Gdns
NR33 . . . . .114 A3
Thoroughfare IP19 . . . . .118 B3
Thoroughfare The
Brundish IP13 . . . . .55 C8
Harleston IP20 . . . . .22 D6
Wilby IP21 . . . . .39 D1
10 Woodbridge IP12 . . . . .147 A5
Thorpe Abbots Rd
IP21 . . . . .21 D4
Thorpe Hall Rd IP21 . . . . . .38 F4
Thorpe La
Ashfield cum Thorpe IP14 . .69 C8
Debenham IP14 . . . . .53 F1
Trimley St Martin IP11 . . . .107 C8
Thorpe Rd
Aldeburgh IP16 . . . . .130 F6
Aldringham IP16 . . . . .129 D2
Thorpe's Hill IP8 . . . . .95 E6
Thorpeness Windmill*
IP16 . . . . .73 B6
Thrandeston Rd IP23 . . . .117 F7
Threadneedle St
Dedham CO7 . . . . .103 F4
1 Hadleigh IP7 . . . . .149 D6
Three Marsh La IP18 . . . .119 B6
Throckmorton Rd
NR35 . . . . .110 D3
Through Duncans
IP21 . . . . .146 E3
Through Jollys IP5 . . . . . .141 D8
Thunderbird Way
IP27 . . . . .109 F1
Thurlestone High Sch
IP1 . . . . .135 A4
Thurleston La IP1 . . . . . . .134 F5
Thurlow CE Prim Sch
CB9 . . . . .74 D6
Thurlow Cl IP17 . . . . .128 B3
Thurlow Cl IP14 . . . . .124 D6
Thurlow Pl 18 CB9 . . . . . .132 F6
Thurlow Rd CB9 . . . . .74 D7
Thurmans La IP11 . . . . . . .152 B8
Thurne Rd NR33 . . . . .114 F5
Thurston CE Prim Sch
IP31 . . . . .49 E4
Thurston Com Coll
IP31 . . . . .49 D4
Thurston Cl 6 IP11 . . . . . .152 C4
Thurston La CO10 . . . . .76 C7
Thurston Rd
1 Beyton IP30 . . . . .49 F2
Lowestoft NR32 . . . . .113 D2
Thurston Sta IP31 . . . . .49 E3
Thurston Sta IP31 . . . . .49 D3
Thwaite Rd
Ditchingham NR35 . . . . . . .110 C7
Thornton IP23 . . . . .53 B8
Wickham Skeith IP23 . . . . . .52 D7
Tibbenham's Score 6
NR32 . . . . .3 D4
Tiberius Cl CB9 . . . . .133 B5
Tide Mill* IP12 . . . . .147 B4
Tide Mill Way IP12 . . . . . .147 A4
Tideway NR32 . . . . .114 E8
Tidys Ct IP33 . . . . .154 B3
Tiger Hill Nature Reserve*
CO8 . . . . .101 E6
Tiggins La IP17 . . . . .128 D8
Tilbury Rd
Great Yeldham CO9 . . . . . . .90 A2
Ridgewell CO9 . . . . .89 E4
Tile Barn La CO11 . . . . . .104 E1
Tilbrooks Hill CB8 . . . . . . .61 B1
Timperley Cl IP7 . . . . .149 D7
Timperley Rd IP7 . . . . .149 E7
Timperleys IP8 . . . . .95 C6
Tinabrook Cl IP2 . . . . .138 E1
Tinker Brook IP13 . . . . . . .71 F5
Tinker St CO12 . . . . .106 C1
Tinker's La
Hadleigh IP7 . . . . .149 D5
Tivetshall St Mary NR15 . . .21 C8
Tinkers La NR34 . . . . .10 D1
Tintern Cl 5 IP22 . . . . . . .139 A2
Tippet Ave IP14 . . . . .124 C8
Titchwell Dr 2 IP3 . . . . . .144 D8
Tithe Ave IP28 . . . . .30 B8
Tithe Cl CB8 . . . . .46 C3
Title Rd IP27 . . . . .13 F2
Titlow Rd 6 IP20 . . . . .22 D6
Toad Row NR34 . . . . .10 F1
Todhunter Ave NR34 . . . . . .9 B6
Tog La CO6 . . . . .102 D2
Tokio Rd IP4 . . . . .140 A6
Toll Gate Rd 6 IP9 . . . . . .150 E3
Tollemache Bsns Pk
IP7 .80 E4
Toller Cl IP12 . . . . .131 C3
Toller Rd IP3 . . . . .139 E3
Tolley Cobbold St 3
IP28 . . . . .30 A8
Tollgate La 3 IP32 . . . . . .123 A8
Tollgate Prim Sch
IP32 . . . . .122 F8
Tollgate Rd IP14 . . . . .140 A6
Tom Jennings Cl CB8 . . . .120 F5
Tomline Cl IP30 . . . . .145 C5
Tomline Rd
Felixstowe IP11 . . . . .153 A3
Ipswich IP3 . . . . .140 A5
Tomline Wlk IP33 . . . . . . .122 B6
Tommy Flowers Dr
IP5 . . . . .141 E7
Tomo Bsns Pk IP14 . . . . . .124 F6
Tomo Ind Est IP14 . . . . . .124 E6
Tomtit's La IP14 . . . . .51 B2
Tonning St NR32 . . . . .113 C1

Tooks Comm La NR34 . . . . .8 F1
Top Rd Haskerton IP13 . . .146 B8
Rattlesden IP30 . . . . .65 D5
St Andrew, Ilketshall
NR34 . . . . .8 E1
Wingfield IP21 . . . . .39 A7
Top St IP12 . . . . .154 C3
Toper La IP33 . . . . .154 C1
Toppesfield Cl 3 IP7 . . . .149 D5
Toppesfield Gdns IP7 . . . .149 D5
Tortoiseshell Cl IP9 . . . . .142 E8
Tostock Rd IP30 . . . . .49 F2
Tot Hill IP14 . . . . .66 C8
Tottington La IP22 . . . . . . .20 B2
Tovell's Rd IP4 . . . . .139 F6
Towells 3 IP13 . . . . .84 F7
Tower Ct 18 CB9 . . . . .132 C5
Tower Field Rd IP12 . . . . . .85 D7
Tower Mill NR34 . . . . .111 C3
Tower Mill La IP7 . . . . . . .149 E6
Tower Mill Rd
Bungay NR35 . . . . .110 B3
1 Hadleigh IP7 . . . . .138 F7
Tower Ramparts IP1 . . . . .155 B3
Tower Ramparts Sh Ctr
IP1 . . . . .155 B3
Tower Rd
Felixstowe IP11 . . . . .152 F4
Lowestoft NR33 . . . . .115 A2
Tower St IP1 . . . . .155 B3
Town End Cl IP9 . . . . .132 D7
Town Farm Cl IP20 . . . . . . .23 C3
Town Farm Est IP12 . . . . .131 B3
Town Gn IP14 . . . . .124 C6
Town Hall Galleries*
IP1 . . . . .155 B3
Town House Cnr IP14 . . . . .68 F7
Town House La IP22 . . . . . .35 A3
Town Stps IP15 . . . . .130 E4
Townhouse Rd IP31 . . . . . .35 C1
Townlands Dr NR34 . . . . . .111 B3
Townlane Rd IP13 . . . . . . .123 B1
Townsend CB7 . . . . .28 C5
Townsend Way NR32 . . . .113 A6
Toyse Cl 1 CB5 . . . . .44 B6
Toyse La CB5 . . . . .44 A6
Trafalgar Cl IP4 . . . . .139 F6
Trafalgar Rd CO10 . . . . . .148 E7
Trafalgar St
4 Lowestoft NR32 . . . . . . .113 C1
Lowestoft NR32 . . . . .115 C8
Trafford Cl 2 IP14 . . . . . . .51 E1
Tranmere Gr IP1 . . . . .134 F2
Traveller's Hill (Tumuli)*
IP28 . . . . .32 E5
Travellers Rd IP13 . . . . . . .69 E5
Traverse The IP33 . . . . . . .154 B2
Treetops IP11 . . . . .152 E7
Treeview IP14 . . . . .124 B6
Trefoil Cl IP7 . . . . .138 F4
Tremlett La IP5 . . . . .141 F7
Trenchard Sq 8 IP26 . . . . . .4 D5
Trent Rd
1 Bury St Edmunds IP32 . . .48 C5
Ipswich IP3 . . . . .139 F2
Trevethan Cl IP32 . . . . . . .122 E7
Triangle Yd 9 NR32 . . . . .113 C2
Trimley Marshes Nature
Reserve* IP11 . . . . .107 B6
Trimley Rd IP10 . . . . .98 D2
Trimley St Martin Prim Sch
IP11 . . . . .98 D1
Trimley St Mary Prim Sch
IP11 . . . . .152 C8
Trimley Sta IP11 . . . . .152 C8
Trinity Ave
Felixstowe IP11 . . . . .152 B3
Mildenhall IP28 . . . . .116 C5
Trinity Cl Fordham CB7 . . . .29 B1
Ipswich IP5 . . . . .140 F7
28 Manningtree CO11 . . . .104 E2
16 Southwold IP18 . . . . . . .119 D5
Woodbridge IP12 . . . . .146 D3
Trinity Distribution Pk
IP11 . . . . .152 B4
Trinity Dr CB8 . . . . .121 B2
Trinity Gdns 3 NR35 . . . . .110 B4
Trinity Gild 7 CO10 . . . . . .78 D4
Trinity Link CB9 . . . . .132 E7
Trinity Mews IP33 . . . . . . .154 A3
Trinity Rd
Lowestoft NR32 . . . . .113 C1
Manningtree CO11 . . . . . . .104 E2
Trinity St Bungay NR35 . . .110 B4
Rose Hill IP3 . . . . .139 E4
Southwold IP18 . . . . .119 D5
Trinity Wlk IP14 . . . . .67 A7
Triple Plea La NR35 . . . . . . .7 B8
Triple Plea Rd NR35 . . . . . . .7 B8
Troon Ct 5 IP28 . . . . .30 A8
Troon Gdns 9 IP4 . . . . . . .136 B1
Trossachs The 1 NR32 . . .112 D2
Troston Mount (Tumulus)*
IP31 . . . . .33 D5
Troston Rd IP31 . . . . .33 E5
Trott's La CO10 . . . . .92 F3
Trotting Horse La CB8 . . . .75 A8
Trunch Hill IP20 . . . . .7 A3
Trunch Rd IP20 . . . . .7 B2
Trundley Cl IP30 . . . . .139 D7
Tuddenham Ave IP4 . . . . .139 E7
Tuddenham CE Prim Sch
IP28 . . . . .30 F2
Tuddenham Cnr IP28 . . . . .46 E6

Tuddenham La IP5 .....136 B2
Tuddenham Rd
Barton Mills IP28 .....116 F2
Ipswich IP4 .....155 C4
Westerfield IP4 .....136 A3
Tudor Ave IP22 .....20 B3
Tudor CE VC Prim Sch
CO10 .....148 C7
Tudor Cl
Chedburgh IP29 .....62 D5
2 Framlingham IP13 .....126 C3
3 Shotley Gate IP9 .....107 A5
Sudbury CO10 .....148 C7
Tudor Ct Ipswich IP4 .....155 C3
1 Occold IP23 .....37 F1
Westhorpe IP14 .....51 E2
Tudor Gn CO10 .....148 C8
Tudor Rd CO10 .....148 C7
Tudor Wlk
5 Honington IP31 .....33 D5
1 Lowestoft NR33 .....114 E4
Tuffen La IP22 .....35 D8
Tuffields Rd IP29 .....63 B3
Tuffs Rd IP23 .....117 D4
Tumbril La IP21 .....22 A3
Tunbeck Cl IP20 .....23 A8
Tunbeck Rd IP20 .....23 A8
Tunbridge Cl **4** GB5 .....44 A5
Tunneys La NR35 .....110 C8
Tuns La IP33 .....154 C1
Tunstall Dr NR32 .....112 F4
Tunstall Gn IP21 .....71 F2
Turin St IP2 .....155 B1
Turin Way **2** NR31 .....3 C6
Turino Ave IP12 .....98 B8
Turkentine Cl **14** CO10 .....92 B3
Turkeyhall La IP14 .....51 F6
Turn La IP12 .....147 A4
Turnberry Cl **3** NR33 .....114 F4
Turnberry Dr **11** IP28 .....48 C6
Turnbull Cl IP15 .....141 E7
Turner Cl
Ditchingham NR35 .....110 C7
Haverhill CB9 .....132 B7
4 Lowestoft NR32 .....113 C6
Sudbury CO10 .....148 E8
Turner Gdns IP12 .....146 D3
Turner La **4** IP9 .....141 D8
Turner La **1** IP4 .....51 C1
Turner Rd Ipswich IP3 .....144 A8
Stowmarket IP14 .....124 B7
Turnpike Hill CB9 .....74 B2
Turnpike Rd
Chippenham CB8 .....45 F8
Red Lodge IP28 .....30 B1
Woodbridge IP12 .....147 B6
Turnstile La **1** IP14 .....53 D6
Turnstone Cl **2** IP28 .....116 D4
Turnstone Dr IP32 .....49 A3
Turret La IP4 .....155 B2
Tut Hill IP28 .....48 B5
Tutelina Rd IP30 .....64 A6
Tutt Hill (Tumulus)*
IP24 .....16 D4
Tuyar Wlk CB8 .....120 E8
Tweed Cl CB8 .....45 F3
Twelve Acre App IP5 .....141 B7
Twin Oak Dr IP13 .....56 B7
Twinnings The IP14 .....124 C3
Twiss Cl **1** IP22 .....20 A3
Two Acres IP9 .....150 F4
Two House Cl IP13 .....127 C7
Two Pole Dro CB7 .....28 A7
Tydemans Ct **1** IP14 .....124 D6
Tye Gn CO10 .....77 A3
Tye La IP8 .....81 D2
Tyler St 3 Harwich CO12 .....106 F3
Ipswich IP1 .....155 B1
Tylers Gn IP11 .....152 C7
Tylers Way **1** IP14 .....124 D3
Tymmes Pl IP13 .....146 C8
Tyrone Cl IP1 .....134 D2

U

Ubbeston Way NR33 .....114 F4
Ufford Pl
16 Haverhill CB9 .....132 F6
8 Ufford IP13 .....84 F7
Ufford Rd Bredfield IP13 .....84 D7
Eyke IP12 .....85 B6
Uggeshall Cl NR32 .....113 A5
Ullswater NR33 .....114 D2
Ullswater Ave **4** IP11 .....153 D7
Ullswater Rd IP12 .....71 C2
Ulster Ave IP1 .....134 D1
Una Rd CO12 .....106 F2
Uncle's La IP19 .....24 B6
Undercliff Rd E IP11 .....153 C4
Undercliff Rd W IP11 .....153 A3
Underhill IP14 .....124 C5
Underwood Cl NR32 .....113 A6
Undley IP27 .....109 B5
Undley Rd IP27 .....109 B4
Unicorn Pl IP33 .....123 C6
Union Hill IP7 .....94 A8
Union La
Lowestoft NR32 .....112 F5
Wortham IP22 .....20 A1
Union Pl 3 NR33 .....115 C7
Union Rd
Lowestoft NR33 .....113 C1
Onehouse IP14 .....66 C6

Union Rd _continued_
Stowmarket IP14 .....124 A7
Union St IP4 .....155 C3
Union St E IP14 .....124 D6
Union St W IP14 .....124 D6
Unitarian Meeting House*
IP1 .....155 B2
**Unitarian Meeting House
The*** IP33 .....154 B2
Unity Rd IP3 .....140 C6
Unity St IP3 .....139 E4
Up St IP31 .....34 C4
Upland Rd IP4 .....140 A6
Uplands Cl NR33 .....114 D5
Uplands Cres CO10 .....148 C7
Uplands Mid Sch
CO10 .....148 D7
Uplands Rd
3 Aldringham cum Thorpe
IP16 .....73 F6
Sudbury CO10 .....148 C7
Uplands Rd N NR33 .....114 D5
Uplands Rd S NR33 .....114 C5
Uplands The
Aldringham cum Thorpe
IP16 .....73 E6
Beccles NR34 .....111 D4
Uplands Way Diss IP22 .....20 C3
Halesworth IP19 .....118 B5
Upper Ave IP19 .....118 B5
Upper Barclay St IP4 .....155 C2
Upper Brook La IP20 .....22 B4
Upper Brook St IP4 .....155 B3
Upper Burnthouse La
IP20 .....22 A5
Upper Cavendish St
IP3 .....140 A5
Upper E St CO10 .....148 D6
Upper Farm Rd CO10 .....89 E4
Upper Grange Rd
NR34 .....111 A4
Upper Harmans La
IP20 .....22 B5
Upper High St IP1 .....155 B4
Upper Melton Terr 10
IP12 .....84 E6
Upper Moorfield Rd
IP12 .....146 F6
Upper Oakley IP23 .....117 F8
Upper Olland St NR35 .....110 B3
Upper Orwell St IP4 .....155 C2
Upper Rd CO10 .....101 C8
Upper Rose La IP22 .....20 C1
Upper St
Brome Street IP23 .....117 F8
Gissing IP22 .....20 F8
Layham IP7 .....149 F1
Stansfield CO10 .....76 C6
Stanstead CO10 .....77 C4
Stratford St Mary CO7 .....103 E5
Upper Tumbril La IP27 .....110 F1
Upperfield Dr IP11 .....153 C6
Upsons Way IP5 .....141 E8
Upthorpe Rd IP31 .....34 F4
Upton Cl **1** IP14 .....124 D6
Upton Pl IP16 .....129 C5
Urban Rd IP20 .....22 D6
Uvedale Gdns IP6 .....125 E4
Uxbridge Cres **3** IP1 .....140 C1

V

Vale Ct IP27 .....5 E4
Vale La
Bury St Edmunds IP33 .....123 C3
Kersey IP7 .....94 A6
Stutton IP9 .....105 A6
Valentine Way IP30 .....64 F7
Valerian Rise **7** IP24 .....16 D6
Valiant Rd IP31 .....33 D4
Valiant St **6** IP28 .....13 B1
Valley Cl
4 Brantham CO11 .....104 E5
Halesworth IP19 .....118 C4
Ipswich IP1 .....135 C1
**Valley Farm Camargue
Horses*** IP13 .....127 A8
Valley Farm La IP7 .....94 E6
Valley Farm Rd IP12 .....147 B8
Buxhall IP14 .....65 F3
Wherstead IP9 .....144 A4
Valley Rd Battisford IP14 .....80 F8
Chilton CO10 .....92 C5
Great Bricett IP7 .....80 D6
Harwich CO12 .....106 E1
Ipswich IP1 .....135 B1
Leiston IP16 .....129 E6
Little Blakenham IP8 .....81 E4
Valley View CO10 .....77 C4
Valley Wash CO10 .....75 D4
Valley Wlk CB8 .....120 E3
Valley Wlk IP11 .....152 F5
Valleyview Dr IP14 .....140 F4
Vallibus Cl **1** NR32 .....112 E4
Van Dyck Cl **9** NR32 .....113 B6
Vandyck Rd **7** IP3 .....144 A8
Vanners Rd CB9 .....132 E5
Vaughan St IP2 .....155 B1
Vaunce's La IP21 .....21 E4
Vaunces La IP21 .....21 E4
Vaux Ave **15** CO12 .....106 F1
Velda CI NR33 .....114 F4
Ventris Cl IP22 .....138 D5
Verdons La IP21 .....39 C4
Verdure Cl **2** NR32 .....112 F5
Vere Gdns IP1 .....135 C2

Vermeer Cl **5** NR32 .....113 B6
Vermont Cres IP4 .....155 C4
Vermont Rd IP4 .....155 C4
Verneuil Ave IP14 .....124 D3
Veryan Dr IP2 .....155 B1
Vetch Wlk CB7 .....132 B7
Veyses End **6** CO7 .....103 E5
Viburnum Gn NR32 .....113 C2
Vicarage Cl CB8 .....59 E5
Vicarage Field CO10 .....148 F3
Vicarage Gdns
10 Debenham IP14 .....53 F2
4 Mildenhall IP28 .....116 B4
Vicarage Hill 7 IP12 .....147 A5
Vicarage La Acton CO10 .....92 A6
Bramford IP8 .....134 B1
Bungay NR35 .....110 E3
Wherstead IP9 .....143 B5
Woodditton CB8 .....60 B6
Vicarage Rd
Belcham St Paul CO10 .....90 D5
Felixstowe IP11 .....152 D4
Laxfield IP13 .....40 B3
Newmarket CB8 .....121 B3
Thetford IP24 .....16 C6
Wingfield IP21 .....39 A8
Winston IP14 .....54 A1
Victor Charles Cl IP27 .....5 E3
Victor Rd IP9 .....33 D4
Victoria Cl **3** IP31 .....49 E4
Victoria Cres **2** CO11 .....104 E2
Victoria Hill IP13 .....117 C4
Victoria Mill Rd IP13 .....126 B2
Victoria Rd
Aldeburgh IP15 .....130 E4
Diss IP22 .....20 D2
Felixstowe IP11 .....152 F3
Haverhill CB9 .....132 D6
1 Lowestoft NR33 .....114 F7
Stowmarket IP14 .....124 E7
Woodbridge IP12 .....147 A5
Victoria St
Bury St Edmunds IP33 .....154 A2
Felixstowe IP11 .....153 A4
7 Harwich CO12 .....107 B2
Ipswich IP1 .....139 A6
6 Southwold IP18 .....119 D5
Victoria Terr
3 Fressingfield IP21 .....39 E8
Lowestoft NR33 .....115 C7
Victoria Way CB8 .....120 E7
Victory Cl IP33 .....123 C2
Victory Ct IP14 .....124 C6
Victory Rd Ipswich IP4 .....140 A7
Leiston IP16 .....129 C5
View Point Rd IP1 .....153 H10
Viking Cl IP12 .....84 B1
Viking Hts **2** IP12 .....84 B1
Viking Rd IP14 .....124 C5
Villa Hill IP12 .....99 B7
Village Way
Lowestoft NR32 .....113 B5
Waldringfield IP12 .....98 D7
Vince's Rd IP22 .....20 D2
Vincent Cl Exning CB8 .....120 E7
2 Feltwell IP26 .....4 E5
Ipswich IP1 .....138 E8
Vincent Drift IP5 .....141 F7
Vine Cl IP12 .....17 E1
Vine Rd IP6 .....69 C2
Vine Wlk IP9 .....150 E3
Vinefields The IP33 .....154 C2
Vinery Cl IP13 .....127 C6
Vinery Rd IP33 .....122 F3
Vines The IP17 .....128 D7
Vinesse Rd CO10 .....102 B2
Vineway The **2** CO12 .....107 A2
Violet Cl
Bury St Edmunds IP32 .....123 F5
Ipswich IP2 .....138 E4
Violet Hill Rd IP14 .....124 A2
Virginia Rd IP11 **11** 30 A8
Viscount Cl IP22 .....20 E2
Vyces Rd IP33 .....126 B3

W

Wacker Field Rd **8** IP12 .....85 E8
Wadd La IP17 .....72 C6
Waddesdon Rd **5** CO12 .....107 B2
Waddlegoose La IP14 .....54 D2
Waddling La NR32 .....112 A7
Wade Cres CO10 .....92 E8
Wade's La Raydon IP7 .....94 E1
Shotley IP9 .....106 E7
Wadehall La NR34 .....10 B5
Wades Gr IP5 .....141 E7
Wades Wood **1** IP30 .....50 D1
Wadgate Rd IP11 .....152 E4
Wadhurst Rd IP3 .....140 D3
Waggoners Ct IP12 .....146 F5
Wagtail Dr IP32 .....123 F7
Wainford Cl **5** NR34 .....9 F4
Wainford Rd NR35 .....110 E5
Wainwright Cl **4** NR33 .....114 C3
Wainwright Gdns IP6 .....81 F5
Wainwright Way IP5 .....141 D8
Wake Ave IP8 .....116 C5
Wakeshall La CO10 .....90 B4
Walberswick Visitor Ctr*
IP18 .....119 B2
Walberswick Way 8
NR32 .....113 A3
Walcot Rd IP22 .....20 D3
Walcot Rise IP22 .....20 D3
Walcott Wlk NR33 .....115 A6
Waldegrave Cl **24** CO11 .....104 D2

Waldegrave Rd CO11 .....104 D2
Waldingfield Rd
10 Acton CO10 .....92 B7
Chilton CO10 .....148 F8
Waldringfield Prim Sch
IP12 .....98 D7
Waldringfield Rd IP12 .....84 C1
Walk The Bacton IP14 .....51 D5
Beccles NR34 .....111 B6
Ipswich IP1 .....155 B3
Walton IP11 .....152 E6
Walker Chase IP5 .....141 C6
Walker Cl IP14 .....140 C5
Walker Gdns NR34 .....26 E5
Walks The NR34 .....10 A8
Wall La CO11 .....105 E2
Wallace Rd IP1 .....134 F2
Walled Gdn The* IP17 .....72 B8
Waller's Gr IP2 .....138 F4
Wallow La IP7 .....80 D4
Walls The CO11 .....104 E2
Walmer Cl NR33 .....115 A5
Walmer Rd NR33 .....115 A5
Walnut Cl Acton CO10 .....92 B8
Felixstowe IP11 .....153 D7
Hopton IP22 .....18 C1
12 Lakenheath IP27 .....13 F2
Walnut Gr IP28 .....30 A4
Walnut Tree Ave IP14 .....85 D8
Walnut Tree Cl **4** IP8 .....134 A2
Walnut Tree La
2 Harkstead IP9 .....106 A5
Sudbury CO10 .....148 C8
Walnut Tree Meadow
IP14 .....68 B6
Walnut Tree Wlk IP14 .....124 C6
Walnuts La IP13 .....127 B5
Walnuts The
Beccles NR34 .....111 E4
3 Ufford IP13 .....84 F7
Walnuttree Hospl
CO10 .....148 B5
Walpole Cl NR35 .....110 D7
Walpole La IP19 .....41 D5
Walpole Rd
Bramfield IP19 .....41 E4
Halesworth IP19 .....118 C4
**Walsham Le Willows CE VC
Prim Sch** IP31 .....35 C2
Walsham Rd
Finningham IP14 .....36 A1
6 Ixworth IP31 .....34 B1
Wattisfield IP22 .....35 C3
Walsingham Cl **11** CO10 .....92 B3
Walsingham Rd IP12 .....122 D3
Walters Cl **9** NR31 .....3 B7
Waltham Cl IP12 .....139 A2
Walton Ave IP11 .....152 E6
Walton Cl **5** Fordham CB7 .....29 A1
1 Stowmarket IP14 .....124 B8
Walton Rd NR32 .....113 D1
Wamil Rd IP28 .....30 B5
Wamil Way IP28 .....116 B4
Wangford Rd
Lakenheath IP27 .....13 F7
Reydon IP18 .....26 D1
Southwold IP18 .....119 B8
Uggeshall NR34 .....26 A3
Westhall IP19 .....42 C3
Wannock Cl NR33 .....114 D4
Wansisden Cnr IP12 .....86 A6
Ward Cl IP7 .....149 D8
Ward Rd IP8 .....138 B2
Ward's View IP5 .....141 E8
Wardlaw Ct **10** IP14 .....53 F2
Wardley Cl IP2 .....138 D2
Wardley Hill Rd NR35 .....8 D8
Ware Rd IP7 .....80 B6
Wareham Ave IP3 .....140 D3
Warene Cl **3** IP13 .....126 C3
Warham Rd CO12 .....106 F1
Warner Way CO10 .....148 E6
Warren Chase IP5 .....141 E2
Warren Cl Elmswell IP30 .....50 E2
Lakenheath IP27 .....109 D5
Warren Cl **1** CB8 .....132 C5
Warren Heath Ave
IP3 .....140 D2
Warren Heath Rd IP3 .....140 D2
Warren Hill La IP15 .....130 D7
Warren Hill Rd IP12 .....146 E4
Warren La
Arwarton IP9 .....106 D6
Hopton IP22 .....50 E2
27 Martlesham Heath IP5 .....98 A8
Woolpit IP30 .....50 F1
Warren Lodge NR31 .....2 B7
Warren Rd
Great Yarmouth NR31 .....9 B8
Herringswell CB8 .....46 A8
Iken se Snar NR31 .....3 C7
Lowestoft NR32 .....113 D4
Red Lodge IP28 .....30 C1
Warren Sch NR33 .....114 C6
Warren The IP18 .....119 E8
Warren's La NR34 .....10 A2
Warrington Rd IP1 .....155 A4
Warrington St CB8 .....121 A2
Warwick Ave
Felixstowe IP11 .....118 C5
Woodbridge IP12 .....146 F6
Warwick Cl **10** CB9 .....132 C6
Warwick Rd IP4 .....139 E6
Wash La Beccles NR34 .....111 B2
Boxford CO6 .....93 D2
Burgh St Peter NR34 .....10 C8
Dennington IP13 .....55 E6
Frostenden NR34 .....26 C3

Wash La _continued_
Great Finborough IP14 .....124 A5
Hinderclay IP22 .....35 E8
Kessingland NR33 .....11 C1
Mendlesham IP14 .....52 E3
Redgrave IP22 .....19 D1
Reydon IP18 .....26 D2
St Peter, South Elmham
NR35 .....23 E7
Shelfanger IP22 .....20 B6
Spexhall IP19 .....118 A7
Stanton IP31 .....34 F3
Topcroft NR35 .....7 A8
Wenhaston with Mells Hamlet
IP19 .....118 E1
Westleton IP17 .....58 B8
Witnesham IP6 .....83 A6
Washington St **4** IP28 .....30 A8
Wassicks La IP14 .....51 E3
Watch House Hill
NR35 .....110 C4
Water Farm Dr IP7 .....94 E1
Water La
Athelington IP13 .....38 F1
Barnardiston CB9 .....75 B4
Barnham IP24 .....16 C2
Botesdale IP22 .....35 F5
3 Bures CO8 .....101 C5
Cavendish CO10 .....76 E1
Debenham IP14 .....53 E2
Denston CB8 .....75 F7
Garboldisham IP22 .....18 D4
Great Bradley CB8 .....74 C8
Great Horkesley CO6 .....102 C4
Great Whelnetham IP30 .....64 A6
Helions Bumpstead CB9 .....88 B4
Kersey IP7 .....94 A6
Lavenham IP22 .....149 E1
Lowestoft NR32 .....113 C2
Polstead CO6 .....102 F8
Steeple Bumpstead CB9 .....88 D3
Sturmer CB9 .....133 D3
Thelnetham IP22 .....18 E1
Thornham Magna IP23 .....37 A1
Weybread IP21 .....22 D4
Worlingworth IP13 .....54 D3
Water Mill La IP12 .....38 C8
Water Run The IP7 .....79 F7
Water Street CO10 .....78 D4
Watercourse The CB8 .....121 A4
Waterford Rd IP11 .....134 D2
Waterhead La IP12 .....147 D8
Watering Cl **11** IP8 .....81 C3
Watering La IP17 .....72 C7
Watering Rd IP12 .....38 D5
Waterloo Ave
Leiston IP16 .....129 B6
4 Roydon IP22 .....20 A3
Waterloo Cl CB8 .....120 D8
Waterloo Rd
4 Ipswich IP1 .....139 A7
Lowestoft NR33 .....115 D7
Sotterley NR34 .....26 A7
Watermill Cl IP7 .....149 E2
Watermill Rd CO12 .....98 C5
Waters Ave NR33 .....114 C3
Waterside IP7 .....29 C5
Waterworks Rd **12** IP28 .....30 A8
Waterworks St IP4 .....155 C2
Watery La **11** IP13 .....146 A8
Watson Cl IP3 .....123 B2
Watson Way IP17 .....99 E4
Watson's Hill IP7 .....79 F1
Watsons Cl **3** NR31 .....3 C7
Watt Cl IP12 .....99 E4
Wattisfield Rd IP31 .....35 C2
Wattisham Airfield IP7 .....80 C6
Wattisham Airfield Mus*
IP7 .....80 C6
Wattisham Rd IP7 .....79 F4
Waveney Cl **3** IP17 .....128 C4
Waveney Cres NR33 .....115 B7
Waveney Dr NR33 .....115 A7
Waveney Hill
Carlton Colville NR32 .....114 B8
Lowestoft NR32 .....112 B1
Waveney Hts IP21 .....21 F2
Waveney Rd
Beccles NR34 .....111 B4
Bungay NR35 .....110 D3
10 Bury St Edmunds IP32 .....48 C5
Ditchingham NR35 .....110 C8
Felixstowe IP11 .....152 E3
Ipswich IP1 .....135 A3
10 Lowestoft NR33 .....115 D8
**Waveney Sports & Leisure
Ctr** NR32 .....113 C3
Waveney Terr 4 CB9 .....132 E5
**Waveney Valley Swimming
Pool** NR35 .....110 D2
Way Bank La CO9 .....89 C7
Wayne Cl NR32 .....113 B5
Wayside Cl IP14 .....124 D3
Weald The NR32 .....112 E2
Weatheralls Cl **9** CB7 .....28 D4
Weaver Cl IP1 .....138 D8
Weavers Cl
2 Hadleigh IP7 .....149 D6
4 Lavenham CO10 .....78 D4
Stowmarket IP14 .....124 C3
Weavers Croft **8** IP20 .....22 D6
Weavers Ct IP14 .....148 C5
Weavers Rd CO10 .....77 A2
Weavers La CO10 .....148 C5
Weavers Marsh La
IP17 .....41 E2
Weavers Way **2** IP6 .....82 A5
Webb Rd IP14 .....124 D3

Webb St 1 IP2 139 C3
Webb's Cl IP14 124 C1
Webbs Ct IP5 141 C7
Webster St NR35 110 A4
Weddell Rd CB9 133 A4
Weeting Castle* IP27 5 E4
Weeting Heath Nature Reserve* IP27 5 C3
Weeting Heath Visitor Ctr* IP27 6 C4
Weeting Prim Sch IP27 5 E3
Weir Pl IP10 98 D2
Weirs Dro CB5 44 A6
Welbeck Cl
Felixstowe IP11 152 C7
North Grove NR34 10 C4
Welbourne Way NR34 10 C4
Welch Cl NR34 10 D3
Welham La IP28 47 D5
Well Bottom CB8 45 D4
Well La 9 CO10 90 A8
Well St IP33 154 B2
Wellesley Rd
Ipswich IP3 139 F5
Troston IP31 33 D4
Wellington Cl
Hadleigh IP7 149 D7
Thistley Green IP28 30 A6
Wellington Espl NR33 115 C6
Wellington Rd
Eye IP23 117 D3
4 Feltwell IP26 4 E5
6 Harwich CO12 107 C3
2 Lowestoft NR33 115 A3
8 Mildenhall IP28 30 A8
13 Troston IP31 33 D5
Wellington St
7 Ipswich IP1 139 A7
1 Newmarket CB8 121 A3
Wellington Terr 5 CB9 132 C5
Wells Cl IP4 139 E6
Wells Cnr IP13 39 F2
Wells Ct IP28 116 B5
Wells Hall Com Prim Sch CO10 148 F2
Wells Hall Rd CO10 148 F3
Wells' La IP20 22 D5
Wells Rd IP20 22 C5
Wells Way IP14 53 F1
Wellum Cl 13 CB9 132 C5
Wembley Ave NR34 111 B4
Wendy Cl 7 IP9 106 C8
Wenham La
East Bergholt CO7 151 D8
Wenham Magna CO7 150 A2
Wenham Rd IP8 150 E8
Wenhaston La IP19 42 D5
Wenhaston Prim Sch IP19 42 C6
Wenhaston Rd IP19 42 B5
Wenhaston Way 2 NR32 112 F3
Wensleydale 5 NR33 114 E3
Wensum Gdns NR32 113 C3
Wentford Ct 7 CB9 132 A6
Wentford View 1 CO10 76 A1
Wentworth Cl
14 Fornham All Saints IP28 48 C6
Hadleigh IP7 149 F5
Weeting IP27 5 E4
Wentworth Dr
Felixstowe IP11 153 C6
7 Ipswich IP8 138 C2
10 Mildenhall IP28 116 B5
Wentworth Rd IP15 130 F4
Wentworth Terr 5 CB9 132 C6
Wentworth Way 2 NR33 114 F4
Wesel Ave IP11 152 D3
Wesley Cl NR34 111 B2
Wesley End Rd CO9 89 B2
Wesley Way IP1 138 F8
West Dock Rd CO12 106 F3
West Dr
Mildenhall IP28 116 B4
Soham CB7 28 C4
West Dr Cres CB7 28 C4
West Dr Gdns CB7 28 C4
West End CB8 60 B5
West End La
Great Thurlow CB9 74 B4
16 Harwich CO12 107 A1
West End Rd IP1 155 A2
West Gr NR33 115 A3
West Hall Dr IP26 6 A8
West Hall Rd
1 Mundford IP26 6 B8
Walsham le Willows IP22 35 F3
West Harling Rd NR16 18 B8
West Herne La IP22 19 A1
West Hill IP16 129 C2
West La IP15 130 E3
West Lawn IP4 140 C8
West Meadows IP1 134 C4
West Mill Gn IP9 104 F7
West Rd
Bury St Edmunds IP33 122 E4
Ipswich IP3 140 E1
West Row Prim Sch IP28 29 E7
West Row Rd IP28 116 A5
West Side Cl NR32 113 C5
West St Harwich CO12 107 B3
Icklingham IP28 31 C4
Isleham CB7 29 B5
Rickinghall Inferior IP22 35 E3
West Stow Anglo-Saxon Village* IP28 31 F2
West Stow Ctry Pk* IP28 31 F2
West Stow Rd IP28 32 B1
West Suffolk Coll IP33 122 E6
West Suffolk Hospl The IP33 123 A2
West Tofts Rd IP26 6 D7
West View Burstall IP8 95 F7
Carlton IP17 128 D6
Stowmarket IP14 124 B6
West View Gdns 4 IP23 36 D2
West Wood 9 IP31 49 A5
Westbourne Ct 6 CB9 132 E6
Westbourne High Sch IP1 134 E1
Westbourne Rd IP1 134 F1
Westbury Ave IP33 122 D5
Westbury Rd IP4 140 B8
Westend La CB9 133 F8
Westerfield La IP6 136 A5
Westerfield Rd
Ipswich IP1 155 C4
Westerfield IP6 135 E4
Westerfield Sta IP6 135 E3
Westerings The 1 CO6 102 C5
Western Ave
Felixstowe IP11 153 D6
Haverhill CB9 132 C7
Western Cl 4 Feltwell IP26 4 D5
Ipswich IP4 140 F4
Western Way IP33 122 D6
Western's End 6 CO11 104 E4
Westfield CO10 90 A7
Westfield Com Prim Sch CB9 132 F5
Westgarth Gdns IP33 122 E3
Westgate 5 IP16 73 F6
Westgate Prim Sch IP33 154 A1
Westgate St
Bury St Edmunds IP33 154 C1
Ipswich IP1 155 B3
Long Melford CO10 77 E1
Westgate St Service Rd IP1 155 B3
Westhall IP21 39 B5
Westhall Rd NR32 113 B5
Westholme Cl IP12 146 F4
Westholme Rd IP1 135 A1
Westhorpe 3 CB5 44 A6
Westhorpe Rd
Finningham IP14 52 A8
Wyverstone IP14 51 E6
Westland 26 IP5 98 A8
Westland Rd NR33 114 E6
Westleton Heath National Nature Reserve* IP17 58 E8
Westleton Rd IP17 57 E8
Westleton Way 17 IP11 152 D5
Westley Bottom Rd CB8 59 A4
Westley La IP29 122 B3
Westley Mid Sch IP33 122 C5
Westley Rd IP33 122 D5
Westley Way IP31 50 E7
Westminster Cl IP4 140 B5
Westminster Dr IP33 122 D3
Westmorland Cl 8 CO11 105 A2
Westmorland Rd IP11 153 D7
Weston Colville Rd CB8 59 E1
Weston Rd NR32 113 B5
Weston Way CB8 120 F6
Westropps 6 CO10 91 E7
Westward Deals CB9 133 F8
Westward Ho IP16 129 C6
Westwood Ave
Ipswich IP1 139 A8
Lowestoft NR33 114 E6
Wet La CO4 102 F3
Wetherby Cl IP1 135 B3
Wetherden Rd
Elmswell IP30 50 F2
Great Ashfield IP31 51 B6
Wetheringsett CE Prim Sch IP14 53 A5
Wexford Rd IP1 134 D2
Weyland Rd IP6 83 A6
Weylands Cl IP14 67 D7
Whalebone Cnr CO4 103 C4
Whapload Rd NR32 113 E1
Wharf La 3 CO8 101 C4
Wharfedale NR33 114 F3
Wharfedale Rd IP1 135 A1
Wharton St 5 NR35 110 B4
Whatfield CE Prim Sch IP7 80 C1
Whatfield Rd
Aldham IP7 94 C7
Elmsett IP7 80 F1
Whatfield Way IP14 124 E3
Wheatacre Dr 3 NR32 3 C4
Wheatfield Rd NR33 114 D4
Wheatfields
3 Botesdale IP22 36 A6
4 Thurston IP31 49 E4
Whatfield IP7 80 C1
Wheatsheaf Cl CO11 105 E2
Wheatsheaf La CO11 105 E2
Wheelbarrow La IP20 23 F5
Wheeler's La IP31 51 A5
Wheelwright Cl IP30 49 C2
Wheelwrights The IP11 152 C8
Whepstead Rd
Hawstead IP29 63 B7
Horringer IP29 122 D1
Wherry La IP4 155 C2
Wherry Quay IP4 155 C2
Wherry Rd
3 Bungay NR35 110 D3
3 Dunnis Hill NR35 110 D3
Wherstead Rd IP2 155 B1
Whights Cnr IP8 138 A1
Whin Marsh 6 IP15 130 E5
Whinchat Cl IP2 138 D3
Whinfield 13 IP5 98 A8
Whinfield Ave 23 CO12 106 F1
Whinfield Ct 16 IP5 98 A8
Whinneys The IP5 141 D8
Whinyard Way 3 IP11 153 D7
Whiskin Cl 7 NR32 112 D2
Whistle Dro IP28 12 D5
Whitby Rd
Bury St Edmunds IP33 122 D3
Ipswich IP4 139 F8
White Elm Rd IP30 50 C1
White Elm St IP3 139 E4
White Foot La IP13 83 E6
White Hall Cl CO10 92 C5
White Hart La 20 CB7 28 D4
White Horse Cl 4 IP11 153 C6
White Horse Hill IP9 142 D1
White Horse La IP30 64 D7
White Horse Rd
Capel St Mary IP9 150 F3
East Bergholt CO7 151 D3
Kedington CB9 133 E8
White Horse St 4 NR32 113 E2
White House Farm La IP21 22 B6
White House Gdns NR34 111 A4
White House Rd IP1 134 D2
White Lion Ct IP7 149 D5
White Lion Rd NR34 10 B8
White Meadow 3 IP14 51 A1
White Womans La IP12 85 B7
White's La NR33 11 B1
Whitedike Dro IP26 4 B4
Whitegates CB8 121 B3
Whitehall Rd IP14 51 F1
Whitehouse Com Inf Sch IP1 134 E1
Whitehouse Ind Est IP1 134 C3
Whitehouse Jun Sch IP1 134 D3
Whitehouse La
Belchamp Otten CO10 90 D5
Earsham NR35 7 C5
Stowupland IP14 67 D8
Whitepost Cnr IP14 54 C1
Whites Cl IP21 39 B4
Whites Field CO7 151 B5
Whitethorn Rd IP3 140 F1
Whitewood Wlk 8 IP27 13 F2
Whithersfield Rd CB9 132 C8
Whiting Rd NR32 112 C2
Whiting St IP33 154 B1
Whitland Cl IP2 143 A8
Whitlands 6 CO10 77 A3
Whitlock Dr CO9 89 F1
Whittle Rd IP2 138 F6
Whitton Church La IP1 134 F4
Whitton Cl NR33 114 E6
Whitton Com Prim Sch IP1 134 E3
Whitton Ct NR33 115 A3
Whitton Gn Prim Sch NR33 114 F5
Whitton La IP1 134 D4
Whitton Leyer IP8 134 C2
Whitton Sports Ctr IP1 134 E4
Whitworth Cl IP2 138 D2
Whyteway IP19 24 B4
Wick La CO12 107 A1
Wick Rd Langham CO4 103 C2
Stoke-by-Nayland CO6 103 A6
Wicken Rd CB7 28 D1
Wickham Com Prim Sch IP13 127 B6
Wickham La IP14 52 A6
Wickham Mkt Sta IP12 71 C2
Wickham Rd IP23 52 F7
Wickhambrook Ct 2 IP11 152 C4
Wickhambrook Prim Sch CB8 61 E2
Wickhambrook Rd IP29 62 A5
Wicklow Rd IP1 134 D2
Wicks La IP14 67 D7
Widgeon Cl IP2 138 F3
Wigg's Way 3 NR32 3 D4
Wiggin Cl IP28 116 D2
Wiggs Acre NR34 10 C4
Wigmore Cl
Ipswich IP2 138 F1
Stoke Park IP2 139 A1
Wignall St CO11 104 C2
Wigston Rd IP33 122 C3
Wigwam Hill IP22 19 F1
Wilberforce St IP1 139 A6
Wilby CE Prim Sch IP21 39 B2
Wilby La IP13 39 E2
Wilby Rd IP21 39 A4
Wilbye Cl IP32 123 E4
Wild Acres 13 CB5 44 A5
Wild Tracks Offroad Activity Pk* CB7 45 E7
Wilde St Est IP28 13 D1
Wilderness Cl 3 IP20 22 D5
Wilderness Hill IP8 95 B6
Wilderness La
Harleston IP20 22 D6
Woodbridge IP12 147 A6
Wildes St NR32 113 E2
Wildflower Way NR35 110 B7
Wilding Dr IP5 141 D7
Wilding Rd IP8 138 C1
Wildmere La IP28 13 D1
Wilford Bridge Rd IP12 147 D7
Wilford Bridge Spur IP12 147 C7
Wilfred Hurry Cl IP8 134 A1
Wilfred Sherman Cl CB8 121 A4
Wilkes Ct IP5 141 E7
Wilkes Way IP14 124 C6
Wilkinson Dr IP5 141 C6
Wilkinson Way IP12 147 A6
Wilks Rd IP33 123 B2
Willbye Ave IP22 20 D3
Willcox Ave IP33 122 C6
William Armstrong Cl 6 IP30 50 F2
William Blake Ct CB9 132 C7
William Booth Way 11 IP11 152 D5
William Groom Ave 2 CO12 107 A1
William St IP1 155 B3
William's Way 4 IP28 29 F6
Williamsport Way IP6 125 F3
Willie Snaith Rd CB8 120 F6
Willoughby Cl IP13 71 A7
Willoughby Rd IP2 155 A1
Willow Cl
Badwell Ash IP31 50 F8
6 Claydon IP6 134 C8
Haverhill CB9 132 B7
Stradbroke IP21 39 B5
1 Sudbury CO10 148 C4
Worlingham NR34 111 F3
Wortwell IP20 23 A8
Willow Cres CB8 121 B2
Willow Gn IP13 54 E7
Willow Gr 3 CO6 102 C5
Willow La
Bedingham NR35 7 B7
Broome NR35 8 C7
Cotton IP14 52 B6
Willow Marsh La
Darsham IP17 42 A1
Yoxford IP17 41 F2
Willow Rd NR33 115 A2
Willow Tree Cl IP13 127 B6
Willow Way
Bury St Edmunds IP33 154 A3
9 Great Bricett IP7 80 D6
3 Harwich CO12 106 F1
8 Rendlesham IP12 85 D8
Willow Wlk
5 Harleston IP20 22 D5
Needham Market IP6 125 D6
Willowbrook Cl NR33 114 A3
Willowcroft Rd IP1 135 A2
Willowvale NR32 112 F6
Willrede Cl NR34 111 B3
Wilmslow Ave IP12 146 E5
Wilmslow Dr IP8 138 C2
Wilson Rd Hadleigh IP7 149 E5
Ipswich IP8 138 B1
Lowestoft NR33 115 C5
Wilton Rd IP26 4 E5
Wimbledon Ave IP27 14 E8
Wimborne Ave IP3 140 D4
Wimpole Cl IP5 140 F6
Wincanton Cl IP4 136 A1
Winchester Cl IP14 124 B6
Winchester Gdns 4 IP6 82 B5
Winchester Rd IP33 122 D4
Winchester Way IP2 142 F8
Windermere Cl IP3 144 B8
Windermere Pk NR32 113 A4
Windermere Rd
6 Felixstowe IP11 153 D7
Stowmarket IP14 124 C6
Sudbury CO10 148 E6
Windgap La IP14 51 D1
Windham Rd CO10 148 E6
Winding Piece 5 IP9 150 E3
Windings Rd 4 IP7 80 F1
Windmill Ave IP30 50 C1
Windmill Cl
Boxted CO4 102 F2
Ramsey & Parkeston CO12 106 C1
Soham CB7 28 E2
3 Somersham IP8 81 C3
Windmill Gn
Ditchington NR35 110 C7
19 Stanton IP31 34 E4
Windmill Hill
Capel St Mary IP9 150 C3
Exning CB8 120 C8
Long Melford CO10 77 D1
Windmill La IP21 38 F8
Windmill Rd IP20 23 A7
Windmill Rise
Bury St Edmunds IP33 154 A1
Hundon CO10 75 D4
1 Wetherden IP14 51 A1
Windmill Row 5 CO10 77 B3
Windrush Rd IP5 141 C8
Windsor Circ
1 Lakenheath IP27 14 A3
Lakenheath IP27 109 F1
Windsor Cl
7 Barnham IP24 16 C2
Lawshall IP29 63 D2
Windsor Pl CO10 148 E5
Windsor Rd
Felixstowe IP11 152 E3
Ipswich IP1 138 F7
Lowestoft NR33 115 C7
Newmarket CB8 120 E4
Southwold IP18 119 B8
Windsor Terr 12 CB9 132 C6
Windward Way NR33 114 E5
Windyridge Rd IP30 65 D5
Winfarthing Rd IP22 20 B6
Winfrith Rd IP3 140 D4
Wingfield Ave IP27 109 D7
Wingfield Meadows IP14 68 B6
Wingfield Old Coll & Gdns* IP21 39 A7
Wingfield Rd
Lakenheath IP27 109 D7
Syleham IP21 21 F1
Weybread IP21 22 C2
Wingfield St
Bungay NR35 110 B3
Ipswich IP4 155 C2
Wings Rd IP27 109 D6
Wings Rd Cl IP27 109 D6
Winnipeg Rd NR32 113 D2
Winsford Rd IP32 123 E6
Winston Ave
Ipswich IP4 140 C8
Lowestoft NR33 114 E7
Winston Cl
5 Felixstowe IP11 152 D5
11 Kessingland NR33 11 C1
Winston Rd
Southwold IP18 119 C7
Winston IP14 53 F1
Winthrop Rd IP33 122 D4
Winthrops The CO10 93 B4
Wissett Cl IP19 118 B4
Wissett Rd
Chediston IP19 41 B8
Halesworth IP19 118 A5
Wissett IP19 24 D1
Wissett Way NR32 113 B4
Wissey View 2 IP26 6 B8
Wissington Uplands CO6 102 A5
Wiston Rd CO6 102 B4
Withers Pl 2 CB7 29 A1
Withersdale Rd
Mendham IP20 23 A5
Weybread IP21 22 D4
Withersfield Rd
Haverhill CB9 132 C7
Withersfield CB9 74 C4
Withingdale Gall The* CO10 91 D7
Withipoll St IP4 155 C3
Witnesham Church La IP6 82 F5
Witnesham La IP6 136 C7
Witnesham Prim Sch IP6 83 A7
Witney Gn NR33 115 A3
Witney Rd 3 NR33 115 A3
Wittons La IP21 38 C7
Wix Rd CO12 106 C1
Wollaston Cl IP32 122 D8
Wollaston Rd NR32 113 D1
Wolsey Art Gall* IP1 155 C4
Wolsey Gdns IP11 153 A3
Wolsey Rd 4 IP14 124 C7
Wolsey St IP1 155 B2
Wolton Rd IP5 141 C7
Wolves Farm La IP7 94 E6
Wolves Wood Nature Reserve* IP7 94 F6
Wood Cl
1 Bentwaters Airfield IP12 85 D8
Kenninghall NR16 19 A8
Tostock IP30 50 B3
Wood Farm La IP18 26 C2
Wood Farm Rd IP13 83 C5
Wood Hall La IP23 37 B1
Wood La Bedingham NR35 7 C6
Bressingham IP22 19 E6
Dallinghoo IP13 70 B1
Dickleburgh & Rushall IP21 21 C2
Fressingfield IP21 40 A8
Henstead with Hulver Street NR34 26 E7
Hepworth IP22 35 A6
Oulton NR32 112 C3
Reydon IP18 26 C1
Scole IP21 21 C4
Thelnetham IP22 35 C6
Wood Rd
Badingham IP13 56 B6
Woolpit IP30 65 F8
Wood Side IP14 124 B5
Wood View 4 IP17 56 F8
Woodbridge Gall* IP12 146 F5
Woodbridge Mus The* IP12 147 A5

Woodbridge Prim Sch 15
IP12 ....147 A5
Woodbridge Rd
Alderton IP12 ....99 D5
Bredfield IP13 ....84 C7
Butley IP12 ....86 A5
Framlingham IP13 ....126 C1
Grundisburgh IP13 ....83 E6
Ipswich IP4 ....155 C3
Sutton IP12 ....85 A1
Tunstall IP12 ....71 E1
Waldringfield IP12 ....98 D6
Wantisden IP12 ....85 E5
Woodbridge Rd E IP4 ..140 C7
Woodbridge Sch IP12 ..146 F5
Woodbridge Sta 147 B4
Woodchurch Ave 6
NR33 ....114 C4
Woodcock Cl IP8 .....133 A5
Woodcock Rd IP2 .....138 E2
Woodcock Rise IP26 ....6 A1
Woodcote IP14 ....124 B6
Woodcrofts Cl 2 IP29 ..63 A1
Woodcutters Way
IP27 ....109 D7
Wooditton Rd
Kirtling CB8 ....60 D3
Newmarket CB8 ....121 A1
Woodditton CB8 ....60 B6
Woodfield Cl NR34 .....25 E7
Woodfield Dr IP14 ....124 E5
Woodfield La
Stowmarket IP14 ....124 D4
Stutton IP9 ....105 C5
Woodfields IP12 ....39 A4
Woodgates Rd CO7 ....151 D7
Woodhall Bsns Pk
CO10 ....148 D8
Woodhall Cl CO10 .....148 C7
Woodhall Com Prim Sch 3
CO10 ....148 D8
Woodhall Rd CO10 ....148 C7
Woodhouse La IP10 ...141 C2
Woodhouse Sq IP4 ....155 C2
Woodland Ave NR34 ...111 F4
Woodland Cl
Onehouse IP14 ....66 C6
Risby IP28 ....47 D5
Thurston IP31 ....49 E3
Woodland Dr
Bungay NR35 ....110 B1
Ellingham NR35 ....8 E7
Woodland Pl 7 IP31 ....49 A6

Woodlands
1 Chelmondiston IP9 ...106 C8
Hadleigh IP7 ....149 B7
33 Harleston IP20 ....22 D6
Lakenheath IP27 ....109 D8
Leiston IP16 ....129 C4
Woodlands Ave 4
NR33 ....114 C3
Woodlands Bsns Pk
IP30 ....49 B3
Woodlands Dr IP24 .....16 C7
Woodlands Rd
Holbrook IP9 ....105 E8
Raydon IP7 ....94 F2
Rushbrooke with Rougham
IP30 ....49 B3
Woodlands Rise IP27 ...14 D8
Woodlands The NR32 ..113 B8
Woodlands Way
Bramford IP8 ....134 C4
Mildenhall IP28 ....116 F5
Woodlane Rd IP23 .....38 C1
Woodlark Cl IP2 ......138 E1
Woodlark Dr 4 IP14 ...124 F7
Woodley Com Sch
IP14 ....124 B7
Woodleys Yd IP18 ....119 D5
Woodpecker Ave 2
NR33 ....114 D5
Woodpecker Cl 10 IP14 ..67 A5
Woodpecker Rd IP22 ..138 D3
Woodrush Rd IP3 .....140 E2
Woods Cl
Ditchingham NR35 ......110 B7
Sturmer CB9 ....133 C3
Woods La IP12 ....147 B7
Woods Loke E NR32 ...113 A3
Woods Loke Prim Sch
NR32 ....112 F3
Woods Loke W NR32 ..112 F3
Woodside
Beccles NR34 ....111 D3
Brampton with Stoven
NR34 ....25 E5
Martlesham Heath IP5 ...98 B8
Woodside Bsns Pk
IP31 ....32 F2
Woodside Cl
Bury St Edmunds IP33 ..123 B1
Lowestoft NR33 ....114 C3
Woodspring Cl 12 IP2 ..139 A2
Woodstone Ave IP1 ...135 C1
Woodthorpe Cl IP7 ....149 F5
Woodthorpe Rd IP7 ...149 E5
Woodville Rd IP4 .....139 F5
Woodward Ave IP14 ...51 F6

Woodward Cl IP2 .....138 D5
Woolhall St 2 IP33 ...154 B2
Woollards Cl IP1 ......139 A6
Woollards Gdns 3 CO10 ..91 E8
Woolmers Cl IP14 .....124 D4
Woolner Cl
7 Claydon IP6 ....82 A5
5 Hadleigh IP7 ....149 E6
Woolnough Cl 6 CB9 ...88 D3
Woolnough Rd IP12 ...146 F6
Woolnoughs The 2
IP5 ....141 D7
Woolpit & District Musuem*
IP30 ....50 D1
Woolpit Prim Sch IP30 ..50 D1
Woolpit Rd IP31 ....34 C2
Woolverstone Cl IP2 ..138 D1
Worcester Rd IP3 .....144 A8
Wordsworth Cl IP17 ..128 B4
Wordsworth Cres IP1 ..134 E3
Wordsworth Rd
4 Bury St Edmunds IP32 ..48 C5
2 Stowmarket IP14 .....124 B8
Worell Dr NR34 ....111 E4
Workhouse Hill
Boxted CO4 ....102 F3
Hartest IP29 ....77 B8
Workhouse La IP17 .....57 E2
Workhouse Rd
Little Horkesley CO6 ....102 B2
Thornham Magna IP23 ...37 A1
Workshop La IP10 .....145 C5
World's End La IP14 ...65 F2
World's End Rd IP13 ...55 B4
Worlingham Mid Sch
NR34 ....111 F3
Worlingham Prim Sch
NR34 ....9 F5
Worlingham Way
NR32 ....113 A4
Worlington Rd
Barton Mills IP26 ....30 E3
Worlington IP28 ....116 A3
Worlingworth CE Prim Sch
IP13 ....54 D7
Worlingworth Rd IP21 ..38 F3
Wortham Ling Nature
Reserve* IP22 ....19 F2
Wortham Pl 1 CB9 ...132 E6
Wortham Prim Sch
IP22 ....36 F2
Worthing Rd NR32 ....113 D3
Wrabness Local Nature
Reserve* IP9 ....105 E2
Wrabness Rd 1 CO12 ..106 D1

Wrabness Sta CO11 ...106 A2
Wragg Dr CB8 ....121 A6
Wratting Rd
Great Thurlow CB9 ......74 D5
Haverhill CB9 ....132 E7
Wren Ave IP2 ....138 D3
Wren Cl
Bury St Edmunds IP32 ...49 A4
Mildenhall IP28 ....116 D4
1 Stowmarket IP14 .....67 A5
16 Thurstow IP31 ......49 D4
Wrens Pk 2 IP31 .....153 D7
Wriggle St IP13 ....70 A7
Wright Cl IP14 ....124 D3
Wright La IP15 ....141 D8
Wright Rd IP3 ....140 C2
Wrights Way
Leavenheath CO6 ......102 A7
Woolpit IP30 ....50 C1
Wroxham Rd IP3 .....139 F3
Wyatt Cl IP30 ....50 F3
Wyatt Way IP24 ......16 B7
Wyatts La CO10 ......101 B8
Wye Rd IP3 ....140 A2
Wyken Rd IP31 ....34 D3
Wyken Vineyard & Gdns*
IP31 ....34 E2
Wykes Bishop St IP3 ..139 E4
Wymering Rd 10 IP18 ..119 D5
Wyncoll's La IP7 ......94 B2
Wyndham Way CB8 ...121 A6
Wynterton Cl IP3 .....140 B1
Wynton Rise IP14 ....124 E4
Wyvern Rd IP3 ....140 C1
Wyverstone Rd
Badwell Ash IP31 ....51 B7
Wyverstone Green IP14 ..51 E6

Y

Yale Bsns Pk IP3 .....144 F8
Yarmouth Pl 3 CB9 ...132 E6
Yarmouth Rd
Corton NR32 ....113 A8
Ditchingham NR35 .....110 D7
Geldeston NR34 ....9 A7
Ipswich IP1 ....139 A6
Kirby Cane NR35 ....8 E7
Lound NR32 ....2 F7
Lowestoft NR32 ....113 B5
Melton IP12 ....84 E6
Ufford IP13 ....127 B1
Woodbridge IP12 ......147 C8
Yarrow Dr NR33 .....114 C4

Yaxley Hall La IP23 .....37 C4
Yaxley Rd IP23 ....37 C3
Yeldham Pl CB9 ......132 E6
Yeoman Cres IP7 .....149 E5
Yeoman Rd IP11 .....152 D3
Yeoman Way IP7 .....149 E5
Yeoman's Cl NR35 ....110 C3
Yeomanry Yd IP33 ...154 A2
Yeovil Rd NR32 ......113 C2
Yerril Gdn CB9 ....132 C5
Yew Cl 1 IP27 ....13 F2
Yew Cl IP2 ....139 A3
Yew Tree Ct 1 IP33 ...122 F3
Yew Tree Rise IP13 ...127 C7
Yewdale NR33 ....114 D2
Yewtree Gr IP5 ......140 F7
Yewtree Rise IP8 ....138 C1
York Cl
Bury St Edmunds IP33 ..122 E5
1 Mildenhall IP28 ......30 A8
Sudbury CO10 ....148 C7
York Cres 12 Claydon IP6 ..82 B5
Claydon IP6 ....134 C8
York Rd
Bury St Edmunds IP33 ..154 A2
Felixstowe IP11 ....153 A4
Foxhall IP5 ....98 A7
Haverhill CB9 ....132 C5
Ipswich IP3 ....140 A4
Lowestoft NR32 ....113 C1
Southwold IP18 ....119 B5
Sudbury CO10 ....148 C6
York Terr IP3 ....154 A2
Yoxford Gdns* IP17 ..57 C8
Yoxford Mews 7 IP12 ..85 B3
Yoxford Prim Sch IP17 ..57 D8
Yoxford Rd
Middleton IP17 ....57 F6
Sibton IP17 ....57 A8

Z

Zanetta Ct NR32 ......113 C1
Zurich Cl 3 NR31 ....3 C6

Name and Address	Telephone	Page	Grid reference

Addresses

Name and Address	Telephone	Page	Grid reference

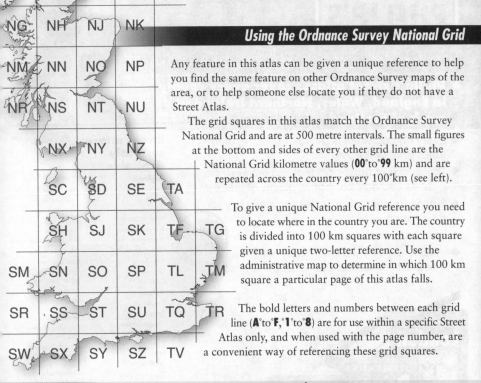

Any feature in this atlas can be given a unique reference to help you find the same feature on other Ordnance Survey maps of the area, or to help someone else locate you if they do not have a Street Atlas.

The grid squares in this atlas match the Ordnance Survey National Grid and are at 500 metre intervals. The small figures at the bottom and sides of every other grid line are the National Grid kilometre values (**00**°to°**99** km) and are repeated across the country every 100°km (see left).

To give a unique National Grid reference you need to locate where in the country you are. The country is divided into 100 km squares with each square given a unique two-letter reference. Use the administrative map to determine in which 100 km square a particular page of this atlas falls.

The bold letters and numbers between each grid line (**A**°to°**F**,°**1**°to°**8**) are for use within a specific Street Atlas only, and when used with the page number, are a convenient way of referencing these grid squares.

Example The railway bridge over DARLEY GREEN RD in grid square B1

Step 1: Identify the two-letter reference, in this example the page is in **SP**

Step 2: Identify the 1 km square in which the railway bridge falls. Use the figures in the southwest corner of this square: Eastings **17**, Northings **74**. This gives a unique reference: **SP 17 74**, accurate to 1°km.

Step 3: To give a more precise reference accurate to 100 m you need to estimate how many tenths along and how many tenths up this 1 km square the feature is (to help with this the 1 km square is divided into four 500 m squares). This makes the bridge about **8** tenths along and about **1** tenth up from the southwest corner.

This gives a unique reference: **SP 178 741**, accurate to 100°m.

Eastings (read from left to right along the bottom) come before Northings (read from bottom to top). If you have trouble remembering say to yourself Along the hall, THEN up the stairs !

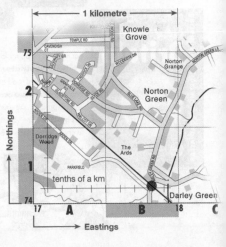

PHILIP'S MAPS

the Gold Standard for drivers

◆ **Philip's street atlases cover every county in England, Wales, Northern Ireland and much of Scotland**

◆ Every named street is shown, including alleys, lanes and walkways

◆ Thousands of additional features marked: stations, public buildings, car parks, places of interest

◆ Route-planning maps to get you close to your destination

◆ Postcodes on the maps and in the index

◆ Widely used by the emergency services, transport companies and local authorities

For national mapping, choose **Philip's Navigator Britain** the most detailed road atlas available of England, Wales and Scotland. Hailed by Auto Express as 'the ultimate road atlas', this is the only one-volume atlas to show every road and lane in Britain.

Street atlases currently available

England
Bedfordshire
Berkshire
Birmingham and West Midlands
Bristol and Bath
Buckinghamshire
Cambridgeshire
Cheshire
Cornwall
Cumbria
Derbyshire
Devon
Dorset
County Durham and Teesside
Essex
North Essex
South Essex
Gloucestershire
Hampshire
North Hampshire
South Hampshire
Herefordshire Monmouthshire
Hertfordshire
Isle of Wight
Kent
East Kent
West Kent
Lancashire
Leicestershire and Rutland
Lincolnshire
London
Greater Manchester
Merseyside
Norfolk
Northamptonshire
Northumberland
Nottinghamshire
Oxfordshire
Shropshire
Somerset
Staffordshire
Suffolk
Surrey

East Sussex
West Sussex
Tyne and Wear
Warwickshire
Birmingham and West Midlands
Wiltshire and Swindon
Worcestershire
East Yorkshire Northern Lincolnshire
North Yorkshire
South Yorkshire
West Yorkshire

Wales
Anglesey, Conwy and Gwynedd
Cardiff, Swansea and The Valleys
Carmarthenshire, Pembrokeshire and Swansea
Ceredigion and South Gwynedd
Denbighshire, Flintshire, Wrexham
Herefordshire Monmouthshire
Powys

Scotland
Aberdeenshire
Ayrshire
Dumfries and Galloway
Edinburgh and East Central Scotland
Fife and Tayside
Glasgow and West Central Scotland
Inverness and Moray
Lanarkshire
Scottish Borders

Northern Ireland
County Antrim and County Londonderry
County Armagh and County Down
Belfast
County Tyrone and County Fermanagh

How to order Philip's maps and atlases are available from bookshops, motorway services and petrol stations. You can order direct from the publisher by phoning **01903 828503** or online at **www.philips-maps.co.uk** For bulk orders only, phone 020 7644 6940